WEALTH AND THE WEALTHY
IN THE MODERN WORLD

Wealth and The Wealthy in the Modern World

Edited by
W.D. RUBINSTEIN

CROOM HELM LONDON

© 1980 W.D. Rubinstein
Croom Helm Ltd., 2-10 St. John's Road, London SW11

British Library Cataloguing in Publication Data

Wealth and the wealthy in the modern world.
1. Upper classes
I. Rubinstein, W D
301.44′1   HT657

ISBN 0-85664-533-8

Printed and bound in Great Britain

CONTENTS

PREFACE

A number of personal and miscellaneous remarks by the editor are perhaps more appropriately made here than elsewhere. Editing a volume of original essays is never an easy task; to co-ordinate — from Australia — the commissioning, writing and publication of five original essays on a novel topic by historians each infinitely more distinguished than myself, is surely the most difficult professional task I have ever undertaken, requiring the skills of a trained diplomat and the patience of a saint. That it has proved possible is due to the enthusiasm and forbearance of my fellow contributors, as well as to the continuing friendship and assistance of the publishers, David Croom and Chris Helm. Despite this I am not yet ready to give to future editors of collections on this subject the celebrated advice of *Punch* to those about to marry ('Don't') and, indeed, I look forward to subsequent volumes in this field, incorporating areas of research which could not be accommodated here. Indeed, I would be most interested in learning from other scholars of any ongoing research in this field which might be suitable for future collections.

I should also like to thank the secretaries and typists at the Australian National University and Deakin University, Betty Gamble, Rosemary Boston, Frances Bensch and Elizabeth Doran, who rendered many of these essays suitable for publication, and Professor Francis West of Deakin University for obtaining translation funds for me. I must also thank Dr Alan Megill for assitance in translation at another stage. Several of the contributors, including myself, have made more specific acknowledgements in their individual essays.

In a volume written jointly by a number of historians, I do not feel it appropriate for me to make a single dedication.

INTRODUCTION

Although it is commonly acknowledged that money makes the world go round, and it has truly been observed that there are differences between the rich and the rest of us, the general public — and even the professional historian more cognisant with the ways of his trade — will be surprised to learn that so little research of a searching and scholarly nature has ever been conducted into the lives and activities of the very wealthy. Indeed, it is perhaps no exaggeration to say that the rich are perhaps the last really major social grouping to come to the attention of the social historian, a generalisation equally true wherever in the Western world serious historical research is conducted. Yet, on the face of it, this is clearly exceedingly odd. On a personal level, great wealth and large fortunes form alike the stuff of our dreams and our nightmares; with sex and power, they are both the goal and the subject matter of our fantasies and daydreams. In the Western world at the present time, literally millions of people weekly play the 'pools', purchase state lottery tickets, or enter the Irish sweepstakes in the entirely fantastical hope of drawing the winning ticket, the miraculous road to millionairedom; there may even be some people who work honestly towards this goal. In the nineteenth century there were gold rushes. On a more public level, the deeds and misdeeds of the fortunate few who started life winning ticket in hand, or who married it, or made it honestly or dishonestly, are the commonplace subject matter of stage and screen, printed page and television, billboard and hoarding, even to an age which scoffs at any drawing of a lesson from it by either a Karl Marx or a Samuel Smiles.

Yet, as remarked above, the general public would surely be surprised to learn that the tremendous increase in the output of social and economic historians during the past 25 years has passed the very rich by virtually untouched. There are, to be sure, some exceptions to this. France, as always in advance of the rest of the world in social historical studies, has produced a number of studies of wealth-holding and wealth distribution of the highest quality; likewise in the United States, the colossal output of historians has inevitably produced its sophisticated and sensitive specialists in this field. Similarly, there are aspects of the lives and careers of the very rich — who, after all, are virtually coextensive with the major historical actors throughout most of civilised life — which have produced their share of fine historical studies, for example the landed aristocracy or the owners and managers of those companies researched by business historians. The subject matter of wealth and income *distribution* has proved the subject of considerable and lively research among economists. Nevertheless, on the whole it is fair to say that the wealthy as such have remained *terra incognita*, a dark historical void where groups or institutions from American slavery to the pre-industrial household have been illumined. There are no journals devoted to their study, no conferences, no 'debates' among historians. Perhaps the best illustration of this simply lies in the fact that, so far as I am aware, this is the first scholarly book ever published in England on the subject of the very wealthy in the modern world.

There are many reasons which might be advanced as to why this state of affairs is true; to a professional historian, one inside the trade and caught up in its rules and private language, these might seem more compelling than to the general public. First, it has been tacitly (and, indeed, explicitly) assumed that it is the function of *political* history to study the rich and powerful, a viewpoint which has taken its cue from Trevelyan's famous definition of social history as 'history with the politics left out'. Although, by definition, the political leaders of a society are among its most powerful men, it is clearly an error to infer that they are necessarily rich, or even representative — in whatever sense may be meant — of the rich (although in most societies probably something of the sort has been true). Political history is not, and cannot be, the scholarly study of the rich. Nor, it must be said, can business history — though, once again, it is widely imagined that business history at least partially serves this function. Business histories typically study the best-known and most long-lived firms as entities in themselves, according to their own accepted criteria of business success; they cannot even attempt to grapple with rich men (and women) who were not businessmen, or with the 'idle rich'. Furthermore, they can touch on the social aspects of the lives and careers of successful businessmen, if at all, only as secondary to their main function.

Secondly — and conversely — there is a widespread tacit feeling among social historians that social history almost necessarily concerns, not the elites of a society, but the broad masses of men and women, most of whom were inevitably poor and humble. According to this view, the role of social history is to study those whom G.K. Chesterton termed 'the secret people': 'the people of England, that have never spoken yet'. Just as scientists have deduced the annual climactic situation three or four thousand years ago from a study of old tree cross-sections, so the social historian attempts to make the inarticulate speak and the illiterate render up a written record by means of a wide variety of ingenious and mathematically advanced techniques aimed at sampling the population as a whole, or at studying a typical village or town in microscopic detail.

Whatever the tremendous feeling of rejuvenation and discovery which these new methods and studies have given to the entire historical profession during the past 25 years, it has necessarily been a concomitant of this attitude that elites in general, and the very rich in particular, have been neglected. Nor must it be forgotten that historians typically study those groups towards whom they feel a considerable empathy, and, given the direction of social history, it is not surprising that such eminent practitioners as Marc Bloch, Eric Hobsbawm or E.P. Thompson have been men of the left — though the point must quickly be made that for the Thompsons and Hobsbawms there are also the Fogels and Engermans. Overall, however, there can be little doubt that social history and its historians have found little time for elites, particularly those based on wealth.

Thirdly, there is the all-important matter of sources. When all is said and done, this constitutes perhaps the most important reason for the neglect of the rich by social historians. Just how does one go about studying them? How does the sophisticated historian even identify them, especially those, perhaps a solid majority of all rich persons at any one time, who are publicly silent and virtually unknown? And, indeed, how does one define 'rich'? In the absence of useful sources and commonly agreed criteria, the serious study of the rich in the past can advance little beyond the anecdotal evidence and *grand guignol* caricatures which are the hallmark of the popular and journalistic accounts of the rich   and which, like the rich themselves, appear to be always with us.

It is probably the last point which has been the most significant factor in the neglect of the rich by social historians. It should be noted that in the closely related field of wealth or income *distribution* — how much of the national cake is held by the richest, median or lowest portions of the population — where important statistics on wealth or income division are available in most nations, economists and economic historians have long produced findings of great importance, not least in the light they throw on the practical effects of political and economic policy on equalitarianism in the modern world. Social historians, however, have lagged behind, believing that relevant sources simply didn't exist or that it would be exceedingly difficult to present naked statistical series with a human face.

Clearly, to advance beyond anecdotal evidence about the rich, it is necessary for the social historian to gain access to records of a new and particularly searching kind, enabling the researcher to identify the top wealth-holders of a country or a region and to ascertain the size of their fortunes. Even should such sources exist, their usefulness is compounded in difficulty by the vested interest which rich men surely have in understating the size of their fortunes wherever these are being ascertained for any purpose even remotely close to the tax-collector, and by the sheer magnitude of numbers through which even the keenest researcher must plough in any series of documents covering the population as a whole, and not just the rich.

Perhaps the most surprising thing about statistical sources available to the historical investigator of wealth in the past, then, is that they do exist. Yet indeed they do, in most Western countries and for broad historical spans. Perhaps the most important of these are the probate records of wealth passing at death, which form the basis of most historical research on this subject in France, America, Britain and Australia, and which quite probably exist in all Western nations in a more-or-less similar format — though it will doubtless require many decades even for comparative lists of the methodology and valuation procedure of the probate process to be compiled. Probate duties are only one of a host of taxes falling upon either income or wealth which historians now recognise comprise the most rigorous and comprehensive way of getting at the real facts of wealth and wealth distribution in the past. Census returns, household surveys, income tax records, taxes which fell upon luxury items owned disproportionately by the wealthy — as existed in nineteenth-century Britain and the Netherlands — wealth and income censuses, land and parochial registers, Stock Exchange records, wartime returns of national capital, and taxes on the rent or imputed rent of inhabited house, are among the many other official taxation series with which historians are now working. In many of these series, particularly — and most usefully — the probate returns, the names, addresses and even occupations of wealth-holders are given, as well as the total of his wealth or income, making possible social analysis of the most rewarding kind. Of course, national taxation returns would not be limited in their coverage or extent to the very rich, but would survey the entire population, rich or poor, and such historical research has or can be done with such material with much wider segments of the population than merely the very rich. And beside the official returns, historians also employ the many studies of the wealthy or of wealth-holders made by newspapers or freelance authors during the past hundred years – many remarkably comprehensive and searching.

Research into wealth-holding and the rich, whether derived from official or unofficial sources, is probably possible in a real sense only for the modern era, that is, very roughly since the Industrial Revolution got under way in the late eighteenth century. In some few societies, for instance the North American colonies, the historian may have source material which extends back to an earlier period, to the seventeenth century, and, of course, the wills and testamentary documents of probate date back to the Middle Ages, while taxation itself is as old as civilisation. Some historians may regard this as curious, in that some of the most notable of all modern works on the rich and elite groups, for instance Lawrence Stone's *Crisis of the Aristocracy*, employ an infinity of relevant quantitative data from an earlier period than the eighteenth century. Yet, whatever the profound importance of such works, they are dissimilar in many ways from research based on the records of a later period, most notably in the absence of global valuation figures detailing the total wealth of an individual, as are available in the modern era. It appears that such valuation figures originated in many different societies during the eighteenth century: certainly this is the case in Great Britain.

Although research by social historians into the very wealthy is only a few decades old, it is not the case that the closely related field of wealth distribution is equally new. Indeed, in this matter we are presented with one of the paradoxes of research in this area. For much of the best of all research into the field of wealth and income distribution throughout Europe and the world was carried out in the early part of this century and in many ways the achievement of these researchers has never been equalled. Such works as Josiah Stamp's *British Incomes and Property* (1916), G.H. Knibb's *The Private Wealth of Australia and Its Growth* (1918) or Corrado Gini's *L'ammontare e la Composizione della Richezza delle Nazioni* (1914), still stand by themselves in their respective fields. Given the lack of electronic calculating aids, the absence of many statistical techniques invented only later, and the difficulties of collecting data which exist in any case, the achievement of this group of researchers is the more astonishing.

Men like Stamp and Gini wrote amidst the background of the first debate among economists and social thinkers about the distribution of wealth and income in modern industrial society, and which produced the reforms of the great 1905-14 Liberal Government in Britain and the Progressive movement in the United States, as well as the growing socialist movement throughout Europe. It was the decline following the First World War of left-wing and progressive concern by the maldistribution of wealth and income which probably was most instrumental in deferring much further important research in this field for nearly 40 years. It was only in the late 1950s and 1960s, paradoxically in the midst of the much-celebrated affluent society, that social scientists, as well as left-wing publicists, rediscovered the existence of remaining pockets of poverty; at the same time they discovered that the distribution of wealth and income throughout most Western societies had altered surprisingly little, certainly much less than might be expected by the growth of the welfare state and the rise to power of social democratic parties. A plethora of works have appeared by the past 20 years documenting this.[1] In many countries the basic statistical measurement from which this viewpoint is derived is the probate inventories of wealth at death, supplemented by household surveys of wealth-holding and income tax figures. There has, in addition, been an important discussion among economists on the role of inheritance in maintaining wealth inequalities.[2] Not unexpectedly, both the conclusions of the radical critics of welfare state inequality and the statistical sources upon which they are based have been attacked by conservative thinkers.[3] This important debate, which obviously possesses an important political dimension, may prove to be one of the great rallying points of Western socialism in the late twentieth century — in Great Britain, for instance, a standing Royal Commission, headed by Lord Diamond, was appointed in 1974 to inquire into the distribution of wealth and income in Britain, and the left wing of the Labour Party has insistently called for the introduction of an effective wealth tax. Indeed, it seems inevitable that any future Labour Government with a parliamentary majority will be compelled to introduce such a tax, in all likelihood against the better judgement and real wishes of its Cabinet moderates. It should finally be remarked that the unequal distribution of wealth and income in contemporary Western societies has also become a stock in trade of sociological analyses of these societies in recent years; unfortunately, practising sociologists have not as a rule gone beyond the statistics offered by economists to produce original statistical analyses of their own.[4]

It would be surprising if *nothing* from the revival of interest in wealth distribution among other disciplines reached the social and economic historian, to whom evidence on wealth, affluence and poverty in the past is meat and drink. Indeed, although this whole

subject has been shamefully neglected, there have been a few historians
who, independently of one another and often working in virtual
ignorance of one another, have done major research in this field.
Modern scholarly research in the area of wealth-holding and wealth
distribution began with Professor Adeline Daumard's pioneering article,
'Une Source d'histoire Sociale: L'enregistrement des mutations par
décès', *Revue d'Histoire Economique et Sociale* (1957), and continued
with her *Les Bourgeois de Paris au XIXe Siècle* (Paris, 1970) and *Les
Fortunes Francaises au XIXe Siècle* (Paris, 1973), and is further
represented in the great French school of social history by such works
as F.P. Codaccioni's on Lille and J. Sentou's on Toulouse.

In English-speaking countries economic historians like Lee Soltow[5]
and more mainstream historians who attempted to relate wealth-holding
and the very rich to broader political and economic changes in society,
most notably Edward Pessen of the City University of New York,[6]
appeared somewhat later. It was not until the mid-1970s that even the
most basic research on the nineteenth-century wealthy derived from the
probate records in Britain was undertaken,[7] although, as noted above,
seventeenth-century historians like Lawrence Stone had written on
similar themes a decade earlier. As the 1980s approach, it is clear that
the study of the modern wealthy by social and economic historians,
and, in a wider perspective, the study of elites by social historians, is
the process of making good the time lost hitherto.[8] However, a great
deal of work remains to be done, and any young scholar interested in
working in what is obviously a rising and still underworked field,
offering the opportunities for quite basic and original research, and
historical discoveries, could do much worse than the area of elite
studies, wealth-holding and wealth distribution, particularly if he is a
specialist in those countries or areas where, it will be evident from the
writings in this book, the surface has hardly been scratched.

It will also be apparent to the perceptive reader that the field
consists of two closely related but none the less essentially separate
areas of study; this dichotomy will be clear in many of the essays in
this work. These two are the historical study of wealth distribution,
the changing share of the cake owned by various segments of the
population at various times, and of top wealth-holders and the wealthy
in society, their salient biographical facts and the manner in which they
interact with the rest of society. Although this work is primarily
intended to focus attention on the second of these areas, the social
historical study of the very wealthy, it quickly becomes clear to any
researcher in the field that he cannot readily separate the two, that

questions of wealth distribution and the changing share of the national
wealth owned by the very rich are intimately bound up with the
identity and careers of individual wealth-holders, and that both the
sources of research and the questions asked in these two fields are
often identical. In the British case, for instance, most research on the
historical distribution of wealth in society and the changing share
owned by the top percentiles is derived from the Inland Revenue's
probate statistics,[9] while, in the research undertaken by social historians
into the lives and careers of the very wealthy, the identity of the top
wealth-holders is taken from the probate records of the Principal
Probate Registry at Somerset House.[10] The major difference between
the two is that, in the latter case, the names, dates of death and size of
fortunes of individual testators can be found by the researcher, while in
the former, only anonymous statistics are available.[11] Given this fact,
it is not surprising that seeming disciplinary lines are crossed very
frequently: for instance, the pioneering scholarly researcher into the
field of intergeneration social mobility in Britain, employing the
'named' probate records at Somerset House, is a leading economist,
Professor Colin Harbury of the City University, while on the other
hand a leading British social historian like Professor Harold Perkin has
made good use of the anonymous Inland Revenue statistics on income
distribution.[12] In reality, the ultimate goal of the sensitive social
historian, to describe and explain the workings of the most important
features of the whole of society, clearly requires the use of both types
of source.

Bearing in mind that a dichotomy exists, and that very much work
remains to be done, the editor of this book in 1976-77 approached a
number of social and economic historians in America and Europe with
the idea of producing a series of essays on the very wealthy and our
current state of knowledge in the fields of wealth-holding and wealth
distribution in the major Western nations since the eighteenth century
(with two essays on the important and well-worked area of the United
States). Each author was to write an essay which would discuss, in a
broad way, who the wealthy were; how wealth was created, controlled
and maintained in each society; the relationship between wealthy
persons and the rest of society; divisions among the wealthy class; social
mobility into the top wealth and income brackets; and the idiosyncratic
features of wealth-holding in each society. Some mention would be
made as well of the sources available to previous researchers in this field,
and of previous important research, as well as of work remaining to be
done. Plainly, this is a guide to an ideal which, for those societies where

insufficient research has been done, would be impossible of total achievement; conversely, for societies like the United States where a vast amount of material exists, in a relatively brief essay much would have to be eliminated. It was also recognised that each essay would, ultimately and inevitably, reflect the training, research and scholarly environment of the author, and especially in so novel a field as this, the final chapters would be as variegated and different both in content and detail, as any set of essays by five different authors living and working in different parts of the world. The emphasis here is on the major industrialised countries of Western Europe and North America since the early nineteenth century, to the exclusion both of non-Western societies and of the smaller Western nations. This is regrettable, but probably inevitable. We had originally scheduled several essays which for reasons of space were unable to appear in the completed volume. For other countries, for instance Canada, Japan, Argentina, Brazil, Austria-Hungary and its successor states, India and the Scandinavian countries, which we should like to have covered, no relevant research at all appears to have been undertaken. For reasons of space, too, early modern Europe, and particularly seventeenth-century Britain, could not be discussed, even though closely related work has been undertaken. A second volume of essays, or a journal on this subject, should one ever eventuate, would certainly provide coverage of many of these areas.

Perhaps the main value of comparative essays of the kind attempted in this volume lies in the possibilities they afford for drawing up a transnational typology of wealth structures, fitting the peculiar features present in each major society — relative size and number of fortunes, occupational distribution, social mobility, political participation by and influence of the wealthy, and so on — into an international schema for each item which could then be related to the more basic socio-economic and political elements common to these countries. For it is clear even with the limited international evidence available at this stage of research in this area that there were very substantial and important relative differences in the most important features of the wealth structures of the societies surveyed here. These differences are often not at all obvious without a determined effort at comparative analysis, and most, so far as I am aware, have never been discussed by historians or economists. But if wealth matters, if wealth-holding is crucial both to the distribution of power and to economic development, clearly it is to this comparative realm that work in this field must eventually turn. In most of the remainder of this essay, I should like to discuss the most important of these comparative dimensions, with the caveat that quite often the research one would most like to see has not yet been done, and that space limitations preclude what could easily be a monograph in itself; it should also be apparent that the very lack of the plethora of studies available in many other fields provides the historian with the rare opportunity to be speculative and conjectural.

Size and Numbers of Fortunes

Perhaps the most basic area in which comparisons among the wealth structures of the advanced countries is useful is in the area of size of fortunes and numbers of top wealth-holders. Although even scholars often talk loosely about 'the rich' in different societies as if they held virtually identical amounts of money and as if they were numerically similar classes of people, in reality nothing could be more different than the size and numbers of the wealthy in different societies and at different times — except in the trivial sense that the wealthiest percentile of the population will invariably number one per cent of the total population. Here, as much as in any aspect of this topic which will be considered here, there appear to be distinct and recognisable typologies among the various societies. Again, however, as so little of the basic research about even the size of fortunes and numbers of top wealth-holders has yet been completed, the delineation of this typology in more than an approximate way must to some extent be educated guesswork — though I would be surprised if such a typology was ever shown to be radically incorrect.

Perhaps the most important and striking single feature about the comparative size differences in top fortunes is the vast and singular level of wealth in the United States between the Jacksonian period (if not before) and the past 20 years (when the rise of OPEC oil wealth, as well as of new and vast private fortunes in other parts of the world produced rivals in size and extent). It would also seem that large fortunes were comparatively more numerous in the United States than elsewhere, but this is more arguable.[13]

When J.P. Morgan died in 1914, leaving an estate of some $80 million, John D. Rockefeller was supposed to have said, 'And to think — he wasn't even a wealthy man'.[14] Rockefeller's fortune, as well as those of his fellow billionaires Henry Ford and Andrew Mellon, and those in the centimillionaire class held by such famous American magnates as the Vanderbilts, Astors, Dukes and Andrew Carnegie, had never previously been equalled in size in modern world history. It is possible that the size of the largest Canadian fortunes were also exceedingly great, probably much larger than the richest British fortunes (though not quite on the American scale).[15] As is pretty generally known and well documented, the peak American fortunes rose from $25 million in 1860 to $100 million by the late 1870s and to one billion dollars by the early twentieth century. The last figure – approximately £200 million – was at least twelve times greater than the peak British fortune of the day. The vast and totally unprecedented size of even second-ranking American fortunes allowed mere run-of-the-mill American millionaires to marry into the highest reaches of the British and continental aristocracies, to buy up the rarest art treasures of Europe, to endow what quickly became among the world's most prestigious universities, and, eventually, to redefine status itself so that the possession of sheer wealth and nothing more was no longer scorned as beneath the dignity of the oldest families.

It appears that in the most advanced European societies, the levels of top fortunes was quite similar to one another, especially in the late nineteenth century. In Britain, where top fortunes were probably somewhat greater than elsewhere, the highest non-landed fortunes rose in size from about £2 million in 1800 to £5 million by mid-century and to about £11 million by 1914. Because of primogeniture and the relative stability in the capital value of land in the nineteenth century, the great British landowners changed far less, the peak probably rising to about £7 million by the First World War. Increasingly, the wealthiest landowners were those who owned substantial urban property or mineral deposits, like the Dukes of Westminster or Devonshire. In France there was a steady rise in the number and size of top fortunes. In Paris, the selected years studied by Professor Daumard (1820, 1847, 1911), the percentage of all estates worth 1 million francs or more rose from 0.4 per cent in 1820 to 1 per cent in 1847 to 4 per cent in 1911, the peak single fortune rising to over 50 million francs in 1911 (over £2 million).[16] As these are only annual samples of French capital, it is highly likely that the absolute peaks were higher still. We know much less about Germany, especially during the earlier part of the nineteenth century, but the late-nineteenth-century industrial and commercial wealth of such men as the Krupps and Baron de Hirsch are legendary, while it is known that 34 individuals declared fortunes of the equivalent of £1.5 million or more in the 1911 Prussian wealth census, with four claiming to be worth £5 million or more.[17]

It seems probable, too, that the fortunes of the greatest Russian aristocrats and landowners were vast, perhaps indeed in excess of anything else in Europe. Until the abolition of serfdom in 1861, however, to speak of the wealth of these men in money rather than

service terms is misleading.[18] Unfortunately, very little research appears
to have been done on this subject.

The smaller and less advanced nineteenth-century European states
appear to have followed a different pattern, with many fewer large
fortunes, and those which existed at a much lower level than in Britain
or Germany. This was the case in Italy, as Dr Zamagni's essay makes
clear, and in all likelihood in the Netherlands, where the great Dutch
commercial achievements of the early modern period were undergoing
a secular decline from the eighteenth century. In Australia, founded
originally as a British penal colony but with a pattern of development
and settlement similar to that of the United States or Canada (but on a
much smaller scale), the number and size of fortunes were small in
comparison with Britain or America. Only a handful of men ever
reached the level of £1 million or more in the nineteenth and early
twentieth centuries. Very few men, if any, amassed great wealth in
Australia's gold rushes.[19]

In a rough way, the size and number of top fortunes appears to vary
at least in an apparently rational way with the level of economic
development and per capita income in each country. Nevertheless,
there are many anomalies which require explanation. America was not
twelve times wealthier than Britain during the nineteenth century, while
per capita income in Australia was certainly higher than in Britain after
1850, yet the number of top fortunes and their extent were smaller.
The industrial and commercial structures and evolution of Britain,
France and Germany were quite different, but their level of fortunes
apparently similar.

Clearly, the most anomalous variation occurred in the United States.
It seems likely that a combination of factors, including the size of the
market, high initial per capita income, wealth of natural resources, lack
of political, social or legal barriers to capitalist expansion, and the
effects of the Civil War and high tariff walls all combined to bring
about the growth of the great American fortunes. It should not be
forgotten, too, that the top American fortunes were 'merely' in the
centimillionaire class until after the beginning of the century, when
men like Ford and Rockefeller expanded their riches by a factor of ten.
Rockefeller, for instance, had already built a great, but certainly not
uniquely large, petroleum fortune based largely upon the sale of
kerosene for home lighting and fuel, when the growth of the American
automobile industry in the first decade of the century provided him
with a wholly unexpected and gratuitous golconda. Rockefeller's
fortune is said to have grown from $200 million in 1901 to $900

million in 1913.[20] It is the unique immensity of the great American
fortunes, perhaps more than any other comparative matter, which
requires an explanation.

Whatever the national differences in the size of fortunes, certain
common trends are evident in their growth and increase in number. In
all Western societies where any evidence, even anecdotal, is available,
the late nineteenth century, and particularly the 1870-80s, marked a
climacteric which separated the merely large business fortunes of the
early and mid-nineteenth century from the much larger fortunes of the
fin de siècle. Everywhere, too, wealth became more vulgar, more flashy,
more ostentatious and conspicuous in display, though on different
scales in different countries. Previously this had not been so to the
same extent. In Britain, for instance, the number of very large
(£100,000 or more) probated non-landed estates did not rise between
1815 and 1850, while the largest individual fortunes did not vary much
throughout most of the entire nineteenth century, until the very end
of the century. The number of millionaire and half-millionaire estates,
however, did experience a marked increase from the 1870s on. The
1870s, too, saw the transformation of the political position and
loyalties of the wealthy throughout most of the Western world. Whereas
as recently as the 1830s and 1840s in Jacksonian America, Orléanist
France and England of the Reform Bill, the newer elements among
both the manufacturing and commercial wealthy were often democratic
or even radical in politics, by the 1870s and 1880s the classical late-
nineteenth-century plutocracy had come into existence; most if not all
great wealth-holders were conservatives by any standard. In Britain the
Liberal Unionist split of 1886 resulted in a wholesale transfer of
commercial wealth to the Conservative Party; thereafter the City of
London, Britain's financial and commercial heart, was as
overwhelmingly Tory as it had once been Liberal.[21] A 'radical
plutocrat', like Sir John Brunner the great chemical manufacturer, was
by the turn of the century by definition a contradiction in terms.[22]

Occupational Distribution

The second aspect of this question which is amenable to comparative
discussion is the occupational distribution of the top wealth-holders
of the various countries. If the comparative size of fortunes is little
explored, the comparative occupations or sources of wealth of the rich
is even less so, and indeed very little can be said of a precise nature
beyond Britain, the United States and Australia. It must be said first,
however, that landed wealth continued to be of major importance in

many countries long after the industrialisation process had transformed the economies of these nations in very basic ways. In Britain, for instance, until the 1880s more than half of all the richest men continued to be landowners. In the earlier part of the nineteenth century, this percentage was much higher, perhaps seven-eighths. Even in Australia, the most highly urbanised society in the world in the nineteenth century, one-third or more of the top wealth-holders deceased down to the Second World War were pastoralists. In early modern times, and in Continental countries certainly until this century, landed wealth continued to be a major segment of the wealth structure. Until the nineteenth century or even after, landed wealth, and particularly its aristocratic portion (as well as middle-class professionals and contractors), often augmented its wealth by government-derived perquisites, pensions or payments of one kind or another, often unbelievably lucrative. In Britain this system of interest and connection was known as 'Old Corruption' or 'the Thing' (*pace* Cobbett), and it clearly had its analogies on the Continent, indeed, in a far more definite way, given the weakness of the bourgeoise notion of parsimony in government and the relative absence of those middle-class (and aristocratic) reformers who modified and eventually destroyed Old Corruption in England from the 1780s on. Nevertheless, in many ways this world of patronage and place was an exceedingly interesting – and ill-explored – phenomenon.[23] Eighteenth-century government and patronage bound up not only the aristocracy and military but such 'middle-class' elements as the Church, lawyers and judges, and old-style mercantile and financial interests like the Bank of England and the East India Company in Britain.[24] In Britain wealth-holding based on Old Corruption, a major element among those deceased in the early nineteenth century, virtually vanished by mid-century in the wake of the new government parsimony of the 1830s and 1840s. There is an urgent need for a proper assessment of this type of wealth in eighteenth and nineteenth-century Europe.

Business wealth includes commercial/financial and manufacturing/industrial categories. These should be regarded as organisational poles rather than as absolutes: some forms of business wealth, for instance newspaper-owning, do not fit neatly into either, while professionals form a world of their own. Nevertheless, organising business wealth around these two polar types is in my opinion fundamental to understanding the structure of nineteenth-century capitalism. As my own research has shown, in nineteenth-century Britain commercial/financial wealth was more important than manufacturing/industrial wealth, and this corresponded with a deep social division in Britain between commercial London and the mainly Anglican South of England, and the manufacturing, dissenting North.[25] The most surprising facet of the nineteenth-century British wealth structure was the predominance of commercial and financial wealth in the new world of the Industrial Revolution. Very few British industrialists or manufacturers were immensely wealthy. That there are salient international differences in this area too, is clear from comparing the British figures with those for post-1865 America presented in Professor Jaher's essay in this volume, where the various manufacturing/ industrial categories account for nearly 60 per cent of his multimillionaire sources of wealth — among them, once again, most of the litany of the great names of high capitalism, Rockefeller (oil), Ford (autos), Carnegie and Mellon (steel) and so on. Financiers and bankers, as well as merchants, traders and shipowners of every description, were much less wealthy and, in all likelihood, less central to the development of the American economy and to social divisions in American society than were their British equivalents — though in the Midwest, the South and rural areas everywhere, there developed a full share of resentment and even hatred towards Wall Street, the big railways and corporations, to the Morgans, Loebs and Harrimans.

In New South Wales, Australia, the only other national area where research has progressed to the extent of making generalisations of this sort possible, there was virtually no domestic manufacturing sector at all, the occupational structure of the wealthy being divided for the most part between pastoralists and the commercial sector almost equally. New South Wales's commercial sector was composed virtually entirely of merchants and shipowners, and the number of wealthy bankers and other financiers being rather small in both the nineteenth and twentieth centuries (down to those deceased in 1939). Australian financial control for the most part remained in the hands of Englishmen; such major bankers as there were in Sydney were career managers who did not independently amass great wealth.

Among the important countries where research in the field of occupational distribution remains to be done is Germany. It would be exceedingly illuminating to know whether German capitalism, with its oft-cited oligarchic bias, most favoured manufacturing or commercial magnates. It seems not improbable, in my view, that research will reveal a pattern more similar to America, where manufacturing predominated, than to Britain. Should this indeed prove to be so it is probable that the weakness of the more 'cosmopolitan' and international-minded

commercial and financial sector can be linked to the strength of
nationalistic and conservative forces generally there, which, as
elsewhere, were innately more favourable to manufacturing — which
aided military development and national strength and whose
entrepreneurs were ethnically more pure — than to commerce and
finance. Naturally, one would not wish to press an essentially
deterministic argument of this sort too far — after all, the United
States, with a predominantly industrial wealth structure, resembled
Britain far more than Germany — but it would certainly be useful and
stimulating to attempt to link German wealth elites with broader
political and social trends in this way.

The Creation of Wealth

Conceptually apart from the occupational distribution of wealth is the
question of how wealth is made — to the non-wealthy majority, the
most intriguing question of all. It seems clear even from the relatively
well-trodden and narrow paths of fortune-gaining in Britain that there
is no simple answer, and that fortunes were made in as many ways as
there were wealthy dynasties. Even at the very peak of the wealth scale
it would be an easy and pardonable exaggeration to say that great
wealth necessarily entails the monopoly of some natural resource, but
in fact this is not so. In fact, if one can contrast the mere
monopolisation of a scarce commodity — of which land, petroleum and
investment capital are perhaps the classical instances — with the more
dynamic and progressive creation of a mass market for a saleable
commodity, it appears that there was at least as much of the latter as
the former, in even the vastest fortunes. The case of a Henry Ford,
literally putting the world on wheels and making a billion in the process,
is clear cut. But surprisingly even the case of a John D. Rockefeller —
at first glance merely the first man to discover in petroleum the means
of hijacking the world — on closer inspection turns out to include at
least as strong an element of market creation as of monopolisation.
Rockefeller's original field was the production and marketing of
kerosene, an area previously dominated by a plethora of small men
whose product varied in quality not merely from company to company
but from barrel to barrel. By ruthless cost-cutting, but also by equally
thorough — and far-sighted — quality control, Rockefeller eventually
came to dominate — but never entirely monopolise — the market.[26]
Rockefeller's drive into China is described by the family's most recent
historian thus:

In China Standard [Oil] created a wholly new market for itself. It gave away millions of cheap lamps so that the Chinese would buy and burn Standard's kerosene. These were the Lamps for the Light of Asia, and Standard started out with a self-made monopoly. This was creative marketing.[27]

This was the American pattern of fortune-making. At its most enlightened, it discovered without theory what a century of economists from Ricardo to Keynes had missed, that capitalism works best not by grinding the faces of the workers in the dirt, but by creating an affluent and acquisitive market — indeed, often by creating the market itself. I am convinced that this discovery must surely be linked with the anomalously vast size of the largest American fortunes, a matter discussed above.

Above we also drew a dichotomy between the London-based British commercial elite and the North-of-England manufacturing elite which, with the great landowners, competed for wealth, status and power in nineteenth-century Britain. This brings to mind another and, in my opinion, exceedingly fruitful way of dividing national wealth structures, that determined by geography and venue — which is usually a convenient shorthand for a large bundle of social, economic, political and religious attitudes, interests and experiences. Sectional analyses of historical movements, based in part on economic distinctions and elite group differences, are, of course, a commonplace and plausible way of thinking. The distinction between 'East Coast' old-moneyed liberal Republicanism and 'Sunbelt' *nouveau-riche* conservative Republicanism in the United States, apparently first formulated by Soviet observers of the American scene during the 1964 election campaign,[28] has been widely taken up even by conservative writers like Kevin Phillips. In America, with its vast sectional differences, based upon substantial cultural and economic distinctions, and above all, the land of the sectionally defined Civil War of 1861-65, such a viewpoint is taken almost routinely by historians. But this perspective has not perhaps spread to the same extent in other societies, and, in particular, much needs to be done about identifying the elite structures of the regions in countries like Germany and Italy.

Social Mobility

Social mobility studies of the rich and powerful are one of the most commonly undertaken types of analysis of these elite groups. Normally, these take the form of comparisons of the social or economic status of the elite group member with his father; others commonly trace the educational backgrounds of elites, inferring original class or status from attendance at fee-paying schools and prestigious universities. Such studies can, of course, be applied to non-elites as well, although it is an almost invariable rule of research in this field that accurate investigation becomes more difficult the further down the social scale one proceeds. Given the general paucity of historical studies on the very wealthy, there are a fair number of such social mobility studies, with several of the essays in this book providing fresh evidence. A sophisticated study of the social origins of the top British wealth-holders deceased in the mid-1920s was undertaken at the time by Josiah Wedgwood in his *The Economics of Inequality* (1929); well-known essays on the American wealthy by William Miller and C. Wright Mills appeared in the early 1950s; since then, there have been many others. Indeed, the relative *ease* with which social mobility studies have and can be mounted have led some critics to question whether the importance of this factor is not thus systematically exaggerated. After all, whatever their social origins, all very rich men have essentially the same interests, and while numbers of 'self-made' millionaires may be evidence of a relatively fluid social system, in personality and political outlook they tend, if anything, to be even more hard-nosed and reactionary than the scions of old-wealth dynasties whose avariciousness has often been gilded over by a patina of culture and moderation, or even liberalism, in politics.

Virtually all social mobility studies of the origins of the top wealth-holders agree on the paucity of real opportunities for one-generation mobility from bottom to top. There is no study of intergenerational social mobility among top wealth-holders in any country, so far as I am aware, which has found that more than 15-20 per cent of all wealth-holders at any one time were 'self-made men' in any sense, although this rate has been exceeded for limited periods among certain wealth cohorts.[29] Most social mobility studies of business elites which find substantially higher rates are artificially biased by including only 'famous' businessmen − who are often famous precisely because they were 'self-made' − and excluding the plethora of wealthy men who inherited great wealth and lived quietly, inactive or only partially active in business life.[30] (This, incidentally, is the real value of making 'wealth' rather than business success or fame the criterion for inclusion in such cases.) Most studies have found far *less* than this 15-20 per cent, even at a remarkably early date. Professor Pessen, for instance, found that only about 2 per cent of the top wealth-holders (as judged by tax returns) in 4 large cities of Jacksonian America were born poor, while

6 per cent came from a background of 'middling economic status'. In contrast in New York nearly 95 per cent of the 100 wealthiest persons 'were born into families of wealth or high status or occupation'.[31] Similarly, the studies in this volume and elsewhere of post-1865 American, British, Australian, German and Italian top wealth-holders confirm this picture in every case. Among the post-1865 American fortune-holders, for instance, only 6-9 per cent came from working-class backgrounds, while over 75 per cent were the sons of businessmen — often themselves exceedingly wealthy — or professionals. Among the wealthiest living men of any country at nearly any time, virtually all will have started life at the very least substantially better off than most of their contemporaries.

But this is not the whole story, although many commentators leave off at this point. Within a single country, there are often wide secular variations in the rates of social mobility to the wealthy class, but within the limitations mentioned above. More importantly, there is a very considerable volume of downward social mobility out of the wealth class. There is a perfectly natural way of breaking up the great fortunes: having children. More precisely put, whenever the number of children of a wealth-holder exceeds one, each will necessarily receive only a fraction of his father's wealth. Given the Schumpeterian propensity of the rich for dissipating their fortunes anyway through philanthropy, estate duties, riotous living or simply bad business decisions, it is actually the rare fortune which stays intact — let alone increases — even 50 years after the death of the great entrepreneur.

A few British examples are equally interesting: for example, I have been unable to trace the heirs of Lord Overstone's (d. 1883) £5 million banking fortune beyond the 1940s, when his chief heir at that point was no more than a half-millionaire; similarly, if the descendants of such mid-Victorian millionaires as Duncan Dunbar, Richard Thornton,[32] Francis Wise or Thomas Wrigley are still very wealthy or socially promiment, they manage to keep this very quiet. And what manifestly fails to transpire is the science-fiction fantasy of a single estate snowballing over the decades into a fortune of simply overwhelming size. Had Vanderbilt's $100 million of 1877 been kept intact and reinvested in the leading growth sectors of the American economy, its size a century later would be simply beyond reckoning. On the contrary, the Vanderbilt dynasty itself is now largely vanished from the rollcall of the very rich.[33] In Britain recent evidence taken from the Inland Revenue probate data has documented a flow of wealth from the very wealthiest to the slightly less wealthy, evidently the product of gifts *inter vivos* by the very wealthiest to a wide number of relatives for the purpose of death-duty avoidance.[34] In sum, even the greatest fortunes tend to dissipate themselves within several generations by perfectly natural means. The nineteenth-century fears of a self-perpetuating, stagnant and even-wealthier caste of great fortune-holders have never come to pass.

Nor, in considering the overall fact of extremely limited opportunities for one-generation social mobility into the wealthy class, can one ignore the many instances of just such Horatio Alger achievement. Psychologically, of course, the relatively few such genuine cases clearly provide both justification for the whole structure of the economic system, and a real inspiration for would-be entrepreneurs, some of whom, after all, are successful in their pursuit of wealth. Even in mid- and late-Victorian England, when class barriers had become stronger than they had ever been in Britain since the Reformation, there were always *some* entrepreneurs who, however astonishingly, scaled the almost insurmountable barriers required to achieve great wealth in one lifetime from a background of poverty. This number has increased in this century, and in particular after the Second World War, when a host of self-made millionaire property-developers, retailers, financiers and manufacturers appeared. The basis of their fortunes was often the small sum given to demobilised soldiers following the end of the war.[35] In the United States, the estimated number of living millionaires has increased perhaps fivefold since 1945; obviously many of these began in backgrounds of need. Much the same is probably true in all other Western capitalist societies. In all likelihood, a fluid and growing economy, such as existed for over two decades in most post-war Western societies, is the best guarantee for social mobility of this type; but at virtually all times and in all social and economic environments but the most repressive, some entrepreneurial skill will meet with success. Historians of this topic must learn to treat the whole subject of social mobility in and out of the wealthy class with much more subtlety and sensitivity than the raw figures themselves suggest. Taking into account the work of sociologists, they must learn, too, to address the larger question of what, if anything, differing rates of social mobility tell us about the evolution of capitalism.

Wealth-holding and Religion

Among the most central lines of division within the wealth class, at least in those societies where such differences exist at all, is that of religion. In Britain, for instance, the distinction between Anglicans and dissenters was one of the most significant of the nineteenth century; in America Protestantism and Catholicism, it is often argued by historians, formed the basis on which major political disputes were hung, both in the past century and in this.[36] In the context of the present discussion of wealth, the importance of religion received its initial scholarly recognition in 1904 when Max Weber first published his celebrated thesis, known to us as *The Protestant Ethic and the Spirit of Capitalism*. Regrettably, not enough research has yet been done to test the Weber thesis as it is relevant to the making of substantial fortunes, and only a few of the essays in this book directly address this question or attempt to assess the issues. In the usual statement of the Weber thesis, as a dichotomy between Protestantism (especially Calvinist-derived) and Catholicism, there seems little doubt that, historically, Protestants seem more adept at making money than Catholics, either in the broad international sphere of comparisons between predominantly Catholic and predominantly Protestant societies, or within pluralistic societies where both Protestants and Catholics were found in substantial numbers. In the United States, for instance, there can be little doubt that Catholics (who have accounted for 25 per cent of the American population since late last century) are substantially underrepresented among the very rich, as Professor Jaher's figures in Chapter 5 make clear – though there are, of course, many spectacular exceptional instances, for instance Joseph Kennedy and his family. However, as in America Catholics disproportionately arrived later than Protestants, sprang from poorer backgrounds and worked initially in unskilled and semi-skilled jobs, the specifically *religious* dimensions of this finding are open to much debate. And there can be little doubt that predominantly Catholic countries like France were perfectly capable of producing their share of highly successful entrepreneurs and wealth-holders.

In the British context, the Weber thesis is often reshaped to debate not the entrepreneurial behaviour of Protestants *vis-à-vis* Catholics but of dissenters (Quakers, Congregationalists, Baptists, Unitarians etc.) *vis-à-vis* Anglicans.[37] Most English social historians now accept the two propositions that dissenters were disproportionately active in 'sparking' the Industrial Revolution and that they were equally disproportionately successful at making money in eighteenth and nineteenth-century England.[38] The only empirical test which has yet been made of these propositions would appear to confirm the Weber thesis in this context.[39] However, my own work on the most successful nineteenth-century British entrepreneurs – those who left the largest fortunes – provides no statistical evidence of any kind to support this viewpoint. Dissenters were no more numerous among business wealth-holders than among the entire population, though a number of individual sects, such as the Quakers, were considerably more successful than they would be expected on a random basis; furthermore, wealthy Anglicans were just as numerous as their numbers would warrant. It seems clear that much more sophisticated statistical work of this sort must be attempted before one can confirm or deny Weber's insight.

The relationship between religion and wealth-holding is further clouded by the fact that nearly everywhere in Western societies there was a religious group who were unquestionably overrepresented among the top wealth-holders of the day: the Jews — overrepresented, that is, whenever they were permitted to engage freely in business at all. Weber specifically denied that Jewish 'pariah capitalism' (sic) was conceptually related to the 'industrial' capitalism engendered by the 'Puritan cast of mind',[40] and, whatever the tastelessness of his phraseology, there can be little doubt that, statistically at any rate, he was perfectly right, for Jews have overwhelmingly earned their fortunes in commercial and financial ventures rather than in industrial and manufacturing enterprises — where, as in Britain, dissenting 'Puritans' were disproportionately prominent. In a perverse way, however, this fact may best serve to undermine Weber's entire project, for it seems, to me at any rate, to be clear evidence that it is not religion, or even effort as such, which is the prime requirement of the successful entrepreneur, but place in the total economy, and in Britain (and probably elsewhere as well, as we have seen) commercial and financial undertakings were inherently more lucrative than manufacturing and industrial enterprises.[41] It was the luck, rather than the pluck, of the Jews to become engaged so heavily in the City of London's financial activities and its equivalents in other Western societies. On a broader scale, the secular success of Protestantism is due not to religion as such, but to the location of Protestants in those northern European countries and their colonies or former colonies overseas, which have made the economic running since the seventeenth century — at least down to the Second World War. For would Weber have been so confident of his analysis had he lived to see the post-1945 success of Catholic countries like West Germany, France and Italy, and the stagnation of Britain?

Wealth-holding and Politics

One of the most controversial aspects of the question of the interaction between the wealthy and the rest of society concerns the political involvement and power of the wealthy. Much of the debate on this issue is, naturally, philosophical or ideological in nature, and cannot readily be answered by quantitative means or, indeed, according to those who hold this view, by an examination of the individual biographies of wealth-holders. According to the well-known Marxist view of the role of individual actors in a bourgeois society, so pervasive and hegemonic is the domination of the capitalist ethos and capitalistic frames of reference, that social democratic parties and leaders, nationalised industries and the trade unions are essentially part and parcel of the system of capitalism;[42] *a fortiori* the rich, no matter how eccentric or far-sighted, work to promote the aims of the system. Naturally, of course, the overwhelming majority of the rich are reactionaries pure and simple, working to extend multinational capitalism around the world, by military force if necessary.

'Moderate' historians and other scholars, particularly those with experience of American conditions, have been much more willing to qualify this overall picture, pointing to the fact that the 'left' in America (or at least the 'liberal' wings of the Democratic and Republican parties) have been led since the New Deal by men of great personal wealth, most notably Franklin Roosevelt, the Kennedys, Averill Harriman and Nelson Rockefeller. Clearly, it is argued, the security and higher educational attainments of at least second-generation wealth negate the greed and acquisitiveness of the founding entrepreneur, producing an enlarged and more 'liberal' view of domestic and foreign policy; in addition, an ill-concealed sense of guilt often permeates the behaviour of the very wealthy towards their vast fortunes; even purely self-made men like Carnegie and John D. Rockefeller devoted most of their declining years to philanthropy. Finally, social psychologists have documented the fact that extreme right-wing, racist and militaristic opinions, particularly the *gestalt* termed the 'authoritarian personality', are much more likely to be held by the working class than by the wealthier members of society; a comparison of the political beliefs of hard-hat construction workers with those of, say, college professors will instantly confirm this.

The historian of wealth who is concerned to link the wealthy and other elites with the entire social structure of a particular society naturally takes a good deal of interest in this debate. His contribution, as a historian, can begin by surveying the historical participation of the very wealthy in the political elite. Studies of the wealth of members of Parliaments in Britain, Australia and France have all shown that the numbers of very wealthy businessmen and professionals who were elected to office rose throughout the nineteenth century, peaking at the century's end and declining steadily after the First World War.[43] This was probably true in the United States as well, where the Senate was known as the 'millionaires' club' at the time. The secular tendency we are describing here, it must be made clear, occurred in *middle-class* parties. Should the 'wealth' of the members of the ever-growing socialist or working-class parties be considered, this trend would of course be more pronounced still. The reasons for this apparently universal (and as yet underdocumented) pattern are varied; they include the tendency of large-scale manufacturers and businessmen to take on the role of the leading patrician figure of his town, election into Parliament being a natural progression; the fact that members of Parliaments were still unpaid or ill-paid, making considerable wealth a prerequisite; and, of course, the potential benefits to be derived from influencing tariff policy, taxation and public spending. But the last two of these reasons are surely inadequate in themselves, since members were unpaid throughout the nineteenth century, while public spending and taxation policies would have become of vastly greater import to the rich after their representation in Parliament had peaked. It is probably in the patrician social role of mid- and late-nineteenth century businessmen, particularly the factory-owners of the new industrial towns — which entailed as well a thorough and persuasive organisation of working-class loyalties — that the main reason for the rise and decline of the wealthy industrialist politician is to be sought.[44] By the time the political structure had been reorganised along exclusively class-based lines just after (or just before) the First World War, making this kind of local hegemony impossible, business life more and more came to be dichotomised between active and intelligent managers and hereditary asset-owners. The professionalisation of politics and politicians, moreover, meant that even very wealthy men, unprepared to make a career at politics or lacking the modern politician's skills, were less preferred than the modern professional, whatever his background.

   In the United States, however, and perhaps in a number of other Western countries as well, the past 20 years in particular have seen the rebirth of the millionaire politician, John F. Kennedy of course providing the model for this type. In the American case, it is probably fair to ascribe the rebirth of this type to the very large expenditures required by any serious candidate for major office, particularly at the national level. Yet these millionaire candidates have proved reasonably or, indeed, remarkably successful in persuading the ordinary man to vote for them. The ascendancy of an Edward Kennedy in Massachusetts or a Nelson Ròckefeller for 15 years in New York cannot be ascribed merely to lavish expenditures — since many of their opponents were wealthy men too — but as much as anything else to the American public's preference for the patrician, or even, in a sense, to its longing for the man on horseback who will rescue them from the dilemmas of self-governance (hence, too, their well-known preference for military horses) — in other words, to their immaturity, to their ability to think in terms of image and style rather than issues. That most such successful millionaire politicians have been (in the American context) men of the left is the greatest irony of all, perhaps the nearest analogy to the Roman world's bread and circuses which the modern age provides. It would be interesting to see if in the contemporary period anything of the sort can be found in other politics: for instance, are conservative French politicians now men of considerable wealth or merely affluent? The relatively few genuinely wealthy men in the last (1970-74) Conservative Ministry in Britain, like Peter Walker, were often self-made men and generally supporters of the 'moderate' Heath wing of the party, rather than Friedmanites, as is Mr Heath's successor Mrs Thatcher. Whether social and political attitudes, even ironical ones, can be derived from personal interest and wealth in the contemporary political scene in other societies is a very large question which remains to be studied in a searching way. Underlying it, and, indeed, underlying most issues surrounding the participation by very wealthy men in politics, is the question inherent in the two viewpoints sketched above: whether men, even (or even especially) very wealthy men, are the creatures of underlying economic and social forces which ultimately they are bound to obey whether they understand them or not, or whether men are essentially independent, and if history develops along its own fortuitous way: whether the bullets which stopped Lincoln and Kennedy, and which failed to stop Lenin, Hitler and Einstein, did not change the course of world events fundamentally and unalterably, in such a way that no bedrock of substructure could ever retrieve. It goes without saying that this raises issues so fundamental that no consensus can ever be reached or even attempted. However, as with almost every other issue related to wealth-holding, the historical research, without which no informed opinion whatever is possible, has barely begun.

Research into these important areas cannot possibly proceed without an adequate and relevant supply of historical sources. As remarked earlier, such sources do exist. The most important of these, at least in countries like France, the United States and Britain where the most research has been done, are the probate records of wealth passing at death. Yet, as one American historian recently remarked, 'Probate records, like tax records, yield to analysis reluctantly.'[45] There are wide and annoyingly anomalous gaps and idiosyncrasies in the probate records of almost all countries, however invaluable these records may be for such research. In Britain, to give some examples of this in a country known to me, real property is not included in the English valuation figures until 1898, and settled realty not until 1926. Net values are unavailable prior to 1881, while prior to 1858 (1876 in Scotland) no central system of probate existed, the probate process being in the hands of local ecclesiastical courts administered by the Church of England. The majority of the population left nothing at all, while the rich increasingly sought to avoid death duties by *inter vivos* gifts prior to their deaths. In colonial Massachusetts, to give another set of such examples, probate valuations included both realty and personalty, while in New Jersey and Pennsylvania only personal property was evaluated.[46] Several of the authors in this book have remarked on similar problems in their respective countries. If probate records are wayward in their coverage, other types of sources used in this field are even worse — for instance, the German census of millionaires undertaken only in 1913 or the Australian War Census of Income and Wealth, a unique work but one compiled only once, in 1915. One of the most striking facets of these essays, indeed, is the aplomb with which the contributors have drawn their conclusions from a wide variety of sources which often cease as suddenly as they began and are relevant only to brief periods of national history. Mastery — and often, indeed, discovery — of such sources is among the most difficult of all the talents required of the specialist in this area, and it is equally among the most exciting and interesting.

Wealth Distribution

The focus of this essay has been primarily on the very wealthy in their interaction with the rest of society, as evidenced by the sources available to the historian in this field, and very little has thus far been said of the aspect of this field dealing with the distribution of wealth and income throughout the whole of society. Perhaps the most basic thing to be said about this at the outset is that wealth is not the same as income, and that income is invariably distributed less unequally than wealth. In the United States, for instance, in 1962 the highest fifth of consumer units owned 76 per cent of the total personal wealth but earned only 57.2 per cent of all income; conversely, the lowest fifth of such units owned a mere 0.2 per cent of all wealth, but earned 7.2

per cent of all income.[47] Similar findings have been made for other societies.[48]

Historically, the distribution of wealth has appeared concentrated in the extreme, especially as the probate returns are the statistical base for almost all such estimates of wealth distribution. In 1858-59 the wealthiest *sixty-seven* English estates accounted for 22 per cent of all property passing by probate! The second main point concerning the historical distribution of wealth and income follows from this, and it is that, broadly speaking, wealth and income have become more equally divided, with income distribution equalising more rapidly and plainly than wealth distribution.

Lee Soltow has impressively discussed the long-term evidence for greater income equality in Britain, his evidence stretching from 1436 (sic) to 1962-63.[49] This trend has increased markedly in the twentieth century, as findings confirmed by evidence for the United States, Australia and elsewhere. [50] With wealth distribution the pattern has been much less marked. For much of this century in Britain there was very little apparent evidence (largely derived from the probate returns) of any appreciable diminution in wealth inequality; lately, however, a greater degree of equality has become evident.[51]

Whatever secular patterns may be true and be seen to be evidenced by good statistical sources, any assumptions about wealth and income inequality rest upon several assumptions which appear on closer examination to be misleading and confused. One is the assumption that the number of very wealthy persons in a society must be decreased if there is to be greater wealth or income equality, or, more precisely put, that countries with fewer wealthy people demonstrate greater equality than countries with more wealthy people. However, a moment's comparison of Britain with the United States — where the rich possess fortunes of unparalleled size and notoriously laugh at taxes, yet where income and wealth are distributed *more* equally — will demonstrate the fallaciousness of this. Britain evidences more inequality because, in a nutshell, it has, relatively, many more poor people than the United States, not because it has fewer rich ones. Defenders of capitalism would argue, moreover, that this is not coincidental: the same socialist mentality which has taxed the British rich to death has also prevented the creation of a mass-based affluent society, as has appeared in the United States. Throughout the whole debate on wealth and income inequalities on a national level, there remains the essential ambiguity that societies which 'clobber' the rich will produce a greater degree of equality than societies which 'coddle' them. The statistical evidence, for whatever it is worth, suggests, however, that precisely the opposite is true. It would be an interesting experiment to compare, at a sophisticated statistical level, whether nations or areas with low levels of wealth taxes and death duties demonstrate markedly greater degrees of inequality than nations or areas with high levels of such taxation. My guess is that, *ceteris paribus*, areas with low levels of wealth taxation would show statistically greater degrees of equality than areas with high wealth taxes. An interesting test case might be provided in the Australian states (Queensland, Victoria and Western Australia) which have recently *abolished all death duties.*[52] A comparison of these states either with the other Australian states which retain death duties or with Britain, the mother country, would be most illuminating, as would a comparison of trends in the three abolitionist states before and after. Again, my guess is that any trends found would be slight, and would, if anything, show relatively greater equality rather than inequality.

Because of the essential ambiguities concealed in a single set of numbers of income or wealth inequalities within a society, it is my opinion too, that, to the historian of wealth-holding, inferences about society derived from such statistics are inherently less valuable than inferences derived from assiduously chronicling and detailing the lives and careers of the wealthy and other elites, and fitting them into a coherent theory of the evolution of a particular society. This is a controversial view, and one probably not shared by some of my collaborators in this volume. However valuable such studies are — and there is no doubt, of course, that they are valuable — they omit the human and, indeed, psychological features wherein wealth influences the social and political structure of a society, and wealth in its turn is perceived in a certain way by the rest of society. No one confronted by the statistical evidence that wealth distribution in Britain remained virtually unchanged in the first 60 years of this century would guess that a social revolution had occurred there, or that the wealthy were infinitely less secure and powerful in the 1960s than in the Edwardian period, and still less could he begin to discern any divisions which may have existed *within* the wealthy class. Instead, he is presented with apparent evidence for solidity and with a statistical pattern which almost predisposes him to divide society simply into a tiny handful of rich and a great majority of poor, with very little in between.

Wealth and the obtaining of wealth can only be seen in depth as part of the wider issue of the bases, both economic and philosophical, of capitalism — although very wealthy persons, landowners, noblemen and merchants, appeared in pre-capitalistic modes of production. It is a real issue — but one which can only be touched upon in passing — whether in such societies wealth was a mask for (titled) status, or status for wealth: or, rather, *when* status became a mask for wealth. In eighteenth- and nineteenth-century Britain, for example, a lucrative and permanent income in the shape of a high agricultural rentroll was an essential prerequisite for ennoblement. When a title was bestowed upon a man lacking such a fitting source of income, this was either for compelling political reasons or because the money was given along with the title, as in the case of the Duke of Wellington, who began life as a younger son of an Irish earl and benefited from a grateful Parliament to the tune of £600,000 as a reward to support his dukedom. An interest in wealth, even then, was at least as strong as an interest in status. In 1789, to cite one of innumerable possible examples, Queen Charlotte wrote to Prince Augustus Frederick,

> The Earl of Huntingdon died about a fortnight ago. . .He has left, it is said, part of his fortune to his nephew L[o]rd Rawdon, and the family estate, Ashby de la Zouch, to his natural son whom he made take the name of Hastings and £2000 a year for this. . .It is also said that he has left to his niece L[a]dy Ailesbury £1500 a year. I hope and wish that to be true, as there never existed a more amiable creature than her.[53]

Ironically, Queen Charlotte's letter also furnished the first royal commentary on the event which eventually was everywhere to diminish title and status relative to wealth, for:

> France furnishes greater, but melancholy news. I often think that this cannot be the 18th Century in which we live at present, for antient [sic] history can hardly produce anything more barbarous and cruel than our neighbors in France.[54]

It was, then, clearly during the nineteenth century that nearly everywhere wealth and its possession became the supreme test of value. The dangers and unfairness of such a morality are obvious: its merits are perhaps less so, though among them could be advanced the emancipation of the Jews and their rise to eminence and prosperity in much of the Western world. For it is only a society in which 'contract' has replaced 'status' — to use Sir Henry Maine's famous terms — that civil liberties can flourish for all people and the successful, regardless of their origins or former disabilities, find their rewards. It was those societies where capitalist values flourished most, like Britain and the United States, which prospered most in the nineteenth century, and

which were the most decent places to live for all of the people,
including the men who were to draw up the theoretical programme of
capitalism's destruction.

It is the legacy of the nineteenth century which constitutes, even
now, the essential background of any serious discussion of the wealthy,
and this is nowhere clearer than in a comparison of communist with
capitalist societies as to how, if at all, status hierarchies are determined
by the possession of money. No matter what one may think of Marxism
either in theory or in practice, it is none the less true that even in the
Soviet Union (which would be attacked by the extreme left as 'state
capitalist') accumulations of wealth, and even high income-earners in
the Western sense, simply do not exist, even at the present time.[55] A
recent study, *Privilege in the Soviet Union*[56] took the threshold of the
lower limit of the Soviet elite of high income-earners in the period
1971-73 at 400 roubles ($500-$600 at the artificially high official rate
of exchange) per month — less than many janitors make in the United
States — though, to be sure, much less would be spent on such items
as rent, medical care and taxation than in most Western countries.[57]
The reported basic salary of the General Secretary of the Communist
Party is only 900 roubles per month; the estimated total wage of the
managers of the *largest* coalmines in the Soviet Union was 656 roubles
per month in 1970; among the managers of the *largest* factories in such
fields as textiles and foodstuffs, only 352 roubles per month.[58] As is
well known, however, such incomes are usually supplemented by
privileged access to Western goods, travel abroad and better housing,
while, needless to say, such statistics are irrelevant to any discussion of
the inordinate and dogmatic power wielded by these men. Nevertheless
(and this applies, *a fortiori*, to China and the poorer Soviet satellite
countries like, say, Bulgaria), Soviet communism has evolved an
economic system where there are, for all practical purposes, no
concentrations of wealth and income as are found in all Western
capitalist countries.[59]

Within the capitalist countries, discussion of this subject has often
centred around the famous distinction, made familiar by James
Burnham and others, about the 'managerial revolution'. Research on
this topic, particularly on an international level, has yet to bring the
wealth dimension into this discussion, but enough is clear from research
in Britain and elsewhere, as well as from the commonsense observations
of sociologists and economists, to see that this 'revolution' is largely
mythical: successful corporate managers are highly rewarded, at least
for the period of time when they are in executive positions, and

personally enter the wealth class as at least junior partners of the actual millionaire asset-owning dynasties. Among the chairmen of Britain's largest companies serving between 1880 and 1970 those who were 'managers' rather than 'asset-owners' (and who were thus often of relatively lowly social origin) themselves left fortunes at death ranging between £70,000 and £700,000, whereas the mean estate left at death in Britain, even now, is only £10,000-£15,000.[60] In America, in 1977, four corporation chairmen earned total salaries (including bonuses) in excess of one million dollars, while sixteen others earned between $750,000 and one million dollars.[61] Among these were such men as Ford's President, Lee Iaccocca, and Executive Vice-President, J. Edward Lundy, most definitely not relatives of the actual Ford dynasty. Such men are, however, by virtually any standard enormously wealthy, and their objective economic interests would be identical with those of any asset-owning millionaire, self-made or inherited. It can, moreover, be argued that the central reckoning-point of the corporate jungle, the bottom line, inherently places greater constraints on the behaviour of such executives, virtually ruling out any eccentric behaviour aimed at disgorging wealth, as was possible with such classical capitalist fortunes as those of Andrew Carnegie or the Rockefellers.

In the contemporary capitalist world, however, there is a real sense in which private accumulations of wealth are less important than previously. The reason for this, ironically, is that there is now too *much* money in private hands. The ability of even the wealthiest American multimillionaire or family of the present day to control economic events is obviously inherently much less in a $2 trillion economy than in, say, the $100 billion economy of 1910; especially as, in real terms, the very wealthiest living Americans are poorer than their counterparts of 70 years ago,[62] and this takes no account of the many sources of countervailing economic and political power which exist within all contemporary Western societies. Economic power increasingly lies with impersonal corporate entities subject to government and trade union pressures, their assets in turn owned not by individuals but by institutions like insurance companies, banks, endowed universities and foundations, pension funds of every description — and trade unions. This wheel of power has no matrix; as Charles Fort put it, one can draw a circle, beginning at any point. In many ways, society would be better off if there *were* a tiny, coherent group of finance capitalists who in actual fact ran things: blame could be assigned and utopia brought into existence by their sudden elimination. Unfortunately, such men do not exist.

Conclusion

Any introductory and general essay concerning a scholarly field so
much in its infancy as that of wealth studies must seem at once
inadequate and idiosyncratic; indeed, it seems to me perfectly plain
that a really satisfactory essay discussing the many facets of this
subject at an international and comparative level cannot yet be
written, and perhaps will not be for 20 years or more. This introduction
can, however, close on a theme which must be far less a matter of
dispute, those areas where further research in this field ought to be
done, if satisfactory answers are to be given, and, indeed, if satisfactory
questions are to be asked. One of the most striking facts which has
become evident to me as editor of this volume is that there is a law of
unequal development about comparative history no less than in
Marxist economics, and the gap between countries, like France or the
United States, where there is much interest in this field, and others
where there is not, is simply immense. (This is, needless to say, no
reflection on the abilities of those historians who have had to write on
this field in these other countries; if anything, it is a compliment to
their achievement.) Certainly the historian of this subject wishes, above
all, that much more detailed research will be set in train in those
countries where little has been done before, especially in those
supremely important societies like Germany and Czarist Russia. As a
prelude, it goes without saying that we require fuller listings of the
source material and resources available to the historian of this field,
and to much more frequent opportunities for liaising over common
problems and discoveries. Given the haphazardness of virtually all
historical research, particularly that which is so much an acquired taste
as this, the wish is unlikely to be father to the deed, at least for a good
many years. In the meantime, one can hope that at least in those
countries like France, Britain and the United States where the surface
has been scratched, research will continue and will deepen, and the
body of scholars in the field will continue to grow.

Such a growth in scholarship may provide us with transnationally
equivalent answers, but it is equally important that we have a common
set of questions. And it is here, perhaps more than in the actual
techniques or programmes of research themselves, that comparative
studies into wealth-holding are most likely to prove disappointing.
Throughout my own writings, I have argued for the importance of
discerning salient lines of division within the wealthy class, and of
linking these in a compelling way with larger divisions within society as

a whole; so long as wealth studies continue to focus narrowly on *horizontal* divisions within society, or simply upon secular changes in the distribution of wealth or income, it is my belief that the most truly illuminating and valuable consequences of such studies will not be brought out. It is this interdisciplinary approach, but one grounded essentially in accurate and sophisticated statistics about the rich and other elites, which is the most fruitful direction in which future research can go.

There is one important dimension of the study of the wealthy which has not been touched upon at all in this discussion, though it is mentioned in several of the essays in the volume. This is the psychological, and its essential purpose is to address the question of whether wealth-making is a form of deviant behaviour. It is important to stress the point that a psychological approach can only deal with self-made men — those who inherit great wealth merely find themselves in a peculiar milieu, and their reactions and lifestyles a matter of socialisation into the milieu. Particularly in America, however, virtually every word ever written on the very rich has quickly turned into a discussion of the bizarre, antisocial, guilt-ridden and even pathological behaviour and lifestyles of the multimillionaires, of which there have been some notable examples in our own time. No one would dispute the fact that the notable self-made millionaires are all unusual men, with excessive drive and ability, and, presumably, all the psychological tensions which accompany these qualities. But to push this argument too far seems to me to be illusory. America's 200 richest self-made men are probably as diverse a group as any group of 200 men, if not more so, with every personality type represented. What applies to America is, I suspect, even truer elsewhere, particularly in Britain where the very rich seem to have been as singularly dull a lot of men as one can conceive, even the conspicuousness of their display being much modified by the relatively rigid patterns of West End and country-house life and by English decorum. If it is the case that *place* in the economy, rather than effort or even any particular degree of ruthlessness or cunning, is the most important quality required to earn a great fortune, then — beyond a fairly minimal degree of business acumen and persistence — it is far from clear that personality or psychology is in any way related to money-making. However, as always, this can be determined only by sophisticated and extensive research at an interdisciplinary level — that is, if employing the tools of psychology does not predispose the discovery of excessive numbers of aberrants. Given the means at their disposal, bizarre or conspicuous consumption or behaviour by the rich could not be well hidden, and it might well be possible to psychoanalyse this group more readily than most in the past. This is one approach historians of this subject must certainly wish to take, at least once the essential preliminary research has been done.

Notes

1. See, for example, Richard Titmuss, *Income Distribution and Social Change* (London, 1962); A.B. Atkinson (ed.), *Wealth, Income and Inequality* (London, 1973); A.B. Atkinson and A.J. Harrison, *The Distribution of Personal Wealth in Britain* (Cambridge, 1978).
2. See, for example, A.B. Atkinson, *Unequal Shares – The Distribution of Wealth in England* (London, 1974) and *The Economics of Inequality* (Oxford, 1975), as well as Colin Harbury's essays, cited in Chapter 1 below (p. 83 n29).
3. See George Polanyi and John B. Wood, *How Much Inequality?* (London, Institute of Economic Affairs, 1974).
4. For example, see the relevant sections of John Westergaard and Henrietta Resler, *Class in a Capitalist Society* (London, 1975). But, on the other hand, for Australia see L. Broom and F.L. Jones, *Opportunity and Attainment in Australia* (Canberra, 1976).
5. See Lee Soltow, 'Long-run Changes in British Income Inequality', *Economic History Review*, 2nd series, 21 (1968), and his more recent *Patterns of Wealthholding in Wisconsin Since 1850* (Madison, Wisc., 1971) and *Men and Wealth in the United States, 1850-1970* (New Haven, 1975).
6. See Edward Pessen, *Riches, Class, and Power Before the Civil War* (Lexington, Mass., 1973).
7. See W.D. Rubinstein, 'The Victorian Middle Classes: Wealth, Occupation and Geography', *Economic History Review*, 2nd series, 30 (1977).
8. For instance, Harold Perkin's recent study of British elite groups 1880-1970, and the references to further research in this area in his articles in *Social History* in 1976 and 1978.
9. See, for example, Atkinson's works cited above.
10. As in W.D. Rubinstein, 'Wealth, Elites, and the Class Structure of Modern Britain', *Past and Present*, 76 (1977), and 'Victorian Middle Classes'.
11. There are certain other qualitative differences between these two sources of a minor nature.
12. Harbury's works are cited in Chapter 1 below; Harold Perkin, *The Origins of Modern English Society, 1780-1880* (London, 1969), pp. 410-28.
13. In 1892, the *New York Tribune* found about 4,047 living American millionaires. Because of primogeniture in landowning and other factors inherent in the structure of British economic development, it is possible that the relative number of British fortunes of equivalent size was just as great. (I discuss this matter in my forthcoming *Men of Property: The Wealthy in Modern Britain.*) The factor of primogeniture and other relevant features of the British scene would presumably be missing in other European societies, where the relative numbers of top wealth-holders were presumably lower.
14. Calvin Tomkins, *Merchants and Masterpieces* (New York, 1970), p. 177.
15. See Gustavus Myers, *A History of Canadian Wealth* (Chicago, 1914, reprinted Toronto, 1972).
16. Adeline Daumard, *Les Fortunes Françaises au XIXe Siècle* (Paris, 1973), pp. 208-9.

17. G.H. Knibbs, *The Private Wealth of Australia and Its Growth* (Melbourne, 1918), p.62.

18. Other great central European magnates, like the Esterhazys in Hungary, must have been immensely wealthy as well.

19. On the other hand, the peak South African gold and diamond fortunes were legendary, and certainly very great by any standards.

20. Alvin Moscow, *The Rockefeller Inheritance* (New York, 1977), p. 82.

21. Rubinstein, 'Wealth, Elites, and the Class Structure'.

22. See Stephen E. Koss, *Sir John Brunner: Radical Plutocrat, 1842-1919* (Cambridge, 1970).

23. There has never been a proper historical study of the decline of 'Old Corruption' in Britain, despite the fact that 'economical reform' was a leading battlecry of the English reform movement of the day.

24. Rubinstein, 'Wealth, Elites, and the Class Structure'. See also John Wade's *The Extraordinary Black Book* (London, 1820-32, reprinted New York, 1970).

25. Rubinstein, 'Wealth, Elites, and the Class Structure'.

26. Moscow, *Rockefeller*, pp. 68ff.

27. Ibid., p. 75.

28. Several discussions in the American press of the Soviet view of the 1964 election included this distinction. See, for example, *New York Times*, 25 October 1964, or S. Menshikov's study of America's plutocracy, *Millionaires and Managers* (Moscow, 1973), and N. Sivachyov and E. Yaykov, *History of the U.S.A. Since World War One* (Moscow, 1976), pp. 337ff.

29. For example (and surprisingly), among British millionaires deceased 1960-69, where nearly one-third were 'self-made'. See W.D. Rubinstein, 'Men of Property: Some Aspects of Occupation, Inheritance and Power Among Top British Wealthholders' in P. Stanworth and A. Giddeus (eds.), *Elites and Power in British Society* (Cambridge, 1974), pp. 161ff.

30. On the other hand, some studies of the social origins of business leaders probably *understate* the real amount of such mobility from bottom to top by focusing on groups like big industrialists, landowners or bankers, which were socially more exclusive and difficult for new men to enter, ignoring such fields as real estate and property development, retailing or entertainment, where higher rates of social mobility could be expected.

31. 'The Equalitarian Myth and American Social Reality: Wealth, Mobility, and Equality in the "Era of the Common Man"', *American Historical Review* (1971), p. 1012.

32. On the dissipation of the great Thornton mercantile and insurance fortune over several generations, see W.G. Hoskins, 'Richard Thornton: A Victorian Millionaire', *History Today* (1962).

33. It is in any case inherently implausible that already-wealthy dynastics would go to the painstaking lengths required to establish a fortune in an entirely new field. Such is normally the domain of entirely new men like Richard Arkwright or Henry Ford.

34. Atkinson and Harrison, *Distribution of Personal Wealth*, especially Ch. 6.

35. See, for example, Oliver Marriott, *The Property Boom* (London, 1969).

36. For evaluations of this point of view see Richard L. McCormick, 'Ethno-cultural Interpretations of Nineteenth-Century American Voting Behavior', *Political Science Quarterly* (1974), and J. Morgan Kousser, 'The "New Political History": A Methodological Critique', *Reviews in American History* (1976). The best historical study informed by this viewpoint is Paul John Kleppner, *The Cross of Culture: A Social Analysis of Midwestern Politics, 1850-1900* (New York, 1970). See also Edward Pessen's interesting article, 'Who Rules America? Power and Politics in the Democratic Era 1825-1975', *Prologue* (1977).

37. See T.S. Ashton, *The Industrial Revolution* (London, 1948), and
E.E. Hagen, *On the Theory of Social Change* (Cambridge, Mass., 1964).
38. M.W. Flinn, 'Social Theory and the Industrial Revolution' in Tom Burns
and S.B. Saul (eds.), *Social Theory and Economic Change* (London, 1967).
39. Hagen, *Social Change*, pp. 261-309.
40. Max Weber, *The Protestant Ethic and the Spirit of Capitalism* (London,
1930), p. 271 n. 58.
41. See Rubinstein, 'Victorian Middle Classes'.
42. See, for instance, Ralph Miliband, *The State in Capitalist Society* (London,
1973), and R.W. Connell, *Ruling Class, Ruling Culture* (Melbourne, 1977). The
inspiration, of course, derives from Gramsci.
43. See Chapter 1 below.
44. For Britain, see Patrick Joyce, 'The Factory Politics of Lancashire in the
Later Nineteenth Century', *Historical Journal* (1975).
45. Gary B. Nash, *Class and Society in Early America* (Englewood Cliffs,
NJ, 1970), p. 63.
46. Ibid.
47. Daniel W. Rossides, *The American Class System. An Introduction to
Social Stratification* (Boston, 1976), p. 127.
48. On Britain, see Atkinson *Wealth, Income and Inequality*, especially
Parts 2 and 4.
49. Soltow, 'Long-run Changes'.
50. For example, H.P. Miller, *Income Distribution in the United States*
(Washington, DC, US Government Printing Office, 1966).
51. See Atkinson and Harrison, *Distribution of Personal Wealth*.
52. Death duties are also levied upon very large estates by the federal
government of Australia, but there are plans afoot to abolish most of these as well.
53. A. Aspinall (ed.), *The Later Correspondence of George III, Volume One,
1783-1793* (Cambridge, 1966), p. 440, dated 17 August 1789.
54. Ibid.
55. An exception to this sweeping statement might have to be made for the
few earners of very substantial royalties or prize monies (as in international
sporting competitions), but even these, of course, cannot *invest* in anything.
56. Mervyn Matthews, *Privilege in the Soviet Union. A Study of Elite
Life-styles under Communism* (London, 1978).
57. Ibid., pp. 22-3.
58. Ibid., pp. 23-4.
59. One distinguished Australian sociologist who is himself a refugee from a
Soviet satellite country illustrates this point by an anecdote about a Western
journalist taken to see the flat of the First Vice-President of the Hungarian State
Bank. Containing no fewer than four bedrooms, it stands in an imposing
apartment bloc on Budapest's most fashionable street. When questioned about
how he reconciled such luxury with his socialist principles, its occupant asked –
not without justice – what the journalist imagined the house belonging to the
First Vice-President of *Austria's* largest bank looked like.
60. These figures are taken from the SSRC-sponsored project on the Economic
Worth of Elite Groups in Britain, 1880-1970, undertaken by Harold Perkin in
1974-75; I acted as Research Associate on this project.
61. *Business Week*, 15 May 1978. Eight American *union heads* earned
$100,000 or more in 1977. Teamster Union President Frank E. Fitzsimmons
topped this list at $160,000 (ibid).
62. In 1978 the two richest American families, the duPonts and Mellons,
were estimated to be worth $2-5 *billion* each but both would have comprised
several dozen family members at least. The Gettys and self-made shipping magnate

Daniel K. Ludwig were estimated to be worth $2-3 billion; the Rockefellers collectively $1-2 billion. No other families or individuals were worth more than $1 billion (which is the equivalent of less than $200 million on 1910 dollars). See Dan Rottenberg, 'America's Richest People', *Town and Country*, May 1978.

1 MODERN BRITAIN

W.D. Rubinstein

Sources and Previous Research

This chapter aims to discuss the most important aspects of wealth-holding and the wealthy in modern Britain under three general headings: sources of information for the historian working in this field, and previous research; main characteristics of the wealthy class since the early nineteenth century, including such dimensions as range of wealth, occupation, social mobility, religious affiliation and landowning among the very wealthy, together with some general observations on the distribution of wealth and income among the entire population and its change over time; and the areas in which research might most usefully be carried on. The author has already attempted to stress the *sui generis* and distinctive features of the British wealth structure, compared with those in similar nations, in the Introduction.

The historian concerned with questions of wealth-holding or distribution in modern Britain is fortunate to possess a series of relevant sources perhaps unrivalled among those of any similar country, because of the lengthy and continuous span of their scope, the relative ease with which the researcher may gain access to much (but not all) of this material, and their centralised and unified manner of organisation.

Probate Records

Unquestionably the most important series of records for the researcher concerned with the wealthy as a social group, or with individual wealth-holders of the past, are the probate records which since 9 January 1858 have covered the estates of every person leaving property in England and Wales in one national repository, since 1874 at the Principal Probate Registry at Somerset House in London. There, in printed annual alphabetical indexes, are detailed the names, addresses, gross size of estate and often other information such as the occupation, of all such persons. These entries serve as the indexes for locating the relevant will or letter of administration, as well as possessing a wide interest and wide range of utility for the social and economic historian. Previous to 1858 in England and Wales the probate process was in the hands of the ecclesiastical (Church of England) authorities, which maintained several dozen ecclesiastic courts among the many

46

bishoprics and peculiar (independent) areas of jurisdiction in England and Wales: consequently, the identification or even the location of probate of the estate of a particular individual is often exceedingly difficult, especially as there is no adequate general index encapsulating all of the many probate courts.[1] However, for a historical study of wealth-holding, this difficulty is not insurmountable, as the great bulk of very large estates were proved in one of the two Prerogative Courts, those of Canterbury (located at Doctor's Commons in London and holding jurisdiction over roughly the southern two-thirds of England and all of Wales) and York (located at York and governing the northern third of England, including Lancashire and Yorkshire). In particular, the will of a very wealthy man (or an aristocrat, bishop, high-ranking military officer or other 'top person') was highly likely to have been proved in the Canterbury Prerogative Court.[2] As part of the research into wealth-holding in Britain undertaken by this author, the records of the two Prerogative Courts and the local ecclesiastical court records currently held by the Lancashire Record Office, Preston,[3] were checked, and all estates totalling £100,000 or more in value were counted. Between 1809 and 1858 a total of 1,220 such estates were proved in the Canterbury, 72 in the York and only 22 in the Lancashire local courts. This overwhelming majority in favour of Canterbury decreased, however, with the passage of time, with 98.5 per cent of the 200 wealthy estates probated in 1809-19 proved in Canterbury, but only 85.6 per cent of the 249 top estates of the 1850-58 period probated there.[4] This probably reflected the rising level of purely provincial wealth.

The probate sources in Scotland and Ireland have a different history. The Scottish printed indexes only begin in 1876.[5] A nationwide manuscript index covering the period 1825-75 exists, arranged chronologically by shire court or county. It is held by the Scottish Record Office, Edinburgh, and access to it is at present heavily restricted.[6] Previous to that, probate records were kept only at the county or shire court level, rather than nationally. Irish records before 1858 were largely destroyed in the Four Courts fire of 1922. An annual alphabetical printed index, similar to the English probate calendars, was published for all of Ireland from 1858 until 1917, and then again for Northern Ireland from October 1921.[7]

It is important to realise that the indexes, containing the gross valuation figure,[8] may be consulted (for free) and the will read (for free or for a small fee) for any person leaving property in Britain from the Middle Ages[10] down to those deceased only a few weeks or months before: this liberalism applies alike to dead Prime Ministers, peers of the realm (but not the Royal Family), one's maiden aunt or erstwhile next-door neighbour. Astonishingly, in view of the Englishman's vaunted love of privacy, this has not resulted in widespread calls for greater secrecy, probably because it has not produced much perceptible abuse (nor, unfortunately, much greater use of these sources by bona fide researchers other than genealogists). Britain's probate records are probably unique among those of the major countries in this respect, and the uses to which this uniquely rich and significant historical source may be put has only just begun to tax the ingenuity of scholars. Because they plainly state the names, size of estate and other biographical information, use of them is probably a necessary precondition for any historical study of the rich in Britain.[11]

Annual Report of the Inland Revenue

The probate records held by the Principal Probate Registry at Somerset House and other similar archives must be distinguished from those probate records collected by the Estate Duty Office of the Inland Revenue, and whose summary statistics have been published annually since the mid-1890s in the *Annual Report of the Inland Revenue* in the Parliamentary Papers. Statistics or inferences drawn from this series have served as the basis for most discussions of wealth distribution in Britain, both in the early part of the century and at the present time. The valuations here differ somewhat from those in the Somerset House archives in recording net rather than gross worth, in continuously including realty, as well as the worth of certain types of settlements excluded by the Principal Probate Registry, and in adding in the value of *inter vivos* gifts 'caught' by the time limit on gifts made prior to death (currently seven years). They are anonymous, and published statistics in the Inland Revenue's *Report* and sources derived from them consist only of tables of range of estates, components of assets etc.,[12] and hence are of greater value to the economist than to the social historian.

Since accurate historical sources relating to *income* were collected for the most part by the Inland Revenue, access to individual returns is subject to the same 150-year rule of confidentiality as are those of the Estate Duty Office. As a result, it is not possible to gain access to individual income tax returns or to abstract the names of the top income-earners in the manner of the top wealth-holders in the probate records.[13] As with the Estate Duty Office figures, the scholar is limited to the wide-ranging but anonymous statistics of taxable income distribution published in the *Annual Report of the Inland Revenue*. With the historical statistics of taxable incomes in Britain, however, another and more formidable difficulty exists, namely that the system of schedules of taxable income in force after 1803 makes it impossible to ascertain the total number of incomes by size of *individual* incomes until the 'supertax' of the Lloyd George period at last presents the scholar with some meaningful statistical data on very large incomes.[14] These notable deficiencies did not, however, deter numerous late-Victorian and Edwardian writers from attempting to use the nineteenth-century income tax (which was levied from 1798 to 1815 and from 1842 onwards) to estimate the size and distribution of incomes during that period, for instance in the cases of Dudley Baxter, Leone Levi and Leo Chiozza Money.[15] Contemporary economic historians concerned with national income growth and distribution have also used these sources and others to measure long-term trends in these areas.[16] However, the limitations of the source materials in this sphere have clearly prevented an exhaustive historical discussion of income distribution, and the utility of the income tax data is rather limited for the nineteenth-century British historian.[17] At the present time, the Inland Revenue is gradually transferring most of its remaining nineteenth-century records to the Public Record Office's new branch at Kew, and it is quite possible that a systematic examination of this new material will shed a considerable light on historical income distribution and related questions.[18]

Other Sources

Along with the probate and income tax records, Britain possesses a number of other statistical sources of very considerable interest and utility to the historian of this subject. Many of these can be found only in manuscript form or lie buried deep within the more obscure volumes of the Parliamentary Papers, often badly indexed, and historians have only scratched the surface in their use. Only three general headings can be discussed here. Perhaps the most promising of these are the statistics of the Inhabited House Duty, a tax which, as the name implies, was levied on all inhabited dwellings between 1778 and 1834, and again from 1851 until 1925. No surviving individual returns exist, but a wealth of manuscript (generally classified at I.R.16 in the Public Record Office) or published sources are available.[19] The special value of this source lies in the fact that assessments were made according to the size of rental or (in the case of freeholds) imputed rental (and not, for example, the rateable value) of a house, which would of course be highly income-elastic. If this source is indeed as fruitful as it seems, a way may thus be found to circumvent the disadvantages of the income tax data in ascertaining income distribution during the nineteenth century.[20]

Secondly, each round of parliamentary reform or mooted reform during the nineteenth century produced an avalanche of statistical tables in the Parliamentary Papers relating the representation, or proposed representation, of constituencies to income and wealth, often in unique detail. (Until the late nineteenth century it was generally assumed that local wealth ought to be a factor in determining representation.) For instance, an 1861 return detailed – so far as I am aware, uniquely – the total number of individual males in each parliamentary city and borough who were charged to any assessed tax or to the income tax under Schedule B or D in the previous year.[21] Several other returns detail the amount assessed under each schedule of the income tax by parliamentary constituency.[22] In particular, a host of such statistical compilations were produced during the debate on reform in the late 1850s and 1860s.[23]

Thirdly, there should be mentioned the unique source of information on British landowners, their acreage and income, compiled by Parliament and published in the Parliamentary Papers in 1874-76, the *Return of Owners of Land.*[24] The statistics contained here were later edited and collated by John Bateman into the famous *Great Landowners of Great Britain and Ireland.*[25] Bateman's work contains the names and biographical information on every landowner possessing more than 2,000 acres or an income of £2,000 per annum or more in the *Return*, with both national and county-by-county totals for acreage and income. This official return, the first since the Domesday Book (and hence often referred to as the 'New Domesday Book') had, according to persistent rumours, a successor compiled during the period of the Lloyd George land tax around 1910: according to these reports, a second *Return* was in progress when the outbreak of the war called a halt with about half the country surveyed. These returns, or at least summaries of them, are said to exist at the Public Record Office, but have not yet been made available to researchers. They would, needless to say, be of the keenest interest to historians of landowning, and should certainly be opened to scholars if they indeed exist.[26]

Examples of research into the fields of wealth-holding and wealth distribution, which rely in whole or in part upon the statistical sources described here, may be found in the areas of economics, economic and social history, and sociology. Of particular note is the widespread and lively debate into the distribution of wealth and income in contemporary Britain, which has itself grown out of the previous debate on this subject in late-Victorian and Edwardian times referred to above.[27] In recent years such economists as J.R.S. Revell, A.B. Atkinson and C.T. Sandford have addressed the question of contemporary wealth distribution, employing the Inland Revenue's probate figures as their major source of debate.[28] Special mention should be made in this context of the major research contributions of Professor Colin Harbury of the City University, London, and his associates, into inheritance and social mobility among top wealth-leavers in the 1960s and 1970s, which he is now pushing back to include wealth-leavers of an earlier period.[29] Professor Harbury's research was inspired in part by the work of Josiah Wedgwood in the 1920s on the same subject in *The Economics of Inheritance*.[30] It is clear that a major debate, and one with the widest larger implications, is taking place among British economists in this field, to which the statistical sources on wealth and income distribution are of central importance.

The fields of economic and social history have been considerably less well served by previous research into British wealth or wealth-holding. The exception to this (and only in a manner of speaking) is, of course, in the domain of business histories, of which there are innumerable examples. Whether this is because, unlike their French and American colleagues, British historians failed until recently to command the minimal quantitative skills necessary for successful research in this area, or because of the widespread preoccupation, especially among social historians, with working-class and labour history, it remains true that, with the possible exception of landed wealth, the wealthy as a group, or indeed research about any social group employing systematic evidence from the probate records or similar sources, can hardly be said to exist before the 1970s.[31] Even so important a work as Harold Perkin's *Origins of Modern English Society* fails to mention more than one or two probate valuations in its discussion of wealthy individuals or elites, although certainly dealing at length with the indices of wealth distribution during the nineteenth century.[32] Professor Perkin has since rectified this by conducting a fully fledged research project on the wealth and social origins of British elites, 1880-1970, making greater use of the probate records than any previous such project.[33] Recently published work employing the probate records to illuminate aspects of elite life include John Foster on the nineteenth-century industrial bourgeoisie, David Cannandine on

landed wealth, and several essays by the present author on wealth-
holding and the structure of nineteenth-century society.[34] Research
projects currently underway or recently completed which use these and
similar sources as an important research tool include investigations into
areas as diverse as the eighteenth- and nineteenth-century judiciary, civil
servants and Cabinet Committees, nineteenth-century scientists and the
Scottish probate inventories of the 1880-1914 period.[35] It is an
interesting commentary on the growth of this field — and perhaps on
changing attitudes as well — that probate valuations do not appear in
Namier and Brooks's *The House of Commons, 1754-1790,* or its
successor volumes — though surely Namier would have been aware
both of their availability and utility — although they do in the more
recent biographical notices of working-class leaders in John Saville and
Joyce Bellamy's *Dictionary of Labour Biography*!

As with social and economic history, British sociology has
incorporated a wealth perspective into its theoretical writings on British
society only recently. Stemming as it does so largely from a quasi-social-
work background, its chief founders either isolated extra-academic
figures like Spencer, or indeed Marx, or associated with the piecemeal
Fabian tradition of empirical investigation into social problems *à la*
Booth and Rowntree, it has until very recently eschewed all-
encompassing studies of the structure of society, and failed as well to
develop an independent Marxist tradition of any intellectual
respectability.[36] However, with the increased popularity (and, many
would argue, overpopularity) of sociology as a university discipline, and
with the rise of a new generation of radical or Marxist thought, this is
changing, and many of the most important of recent studies by British
sociologists touch broadly on the structure of modern society from a
perspective entailing a class and wealth-distribution viewpoint.[37]
Several well-known anthologies of articles on the principal facets of
power-holding and its base in political economy are evidence of this
new-found interest,[38] as are several stimulating works from an explicitly
Marxist perspective.[39] However, *original* research by sociologists in this
field has been surprisingly slim, their historical and quantitative analysis
drawn heavily from the aforementioned work of economists on wealth
distribution or from writings of non-sociologists, such as
W.L. Guttsman's *The British Political Elite* or even Anthony Sampson's
(admittedly invaluable) *Anatomy of Britain.*

Mention of Sampson's gossipy journalism on British elites and
decision-makers reminds us of the time-honoured tradition of writings
on the wealthy and on successful entrepreneurs in the popular vein, a

tradition at least as old as *Fortunes Made in Business* of 1883, the *Financial Times*'s series on putative British millionaires of 1897, and such volumes as T.C. Bridges and H. Hessel Tiltman, *Kings of Commerce* (1928), and continued in such contemporary analyses as Thomas Wiseman, *The Money Motive* (1974), Raymond Pinter, *Fortunes To Be Made* (1970), and Alan Jenkins's *The Rich Rich* (1977).[40] At the level intermediate between serious scholarship and journalism are a number of extremely useful popular studies of aspects of contemporary British wealth, like Roy Perrott's *The Aristocrats* (1968) and Oliver Marriott's *The Property Boom* (1969). Yet the impression persists that serious social analysis of the wealthy in Britain, both historically and in the contemporary world, has not been notably strong.[41]

The Statistics of Wealth-holding

This section, which forms the heart of this chapter, is largely based upon my own research into this subject, and is on the whole statistical in its presentation.[42] My study of wealth-holders in Britain surveyed all persons leaving £500,000 or more between 1809 and 1939, with the addition of two groups of 'lesser wealthy' — those leaving £150,000 or more between 1809 and 1829, and £250,000 or more in the period 1850-69, in order to increase the size of the group in the earlier period, and subject to the exclusion of real property as mentioned above. In addition, the other variety of sources available to the historian on wealth and income noted above have also been drawn upon where necessary to further illuminate the discussion.

Range of Wealth and Number of Wealth-holders

Perhaps the most basic matter which can be discussed is that of the range of wealth and number of wealth-holders. How much does it take to be rich, to be numbered among the country's richest men? Clearly, this will vary widely from place to place and time to time. Because of the relative completeness of the probate figures, these questions can be answered with a considerable degree of definitiveness in the case of Britain, bearing in mind again the special matter of landed wealth.

During the late eighteenth and very early nineteenth centuries, it appears that a personal fortune of £500,000 to £1 million would have been sufficient to place its holders among the very richest of Englishmen: this figure was exceeded seldom if ever by any personal fortune in this period. In this range of wealth were such men as John Moore, Archbishop of Canterbury (d. 1805), who left £1 million;

Samuel Fludyer (d. 1786), 'probably the richest clothier in England', who left £900,000; the miser John Elwes, probably worth £800,000 in 1789; the financier Abraham Franco (d. 1777), the banker John Denison (d. 1806), and the great potter Josiah Wedgwood (d. 1795), each worth £500,000-600,000 at their deaths.[43] Since usable probate figures begin only in 1809, this list cannot be regarded as comprehensive: yet it would be surprising if any vastly greater British fortune existed at the time. This level of wealth is, indeed, probably not greater than the largest personal fortune of the seventeenth century: examples merely occurred more frequently.

From 1809 fairly precise figures can be given for the largest personal fortunes. Dividing the span down to 1939 into successive 30-year intervals, some indication of the change in the top levels of personal wealth-holding can be gained from Table 1.1, a list of the three largest estates of each such period.

Since these figures exclude realty for most of the period surveyed, they probably exaggerate the upward rise in the peaks of British wealth-holding. Although the wealth of those landowners who were lucky enough to own them continued to rise with the increasing value of urban property and mineral deposits, in whose development they played so prominent a part, it is probably the case that the personalty of an early-nineteenth-century landowner like the first Duke of Sutherland (which is recorded in Table 1.1) would, if added to his purely landed wealth (which is not), exceed even the fortune of a Rothschild: 'I believe he was the richest individual who ever died', was Greville's comment at his death.[44] By the end of the nineteenth century, the Duke of Westminster was said to be worth £14 million on his London holdings alone,[45] with the very greatest landed magnates like the Dukes of Devonshire, Bedford or Portland, or the Earl of Derby, not far behind. Indeed, C. Northcote Parkinson has recently stated that even in 1885 Westminster may have been wealthier than the richest American millionaire, W.H. Vanderbilt.[46]

None the less, these figures serve to indicate the progressive rise in the size of the greatest personal fortunes during the nineteenth century, and the extent to which the growth of the British economy allowed a handful of the keenest or luckiest businessmen to enrich themselves. To be sure, each of these men was highly anomalous, and none more so than the very richest of the wealth cohort.[47]

Ascertaining the size of the bulk of Britain's wealth class – those with fortunes in excess of £100,000 – is hampered by the paucity of collected and published nineteenth-century probate statistics. Until the

Table 1.1: Top Wealth-leavers, 1809-1939

			£ millions*
1809-1839:	1.	Nathan M. Rothschild (d. 1836), merchant banker	c. 5
	2.	George, first Duke of Sutherland (d. 1833), landowner	c. 2
	3.	Sir Robert Peel, 1st Bt (d. 1830), cotton manufacturer	c. 1.5
1840-79:	1.	James Morrison (d. 1857), warehouseman and merchant banker	c. 4
	2.	Thomas Brassey (d. 1870), railway contractor	3.2
	3.	Giles Loder (d. 1871), Russia merchant	2.9
1880-1909:**	1.	Charles Morrison (d. 1909), warehouseman and merchant banker	10.9
	2.	Herman, Baron de Stern (d. 1887), merchant banker	3.5
	3.	Wentworth Beaumont, first Baron Allendale (d. 1907), landowner	3.2
1910-39:	1.	Sir John R. Ellerman, 1st Bt (d. 1933), shipowner and financier	36.7
	2.	Edward A. Guinness, first Earl of Iveagh (d. 1927), brewer	13.5
	3.	James Williamson, first Baron Ashton (d. 1930), linoleum manufacturer	10.5

*Most of the millionaire estates proved before about 1860 were sworn in the probate calendars at 'Upper Value' (i.e. above £1 million) or 'Above £1m'. The figures given here are based on contemporary estimates.
**Sir Julius Werhner (d. 1912) and Alfred Beit (d. 1906), the South African gold magnates, left, respectively, £10 million and £8 million in Britain. Samuel J. Loyd, first Baron Overstone (d. 1883), the banker, left £2.1 million in personalty plus land which had cost about £3.1 million to purchase.

Inland Revenue statistics first become available in 1894, in order to construct a continuous series, it is necessary to abstract such a list from the probate calendars by hand. The results of this exercise, summarised by five-year averages, are given in Table 1.2.

Several important trends may be discerned from Table 1.2. The period of the Napoleonic Wars and first 15 post-war years witnessed a sharp rise in the number of wealthy deaths, most likely a product of the inflation of that time and fanned by the deaths of newly rich war

Table 1.2: Estates of £100,000 or More, Five-year Annual Average Number, 1809-94, with Percentage Change over Previous Period

Years	Average Annual Number	Percentage Change
1809-14 (6 years)	16.5	–
1815-19	18.2	+ 11.0
1820-24	25.6	+ 40.7
1825-29	29.0	+ 13.3
1830-34	29.4	+ 1.4
1835-39	30.4	+ 3.4
1840-45	30.2	– 0.7
1845-49	29.2	– 3.3
1850-54	31.6	+ 8.2
1855-58*	37.0	+ 19.0
1858-59	49.5	+ 33.8
1860-64	55.4	+ 11.9
1865-69	76.2	+ 37.5
1870-74	114.8	+ 50.7
1875-79	115.0	+ 0.2
1880-84	141.6	+ 29.1
1885-89	149.6	+ 2.1
1890-94	185.5	+ 30.0

*Series broken by the institution of the Principal Probate Registry from 9 January 1858.

Source: Prior to 1858, from the Canterbury and York Prerogative, the Lancashire and Scottish court records (from 1825 to 1875), as explained above. From 1858, from the English/Welsh, Scottish and Irish probate calendars. It should be noted again that these numbers include personal estates only. Since they were the result of manual abstraction, there is a possible element of human error built into them.

contractors.[48] There then ensued a period of 25 years in which the number of wealthy deaths hardly varied. This is clearly unexpected, especially as the national income expanded from £291 million in 1821 to £423 million in 1851.[49] The reasons for this are unclear, and can at present only be the basis for speculation.[50] This period was followed by another continuing rise thereafter until the mid-1880s, with two plateaus in the years 1875-79 and 1885-89. The most dramatic period of growth in top fortunes[51] occurred in the early 1870s, with a doubling of the annual number of wealthy deaths in only ten years. This is consistent with an increased contemporary awareness of the

Table 1.3: Estates of £100,000 or More, Five-year Annual Average
Number, 1895-1939, with Percentage Change over Previous Period*

Period	Average Annual Number	Percentage Change
1895-99	264.6	_**
1900-04	292.8	+ 10.7
1905-09	303.8	+ 3.8
1910-14	299.8	− 1.4
1915-19	351.8	+ 17.3
1920-24	372.0	+ 5.7
1925-29	495.0	+ 33.0
1930-34	466.2	− 5.8
1935-39	540.0	+ 15.8

*The valuations here are *net*; in Table 1.2 they were *gross*. The difference consists of personal debts and funeral expenses and generally totalled 3-10 per cent among those wealthy estates where I have seen both figures.
**Represents an increase of 42.6 per cent over the 1890-94 figures cited in Table 1.2, although the totals are not strictly comparable.

wealthy in British society, and coincident with the publication of such works as Trollope's *The Way We Live Now* (1875), Samuel Smiles's *Character* (1871) and *Thrift* (1875), Henry George's *Progress and Poverty* (1879), and the compilation of the *Return of Owners of Land.*

From 1895 onwards, official statistics are available from the Inland Revenue of the annual numbers of large estates which include both realty and personalty, as well as *inter vivos* gifts made prior to three (later five and then seven) years before death. On the other hand, increased estate-duty avoidance among the rich, especially after the First World War, render these figures more suspect. Table 1.3 details these changes in the same manner as Table 1.2.[52]

Again, some broad trends are evident from Table 1.3. The slow increase in the last pre-1914 years' totals is perhaps surprising; part of the explanation for this may lie in increased death-duty avoidance by the rich, although it is notable that the worst three-year period for large estates at this time was 1902-05, before the Lloyd George tax increases. The rapid decline in land values and the growth of foreign investment may also have been factors. During the First World War, the number of large estates, though increased, failed to keep pace with inflation. There then ensued another period of increase during the 1920s, the totals reaching a level about 54 per cent above the pre-1914 numbers. During the Depression of the 1930s, the number of large estates declined, but at nothing like the same rate as the economy as a whole. Even at the very worst stage of the Depression the average annual number of estates over £100,000 considerably exceeded the numbers proved in 1920-24 (434 in 1931-32, 440 in 1932-33, 458 in 1933-34), and the late 1930s, as is now becoming increasingly clear, represented an Indian summer of British capitalism fully reflected in the statistics of wealth. Prior to the Second World War, the two years with the most estates proved in excess of £100,000 were 1937-38 (618) and 1936-37 (597), not 1929-30 (581), 1928-29 (535) or, certainly, 1913-14 (318).

As discussed above, the utility of the income tax statistics in gauging the size of the wealthy class is vitiated almost entirely by the schedule system in force from 1803. Only scattered attempts exist to rework such statistics as can be found for the distribution of nineteenth-century income, their accuracy unknowable, but certainly open to serious question.[53] In fact, no fully satisfactory figures for the number of high income-earners exist until 1911-12, when, in the wake of the 'supertax', statistics of the number of individual incomes of £5,000 or more first became available. The data for the years between 1911 and 1940 are summarised in Table 1.4, presenting five-year annual averages for all incomes over £5,000, with those at the very top further distinguished.

The variations between the trends in high income-earning evident here, and the probate valuations given above, require some comment. Of particular note is the extremely sharp rise during the years of the First World War — lending some evidence to the popular notion of 'war profiteering' at the time — and the continuing further marked increase during the early 1920s. However, in contrast to the trend apparent among the top wealth-leavers, there was a slower growth, and, at the very top levels, an actual decline during the prosperous late 1920s, and a very marked decline during the Depression. Although an increase in large incomes occurred during the late 1930s, it was not as rapid as among the wealth-holders, and the numbers at this period never reached those attained during the 1920s.

Occupations of Wealth-holders

The occupations of the wealth-holders deceased between 1809 and the present time is perhaps the most fundamental item of social analysis which can be discussed.[54] This author has elsewhere described the occupational distribution of the top wealth-holders deceased to 1914, and perhaps can do no more here than to concisely summarise those findings.[55] Table 1.5 offers an abbreviated ranking of the occupations

Table 1.4: Incomes of £5,000 or More, Five-year Average Number, 1911/12-1939/40, with Percentage Changes over Previous Period*

Years	£5,000+	Change (%)	£50,000-£100,000	Change (%)	£100,000+	Change (%)
1911/12-1914/15**	13,134	–	182	–	75	–
1915/16-1919/20	18,047	+ 37.4	307	+ 68.7	115	+ 53.3
1920/21-***1924/25	26,805	+ 48.5	452	+ 47.2	157	+ 36.5
1925/26-1929/30	28,359	+ 5.8	403	–10.8	146	– 7.0
1930/31-1934/35	22,572	–20.4	255	–36.7	86	–41.1
1935/36-1939/40	25,182	+11.2	288	+11.3	92	+ 7.0

*These are current figures and have not been modified for inflation.
**Four years only.
***Excludes the Irish Free State from 1922-23 onwards. The *Annual Report* gives these figures for both Great Britain and Northern Ireland. The difference between the two (i.e. the number of large southern Irish incomes earned in 1922-23) was: £5,000-10,000, 284; £10,000-20,000, 50; £20,000-50,000, 7; £50,000-100,000, 0; £100,000+, 1.

Source: *Annual Report of the Inland Revenue* in the Parliamentary Papers, 1912 onwards. The final revised figures have been used wherever given.

of the wealth-holders, arranged according to the *Standard Industrial Classification* used by the British government in numerating occupation distribution. Its main virtue is that it clearly separates manufacturing and industrial activities from commerce and finance, leading to perhaps the most important point to be made about the occupational distribution of wealth-holders.[56] As real property is excluded from the probate valuations, the landowners' numbers were determined by multiplying the number of landowners whose income exceeded an appropriate figure in Bateman's *Great Landowners* (normally £33,000 per annum in the case of millionaires) by the years' rental required to ascertain the capital value of his land, which varied throughout the nineteenth century.

The most important conclusion to be derived from Table 1.5 is the predominance of commercial and financial occupations as the main source of nineteenth-century British business wealth, and the relative infrequency of great fortunes built up in manufacturing and industry.

Table 1.5: Occupations of Wealth-holders Deceased 1809-1914, Concise Ranking*

Millionaires	1809-58	1858-79	1880-99	1900-14
Manufacturing	5 (55.5)**	13 (43.3)	22 (37.3)	20 (27.4)
Food, drink and tobacco	0 (0.0)	1 (3.3)	14 (23.7)	14 (19.2)
Commercial	3 (33.3)	16 (53.3)	23 (39.0)	38 (52.1)
Professional, public administration and defence	1 (11.1)	0 (0.0)	0 (0.0)	1 (1.4)
Land	181	117	38	27

Half-millionaires	1809-58	1858-79	1880-99	1900-14
Manufacturing	11 (22.9)	32 (31.7)	60 (38.0)	59 (32.6)
Food, drink and tobacco	1 (2.0)	2 (2.0)	23 (14.6)	22 (12.2)
Commercial	28 (58.3)	60 (59.4)	66 (41.8)	91 (50.3)
Professional, public administration and defence	8 (16.7)	7 (6.9)	9 (5.7)	9 (5.0)
Land	349	165	137	80

Lesser Wealthy	1809-29	1850-69
Manufacturing	17 (12.7)	44 (31.9)
Food, drink and tobacco	8 (5.8)	12 (8.7)
Commercial	66 (49.3)	73 (52.9)
Professional, public administration and defence	43 (32.1)	9 (6.5)

*This table, and all subsequent tables in this section, include male British wealth-holders only, excluding women and foreigners leaving very large estates in Britain.
**Figures in brackets denote percentages. Percentages are given for non-land wealth-holders only.
Source: Central Statistical Office, *Standard Industrial Classification* (1958).

The lead of commerce persists among all of the cohorts in Table 1.5 with the exception of the early millionaires and the 1880-99 group. At the individual level, most of the very largest British business fortunes of the nineteenth century were in commerce or finance, such as those of the Rothschilds, the Morrisons or Lord Overstone. Very few factory-owners or 'cotton lords' were immensely wealthy, most leaving not more than £100,000 or so.[57]

The present author has also done some work on the wealth-holders leaving £500,000 or more between 1920 and 1969.[58] The data here is perhaps less 'firm', especially at the half-millionaire level, for the most

Table 1.6: Occupations of Non-landed Wealth-holders Deceased 1920-69, Concise Ranking

Millionaires	1920-39	1940-59	1960-69
Manufacturing	44 = 28.8%	23 = 23.5%	19 = 28.8%
Food, drink and tobacco	40 = 26.1%	29 = 29.6%	11 = 16.7%
Commerce	61 = 39.9%	41 = 41.8%	30 = 45.5%
Professionals etc.	7 = 4.6%	4 = 4.1%	4 = 6.0%
Others	1 = 0.7%	1 = 1.0%	2 = 3.0%
Unknown	0	0	0
Total	153	98	66
Half-millionaires	1920-39	1940-59	1960-69
Manufacturing	107 = 30.7%	74 = 32.6%	48 = 35.8%
Food, drink and tobacco	57 = 16.3%	35 = 15.4%	11 = 8.1%
Commerce	167 = 47.9%	89 = 39.2%	51 = 37.8%
Professionals etc	11 = 3.2%	19 = 8.3%	15 = 11.1%
Others	5 = 1.4%	3 = 1.3%	2 = 1.5%
Unknown	2 = 0.6%	7 = 3.1%	8 = 5.9%
Total	349	227	135

recent cohorts. Unlike Table 1.5, landowners – about whose real property comprehensive data is available from 1926 – are excluded from that set of data. (See Table 1.6.)

It is clear that the same broad patterns of occupational distribution found during the nineteenth century persist into this. The comparative differential in the percentage of food-drink-tobacco wealth-holders – much more numerous among millionaires than half-millionaires – is striking. Although the percentage of commercial wealth-holders remains comparatively high – though not so high, overall, as during the nineteenth century – there is a clear decline (which cannot, of course, be inferred from the raw statistics) in the frequency of the wealth-holders from long-established merchant banks, mercantile and shipping companies and the like, their place taken by newer, often 'self-made' financial wealth-holders frequently operating independently or within very small firms or partnerships, such as the post-war property speculators, or Lloyds of London insurance or stockbrokers. Although there is some evidence of the decline of the nineteenth-century city financial dynasties during the inter-war period,[59] the relative success of the City and of finance and commerce generally in the recent British economy leads one to suspect that it is quite probably in this area, above all, that large-scale estate-duty avoidance has taken place, and that their totals probably understate the degree of wealth left by financial and commercial wealth-holders during the recent past, especially those from the older merchant banks and the like. It is probably not surprising that City families would be the readiest to avail themselves of clever lawyers and accountants, themselves based primarily in London.

Venue of Business Interests

Just as occupation constitutes a basic element of social analysis, so the geographical venue of the business interests of the wealth-holders is important in pinpointing the locale of wealth. Again, the main conclusions concerning the venue of the business activities of the nineteenth-century wealth-holders were drawn by this author in previous writings, and need only be summarised here.[60] Since Victorian business wealth was so disproportionately centred in its financiers and merchants rather than among its manufacturers, it was likewise to be found disproportionately in London, and above all in the City of London, the 'Clearing-house of the World', and in provincial ports and *entrepôts* like Liverpool, Bristol and Glasgow. Among non-landed millionaires, for example, five of eight deceased 1809-58, 16 of 30 deceased 1858-79, 21 of 54 deceased 1880-99, and 40 of 70 among the 1900-14 cohort, earned their fortunes in London, most in the City of London.[61] Greater Manchester – including Manchester's network of outlying towns like Oldham – produced only six millionaires during this whole period, compared with eleven in Merseyside (Greater Liverpool) and 14 in Clydeside (Greater Glasgow). Similar percentages are found among the half-millionaires and the 'lesser wealthy' – amongst this last group, the pattern is more marked still.[62]

As with the occupational distribution of the wealth-holders, some new data is available on the venue of the non-landed wealth-holders deceased 1920-69, which is given in Table 1.7.[63]

Only the main conurbations are detailed in Table 1.7. As it did during the previous century, London remains the most important single element in the wealth structure, its significance among millionaires, indeed, rising sharply between 1940-59 and 1960-69. Most of the other conurbations too remain about as they were in the nineteenth-century wealth structure, with Clydeside, as might be expected, exhibiting a continuing decline after the First World War and Greater Birmingham increasing in significance, especially among half-millionaires. If, as suggested earlier, there is a greater amount of

Table 1.7: Venues of Non-landed Wealth-holders' Business Interests, 1920-69, by Main Conurbations

Millionaires	1920-39	1940-59	1960-69
City of London	32 = 20.9%	15 = 15.3%	14 = 21.2%
Other London	15 = 9.8%	11 = 11.2%	14 = 21.2%
Total London	47 = 30.7%	26 = 26.5%	28 = 42.4%
Greater Manchester	6 = 3.9%	4 = 4.1%	2 = 3.0%
Merseyside	12 = 7.8%	2 = 2.0%	2 = 3.0%
West Yorkshire*	11 = 7.2%	7 = 7.1%	4 = 6.1%
Greater Birmingham	5 = 3.3%	3 = 3.1%	3 = 4.5%
Clydeside	12 = 7.8%	5 = 5.1%	3 = 4.5%
Totals all non-landed wealth-holders	153	98	66
Half-millionaires	1920-39	1940-59	1960-69
City of London	72 = 20.6%	41 = 18.1%	25 = 18.5%
Other London	33 = 9.5%	38 = 16.7%	22 = 16.3%
Total London	105 = 30.1%	79 = 34.8%	47 = 34.8%
Greater Manchester	26 = 7.4%	4 = 1.8%	7 = 5.2%
Merseyside	25 = 7.2%	15 = 6.6%	8 = 5.9%
West Yorkshire	22 = 6.3%	6 = 2.6%	7 = 5.2%
Greater Birmingham	11 = 3.2%	12 = 5.3%	13 = 9.6%
Clydeside	24 = 6.9%	14 = 6.2%	6 = 4.4%
Totals all non-landed wealth-holders	349	227	135

*West Yorkshire consists of Leeds and Bradford, and their outlying areas.

estate-duty avoidance among old-style City financiers and merchants than among other men of comparable wealth, the centrality of London in the modern wealth structure is more marked still, perhaps as much so as during the Victorian period. This is certainly true if two other facts are taken into account, London's magnetic role as the urban centre of the aristocracy, landed wealth, and 'society', and its attractiveness (needless to say) *vis-à-vis* provincial urban England for wealthy foreigners resident in Britain down to the latest wave of Arab oil princes, and the decline of a self-confident and socially distinctive provincial urban elite, based on autonomous domination of the industrial heartland of Britain, replaced either by the national (or multinational) corporation or by a resident elite socialised at the same public schools and universities. On the other hand, and despite these trends, the twentieth century has witnessed its share of local self-made entrepreneurs, often owing as little to London as their nineteenth-century counterparts: men like Nuffield in Oxford, Rootes or Austin in Birmingham, Bristol's aeroplane-builders, or, slightly earlier, Leverhulme of Merseyside. Yet such men often left incompetent heirs, and control of the family firm quickly passed into other hands – the recent history of Britain's main automobile firms is painfully familiar. Lord Leverhulme was succeeded as Chairman of Unilever on his death in 1925 by Francis D'Arcy Cooper, a London accountant, one of the first of the new breed.

Social Mobility

One of the most interesting and important modes of analysis of the wealth-holding groups is that of social mobility, the degree to which the wealth-holders themselves sprang from wealthy backgrounds or to which they were 'self-made men'. Biographical information on the non-landed wealth-holders was traced to ascertain this in a comprehensive way; these sources included published obituaries and biographies as well as genealogical works like Burke's *Peerage* and *Landed Gentry*, and, where necessary, the purchase of birth certificates and marriage licences (which list the father's occupation).[64] The father's own probate valuation was traced wherever possible, together with the extent of his landed income. Still, despite the best efforts of the researcher, many unknowns remain, especially for the earliest cohorts and at the 'lesser wealthy' level.[65] Table 1.8 spells out this information as traced.

It is obvious – and surely any other result would be most unexpected – that the great bulk of Britain's non-landed-wealth elite were themselves the offspring of affluent or wealthy fathers (although of extremely wealthy or socially prestigious fathers in fewer than half the cases) and were only rarely born poor or even into the lower-middle class. This pattern shows considerable variations among the various cohorts, the percentage of upper-class fathers rising steadily to a peak among the 1940-59 group and then declining in the 1960s.[66] Conversely, the size of the lower-middle group reached a peak in the late nineteenth century, at 26.7 per cent and 18.1 per cent of the millionaires and half-millionaires, and then declined, rising again (among millionaires only) in the 1960s. The percentage of genuinely self-made wealth-holders, those with poor fathers, was at all times very small – though, after the early nineteenth century, never non-existent – rising above

Table 1.8: Social Class of Fathers of Non-landed Wealth-holders*

Millionaires	1809-19	1820-39	1840-59	1860-79	1880-99	1900-19
Upper	0	0	3 = 60.0%	13 = 48.1%	31 = 51.7%	57 = 56.4%
Upper middle	0	4 = 100.0%	0	7 = 25.9%	11 = 18.3%	15 = 14.9%
Lower middle	1 = 100.0%	0	1 = 20.0%	5 = 18.3%	16 = 26.7%	18 = 17.8%
Lower	0	0	1 = 20.0%	1 = 3.7%	1 = 1.7%	5 = 5.0%
Unknown	0	0	0	1 = 3.7%	1 = 1.7%	6 = 5.9%
N =	1	4	5	27	60	101

Half-millionaires	1809-19	1820-39	1840-59	1860-79	1880-99	1900-19
Upper	1 = 25.0%	4 = 16.0%	9 = 33.3%	35 = 35.7%	52 = 32.5%	100 = 39.5%
Upper middle	0	0 = 40.0%	11 = 40.7%	27 = 27.6%	42 = 26.2%	71 = 26.7%
Lower middle	0	2 = 8.0%	2 = 7.4%	10 = 10.2%	29 = 18.1%	41 = 15.4%
Lower	0	0	0	5 = 5.1%	5 = 3.1%	11 = 4.1%
Unknown	3 = 75.0%	9 = 36.0%	5 = 18.5%	21 = 21.4%	32 = 20.0%	38 = 14.3%
N =	4	25	27	98	160	266

Table 1.8 *(contd.)*

Post-1919 Father's Social Class

Millionaires

	1920-39	1940-59	1960-69
Upper	91 = 59.5%	63 = 64.3%	33 = 50.0%
Upper middle	24 = 15.7%	17 = 17.3%	7 = 10.6%
Lower middle	28 = 18.3%	11 = 11.2%	14 = 21.2%
Lower	9 = 5.9%	4 = 4.1%	9 = 13.6%
Unknown	1 = .7%	3 = 3.1%	3 = 4.5%

Half-millionaires

	1920-39	1940-59	1960-69
Upper	133 = 38.1%	100 = 44.1%	46 = 34.1%
Upper middle	106 = 30.4%	58 = 25.6%	47 = 34.8%
Lower middle	59 = 16.9%	32 = 14.1%	19 = 14.1%
Lower	19 = 5.4%	17 = 7.5%	5 = 3.7%
Unknown	32 = 9.2%	20 = 8.8%	18 = 13.3%

Lesser Wealthy

	1909-19	1920-29	1950-59	1960-69
Upper	17 = 19.8%	17 = 20.5%	27 = 46.6%	23 = 23.7%
Upper middle	14 = 16.3%	16 = 19.3%	9 = 15.5%	21 = 21.6%
Lower middle	2 = 2.3%	3 = 3.6%	4 = 6.9%	2 = 2.1%
Lower	0	0	0	3 = 3.1%
Unknown	53 = 61.6%	47 = 56.6%	18 = 31.0%	48 = 49.5%
N =	86	83	58	97

Table 1.8 *(contd.)*

*It should be noted that the cohorts used here are divided into 20-year
intervals; in previous tables those deceased 1809-58 (when the records of the
Principal Probate Registry begin) are taken as a single group.

The definition of status groups used here may require some elaboration.
'Upper-class' fathers include large landowners or aristocrats, big businessmen
and upper professions; in general, any father whose own probate valuation
was £25,000 or more was placed here. The 'upper-middle' class included
medium-sized landowners, moderate-sized businessmen and other professionals
(in general to a probate value of £10,000-25,000). The 'lower-middle' class
consisted of farmers, small businessmen and most shopkeepers, and clerks
(equal to a probate valuation of about £3,000-10,000). Working-class and poor
fathers make up the 'lower class'. Assignments to one or another class are in
many cases approximations, and certain problems remain, for example,
non-patrial inheritance by the wealth-holder.

10 per cent only among the millionaires deceased in the 1960s.[67] It is
probable, however, that the low degree of social mobility indicated here
is overstated by the fairly substantial number of 'unknowns', as a group
almost certain to contain many more lower-status fathers, and hence
more self-made sons, than is the case among the 'knowns'.[68] There is,
in fact, considerable evidence, presented by the present author
elsewhere,[69] that the rate of social mobility from lower social-class
backgrounds has at most periods been consistently higher than among
the top wealth-holders of the United States, when measured against a
comprehensive group of American wealth-holders identified on the
same objective bases as the British group (and not merely on the basis
of 'fame' or some non-objective criterion biased in favour of the well-
known self-made men). Given the very real existence of class barriers to
mobility and the absence of educational opportunities for the poor in
nineteenth-century Britain, it is remarkable that even a single
entrepreneur starting from scratch should have amassed £500,000 or
more in just one working lifetime. Given the role of inheritance and
inherited wealth in the composition of the total British wealth structure,
it is equally remarkable that 'new' wealth should have represented as
sizeable a fraction of the total as it did. These facts suggest two general
conclusions which would repay more careful study: that the very lack
of entrepreneurial drive among the descendants of self-made men
presented a greater opportunity for wealth accumulation by the self-
made man of a subsequent generation; and that middle-class British
inheritance patterns — most notably the tendency for large fortunes to
be divided equally among all sons rather than left *en bloc* to the
eldest — deterred a renewed entrepreneurial drive among the

descendants of business wealth-holders.[70]

Religious Affiliations

The final matrix of biographical analysis of wealth-holding which will
be considered here is the religious affiliations of the wealthy, a most
important line of division within the wealthy class, and, it is often
claimed, a most significant motivating factor in producing
entrepreneurial drive and success.[71] In considering the evidence
presented in Table 1.9 about the connectedness of religion and wealth-
holding, two important facts should be kept in mind: first, in common
with the other tables in this section, only non-landed wealth-holders
are considered. If the great landowners are brought into the picture –
and many historians consider them to have been essentially capitalists
of the land – the Anglican (and Church of Scotland) percentages rise
considerably, while the dissenting percentages decline. Secondly, only
the *original* religion (rather than the adult or final religion) has been
used in this table, and anyone with a *traceable* dissenting ancestor back
to his grandparents has been counted as a dissenter, *even if* that person
was himself a practising Anglican, ensuring that the son or grandson of
a wealthy dissenter who converted to Anglicanism will still be
considered a dissenter.[72] Table 1.9, detailing the religious affiliations
of the non-landed wealth-holders, has been arranged somewhat
differently from the other tables, by *date-of-birth* cohort among those
deceased up to 1919, and excluding the more recent groups, when
religion becomes increasingly irrelevant and information on original
religious affiliation often impossible to trace.[73]

It is generally agreed that in early-nineteenth-century England the
dissenting portion of the population was a very small one and one
probably declining in number among 'Old Dissenters' (Baptists,
Congregationalists, Unitarians, Quakers etc.), rising in numbers again
only with the Methodist revival in the wake of Wesley.[74] However,
the famous Religious Census of 30 March 1851 revealed that by then
20.2 per cent of the English and Welsh population attended non-
Anglican (including Roman Catholic) services, while only 19.7 per
cent attended Anglican services.[75] Without going into excessive detail,
a percentage breakdown of the main religious denominations of the
United Kingdom (including Ireland) would probably find that in the
early nineteenth century about 60 per cent of the total population was
nominally Anglican (with the observant population considerably fewer),
about 25 per cent Roman Catholic, about 15 per cent Presbyterian
(Church of Scotland etc.), and about 5 per cent dissenting or members

Table 1.9: Original Religions of Non-landed Wealth-holders, by Year-of-birth Cohorts

Millionaires

Millionaires	1720-39	1740-59	1760-79	1780-99	1800-19	1820-39	1840-59	1860-79	Row Totals
Anglicans	1 = 100%	4 = 100%	2 = 40%	10 = 67%	25 = 57%	36 = 49%	12 = 39%	2 = 50%	92 = 51%
Dissenters	0	0	1 = 20%	3 = 20%	7 = 16%	11 = 15%	4 = 13%	0	26 = 15%
Church of Scotland	0	0	0	2 = 13%	9 = 20%	10 = 14%	5 = 16%	2 = 50%	28 = 16%
Roman Catholics	0	0	0	0	0	0	0	0	0
Jews	0	0	2 = 40%	0	4 = 9%	13 = 18%	9 = 29%	0	28 = 16%
Lutherans	0	0	0	0	0	3 = 4%	0	0	3 = 2%
Greek Orthodox	0	0	0	0	0	1 = 1%	1 = 3%	0	2 = 1%
Others	0	0	0	0	0	0	0	0	0
Column Totals	1 = 0.6%	4 = 2%	5 = 3%	15 = 8%	45 = 25%	74 = 41%	31 = 17%	4 = 2%	179

Unknowns (by religion) = 19

Half-millionaires

Half-millionaires	1720-39	1740-59	1760-79	1780-99	1800-19	1820-39	1840-59	1860-79	1880-99	Row Totals
Anglicans	2 = 50%	11 = 85%	13 = 62%	37 = 61%	56 = 57%	94 = 54%	38 = 48%	9 = 75%	0	260 = 56%
Dissenters	0	1 = 8%	1 = 5%	12 = 20%	17 = 17%	28 = 16%	11 = 14%	0	0	70 = 15%
Church of Scotland	1 = 25%	1 = 8%	4 = 19%	4 = 7%	16 = 16%	33 = 19%	13 = 16%	1 = 8%	1 = 33%	74 = 16%
Roman Catholics	0	0	0	2 = 3%	0	2 = 1%	3 = 4%	0	0	7 = 2%
Jews	0	0	2 = 10%	5 = 8%	5 = 5%	11 = 6%	11 = 14%	2 = 17%	2 = 67%	38 = 8%
Lutherans	1 = 25%	0	0	0	0	0	0	0	0	0 = 0.3%
Greek Orthodox	0	0	1 = 5%	1 = 2%	2 = 2%	4 = 2%	3 = 4%	0	0	11 = 2%
Others	0	0	0	0	2 = 2%	2 = 1%	1 = 1%	0	0	5 = 1%
Column Totals	4 = 1%	13 = 3%	21 = 5%	61 = 13%	98 = 21%	174 = 37%	80 = 17%	12 = 3%	3 = 1%	466

Unknowns (by religion) = 114

Table 1.9 *(contd.)*

Lesser Wealthy	1720-39	1740-59	1760-79	1780-99	1800-19	1820-39	Row Totals	(of which, Dates Unknown)
Anglicans	18 = 82%	29 = 67%	16 = 62%	37 = 70%	8 = 89%	1 = 50%	109 = 79%	27
Dissenters	1 = 5%	7 = 16%	5 = 19%	7 = 13%	1 = 11%	1 = 50%	22 = 14%	4
Church of Scotland	1 = 5%	4 = 9%	4 = 15%	5 = 9%	0	0	14 = 9%	6
Roman Catholics	1 = 5%	0	0	0	0	0	1 = 1%	0
Jews	0	1 = 2%	1 = 4%	2 = 4%	0	0	2 = 3%	2
Lutherans	0	2 = 5%	0	0	0	0	2 = 1%	0
Greek Orthodox	0	0	0	2 = 4%	0	0	2 = 1%	0
Others	1 = .6%	0	0	0	0	0	2 = 1%	0
Column Totals	22 = 14%	44 = 28%	26 = 17%	53 = 34%	9 = 6%	2 = 1%	156	
Unknowns (by religion) = 128								

of immigrant sects like the Jews or Lutherans. By the mid-nineteenth century, these figures were, respectively, about 55, 15, 15 and 15 per cent. It is these figures with which any statistics on entrepreneurial behaviour must be compared.

Despite the fact that the importance of dissenters in the Industrial Revolution and as successful businessmen is a stock in trade of contemporary economic historiography, only one previous attempt appears to have been made to measure empirically the proportion of dissenters among leading industrial figures – the effort of Everett E. Hagen in *On the Theory of Social Change*.[76] Hagen found that of 71 leading 'innovators' of the Industrial Revolution period, 41 per cent of the English or Welshmen were dissenters, a percentage certainly far exceeding random expectation.[77]

The evidence presented in Table 1.9 suggest that, at least as far as wealth-holding is evidence of entrepreneurial success,[78] there is virtually no objective evidence of any kind to support the contention that dissenters were prominent among the top money-makers of nineteenth-century Britain. Indeed, excepting for the overrepresentation of Jews and other immigrant groups, and the underrepresentation of Catholics, there are virtually no discernible patterns other than what would be expected purely on the basis of random chance. The overrepresentation of Jews and other immigrant groups, especially at the very highest levels of wealth-holding, is evidence that the type of business in which an entrepreneur was engaged, rather than his religious background, was probably the key element in his success at accumulating great wealth: commerce and finance were much more lucrative than manufacturing, and it was in commercial trades, above all in the City of London, that Jews and other immigrants, as well as many Anglicans, were to be found. Manufacturing, in which a disproportionate number of dissenters were to be found, was, as we have seen, far less likely to be productive of vast fortunes.[79] This is suggestive of a corollary, that *effort* is not as important to entrepreneurship as *place* in the total economy. A Calvinist cotton-manufacturer might in fact have worked three times harder than a London stockbroker, but built up a fortune only a fraction as large. It further suggests that what patently requires a fresh examination is not the success of dissenters but of Anglicans, who lacked the mutual self-help networks, often hereditary, provided by the chapel or meeting house (or, indeed, by the synagogue), and whose own peculiar institutions, such as the public schools and universities, led away from business life altogether, into the army, the Church, civil service, or Imperial administration.

Political Office-holding

The overlap between political office-holding and wealth-holding is an
interesting facet of this subject, for it appears to be one area in which
fundamental change has definitely occurred in the recent past. Since
most early and mid-nineteenth-century MPs were either members of
the landed aristocracy or their close relatives, it can be assumed that
most were rich – although the question of exactly how rich founders
on the rock of the exclusion of realty from the valuation figures. It is
perhaps not until the late nineteenth century, when substantial
numbers of very wealthy businessmen entered Parliament, that the
question can be fully discussed. In a previous paper, the present author
traced the probate valuations of all deceased Members of the 1895,
1906, 1922 and 1950 Parliaments whose dates of death were known.[80]
It is worth reproducing the main findings in Table 1.10.

The great bulk of non-Labour MPs serving in the first three
Parliaments surveyed here were rich, or at least highly affluent, by any
conventional definition of wealth, leaving £50,000 or more (implying
an income of £2,000-3,000 per annum when £700 was taken as the
lower limit of the upper-middle class), and a sizeable minority were
immensely wealthy, leaving £500,000 or more. The 1895 Parliament
was, however, somewhat wealthier than the 1906 House with its large
contingent of small businessmen and professionals, as well as trade
union figures, in the Liberal ranks.[81] The 1895 Parliament probably
represented the zenith of a trend toward ever-wealthier MPs (it appears
that the 1846 and 1868 Houses, on which the present author has done
some preliminary work, contained many fewer wealthy businessmen),
their wealth, even among the non-Labour parties, declining in this
century. By the 1950 Parliament, only 5 per cent of the Tory MPs
traced left £500,000 or more; most of those still living would probably
have been younger self-made politicians of the type of Heath, Powell
or Thatcher, who presumably would depress the average still further.
The addition of the Labour Party of course brought into the figures a
large number of Members who were poor or very nearly poor.[82] The
key to this decline – which has also been observed in Australian and
French politics[83] and is probably a feature of parliamentary life in this
century – is the elimination of the older type of neofeudal-rooted local
industrial capitalist, typically the largest employer of labour in an
industrial town, and his replacement either by career politicians whose
backgrounds may have been almost anything and who had not yet risen
to the top of the business or professional tree when their parliamentary

Table 1.10: The Wealth of Members of Parliament, 1895, 1906, 1922 and 1950

Valuation	1895 Con.	1895 Lib. Un.	1895 Lib.	1906 Con.	1906 Lib. Un.	1906 Lib.	1906 Lab.	1922 Con.	1922 Lib.	1922 Lab.	1950 Con.*	1950 Lib.	1950 Lab.
Under £1,000	9	2	4	3	1	8	2	3	1	20	0	–	5
Under £10,000	24	2	21	9	2	51	16	34	20	55	7	–	42
Under £50,000	78	7	33	26	4	82	3	69	25	13	10	–	18
Under £100,000	47	11	31	23	5	68	–	38	11	4	5	2	5
Under £200,000	49	12	17	16	6	36	–	44	10	0	11	–	–
Under £300,000	24	3	9	8	1	13	–	24	5	1	3	–	–
Under £500,000	23	5	3	10	1	16	–	10	4	–	3	–	–
Under £1 million	17	5	7	7	1	15	–	10	1	–	2	–	–
Under £2 million	8	5	7	5	1	9	–	6	1	–	0	–	–
Over £2 million	6	2	3	2	2	3	–	4	–	–	0	–	–
Total known	285	54	141	109	23	301	21 Unk.)	247	78	93	41	2	70
Unknown	47	6	36	21	2	79	22 Still living)	91	34	51	–	–	–
Percentage of known above £500,000	11	20	12	13	15	9	–	8	3	–	5	–	–
Percentage of known between £100,000 and £500,000	32	38	23	31	31	22	–	31	23	–	40	–	–
	43	58	35	44	46	31	–	39	26	–	45	–	–

47% abcve £100,000 (1895); 44% (1906)

*Includes 1951 Parliament (Conservatives only).

careers began.[84] Much could also be said, in this context, of the social
origins and wealth of the highest officials of the civil service,
nationalised industries and other state or quasi-state organisations, a
prospect which must await a further detailed analysis.[85]

Landed Wealth

Since, as a rule, it has been excluded from the previous discussion,
something must be said of landed wealth as a most significant element
in the British wealth structure. As Table 1.5 made clear, the number of
wealthy landowners vastly exceeded the number of business and
professional wealth-holders until the last decades of the nineteenth
century: until the 1880s, more than half of Britain's wealthiest men
were landowners; probably until the 1920s, Britain's half-dozen
wealthiest men included among them more than three landed aristocrats.
Enjoying a social prestige unrivalled throughout Europe, producing the
nation's statesmen from 1688 to Churchill, major thinkers and literary
figures from Byron to Bertrand Russell, and attracting supporters from
vastly different social milieux from Burke to Namier, the landed
aristocracy continued to dominate the British political elite until 1906,
and perhaps never more so than during the nineteenth century, a fact
remarked upon by innumerable contemporary writers. One of the most
striking aspects of the British landed aristocracy of the nineteenth
century, in the opinion of this writer, was its transformation into an
increasingly caste-like and homogeneous group, in contrast to what
Professor Perkin has termed the 'open aristocracy' of the eighteenth
century. Against the traditional pattern, it was simply no longer true
that many newly-rich nineteenth-century businessmen bought land on
an immense scale. Only a tiny handful of post-1780 wealthy
businessmen or professionals purchased vast amounts of land, most
notably the Peels, Lord Overstone the banker, Sir Josiah Guest the
ironmaster, James Morrison, the China merchant Sir Alexander
Matheson, the Baird family of Scottish ironmasters and the Barings.
The landed acreage held by the non-landed (i.e. business and
professional) millionaires deceased between 1840 and 1914 is detailed
in Table 1.11, which gives some indication of the extent to which the
newly rich remained aloof from wholeheartedly joining the landowners'
ranks.

In 1883, only a tiny fraction of Britain's agricultural land could
have been in the hands of relatively new men. Compounding this
tendency was the well-known antipathy to bestowing peerages upon
the nation's leading industrialists, until the 1880s when the flood

Table 1.11: Landed Acreage of Non-landed Millionaires, 1840-1914*

Acreage	1840-58	1858-89	1880-99	1900-14
50,000+	1	1		
25,000-50,000		1	1	
10,000-25,000	2	5	7	2
5,000-10,000	1	1	5	1
2,000-5,000		2	9	6
Unlisted	0	20	38	65
Percentage unlisted	0.0	66.7	63.3	87.8

*A number of self-made millionaires deceased in the last part of the span surveyed here might of course not yet have been wealthy in 1883. Millionaire deaths prior to 1840 were too few to be statistically meaningful.

Source: John Bateman, *Great Landowners of Great Britain and Ireland* (1883 edition).

began.[86] It should further be emphasised that, although their landed wealth made them the richest stratum of the British elite during the nineteenth century, the gains which came from non-landed activities, including the development of new urban areas and the exploitation of mineral resources, were distributed in a grossly uneven way even among landowners with high titles. Only a very small minority among even the landowners with the highest annual incomes from agricultural land left *personal* estates of £500,000 or more. According to Bateman's figures some 65 landowners were in receipt of gross annual rentals of £50,000 or more, and in the course of the period 1809-98 (when the valuation figures begin to include unsettled realty), perhaps five holders of each title or principal heir of untitled landowners were deceased, indicating that more than 200 landowners whose income was £50,000 per annum or more died and left estates to probate. Yet the total number of landowners leaving £500,000 or more according to the probate calendars was no more than 26.[87] As David Cannandine has recently emphasised, it was those landowners who possessed both large landed and personal fortunes (the latter often the product of the sale of land) who could best carry on in the old grand manner, or continue their lead in the political sphere, especially after the agricultural depression began about 1879. Such particularly fortunate magnates remained powerful national figures until the Second World War and possibly even after.[88]

The Wealthy After 1945

The last matter to be considered here is the question of the status of
the very wealthy in post-1945 Britain, a subject which must be limited
in its range by the historical nature of these essays, and to which some
attention has already been paid in the previous discussion. In general,
and based both on statistical as well as anecdotal and impressionistic
evidence, it seems fair to divide the fortunes of the rich in the post-war
period into the following main chronological periods:[89]

1. The era of austerity and increased equalisation of incomes and
wealth, begun during the Second World War and continuing until the
mid-1950s (i.e. well after the end of the 1945-51 Labour Government).

2. A period of easier times and greater affluence lasting from the
mid-1950s until the early 1970s, and marked by a spottiness in growth
among the various occupational elements in the wealth structure, with
the birth or increase of truly great fortunes in such fields as property
development, agricultural landowning, and consumer products and
services at the expense of basic manufacturers and (perhaps) of finance
or commerce of the older variety.

3. Another period of contraction – indeed, during the years 1974-76,
near ruination – in the fortunes of the very rich (and especially in those
speculative areas which had expanded during the 1955-72 period),
which may represent a permanent shift in the balance of property-
holding and income distribution in Britain, although very recent data
for 1977-79 suggest a recovery from this low point.

Some statistical evidence for this periodisation can be gleaned from
Table 1.12, presenting the distribution of very large incomes from
1945/6 until 1968/9.

It should be remembered, in considering these numbers, that the
equivalent figures for the 1935/6 to 1939/40 period, when the pound
was worth more than twice its post-war value and taxes were

**Table 1.12: Pre-tax Incomes of £50,000 or More, Annual Average
Numbers, 1945/6 to 1968/9**

	£50,000-100,000	£100,000+
1945/6-1949/50	213.0	50.6
1950/1-1954/5	180.6	39.6
1955/6-1959/60	224.0	56.4
1960/1-1964/5	408.6	102.2
1965/6-1968/9 (four years)	434.6	119.8

substantially lower, were 288 and 92, and that during the early 1920s the figures were 452 and 157. The same periodic trends are evident among the numbers of top fortunes left in the post-war era, which declined to an annual average of 5.4 millionaire estates during the 1950s (only two were left in 1957-58), compared with nine during the 1930s. These numbers again increased during the 1960s and early 1970s, reaching a peak of 21 millionaire and 61 half-millionaire estates left in 1972/73.

To be sure, enormous fortunes, in current values absolutely unprecedented in British history, were gained during the 1950s and 1960s, especially in property development and consumer products.[90] The *Daily Express* of 31 March 1969 published a putative list of Britain's top living wealth-holders (individual and family), headed by Garfield Weston, the Canadian-born food and restaurant king who was credited with worldwide holdings worth £200 million, the rejuvenated Pilkington family of glass makers (£200 million), Lord Cowdray (£150 million), Sir John Ellerman (£150 million), and the Moores, the Littlewoods football pool dynasts (£125 million). The *New York Times* of 24 April 1969 revealed that Lord Cowdray's interests, which stretched from Shell to Penguin Books, definitely exceeded £100 million in value; several property-developers, most notably Lord Samuel and Harry Hyams, were regularly credited with fortunes of £500-1,000 million (sic) at the height of the property boom in the early 1970s; while Sir John Ellerman, son of Britain's greatest pre-war wealth-leaver, actually left £52.3 million at his death in 1973. Because of the commonness of estate-duty avoidance (and perhaps because of the newness and instability of many such fortunes), wealth of this magnitude seldom appeared in full in the probate valuations at the death of their holder — Ellerman's vast estate was much the largest of the post-war vintage.

Notwithstanding these vast fortunes, there is ample evidence both that the bubble of great wealth burst fairly convincingly in the wake of the OPEC inflation of the mid-1970s, and that both income and wealth have become increasingly more equally distributed, especially during the 1970s.[91] This is a continuation, at a vastly increased rate, of a trend which dates back to the Middle Ages, and is probably common to all advanced societies.[92] To what extent deliberate measures of redistributive taxation have accelerated this trend is, however, more arguable.[93] And no statistics can encapsulate the enormous social and psychological changes in the position of the wealthy in post-war Britain relative both to their old status and to the rest of society: the end of servant-keeping, of residual deferential behaviour, of 'society' in its old form, the necessity for continuous legal and quasi-legal dodges, often unsuccessful, to keep one step ahead of the tax-collector, the power of the trade unions: all, paradoxically, coexistent with a British working and middle class notably less well-paid and productive than its counterparts in other societies.

Areas of Future Research

It is clear that historians and students of British social structure have only scratched the surface of this immense field, and in this final section, I should like to suggest some of the obvious directions in which research could go. It seems definitionally true that, having mapped the peaks of wealth, further research can turn in only one direction, namely downwards. The next really important research in the field of wealth-holding and its relationship to the rest of society will probably take the form of local studies of individual communities; these, it is hoped, they will survey not only compact industrial towns, of which John Foster's study of Oldham, South Shields and Northampton is already the model,[94] but also the more difficult and opaque commercial towns, above all London and that central mystery, the City.

This task is, however, rather more difficult than it first looks, as the probate calendars generally record only the residence at death of the wealth-holder, rather than his business address (although often this is given as well), and many successful businessmen would have retired to the countryside or a resort. However, although there might be some omissions, with proper checks on the possible loss of important local figures who subsequently moved elsewhere, serious and sensitive investigations of the wealth structures of local communities would doubtless prove of considerable importance to our understanding of nineteenth-century urban society.

It is not quite correct to state that wealth studies in Britain can move only in a downward direction: they can look backward as well. Although it is true that comprehensive investigation of the wealthy can begin only in 1809, it will perhaps be possible to incorporate other evidence – for instance the tithe and similar records – dating back to the eighteenth century or before.[95] Inventories of property (including individual chattels) accompanying wills exist in considerable quantity – there are 30,000 in the Canterbury Court records – up to about 1750, when thereafter they are 'seldom met with',[96] and a global valuation of property (but with all estates of £10,000 or more sworn as 'Upper Value') takes their place. It might prove exceedingly difficult and tedious work — and perhaps only local studies could ever be attempted — but it would be illuminating to push the research on various aspects of this question back to the seventeenth century, linking up with the significant work of Stone and others at that end.

There is also a very great deal remaining to be done on the nineteenth-century wealthy. There needs to be much more sophisticated work on the changing clientele of the public schools and universities, incorporating sophisticated data about the social status of the fathers of students, including their occupations and wealth.[97] We need much better such analyses of the professions, including such important institutions as the military and Anglican Church which Professor Perkin did not survey in his study, and extending the data on other elites back before 1870. There is a need for more comprehensive studies of inheritance and marriage patterns among elites: so far as the author is aware, no one, for instance, has as yet attempted to trace whether the old chestnut that the younger sons of gentry and even aristocratic families went into business life is true. No one has as yet traced the educational backgrounds of the descendants of the very wealthy, or determined in a precise way at what stage public school education became the norm among the sons of nineteenth-century business-leaders. In a different area, no one has attempted to determine the general distribution of wealth in Britain before 1895 from the probate records — a procedure unquestionably entailing considerable samplings of the many local probate courts which existed before 1858, but which would add much to Soltow's study of income distribution and to the work of Atkinson and others on twentieth-century wealth distribution.

Finally, important as these individual historical studies unquestionably would be, they can at best only be instrumental and anterior to a new general study of British social structure from before the Industrial Revolution to our time, incorporating the new quantitative material and addressing itself as well to the question of class and class relationships, to the subject to power, and to political ideology, organisation and change. This work will not be easy, and it will be less easy still for the historian to rid himself of any of the presuppositions and ideologies which already hold the field among the standard histories of modern Britain, whether Tory, Whig, 'pluralist' or Marxist. But in my opinion it would be one of the most important tasks which the modern British historian can undertake, and would go a long way toward rescuing historians, even social and economic historians, from the charge that they are excessively concerned with the trivial and the unimportant.

Notes

1. The best work on the tracing of wills in the ecclesiastical courts is Anthony J. Camp, *Wills and Their Whereabouts* (London, 1974). A general index of all estates proved in England and Wales, 1796-1863 (and superseded by the superior Somerset House indexes from 1858 onwards), may be found at the Public Record Office, Chancery Lane, London, classified at I.R.27, but they are difficult to use and not strictly alphabetical. There is an urgent need among genealogists and social historians for a good national index of estates for the period before 1858.

2. It was so required if an estate contained Bank of England funds ('consols'). Walter Thornbury, *Old and New London* (n.d. [1873]), vol. 1, p. 289.

3. These are the records of the Episcopal Consistory Court of Chester and the Consistory Court of the Archdeaconry of Richmond. The Canterbury Prerogative Court records searched are those held by the Public Record Office and classified at PROB. 8, the calendars of wills (and excluding PROB. 6, 7 and 9, the calendars of letters of administration and of limited wills and administrations). Hence these figures probably slightly *understate* the Canterbury totals.

4. Specific valuations above £100,000 are first given in the Canterbury Court calendars in 1809; previously, the unspecified term 'Upper Value' was used to denote any such estate; hence it is difficult to make a quantitative study of wealth-holding prior to 1809. For more on the individual court totals, see W.D. Rubinstein, 'Men of Property: The Wealthy in Britain 1809-1939', unpublished doctoral dissertation, Johns Hopkins University, Baltimore, 1975, p. 14; W.D. Rubinstein and D.H. Duman, 'The Probate Valuations as a Tool of the Historian', *The Local Historian* (London, 1974); Gerald Hamilton-Edwards, *In Search of Ancestry* (London, 1966), p. 56.

5. This index is available both at the Scottish Record Office, Edinburgh, and in storage (but available to researchers) at Somerset House; the latter's run of volumes, however, does not extend later than 1958.

6. This is because this index (known as I.R.9) is technically in the possession of the Inland Revenue, who have in the past maintained a 150-year rule of confidentiality in access to documents held by them. This absurd rule is gradually being modified. The present author was allowed to consult the 1825-75 Scottish probate index in the course of his research.

7. Indexes for 1918-21 were compiled only for Armagh, Belfast and Derry. The number of very large Irish estates, needless to say, is comparatively tiny, with fewer than 100 fortunes of £100,000 proved between 1858 and 1899. For an excellent summary of the Scottish and Irish situations, see Camp, *Wills*, pp. 196-225.

8. The valuation appearing in the printed (or manuscript) probate records is the global figure for the gross value of the personal estate. Real (landed) property was excluded from these figures entirely in England and Wales until 1898 and in Scotland until 1965. From 1898 to 1926, only unsettled realty was included in the valuation figures and only from 1926 has all realty been included. See Rubinstein, 'Men of Property', pp. 23-31.

9. The pre-1858 wills and letters of administrations held in the Public Record Office and other archives may, however, be consulted for free.

10. Discussion here of the valuation figure and of usable indexes to the wills is not, of course, meant to imply that wills and other testamentary documents originated only in the modern period: Anglo-Saxon wills exist, while those held

by the ecclesiastical courts date back to the thirteenth century. See Camp, *Wills*, p. ix.

11. Large or notable recent wills are published daily in *The Times* and other newspapers; since 1901 a list of the largest estates proved during the previous year has appeared in the annual *Daily Mail Yearbook*.

12. At death, the executor or administrator of an estate must lodge an inventory of the assets and liabilities of the deceased with both the Principal Probate Registry (for testamentary and legal purposes) and with the Estate Duty Office (for taxation purposes): hence the duality of offices and differences in valuation. The Estate Duty Office records are subject to the 150-year rule of confidentiality of the Inland Revenue, and researchers have never to my knowledge been granted permission to examine individual records. There is a discussion of the varied and often interesting statistical series to be found in the *Annual Report of the Inland Revenue* (especially good during the inter-war years) and in A.B. Atkinson and A.J. Harrison, *The Distribution of Personal Wealth in Britain* (Cambridge, 1978).

In contrast, few if any tables detailing the numbers of estates by range of wealth for the whole population were published prior to 1895, when (as a consequence of the Harcourt death duties) detailed statistical information on wealth distribution was published for the first time. Hence it is largely impossible to discuss statistically the distribution of wealth from the probate sources prior to 1895. Two exceptions, however, are the 1825 Table from the Parliamentary Papers reprinted in A. Aspinall and E. Anthony Smith (eds.), *English Historical Documents, 1783-1832* (London, 1959), p. 574, detailing the size of estates proved by the Canterbury Court in 1824 (and hence skewed toward the wealthy), and in the *Twenty-second Annual Report of the Registrar-General of Births, Marriages and Deaths* (PP 1861, XVIII, 545), which contains apparently unique statistics correlating the size of estates in 1850 by the *occupation* of the deceased. (I am grateful to Dr Michael King for this reference.)

In contrast to studies of *wealth* distribution, *income* distribution has been estimated many times prior to 1895, for example, by Gregory King in 1695.

13. It is, in any case, extremely unlikely that individual income tax records are kept when no longer current.

14. Under the schedule system, the income of a single individual (or profits of a firm) were assessed under any one of the five schedules: A (on rents); B (on farming profits); C (on Bank of England and other government securities); D (on the profits of trades and the professions); and E (on the profits of corporations and salaries etc. of corporate employees). A number of other important difficulties in using the nineteenth-century income tax exist, most importantly that 'individuals' assessed under Schedule D include both persons and companies. The best guide to the nineteenth-century income tax remains Josiah C. Stamp, *British Incomes and Property* (1916); see also Arthur Hope-Jones, *Income Tax in the Napoleonic Wars* (Cambirdge, 1939); P.K. O'Brien, 'British Incomes and Property in the Early Nineteenth Century', *Economic History Review*, 2nd series (1959); W.D. Rubinstein, 'The Victorian Middle Classes: Wealth, Occupation and Geography', *Economic History Review*, 2nd series, 30 (1977); and, more generally, B.E.V. Sabine, *A History of the Income Tax* (London, 1966).

15. Dudley Baxter, *National Income* (London, 1868); Leone Levi, *Wages and Earnings of the Working Classes* (London, 1867); L.G. Chiozza Money, *Riches and Poverty (1910)* (London, 1911); Stamp's attempt (*British Incomes*, especially pp. 430-65) is of a different order from the others in its sophistication and likely accuracy.

16. The basic work, appearing considerably earlier, is A.L. Bowley, *The*

82   *Modern Britain*

Change in the Distribution of the National Income 1880-1913 (Oxford, 1920).
Among the recent efforts are H.F. Lydall, 'The Long-term Trend in the Size
Distribution of Income', *J.R. Statistical Society*, 122 (1959); Phyllis Deane,
The First Industrial Revolution (Cambridge, 1965), especially Ch. 1; Lee Soltow,
'Long-run Changes in British Income Inequality', *Economic History Review*,
2nd series, 21 (1968); Sidney Pollard and David W. Crossley, *The Wealth of
Britain, 1085-1966* (London, 1968); Harold Perkin, *The Origins of Modern
English Society* (London, 1969), especially Ch. X.

17. In my essay, 'Victorian Middle Classes', I have attempted to use the
income tax sources to demonstrate the numerical superiority of high income-
earners in London. The 'supertax' and general statistics of income tax in this
century awaits a detailed study.

18. This material is classified under the heading I.R. (for Inland Revenue)
in 78 classes, of which (as of early 1978) fewer than half are as yet open to the
public. Of particular interest to scholars are I.R.2, detailing assessment under
each schedule by parish at seven-year intervals; and I.R.16, the Tax Abstracts
and Statistics by surveyor's district. Mention should also be made of the series E.
(for Exchequer), 182 (still held at Chancery Lane), containing the surviving
records of the first (1798-1815) income tax.

19. Yearly summaries can be found in the *Annual Report of the Inland
Revenue* from the late nineteenth century. Statistical tables on the county-by-
county distribution of assessments can be found scattered throughout the
Parliamentary Papers, especially during the years 1828-33 when parliamentary
redistribution was mooted.

20. The tacit assumption being that there is a relatively fixed ratio between
income and rent. Since everyone lives in a house, every family unit should
presumably count once and only once. Being based on actual expenditure, and
expenditure which is highly income-elastic, this source would also circumvent
the problem of self-definition found in the Census and similar returns: a man
may claim to be a barrister when he is not, but no one can spend £150 a year on
rent unless he has £150 – and a good deal more.

Unfortunately, there inevitably seem to be major difficulties in the use of this
material. Boarding houses etc. were counted only once rather than as multiple
dwellings, while shops with living-in owners or employees were often counted as
inhabited houses. There were also very considerable regional variations in the
rates of house rents (above all in London) after the 1870s. I hope to examine
this source in detail. See the ubiquitous Stamp, *British Incomes*, pp. 107-41 and
444ff., and Stephen Dowell, *A History of Taxation and Taxes in England* (1884,
reprinted 1965), vol. 3, pp. 178-92.

Inhabited House Duty was one of the so-called assessed taxes which fell upon
carriages, coats-of-arms, windows, hair powder etc. See Dowell, *History of
Taxation*.

21. PP 1861, L, 785.

22. For example, *Parliamentary Constituencies (Population)* (PP 1882, LII).
A return of April 1860, *Property and Income Tax* (PP 1860, XXXIX, pt 11),
details the assessments under Schedules A, B and D for every parish in the
United Kingdom.

23. See, for example, the references in F.B. Smith, *The Making of the Second
Reform Bill* (Melbourne, 1966), especially Chs. 3-5.

24. PP 1874, LXXII, pts I and II (England and Wales); PP 1874, LXXII, pt III
(Scotland); PP 1876, LXXX (Ireland).

25. First edition 1876; fourth edition 1883. A reprint of the 1883 edition,
edited by David Spring, was published by the Leicester University Press in 1971.

26. The main source of information about social stratification has traditionally

been the Censuses, taken in Britain every tenth year since 1801 (except 1941).
The Census' Enumerators Books, containing the names, occupations etc. of all
persons resident in Britain, are available to the historian for the Censuses taken
1841-71, and are declassified at the end of 100 years. An example of use of them
by a recent social historian is Alan Armstrong, *Stability and Change in an English
County Town: A Social Study of York 1801-1851* (Cambridge, 1975).

27. And which for some reason virtually died out for nearly 40 years until
the 1960s. Some exceptions in the interim were Bowley, *Change in Distribution*;
Josiah Wedgwood, *The Economics of Inheritance* (London, 1929); D. Seers,
The Levelling of Incomes Since 1938 (Oxford, 1951).

28. J.R.S. Revell, *The Wealth of the Nation* (Cambridge, 1967); A.B. Atkinson,
Unequal Shares – The Distribution of Wealth in Britain (London, 1974), *The
Economics of Inequality* (Oxford, 1975); Atkinson and Harrison, *Distribution of
Personal Wealth*; C.T. Sandford, *Taxing Personal Wealth* (London, 1971). The
drawbacks of the probate data for inferences about the living population have
been skilfully outlined, in the context of a conservative attack on the common
conclusions of such studies, by George Polanyi and John B. Wood, *How Much
Inequality?* (Institute of Economic Affairs, 1974).

29. Professor Harbury's main writings include 'Inheritance and the
Distribution of Personal Wealth in Britain', *Economic Journal*, 72 (1962),
'Inheritance and the Characteristics of Top Wealth Leavers in Britain', *Economic
Journal*, 83 (1973) (with P.C. MacMahon), and 'The Inheritances of Top Wealth
Leavers: Some Further Evidence', *Economic Journal*, 86 (1976) (with
D.M.W.N. Hitchens). Also of note is G.J. Fijalkowski-Bereday, 'The Equalizing
Effects of Death Duties', *Oxford Economic Papers*, 2 (1950).

30. Wedgwood, *Economics of Inheritance*. Hon. Josiah Wedgwood (1899-
1968), son of the first Baron Wedgwood, was a radical in the family tradition: his
book is dedicated to R.H. Tawney. This did not, however, stop him from serving
as Director of the Bank of England and the District Bank, and as Chairman of the
family pottery firm from 1947-67.

31. The standard works on English landowning in modern times remain
G.E. Mingay, *English Landed Society in the Eighteenth Century* (London, 1963),
and F.M.L. Thompson, *English Landed Society in the Nineteenth Century*
(London, 1963).

32. Perkin, *Origins of Society*, Ch. X.

33. This was undertaken under the auspices of the Social Science Research
Council in 1974-75; the present author acted as Research Associate. The final
report to the SSRC of this project, 'Elites in British Society Since 1880', is
available at the British Library, and Professor Perkin intends to write a full study
of British elites in the near future.

34. John Foster, *Class Struggle and the Industrial Revolution* (London, 1974),
especially Ch. 6; David C. Cannandine, 'The Landowner as Millionaire',
Agricultural History Review, 25, pt II (1977). My essays, aside from those cited
above, include 'British Millionaires, 1809-1949', *Bulletin of the Institute of
Historical Research*, XLVIII (1974); 'Men of Property: Some Aspects of
Occupation, Inheritance, and Power Among Top British Wealthholders' in
P. Stanworth and A. Giddens (eds.), *Elites and Power in British Society*
(Cambridge, 1974), and 'Wealth, Elites, and the Class Structure of Modern
Britain', *Past and Present*, 76 (1977). I will be completing a comprehensive study
of wealth-holding in modern Britain in the near future.

35. By, respectively, Dr D.H. Duman (Ben-Gurion University, Israel),
M. Didier Lancien (University of Aix-en-Provence, France), Dr Michael King
(University of Nottingham) and Dr W.L. Kennedy (University of Essex) – an
indication of the international scope of British economic and social history at the

present time.

36. See Philip Abrahms, *The Origins of British Sociology, 1834-1914* (Chicago, 1968). Booth's analysis of the geography of social classes in London in the late nineteenth century is unsurpassed. Statistical analyses of British social structure include A.M. Carr-Saunders and D. Caradog Jones, *A Survey of the Social Structure of England and Wales* (London, 1927); A.M. Carr-Saunders, D. Caradog Jones and C.A. Moser, *A Survey of Social Conditions in England and Wales* (Oxford, 1958); David C. Marsh, *The Changing Social Structure of England and Wales 1871-1961* (London, revised edition 1965).

37. For example, W.G. Runciman, *Relative Depravation and Social Justice* (London, 1966); Anthony Giddens, *The Class Structure of the Advanced Societies* (London, 1973); John Westergaard and Henrietta Resler, *Class in a Capitalist Society* (London, 1975).

38. For example, Stanworth and Giddens, *Elites and Power*; John Urry and John Wakeford (eds.), *Power in Britain* (London, 1973).

39. For example, Robin Blackburn (ed.), *Ideology in Social Science* (London, 1972); Ralph Miliband, *The State in Capitalist Society* (London, 1973); Ken Coates (ed.), *Can The Workers Run Industry?* (Nottingham, 1968); Andrew Glyn and Bob Sutcliffe, *British Capitalism, Workers, and the Profits Squeeze* (London, 1972). H. Frankel, *Capitalist Society and Modern Sociology* (London, 1970), is an interesting refutation of Crosland's social democratic view of the transformation of modern capitalism, with much statistical analysis. S. Aaronovitch, *Monopoly. A Study of British Monopoly Capitalism* (London, 1955) is the real thing, 'Imperial Octopus' (Ch. 4), 'Monopolies and Propaganda' (Ch. 8) and all.

40. Mention must at least be made in passing of the considerable body of work now extant, often at the level of county analysis, on elites, the nobility, gentry and merchant classes, during the seventeenth century. The central work is of course Lawrence Stone, *The Crisis of the Aristocracy* (Oxford, 1965). Even more relevant to the subject of this essay is Richard Grassby, 'The Personal Wealth of the Business Community in Seventeenth Century England', *Economic History Review*, 2nd series, 23 (1970), and several other articles by the present author.

41. Nothing has, or can, here be said of the wealth as portrayed in literature or popular writing. Since virtually every work of fiction is in some sense a mirror of social reality, this topic is as vast and variegated as modern British literature itself, and a good deal could be said of the treatment of the rich in the likes of Jane Austen, Thackeray, Dickens, Trollope, George Eliot, Galsworthy, Michael Arlen, George Orwell, Anthony Powell, C.P. Snow and innumerable others, to say nothing of popular and light fiction, 'thrillers' and their kind.

42. For fuller presentations see my doctoral dissertations and previous articles.

43. R.A. Soloway, *Prelates and People: Ecclesiastical Thought in England 1783-1852* (London, 1969), p. 72, n. 3; Sir Lewis Namier and John Brooks, *The House of Commons, 1754-1790* (HMSO, London, 1964), p. 103; Thornton Hall, *Romances of the Peerage* (1914), p. 245; *Anglo-Jewish Notabilities, Their Arms and Testamentary Dispositions* (n.d.), p. 227; *Gentleman's Magazine* (1806), p. 1,181; Sidney Pollard, *The Genesis of Modern Management* (London, 1965), p. 121. See also Richard Grassby, 'English Merchant Capitalism in the Late Seventeenth Century. The Composition of Business Fortunes', *Past and Present*, 46 (1970). Professor R.S. Neale, who is working on the early-eighteenth-century noble placeman and financier the Tuke of Chandos, indicates that his personal fortune may have exceeded £1 million.

44. Eric Richards, *The Leviathan of Wealth* (London, 1973), p. 12.

45. *The Times*, 23 December 1899.

46. C. Northcote Parkinson, *The Rise of Big Business* (London, 1977), p. 109.

This may well in fact have been incorrect, as Vanderbilt was by his own
admission worth $194 million, or more than twice as much as Westminster's.

47. For instance, Charles Morrison, who was nearly three times wealthier than
the second richest man of his day, was the eldest son of millionaire James
Morrison, proprietor of the Fore Street textile warehouse in London. Unmarried,
living quietly outside the public gaze, he 'habitually kept a large sum in gold as a
reserve against serious financial loss' (*The Times*, 26 May 1909).

Even more striking is the case of Sir John Ellerman, whose fortune, left at the
bottom of the Depression, almost defies belief. A self-made man (his father had
left £600), Ellerman began as an accountant, forming his own London
accountancy firm at 24 and acquiring the old-established Liverpool shipping firm
of Frederic Leyland & Co. at 29. The full story of his vast and invariably
successful ventures into shipping, finance, brewing and property development
may never be known. See James Taylor, *Ellerman's, a Wealth of Shipping*
(London, 1976), especially Part One.

48. See Arthur Bryant, *The Age of Elegance* (London, 1956), p. 310.

49. B.R. Mitchell and Phyllis Deane, *Abstract of British Historical Statistics*
(Cambridge, 1971), p. 366.

50. Among the more obvious seem to be: an illusory product of a shift to local
probate courts not included in these figures and away from Canterbury and York;
a shift of property by the wealthy away from unsettled personalty not covered in
the valuation figures (at the peak of the land price rise prior to 1837, purchase of
a small estate of 3,000-4,000 acres required an expenditure of about £100,000),
or to foreign investment; a shift in the lifestyles of wealthy men to greater
profligacy; a redistribution of the national cake away from the very rich to the
poor or to middle-rank or small entrepreneurs, such as the typical factory-owner
is known to have been. None of these, excepting possibly the last, strikes me as
very conclusive or even likely.

51. Assuming – as everyone who uses this material must do – that the number
of wealthy deaths is a random sample of the number of living wealth-holders, and
varies directly with their numbers. This point is arguable. See Polanyi and Wood,
Inequality?, p. 25.

52. There are also the effects of inflation to be considered when discussing
changes in the meaning of 'wealth'. The figures here are, however, in current
values, without allowing for inflation.

53. See the discussion in Stamp, *British Incomes*, Chapter XIII. Stamp
reworked the income tax and Inhabited House Duty to estimate that the number
of individuals with incomes over £150 per annum rose from 307,000-320,000 in
1860-61 to 1,202-000-1,253,000 in 1909-10.

Some statistics also survive for the earliest period of the first income tax
before the schedule system went into force. In 1801 there were a total of
320,759 incomes of £60 or more, including 6,927 in the range £1,000-2,000,
3,657 between £2,000-5,000 and 1,020 above £5,000. Ibid., pp. 431 and 514.
See also Hope-Jones, *Napoleonic Wars*, pp. 19, 26 and 77.

54. As mentioned previously, in this and succeeding parts of this section we
are concerned exclusively with the wealth-holders; top income-earners are not
brought into the discussion.

55. Rubinstein, 'Victorian Middle Classes', pp. 605 ff.

56. There is surprisingly little difficulty in assigning each wealth-holder to an
occupational category, as one or another of these was clearly his main pursuit in
the great majority of cases. Rentiers were assigned to the fields in which the
family fortune was earned. The extended *Standard Industrial Classification* has
24 main headings.

57. See the remarks of V.A.C. Gattrell on the 'advisability not of scale, but,

to the contrary, of moderation in enterprise' among nineteenth-century cotton-manufacturers, 'Labour, Power, and the Size of Firms in Lancashire Cotton in the Second Quarter of the Nineteenth Century', *Economic History Review*, 2nd series, 30 (1977), p. 107.

58. Of those wealth-holders deceased between 1915 and 1919 (and excluded from either table of occupation), the following occupational distribution occurs:

	Millionaires	Half-millionaires
Manufacturing	8	38
Food, drink and tobacco	3	8
Commerce	16	33
Professions etc.	0	1
Unknown	0	2

There are, in addition, seven millionaires and nine half-millionaire landowners among this group.

59. Chaim Bermant, *The Cousinhood. The Anglo-Jewish Gentry* (London, 1971), p. 406.

60. Rubinstein, 'Victorian Middle Classes', p. 608 ff.

61. Ibid., p. 609. These venues are exclusively those of the main business interests (factory, mine, bank etc.) of the wealth-holders, not where they lived or retired to. Certain wealth-holders, like engineering contractors or some multiple retailers, cannot be classified in this way, nor can landowners.

62. Ibid., pp. 610 ff.

63. The venues of the non-landed wealth-holders deceased 1915-19 among the major conurbations was:

	Millionaires	Half-millionaires
City of London	6	15
Other London	3	11
Total London	9	26
Greater Manchester	1	4
Merseyside	2	8
West Yorkshire	1	0
Greater Birmingham	1	2
Clydeside	5	7
Total non-landed	27	82

64. These are available in England and Wales from 1837, and in Scotland from 1856. Scottish death certificates also record the occupation of the father of the deceased, which is not the case with English/Welsh death certificates.

65. Biographical information of this sort about the more obscure merchants and other businessmen, especially in London, is almost impossible to obtain.

66. The figures presented here indicate a somewhat greater degree of social mobility than was found in the two previous studies of intergenerational wealth transmission, those of Wedgwood (*Economics of Inheritance*, pp. 155 ff) and Harbury ('Inheritance and Distribution'), where the 50th percentile of fathers' valuations among sons' estates proved in 1924-26 and 1956-57 exceeding £200,000 was about £100,000 in most cases. The major reason for this is probably the exclusion of the great landed fortunes in the present statistics, which in all such cases would have been inherited from equally wealthy forbears. It is interesting to note that Harbury's most recent study of 1973 wealth-leavers found a 'significant decline' in real terms in the valuations of the wealth-holders'

fathers, as against his previous (1956-57) data (Harbury and Hitchens, 'Top Wealth Leavers', p. 321).

67. It is likely that most people, on a commonsense definition, would include as 'self-made men' both the 'lower' and 'lower-middle' (shopkeepers, clerks etc.) groups, in which case the 'self-made' percentage would be considerably higher, totalling nearly 35 per cent of the 1960-69 millionaires.

68. Chiefly because the 'knowns' will include all of the aristocratic and socially prestigious fathers, who are readily traceable in published genealogies, biographical dictionaries, peerages etc., while the 'unknowns' will include no such persons. It is also true that many unknowns combine only one forename with a common surname, while during the nineteenth century in the main only middle-class (or above) children were given several forenames.

69. Rubinstein, 'Men of Property', pp. 164-66.

70. Ibid., pp. 154-60. These tendencies were much more apparent in manufacturing industry than in finance or commerce, where, for example, the great merchant banks continued to be family-run to this day, with no apparent loss of business drive. See Rubinstein, 'Wealth, Elites, and the Class Structure', pp. 115-17; D.C. Coleman, 'Gentlemen and Players', *Economic History Review*, 2nd series, 26 (1973).

71. This, of course, is the famous Weber thesis, the alleged causal connection between entrepreneurial drive and the Protestant religion (in its post-Reformation British context, English dissent), first postulated by Max Weber in 1904. In this vast debate, the most useful and significant works include Kurt Samuelssen, *Religion and Economic Action* (New York, 1961), Robert W. Green (ed.), *Protestantism, Capitalism, and Social Science. The Weber Thesis Controversy* (second edition, Lexington, Mass., 1973), and S.N. Eisenstadt, *The Protestant Ethic and Modernization, a Comparative View* (New York, 1968). Weber's own formulation is available in English in his revised 1920 version as *The Protestant Ethic and the Spirit of Capitalism* (London, 1930), translated by Talcott Parsons.

72. The effect of this is probably to increase the percentage of dissenters among the totals of Table 1.9 by 2-3 per cent. The main point of doing this is to counter the argument (put forward by, for example, Michael Flinn in 'Social Theory and the Industrial Revolution' in Tom Burns and S.B. Saul (eds.), *Social Theory and Economic Change* (London, 1967)) that entrepreneurial values are transmitted by subtle child-rearing methods, commonly found among certain dissenting sects like the Quakers and Unitarians (but not among, for example, the Methodists), and presumably retained following a formal religious conversion.

73. It is difficult enough for the nineteenth-century groups. To find a rich man's date or even his father's occupation (at least after 1837) are relatively easy compared with ascertaining information about that man's religion unless, as with Jews or Greek Orthodox wealth-holders, ethnicity and religion are identical. Information about original religion must often be inferred from such sources as the man's or his parents' marriage licence (which tells the place of marriage), from attendance at a denominational school etc., and there remain many 'unknowns'. These unknowns are not randomly distributed, but are clustered mainly in London and among mercantile and commercial groups there. There are no local London newspapers or other biographical sources of an equivalent degree of excellence as those in the northern industrial towns (where dissenters were disproportionately to be found). Thus, the percentage of Anglican wealth-holders is probably understated yet again.

74. The best recent discussion of numbers is A.D. Gilbert, *Religion and Society in Industrial England* (London, 1976), pp. 23-48.

75. These are the reworkings of the Census figures by Perkin in *Origins of Society*, p. 201.

76. E. Hagen, *On the Theory of Social Change* (Cambridge, Mass., 1964), pp. 261-309.

77. In the opinion of the present author, Hagen's work is fatally flawed on a number of conceptual grounds, the most important being a confusion between 'innovators' (i.e. inventors and pioneers of technical change) and entrepreneurs. Since the Weber thesis is concerned with *business* success, references to *innovators* are non sequiturs.

78. Since the probate valuations measure wealth at death, they favour, as it were, the prudent and the thrifty over the profligate, and hence — presumably — the typical dissenter or men in their mould.

79. See the acute remarks of one recent historian of the Lancashire cotton trade, V.A.C. Gattrell, on the 'constraints on growth. . .a curious reticence about the advantages of expansion [among contemporaries in the cotton industry] witnessed in numerous contemporary recommendations of the advisability not of scale, but, to the contrary, of moderation in enterprise'; Gattrell, 'Lancashire Cotton'.

80. Rubinstein, 'Men of Property', pp. 106 ff.

81. J.A. Thomas, *The House of Commons, 1832-1901: A Study of Its Economic and Functional Character* (Cardiff, 1939), pp. 25 ff.

82. It will be interesting to see if the so-called 'embourgeoisation' of the Labour Party will bring up the average wealth of its recent MPs, possibly to close equality with the Tories.

83. R.W. Connell, *Ruling Class, Ruling Culture* (Cambridge, 1977), p. 53; Jean Estebe, 'Les Gouvernants de la III[e] Republique et leur Fortunes, 1871-1914', *Revue D'Histoire Economique et Sociale*, 54 (1976).

84. This is not to say that other forms of capitalist wealth were unrepresented in nineteenth-century Parliaments: both landowners and rich bankers and merchants abounded, and both have become much less numerous. The payment of backbench British MPs from 1908 on was a turning-point; however, as is well known, personal wealth was still an important criterion of selection in the Conservative Party until after 1945.

85. See Perkin, *Origins of Society*, Ch. X, for a discussion of many of these groups.

86. This has been well documented by Ralph E. Pumphrey in 'The Introduction of Industrialists into the British Peerage: A Study in the Adaptation of a Social Institution', *American History Review*, 65 (1959).

87. There is, of course, no necessary relationship between possession of a landed income of £50,000 per annum and a personal fortune of £500,000: these are merely taken as convenient benchmarks situated at roughly equal points on the wealth pyramid. On the other hand not all of these 26 landowners were credited with landed incomes of £50,000 or more in Bateman.

88. Cannandine, 'Landowner as Millionaire', and 'Aristocratic Indebtedness in the Nineteenth Century: The Case Reopened', *Economic History Review*, 2nd series, 30 (1977), especially pp. 647-69.

Something should also be said at this point of the wealth of the monarch and the Royal Family. As the sovereign is not liable to taxation, no probate valuations have ever been published, and contemporary estimates of the wealth of the Queen range up to £500 million or more — but only if quasi-public and unsaleable royal possessions like royal palaces are taken into account. Her *personal* wealth is certainly very considerably less. The only direct member of the Royal Family who ever left £500,000 or more was the Duke of Gloucester (d. 1974), worth £734,262 gross (£450,777 net) at his death — the 33rd largest estate probated in 1975-76.

89. An essentially similar periodisation (although he dates the trend away

Modern Britain

Modern Britain   89

from greater equality from the late 1940s) is made by Richard Titmuss in his famous work *Income Distribution and Social Change* (London, 1962), especially Ch. 3.

90. There were seven fortunes of £5 million or more left between 1940 and 1969. The four largest belonged to James A.E. de Rothschild (d. 1957), merchant banker, £11.7 million; Guy A. Vandervell (d. 1967), engine bearing manufacturer, £10.9 million; Hugh, second Duke of Westminster (d. 1953), land and property owner, £10.7 million; and Charles L. Arnold (d. 1968), electrical equipment manufacturer, £5.8 million, and five in the period 1970-76, headed by Ellerman's £52.3 million and Felix D. Fenston (d. 1970), property-developer, £12.7 million.

91. See Polanyi and Wood, *Inequality?*, and *The Royal Commission on the Distribution of Income and Wealth*, Report No. 1 (Cmnd 6171, 1975). For a contrary view, see Atkinson, *Unequal Shares*.

92. Soltow, 'Long-run Changes'. Soltow concludes: 'The argument is thus one that there was a continuing widening of opportunity for non-propertied income groups. Statistical evidence indicates that income inequality, particularly in upper-income groups, has decreased for several centuries. This trend has been accelerated in the twentieth century' (ibid., p. 29).

93. Titmuss, Income Distribution, p. 53, citing H.F. Lydall.

94. Foster, *Class Struggle*, and 'Nineteenth Century Towns – A Class Dimension' in H.J. Dyos (ed.), *The Study of Urban History* (London, 1968).

95. See, for example, the use by George Rudé of Land Tax Registers and Poor Rate Books to assess the social and economic status of late-eighteenth-century Westminster electors, in *Wilkes and Liberty* (Oxford, 1962), pp. 74 ff.

96. Camp, *Wills*, p. xix.

97. The pioneering work on this subject remains T.J.H. Bishop and Rupert Wilkinson, *Winchester and the Public School Elite* (London, 1967).

2 WEALTH AND AFFLUENCE IN FRANCE SINCE THE BEGINNING OF THE NINETEENTH CENTURY

Adeline Daumard

The abolition of legal privileges attached to birth, the development of the mentality of individualism even in the most traditional areas, and the insufficient development of public and private assistance which did not completely replace the role played by the Church prior to 1789 are the causes of the importance which the French attached to wealth in the nineteenth century. In the absence of a better criterion, a hierarchy based on wealth became evident. On the other hand, the possession of an inheritance became a vital necessity for those who were in danger of poverty in case they were unable to work. When industrial and financial capitalism began its ascent, particularly after 1840, many new fortunes, modest or affluent, were formed. Workers without means other than their wages converged on the towns and money acquired an even more important place in the life of society. Conditions altered in the twentieth century. The number of salaried people occupying well-paid and high-status positions increased continuously. A system of social security and retirement benefits was progressively developed. The abolition of the gold franc and monetary fluctuations destroyed the conditions for saving. Today it is undoubtedly less necessary than previously, but wealth has perhaps become more important than before because of the difficulties of amassing a patrimony with limited savings.

However, it is not possible to compare *a priori* wealth and the social hierarchy. In order to study private fortunes, one must first try to evaluate the growth of fortunes brought about by economic development and by the consequences of the economic and political crises which are the hallmarks of French history since the beginning of the nineteenth century. This requires the evaluation of the distribution of property, of the contrast between regions, and of the differences between the various social spheres and the concentration of wealth. It requires the comparison of the conditions of wealth with social conditions; such a comparison will supply answers about the nature and foundations of contemporary French society.

Until 1914, savers and capitalists alike based their fortunes on

90

complete confidence in the gold franc. A change occurred after the
First World War, which signified the beginning of a new era. But before
we depict the nature of wealth and affluence, an analysis of the data
and a description of the methodology will allow us to define the notion
of private wealth.

Before we can analyse wealth, it will be necessary to define it. In the
nineteenth century particular consideration was given to real property.
Even as late as 1870, when the government inquired into 'wealth
valued for the annual revenue' (*fortune évaluée en revenu annuel*),
of the country councillors (conseillers généraux), information about
rural properties and houses was usually required.[1] Even the census, up
to 1848, gave a privileged place to information on realty. But this was
a result related to the facility of direct taxation rather than to
deliberate choice. On the other hand, probate duties were a taxation
imposed on wealth in its widest sense. According to the regulations of
a law which remained valid during the entire nineteenth century and
with certain modifications until 1956, all possessions which were part
of an inheritance were liable to taxation, with two exceptions: real
estate in foreign countries, because it was taxed locally, and French
public funds from before 1850, a measure adopted in order to help
investors in government stock ruined by the Revolution. New laws were
effected in the later nineteenth century in order to adapt to the
conditions of modern capitalism, but these closed loopholes in the old
law and did not contain any basic new principles.[2]

The taxes on private wealth imposed following an inheritance were
therefore applied to all goods with a market value. Among these, goods
which had a utilitarian value, such as clothing and tools, were evaluated
very low in the probate declarations of the nineteenth century. Others
which produced income had their value enhanced. This depended upon
the form of investment and the influence which flowed from landed
property, private industrial or commercial investments in private
enterprises, the possession of personal capital, credit, financial stocks,
particularly in government bonds or shares in public companies.

Among contemporary inquiries were new studies concerned with
inheritances. Some were concerned only with 'domestic inheritance'
(*patrimoine domestique*) excluding capital invested in individual
enterprises. They had as their object mainly the study of their
management as consumers or savers. Most of these inquiries disregarded
cash, hidden gold, jewellery and objects in collections, not because of
any principle, but because they were not declared. For the same
practical reason, because of the difficulties connected with their

valuation, fungible goods such as furniture, motor cars etc. are disregarded. On the other hand, sometimes the notion of heritage is extended, for example, when we take into consideration social rights it becomes obvious that differences between fortunes are modified. Finally, there is the delicate question of debts. When liabilities are deducted from assets in some estates nothing remains, or they may even have a negative value. But not everyone may obtain credit. Gross and net assets may have their significance, but in reality the historian has no choice but to work with the documentation he has.

New questions arise if one intends to compare the status of fortunes with social status.

Is it advisable to distinguish what is called inheritance from the total patrimony? A certain prestige is attached to family assets: the survival of the spirit of the *ancien régime* before 1914, the suspicion of *nouveaux riches* afterwards. Conversely, there was always opposition to the inheritance of assets 'acquired by hard work and savings', fruits of two of the cardinal virtues of the nineteenth-century bourgeoisie, the crowning of effort with success and the moral force which secures the future by sacrificing the pleasures of today.[3] In our times this first patrimony, particularly when it is of modest size, finds numerous defenders, but with two differences: whereas it is unanimous when the family house is in question, opinion is more divided when investments or stocks are concerned, as it would be more justifiable to give privileged status to utilitarian goods than to productive capital.

Under the influence of the Civil Code, most married French people live in a system of the communal possession of assets which, in spite of many variants, has a common trait: each spouse retains the property of his or her inheritance, but the husband, with few exceptions, manages the entire fortune and disposes of the assets of his wife under the condition that the rights of the wife are preserved in case of the dissolution of the marriage.[4] Therefore it is the totality of these assets, i.e. those of the husband and of the wife as well as those acquired during the marriage, which forms the real wealth of the household and thus its place in the hierarchy of fortunes. Is it necessary to go further? Many of the recent inquiries on patrimonies consider that the household is a community of all persons living in the same dwelling. This leads to an increase in the total wealth since the assets of the spouses are added to those of adult children, of parents of the spouses etc. This can be justified when it is intended to compare the value of the patrimony with, for instance, consumption capacity. But the 'head' of the household extended in this manner lacks the power to dispose of the assets or the incomes of those people living under his roof. As a rule, when the total resources of the husband and wife are taken as the basis for the calculation of income tax, other persons lodged by the head of the household are considered as separate contributors. Grouping together all these assets, as is sometimes done in some contemporary inquiries, risks deforming the hierarchy of fortunes which characterises the various social spheres.

Finally, difficult problems of classification remain to be clarified. Various types of assets can be regrouped differently, depending on whether it is intended to put the stress on the role of personal wealth in economic development or on the social role of riches. The choice of variables permitting an analysis of the distribution of assets has an even more decided importance. When we study the geographical distribution of wealth, these can contribute to assumptions about the inequality of economic development in different regions and about the effects of urbanisation on patrimonies. When we research the contrasts connected with age and sex, our apparently easy groupings are sometimes artificial due to the marriage of persons of different ages and of professions which are not comparable. The trade or profession and often the rank are frequently applied criteria. In order to be usable in allowing comparisons between distant regions and periods, these classifications require important simplifications and regroupings which often have a great influence on the conclusions.

Some of these difficulties are, in practice, more theoretical than real. Everyone who studies private wealth-holding during the past two centuries is dependent on the sources. The choice and the methods are imposed to a certain degree by the contents of the documents.

When evaluating private wealth, one often relies on the estimates of national wealth and the more or less complete official statistics, such as are at present available in the National Accounting Office (*Comptabilité nationale*).[5] But the value of the data for certain assets is quite uncertain and the calculation of French private wealth derived from this data contains a large amount of personal estimates. This means that comparisons between different times are quite hazardous.

From the end of the nineteenth century, the value of 'yearly inheritances' (*annuité successorale*) was used in order to determine the variations in private wealth.[6] The Department of Finance has published the value of assets passed by inheritance every year since 1826. By multiplying this value by a coefficient corresponding to a mean interval separating two generations, it is possible to evaluate approximately the total amount of wealth in private hands, because in principle all inheritances are subject to the tax. In reality, there exist two factors making for error. Neither the totality of assets nor their exact value are known, due to fraud, concealment and legal exemptions. Additionally, a share of the total private wealth is transferred prior to the death of the owner as *inter vivos* gifts. Secondly, it is difficult to calculate precisely the coefficient allowing the evaluation of the wealth of all living persons on the basis of inheritance. Attempts have been made to reduce the margin of error by taking into account the mortality rates of different age cohorts and by re-evaluating the various categories of assets on the basis of statistical data, in order to reduce the effects of fraud. But such calculations based on simple estimates are more rigid than rigorous.[7] Nevertheless, the probate statistics remain a fundamental source. In the twentieth century, until their disappearance in 1964, they were more and more detailed, and in particular made it possible to know the composition of inheritances and their distribution by *départements* according to their size. Although estimates of the total private wealth made on this basis remain very approximate, analysis of the data indicates general trends in the evolution of French private wealth, with the stipulation that changes in the law relating to inheritance are taken into account.[8]

In order to relate wealth to the social structure, it is necessary to rely on monographic sources. Marriage contracts and inventories made after death by public notaries, often very detailed, exist in the nineteenth century only for a small percentage of the population.[9] The probate declarations have the advantage of being more concise and of existing on a much wider basis; even deceased persons who did not leave any taxable assets were recorded for the purpose of registration. A direct examination of these declarations supplies more valuable information than do the published official statistics. They contain accurate data concerning the situation of the deceased, of the marriage partner and of his heirs. When a married person died in most cases it is possible to reconstitute the estate of the married couple and the composition of their assets on a very detailed basis. But every study of wealth based on inheritance entails distorting reality if too great an importance is given to the elderly. Finally, the slowness and the difficulties connected with searches in the Registrar's Archives (the department which is responsible for the probate declarations) has compelled all researchers to limit their studies to a period of only a few years and to a few representative places. On the other hand, all such historical research is based for each period and for each place on hundreds, and in large cities even on thousands, of cases.[10] The obtaining of access to the probate documents is more difficult for the recent period, because of the necessity not to violate the confidentiality of private life.

The most recent inquiries on patrimonies are often based on questionnaires devised by the researcher himself. The inquiry on the wealth of the French people in 1975, for instance, was based upon the answers of nearly 3,000 households selected on the basis of a random sample of the whole population.[11] Compared with the probate declarations their advantages are obvious: all age groups, all regions, all strata of society can be taken into account, supposing that the statistics concerning the distribution of households according to profession, age, sex and domicile may be utilised to supply an accurate image of the actual society.[12] But the method has many disadvantages. In a sample where there were 2,800 usable responses, the upper classes and the richest categories risk being underrepresented, because numerous members of 'high society' refuse to answer the questions of the investigator. Conversely, using the components of patrimonies tends to underestimate, particularly, the wealth of more modest households. Durable goods such as furniture, electrical appliances or motor cars, are excluded, but the acquisition of such goods consumes a large part of ordinary savings. Houses acquired outside of France were not taken into consideration, but the immigrant workers included in the sample, for instance the Portuguese, often use their early savings in order to acquire a block of land or build a house in their native country. On the other hand, direct investigations which are not based on taxation documents contain approximately the same percentage of concealment or understatement as the probate declarations, especially among the less visible assets, like financial assets (*les actifs financiers*) and transferable securities.[13]

With such heterogeneous data, long-term comparisons are very difficult. The depreciation of the franc following the abandonment of the gold franc is the principal reason for making a clear division in 1914. When investigating the nineteenth century extended to 1914 the historian has access to documents when constructing his working hypotheses. But for the twentieth century, on the other hand, he can only comment on official statistics or on results which are not always his own.

The French nation which entered the First World War was in many respects different from that which was produced by the Revolution and by the Empire in 1815. The notions of wealth, affluence and poverty, the composition of fortunes and the nature of savings had

changed; but before we point out the character and extent of this
evolution it is necessary to stress the stability which was characteristic
of that century.

Up to 1914 the percentage of poor people in French society was
considerable. In the most important and enterprising towns, the reality
which occurred year after year from the start of the Restoration — in
Paris, Lyon, Bordeaux, Lille or Rouen, for instance — was that 70 to
80 per cent of adults died leaving nothing at their deaths. This is a
minimum percentage, since many people who possessed only worthless
trifles such as straw mattresses and pots and pans were in a similar
position to those who left nothing at their deaths. Certainly such
people were not poverty-stricken in the proper meaning of the term,
because they were able to exist from their wages alone, but they were
at least the 'virtual needy' (*indigents virtuels*) because they had no
reserves: any interruption in their work drove them back into extreme
poverty. This position was not limited only to aged persons dying at
a higher rate than others. In analysing the housing conditions of
Parisians, numerous administrative reports from before 1848 estimate
that 'the really non-indigent part [*partie réellement non indigente*] of
the population resides in a quarter of the dwellings'.[14] In the small
towns and villages, the ratio of deaths not requiring probate
declarations was smaller, being of the order of 30 to 40 per cent. But
as large urban centres increase in importance, so too does this
proportion. Two Frances stand in opposition. In the rural, more
traditional France there was plenty of poverty, but absolute destitution
is much rarer. This influenced the conditions of life in certain provincial
towns which for a long period remained close to the life of the
countryside, such as Toulouse, where the proportion of poor people
was much smaller than in other large towns. In contrast, in urbanised
France, where essential enterprises and wealth were concentrated in the
nineteenth century, poverty was particularly widespread, being as high
in the years 1820-30 as at the beginning of the twentieth century.
Economic growth and the development of financial and industrial
capitalism, which began in France in the 1840s, have increased the
degree of poverty in the cities where the remaining vestiges of rural
life were obliterated; but the degree of poverty did not increase in the
largest, most advanced cities where it existed before. Poverty is not a
direct result of urbanisation, but characteristic of urban life.

Wealth remained very concentrated from 1815 to 1914. Between
1902 and 1913, according to the probate statistics, and for the whole
of France, only 0.2 per cent of taxed inheritances (left by about 0.1 per

Table 2.1: Distribution and Concentration of Assets, 1911

Localisation	0	less than 2,000	Level (in francs) 2,000–50,000	50,000–1,000,000	more than 1,000,000	Total
France						
Number of deaths	37.0	33.1	27.2	2.6	0.1	100
Number of inheritances		53.0	42.6	4.2	0.2	100
Value of inheritances		2.5	26.4	43.1	28.0	100
Paris						
Number of deaths	71.8	7.9	13.0	6.2	1.1	100
Number of inheritances		27.9	46.0	22.1	4.0	100
Value of fortunes		0.1	3.3	29.6	67.0	
Lyon						
Number of deaths	70.0	15.8	9.2	4.8	0.2	100
Number of inheritances		52.6	30.7	15.9	0.7	100
Value of fortunes		0.4	10.9	52.6	36.1	100
Bordeaux						
Number of deaths	70.0	6.6	16.8	6.1	0.5	100
Number of inheritances		22.2	55.8	20.4	1.6	100
Value of fortunes		7.5	40.1	42.9	47.6	100
Toulouse						
Number of deaths	40.0	19.1	35.5	5.3	0.1	100
Number of inheritances		31.9	59.2	8.8	0.2	100
Value of fortunes		1.1	27.6	53.3	18.0	100

Source: A. Daumard, *Histoire Économique et Sociale de la France* (5 vols., Paris, 1979), vol. 4.

cent of all French adults deceased during this period) exceeded one
million francs. This amount represented about 30 per cent of all
transferred assets. Small inheritances were much more numerous but
less than 4 per cent of owners (3 per cent of all deceased adults) left
more than 50,000 francs to their heirs, who received more than 70 per
cent of all assets left at death. This was not a new situation, as was
established by an investigation of the inhabitants of large towns.
Around 1820 the poorest 30 per cent of the deceased owned only 0.1
per cent of all assets left in Paris, 0.5 per cent in Bordeaux, 1
per cent in Toulouse. The proportions were identical in 1911. At the
other end of the scale, 30 per cent of all wealth in the Restoration
period was owned by 1 per cent of Parisians, 1 per cent of Bordelais,
2.5 per cent of Toulousians; in 1911, by 0.4 per cent of Parisians, 1 per
cent of Toulousians, and 2.5 per cent of Bordelais. The similarities are
more important than the differences: most of the wealth was owned by
a very small number of persons. This is characteristic of the whole
period until 1914, although the concentration of wealth increased
slightly during the century.

From poverty to affluence, from affluence to wealth, all shades
existed. Very pronounced contrasts separated the base from the summit
with patrimonies classed according to their descending importance, but
with an enlarged area below the measurable containing all those who
left nothing. Schematically, up to 1914 there existed three major types
of asset distribution. The older type evokes the image of a pyramid of
irregular angles with a very large base and a high apex. Such a
distribution, which existed in certain large cities like Lyon in 1845, is
characteristic of all of France at the beginning of the twentieth century,
as a large number of French people, particularly peasants and villagers,
were owners of very small patrimonies. The distribution of assets in
small towns such as Bayeux or Honfleur at the end of the nineteenth
century calls to mind the trunk of a thick-set pyramid. The number of
fortunes at each level is very similar and the contrasts between base and
summit very much reduced, with the exception of some very rare cases
where one large local fortune exceeds and dominates the remaining
total. This is indicative of one aspect of the distribution of wealth in
France. Very rich families who make their residence in villages or small
towns are quite rare. In larger towns the distribution of fortunes takes
a new form. Their irregular angles suggest the shape of a reversed
spinning-top, with the point extended and the sides more or less
swelled. Evident in Paris and Bordeaux before 1848, this structure
appeared in Lille under the Second Empire and spread widely over the
whole country at the beginning of the twentieth century. It is

Figure 2.1: Distribution of Assets According to Social Milieu

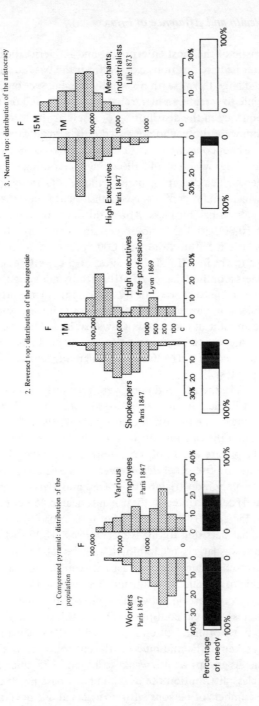

1. Compressed pyramid: distribution of the population

2. Reversed top: distribution of the bourgeoisie

3. 'Normal' top: distribution of the aristocracy

Workers
Paris 1847

Various employees
Paris 1847

Shopkeepers
Paris 1847

High executives
free professions
Lyon 1869

High Executives
Paris 1847

Merchants, industrialists
Lille 1873

Percentage of needy

Source: Daumard, *Histoire Economique*, vol. 3, p. 888

characteristic of the most enterprising and modern cities.

All intermediate positions existed from the base to the summit at least in the large towns, with no wholly missing sections. Nevertheless, it is possible to establish a hierarchy of wealth based on the greater or lesser frequency in the distribution of assets at the various levels. At the bottom were those who possessed only a small capital insufficient to produce an income which would assure survival, but which comprised a modest savings which would allow the overcoming of temporary difficulties such as unemployment or illness, or, in the case of young people, which would permit the establishment of a tradesman's workshop or a small business. Above this level are the owners of capital valued at 10,000-20,000 francs in certain small towns at the beginning of the twentieth century, or of 20,000-50,000 francs in Paris and in most large towns in 1911. The smallest of these estates conferred upon their holders a limited degree of affluence by allowing them to exist without resorting to charity, or by assuring them a yearly income comparable to the wage earned locally by the lowest paid workers. When the amount of capital owned was so large that it could produce an income higher than the average among manual workers, it was possible to speak of it as a 'fortune', ranging from the most modest to the very greatest.[15]

At all times, the rich and poor were very unevenly distributed throughout France. A calculation based upon the probate statistics at the beginning of the twentieth century shows the following results: Parisians and other inhabitants of the Seine *département* owned 32 per cent of the private wealth of the country. Altogether, Frenchmen living in the Seine and five other *départements* (Nord, Lower Seine and Rhone — mainly industrial; Seine-et-Oise and Marne — mainly agricultural) concentrated in their hands nearly 45 per cent of the total wealth of the country. The analysis of urban fortunes confirms that this trend has persisted for many years. From 1820 to 1911, the wealth of Parisians was largely predominant and the relative poverty of Toulousians underlines the contrast between the economically enterprising towns and the traditional cities (see Table 2.2).

Finally, a comparison between wealth-holding and social class demonstrates a certain continuity. During this period we find again the three types of distribution illustrated in the schema here in examples taken in the mid-nineteenth century. Even in the most homogeneous groups wealth was distributed hierarchically. In the working class distribution the pyramid has a base much enlarged by the large numbers of persons with no assets at all: poverty — or, for

Table 2.2: Comparison of the Evolution of Fortunes in Large French Towns

	\multicolumn{4}{c}{Value of inheritances left during one year of the period}			
	1820-26	towards 1847	1869-73	towards 1910
	\multicolumn{4}{c}{Total value (in million francs)}			
Paris	144	301		1920
Lyon		22.3	65.5	111.6
Bordeaux	7.9		51.8	105.8
Lille	4.5		53	129.5
Toulouse	6.1	8.8	20.1	28.3
	\multicolumn{4}{c}{Mean value (in francs)}			
Paris	34,600	66,000		191,700
Lyon		13,800	42,800	57,700
Bordeaux	23,800		49,500	96,300
Lille	14,400		100,100	142,300
Toulouse	7,500	10,400	22,600	23,400

Sources: A Daumard *et al.*, *Les Fortunes Français au XIXe Siècle* (Paris, 1973), p. 118; Daumard, *Histoire Economique*, vol. 3, p. 862.

certain people, scarcity — was a quasi-general rule; some degree of modest affluence appeared at the pyramid's summit. The 'reversed spinning-top' schema is typical of the middle-class distribution of wealth. One can neglect the percentage of the 'needy' who did not leave any taxable inheritance: these are ruined people or those close to the borders of the working class. Depending on the social group, town or epoch studied, the base from which the distribution starts can vary, as can the apex, but the proportion of intermediary estates, modest or middling, is the most important. In the aristocratic distribution, which is much less common, the extreme and median values are not very widely represented, while great wealth, still exceptional, is more frequently encountered, and the number of intermediary fortunes is relatively higher. Nevertheless, it is difficult to strictly disentangle social class from the hierarchy of wealth because the levels of fortune of the different classes intermingled in their extreme values. There were no strictly discontinuous patterns, and overlapping was the rule.

However, if the characteristics of the distribution of wealth are closely studied, it can be established that a profound evolution took place.

   Between 1820 and 1914 private wealth increased considerably. The evolution of incomes from inheritance proves this (see Figure 2.3). This tendency is the same when the mean value of inheritances is calculated in relation to the total number of deaths. But this evolution is not continuous. After a period of stagnation, an increase starts around the year 1840, and continues with some irregularities up to around the year 1880. From around 1,800 million francs at the end of the July Monarchy (1848), this sum rose to more than 3,000 million francs at the end of the Second Empire (1865-70), and to 5,000 million francs by 1880. Subsequently another period of stagnation appears and from 1885/90 until about 1910 the growth is only around 20 per cent instead of the 50 per cent increase in the period 1860-80. Private wealth-holding was clearly subject to the effects of the economic recession which occurred toward the end of the nineteenth century. On the other hand, the economic recovery, which was very marked before 1914, had little effect on the total value of all estates. Is it that this economic recovery had less of an influence on wealth-holding than that of the Second Empire? Another explanation is also plausible. Possibly the probate valuations understate the values of the top fortunes. Some of these were collected only recently; possibly, too, the reform of the probate procedure in 1901 increased concealment and fraud.

   This growth in wealth modified the distribution of wealth. While the inequality of wealth between regions remained strong, the contrast between Paris and the other large provincial towns in general decreased at the same rate as the economic activity of these towns increased: for instance, while in 1820 the average estate subject to probate of the inhabitants of Lille did not amount to half of the value of Parisians, in 1911 it had risen to three-quarters of the Parisian value. Not all possessing classes profited equally from this economic development. While the degree of wealth concentration was great, what became of the intermediary fortunes? This question preoccupied the French people very much. But it is difficult to solve because the notion of intermediary levels of wealth varies so greatly with the locality and the epoch. The possession of 500,000 francs already constituted great wealth under the Restoration, whereas in the last third of the nineteenth century the economist Foville coined the phrase 'living like a millionaire' (in the manner of those whose inheritance attained a million francs) as a designation for the wealthiest classes. Even more uncertain are the lower limits of wealth. Taking as a basis the distribution of fortunes according to their levels as well as the presumed income from capital, we have fixed, very approximately, the lowest limits of this class at 20,000 francs at the beginning of the period and 50,000 francs at the end. On this basis it is possible to estimate, at least for the towns, the size of fortunes which assured a degree of affluence, great or modest, to their owners. They amounted in Paris to 22-24 per cent of the number of inheritances (depending on the year) and to 7 per cent of all adult deaths. This group accounted for 62 per cent of the total value of all assets passing in 1820, but only 30 per cent in 1911. The relative number of fortunes of a middling value remained nearly stationary, whereas their importance in the economic life and wealth structure of the country decreased considerably.

Certain classes benefited particularly from this increase in private wealth. However, the old thesis which attributed to the industrialisation of the nineteenth century the aggravation of the gap between rich and poor cannot be maintained. The differences between poverty and wealth remained materially of the same order from 1820 to 1911. The ratio between those adults who were the most deprived (a median established by taking into account the large numbers of people who had no assets) and the average fortunes of the wealthiest groups was 1:10,000; an analysis of estates in Paris or Lille makes this apparent.[16] On the other hand, in Lyon the difference between the poorest proletarians and the merchants and manufacturers grew wider. This was more the result of the enrichment of the class of the big businessmen than the impoverishment of the needy who, at the beginning of the nineteenth century, were already very far from the apex of the scale of wealth. These developments are not contradictory but complementary. But the process of enrichment due to economic development did not lead to a transfer of assets. Those least favoured were the small employers, shopkeepers or craftsmen working on their own account. In Paris, for example, they were the owners of 17 per cent of the total wealth in 1820, but only 3 per cent in 1911. The mean value of their fortunes grew from 28,600 to 44,000 francs – an increase of 54 per cent – whereas the mean value of fortunes in the capital doubled in that time. This cannot be described as a ruining, only as a relative reduction, of their social status. This is an aspect of what contemporaries described as a crisis of the middle classes, and above all a crisis of small businesses. The position of 'men of talent' – members of the liberal professions, civil servants, personnel in the ranks of private business – can be classified as being of the same type. All of these participated only slightly in the general enrichment, above all in large cities where, since the beginning of the nineteenth century, the administrators and managers were most numerous. The principal

benefactors of the general enrichment were big businessmen. The mean
fortunes left by heads of large enterprises in Paris reached nearly 1.5
million francs in 1911 — nearly seven times as much as in 1820. This
rise was just as great in the provinces. In Lyon and in Lille the
manufacturers had the largest mean fortunes, while in Paris it was the
merchants and bankers in first place.

These changes which affected the very largest fortunes are highly
indicative of the evolution of wealth from 1815 to 1914.

Between 1902 and 1913, the probate statistics indicate that 6,500
estates exceeded one million francs during this period (the actual
number — 5,327 — excludes the two years 1906 and 1908; the figure
here has been arrived at by extrapolation). The probate returns of the
Seine *département* represented 58 per cent of the number and 66 per
cent of the total value of all estates. Among the very rich, the
preponderance of Paris was more pronounced still. Of the 500 estates
valued at 5 million francs or more, 68 per cent were proved in the
Seine *département*, representing 78 per cent of the total gross value of
all estates. The other *départements,* those of Nord, Rhone and Seine-
Inférieure, contained 8 per cent of all very large estates and 5 per cent
of their total value; the remainder were dispersed throughout the other
départements. Statistics of this type are not available for the nineteenth
century, but the electoral rolls — which were based on property
qualifications — supply some indications. A major part of all electors
whose property qualifications amounted to 1,000 francs can be
considered as having been rich, while those with property qualifications
exceeding 5,000 francs were among the owners of large fortunes.
Around 1840 only 15-16 per cent of all rich electors voted in Paris and
its suburbs. Moreover, the electoral roll of the Seine *département*
contained only two of the fifteen electors with property qualifications
exceeding 15,000 francs.[15] But it would be erroneous to conclude from
this that in the course of the nineteenth century wealth migrated to
Paris from the provinces. The great personal fortunes which already
existed in Paris were not well-represented by the amount stated as the
property qualifications (in 1842, for instance, the head of the family
which owned the Banque Mallet had a property qualification below
1,000 francs), and, above all, the residence of these people did not
always coincide with the locality of their main enterprises. For example
the Comte Roy, the peer of France raised to the nobility during the
Restoration and considered to be one of the richest landowners in
France, was registered on the electoral roll of Marne with a property
qualification of 24,000 francs. He was the owner of a castle in the

country, immense forests in the east of France and lands and ironworks in Normandy, but he was domiciled in the rue de Chaussée d'Antin and managed his business affairs from Paris. He had local political connections, but his influence in the country was enormous in relation to his life in the capital. In the same way many of the wealthy provincial electors were in reality Parisians, and when they died their probate declaration was made in Paris — their principal venue — in accordance with the law.

The electoral rolls with their property qualifications indicate the profession and rank of each elector. This allows us to establish that among electors with a property qualification exceeding 5,000 francs, 14 per cent were merchants, bankers and manufacturers. Nearly half of these electors were people with noble titles and the proportion increased to two-thirds among electors with property qualifications above 10,000 francs. A part of this nobility had acquired its titles quite recently. Because their titles dated from the Empire or the Restoration, they were considered to be 'commoners' by the old nobility. None the less, the famous names of the *ancien régime* continued to hold an important role at the summit of the wealthy class. The probate statistics of the twentieth century do not supply any indications of the social origins of testators, but one fact is significant: all estates declared between 1902 and 1913 were valued at less than 100 million francs, with two exceptions — one left in 1905 and another in 1912. They were of the order of 250 million francs and their dates coincide with those of the deaths of Alphonse and Gustave de Rothschild.

Local studies underline the fact that wealth progressively changed in character. In Paris in 1820 the nobility, mostly those of the *ancien régime*, had an enormous preponderance among the largest fortunes: 40 per cent of the number, 70 per cent of the value. In the mid-nineteenth century the nobility was far from ruined. In 1847 the mean fortune of Parisian noblemen exceeded that of other groups. But the number and value of the great Parisian fortunes had increased, and the nobility represented only 38 per cent of the wealthiest Parisians and their fortunes only 30 per cent of the total. In 1911 the nobility maintained its individual position, and in the capital, where most of the great families had their residence, the mean fortune remained very high. Nevertheless, an important change did take place: less than one per cent of fortunes higher than one million francs belonged to the nobility and a maximum of 15 per cent of the total value of all assets belonged to them.[18] The business aristocracy had not as yet completely supplanted these traditional fortunes, but its importance at the apex of the hierarchy of wealth was now well-established.

Is the contrast between wealthy noblemen and the wealthy business aristocracy still meaningful at the beginning of the twentieth century? This question cannot be answered from the point of view of wealth alone, but the analysis of wealth adds some elements to the answer.

In certain cases, when the deceased left a widow and the marriage had been established on the basis of common assets of the spouses, the probate declarations allow us to gauge approximately whether the household grew or declined in wealth. The analysis is based on a comparison between the assets of the spouses (formed by their contributions to the marriage, plus gifts or inheritances obtained) and the total wealth of the household at the time of the death of the deceased partner, increased by dowries given to the children but reduced by any debts outstanding. Compared with the groups which left the smallest and largest inheritances, the nobility in Paris in 1911 appears to be the class least favoured in this regard. In 35 per cent of such cases, the final fortune of the household was smaller than the value of the assets brought in by the spouses. This percentage is greatly in excess of those which characterise other social groups where a decline in wealth is less frequent and enrichment more common.[19]

This contrast can partly be explained by the composition of those fortunes which belonged to the wealthy nobility and to the bourgeois aristocracy. Table 2.3 shows that the rich nobility adapted itself to the new forms of financial capitalism, but that the composition of fortunes remained more traditional in the nobility than in the wealthy bourgeoisie. The place of real estate remained extremely important, particularly that of 'provincial' real estate which consisted mainly of large properties bringing in only small incomes in relation to the capital invested. But, on the other hand, the business aristocracy in the twentieth century possessed real estate for renting which had, in Paris up to 1914, brought in high revenues, as well as important hotels, mansions and villas, whereas the value of the land they possessed was ridiculously small: only 2 per cent of their total wealth. Certainly the nobility was not uninterested in the Bourse. Stock-dealing was already quite high in 1847, and in 1911 was identical to that which characterised the large bourgeoise fortunes. But a more detailed examination underlines the differences: the place in their fortunes of fixed-value bonds was higher, 37 per cent instead of 28 per cent, and the place of foreign stocks and shares was less, 18 per cent instead of 22 per cent. We are therefore led to believe that the tendency to speculate on the Stock Exchange was less widespread in the traditional spheres of society – and this label must be attached to most of the old noble families – than in the big business bourgeoisie, and this is reflected in the composition of their patrimonies.

Since the mid-nineteenth century the place of stocks and shares in the composition of private wealth increased continuously and was most important among the largest patrimonies. In parallel fashion, the amount of money invested abroad increased considerably. But, contrary to popular belief, the 'rentiers of the world' were the rich rather than the modest savers: the greater the fortune, the greater the number of foreign investors and the more significant the share of foreign investment in the total portfolio. The analysis of private Parisian wealth given in Table 2.4 is one piece of evidence which demonstrates this. The French placed only a relatively minor part of their assets and their savings in foreign countries, and the rich and affluent, while more interested in foreign investment, placed only a small part of their disposable assets outside France. The acquisition of foreign holdings was the result of complex factors. Stocks with fixed incomes and particularly public stocks (*fonds publics*), especially Russian stocks, provided an income which was very much higher than that of French stocks. The acquisition of such stocks had as its purpose the provision of a high income, the desire for which was of course general. In the portfolios of the richest capitalists stocks and shares constituted an important part of all foreign holdings, especially for the big businessman. These investments were geographically very widespread, as will be seen on the accompanying map (Figure 2.2). Such men desired to diversify their risks, and they therefore preferred solid concerns which yielded lower revenues. Simultaneously, they invested part of their wealth in more speculative shares which were likely to increase in value and yield large dividends. From the beginning of the nineteenth century, all fortunes were divided into two such parts as soon as they grew to a certain size. One was reserved for 'investments by the heads of the family' (*placements de pères de famille*) in urban real estate or land purchases, or in Stock Exchange debentures: this constituted a 'reserve' which, while it could increase in value, could not in principle be disposed of except to set up the next generation in adult life. The other part, more important among the mercantile and industrial classes, was utilised for speculation in businesses, land deals and on the Bourse. The spirit of enterprise thus combined with prudence allowed one to grow rich without endangering the position of the family.

Inheritance statistics, interrupted in 1914, were again regularly

Table 2.3: Composition of Parisian Fortunes Higher Than One Million Francs

	1847 Nobility	1847 Bourgeois aristocracy	1911 Nobility	1911 Bourgeois aristocracy
Real estate				
Paris	16.5	28.3	18.2	19.4
Provinces	49.5	23.0	19.2	6.2
Total	66.0	51.3	37.4	25.6
Stock Exchange				
French Government bonds			14.0	5.1
Foreign Government bonds			8.7	11.5
French debentures	2.0	8.5	12.0	8.1
Foreign debentures			2.7	3.8
French industrial shares			5.4	14.4
Foreign industrial shares	6.6	8.8	7.0	6.4
Total	8.6	17.3	49.8	49.3
Interest				
Commercial loans, partnerships	0.5	15.3	0.3	12.6
Trust moneys	15.2	12.0	2.1	4.0
Deposits, cash moneys	1.5	3.5	4.2	6.1
Personal chattels	3.2	0.3	5.0	1.8
Various	5.0	0.3	1.2	0.6
Total	100	100	100	100

Source: Taxes imposed on private wealth following an inheritance.

Table 2.4: Placement of Funds by Parisians in Foreign Countries, 1910

| | Size of fortunes (francs) | | | |
	less than 50,000	50,000- 1,000,000	above 1,000,000	Total
Number of fortunes which possessed foreign securities (%)	14	54	78	26
Part of foreign securities in the total value of fortunes (%)	11	14	22	19
Geographical distribution of foreign investments				
Russia	36.9	21.6	15.2	18.4
Rest of Europe	27.9	31.7	36.6	34.3
Ottoman Empire	5.0	5.5	3.0	3.7
Africa	9.6	16.4	16.8	15.7
Asia (excl. Turkey)	4.6	6.1	5.7	5.9
North America	3.2	7.8	7.1	6.6
Latin America	12.8	10.9	15.6	15.4
Total foreign portfolio	100	100	100	100

Source: Daumard, 'Foreign Investments in the French Patrimonies of the XIX Century', *Revue of Economic and Social History*, no. 4 (1974).

published from 1925 to 1964, but in recent years have become less detailed. In addition, small inheritances have been exempt from paying probate duties since 1956. The number and value of estates worth less than one million old or 10,000 new francs has become unknown since the 'new franc' replaced the old unit of currency in December 1958. It is no longer possible to estimate the number of persons who possessed modest reserves without attaining real affluence. The utilisation of the available data creates other difficulties as well. Because of the devaluation of the franc, long-term comparisons require the conversion of nominal values into real values, but the indices which allow the conversion of 'current' into 'constant' francs are imperfect.[20] Besides, more and more one can question the significance of the probate data. Certain assets completely escape from the legal necessity to pay probate duties. The estates of Frenchmen who died for France in the Second World War were completely exempt from probate duties and therefore from a probate declaration. The 'Pinay Loan' issued in 1952 was also exempted from probate duties and it is widely admitted that the value of some large estates was reduced to a minimum thanks to 'deathbed transfers' made through the solicitude of shrewd heir-

Figure 2.2: Investments of Rich Parisians in Foreign Countries in 1910

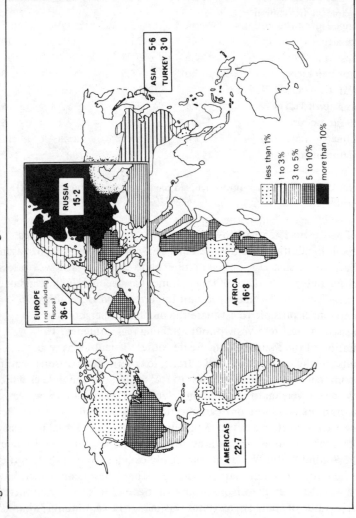

Source: Daumard, *Histoire Economique*, vol. 4, 1, p. 429.

presumptives. It may be that fraudulent transactions have increased greatly since the end of the First World War. The ever-increasing value of stocks and shares labelled as belonging to the 'bearer', the importance of anonymous Treasury bonds, the increase in probate duties, have all encouraged the concealment of assets by their owners; finally, the uncertainties of the future have led others to invest in gold or collector's items which are very difficult for the Treasury to evaluate. Others, particularly among the very rich, tried to conceal their wealth in foreign countries. But it must not be assumed that this behaviour changed with the end of monetary stability. Fraud and tax evasion were already widespread before 1914. Based upon various estimates, it is possible to calculate that only 54 per cent of the value of French shares belonging to privately owned wealth were mentioned in probate declarations in 1934. Estimated on the same basis, this proportion amounted to 57.5 per cent in 1908.[21] Even taking the imprecision of such estimates into account, it can plainly be seen that this tendency has been persistent. Concerning the evasion of duties on foreign investment, it can be assumed that the very wealthy already practised this before 1914. In order to counteract this, Caillaux, the Minister of Finance, had in 1908 opened negotiations with foreign countries over this matter and concluded an agreement concerning this with the Chancellor of the Exchequer.[22] Inheritance statistics can at least be used to demonstrate general trends in the evolution of wealth-holding.

Starting with the First World War and for many years afterwards, the private wealth of the French decreased considerably. The evolution in the amount of inheritances (see Figure 2.3) is among the best evidence of this. An increase in the nominal value here hides the considerable reduction in the real value. Until 1964 this value was much lower than that attained in the years 1902-13. Were circumstances the same? Before 1914, for the whole of France, about 65 per cent of adults left property which was the object of a probate declaration. Beginning in 1951 this proportion decreases. It attained only 50 per cent in 1955 because the administration became ever more tolerant in regard to small estates. But this only slightly decreased the total amount of transmitted assets. In fact, when in 1956 estates worth less than one million francs were no longer liable to probate duty, the number of declared estates decreased by 70 per cent (65,000 instead of 239,000), but the value of their assets decreased by only 11 per cent (260,000 million in current francs instead of 291,000 million). When we take into account the indices based on real value, its evolution can be summarised in the following way: taking 1913 as 100, the total amount of the inheritances passing was 33 in 1955 and 64 in 1964. The difference between the mean values of assets inherited, as is shown in Table 2.5 is not as great, but the decrease remains enormous. It is sometimes assumed that an increase in the number of *inter vivos* gifts partly explains the decrease in the value of inherited assets. In fact, the proportion of such gifts in relation to the total value of all inheritances increased from 15 per cent in 1910 to 25 per cent after the Second World War. But when we add the value of such gifts to that of inheritances, the index changes only from 35.5 in 1955 to 67 in 1964.

The decline is not continuous. Sometimes very low, the amount of inherited assets rose rapidly during periods of economic prosperity, but the indices showing the purchasing power of money reach their highest point after the crisis: 78 for the median value of estates in 1932, 69 in 1935 for the total amount of assets. The world crisis of the 1930s and even more the Second World War reduced the fortunes and the wealth of Frenchmen in spite of the inflation connected with the temporary and artificial advance in the price of real estate and shares in 1942 and 1943.[23] A growth occurred after reconstruction. It was rapid up to 1964, the date when inheritance statistics break off.

According to the 1975 sample, the mean fortune of Frenchmen amounted to 186,000 francs, or ten times that of the mean value of inheritances declared in 1950 and 2½ times the amount declared in 1913 (these are in the real rather than the nominal value of the franc[24]). However, the values are not exactly comparable. Debts are deducted from the assets of inheritances. In 1975, on the contrary, the value of loans, particularly those contracted in order to become the owner of one's dwelling, is considered an asset.

On the other hand, the total value of inheritances is less than the total value of household wealth because inheritances include only the value of estates liable to taxation. One must take into account as well the fact that personal wealth tends to decline in old age: gifts are made to children, old people live on their capital. Conversely, young people (who were included in the 1975 study) would not have had time to save, nor would they have received the inheritances which they will eventually obtain. Furthermore, the total value of wealth in 1975 was underestimated: certain assets were excluded from the questionnaire, and the greatest fortunes were missed by the study.[25] Given that exact calculations are not possible in these conditions, one must conclude that French private wealth has grown (in real terms) by a factor of 1.5-2 from 1910/13 to 1975. But this figure does not take into account either real estate situated outside France or the value of foreign investments.

Table 2.5: Evolution of the Average Value of Inheritances and Fortunes in France

	Number of cases (thousands)	Nominal mean value*	Real mean value Value in 1914 (francs)	Index
Inheritances				
1913	360.5	15,300	15,400	100
1932	278.2	54,700	12,000	78
1950	275.9	462,700	3,800	25
1955	239.4	1,218,100	7,800	51
1964	123.9	68,000**	28,600	186
Fortunes				
1975	2.8	186,800	37,600	244

*Expressed in current francs, therefore in 'new francs' for 1964 and 1975 (since December 1958, 1 franc = 100 old francs).
**Since 1964, only inheritances above 10,000 francs are objects of a probate declaration.
Source: Inheritance statistics published by the Finance Department; A. Babeau and D. Strauss-Kahn, *La Richesse des Français* (Paris, 1977).

Despite all the reservations we have made regarding the value of the evidence, the inheritance statistics allow us to ascertain that the regional contrasts in the distribution of wealth were reduced after the First World War. According to Cornut's calculations the difference between the mean value of fortunes belonging to the inhabitants of the richest *départements* and those of the poorest decreased considerably in 1934 and even more in 1953: from a ratio of 1:16 in 1914, it declined to 1:5 between the wars and to 1:3 in 1953.[26] A direct analysis of inheritance statistics allows us to see that from 1929 (i.e. even before the Depression) the contrasts between the North and the South, between the traditional zones and the *départements* integrated into the modern world, had reduced the part played by Paris and the Seine *département*, where the majority of the very large French estates were declared. This diminution was even more pronounced after 1950.[27]

Given such heterogeneous data, it is difficult to ascertain exactly the evolution of the concentration of wealth. The presentation of results complicates the task still more. The results actually have to be regrouped arithmetically. The inheritance statistics indicate the number and amount of estates according to their value, but the level has varied

Figure 2.3: Total of Property Transmitted by Inheritance in France

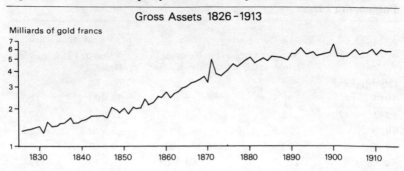

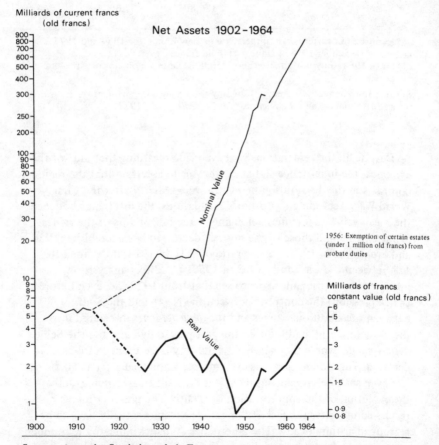

Source: Annuaire Statistique de la France.

Table 2.6: Evolution of the Concentration of Assets in France in the Twentieth Century

Part in the total number of inheritances or fortunes	Part of the total amount of assets (percentage) mean			
	1902-13	1929	1950	1975
Low level				
50 % of the total	2	4	7	5
80 % of the total	11	18	23	31
Intermediary level				
15 % of the total	9	17	24	30
High level				
5 % of the total	80	65	53	39
1 % of the total	50	45	31	
0.2 % of the total	30	26	20	15

Sources: Patrimonies of households reconstituted by Babeau and Strauss-Kahn, *La Richesse*, for 1975; inheritance statistics for previous years.

at different times: in 1950, for instance, all inheritances worth less than 250,000 francs were collected, which corresponded to 63 per cent of the total (and to 11 per cent of the value of all assets). The approximate results which could be established from these figures can be represented graphically so as to give the cumulative percentage of the number of estates and their values at different levels for all estates.

Between the two world wars the general concentration of assets for all of France retained the characteristics very close to those which existed at the beginning of the twentieth century. As before 1914, more than 50 per cent of the value of all estates were left by one per cent of the recorded wealth-leavers and the distribution retained the form of a pyramid very similar to that in the past. Until 1939 the proportion of inheritances which were not obliged to make a probate declaration was of the order of 35 per cent of deceased adults. However, as is shown in Table 2.6, the proportion of assets belonging to the smallest estates increased, whereas the largest estates decreased. But in the *département* of the Seine the value of middling fortunes decreased: in 1911, 18 per cent of estates, those worth between 50,000 and one million francs, constituted 37 per cent of the total value of assets. In 1929 the corresponding estates, worth from 250,000 to 5 million francs of that time contained 40 per cent of all assets while containing only 12.5 per cent of the number of declarations. The very largest estates, amounting to one per cent of the total, accounted for 43 per cent of the value of all estates in 1911 and 49 per cent in 1929. Should it be necessary to oppose the evolution of fortunes possessed by the inhabitants of the countryside and of the small towns which formed the majority of inheritances throughout the whole of France, against urban fortunes, of which the Seine — a *département* with a negligible rural population — is a symbol?

This evolution became more pronounced after the Second World War. The concentration of assets in 1950 indicates, for various layers of the population, a general transfer of wealth toward the smaller and middle-sized estates. (The method employed of assessing their numbers makes comparisons more difficult for the *département* of the Seine.) It seems possible that the great preponderance in favour of the largest estates was somewhat lessened. In 1929, 2.3 per cent of all estates accounted for 65 per cent of all assets, but in 1950, 3.1 per cent of estates represented 56 per cent of the total value of all assets. The degree of concentration continued to decrease, judging by the distribution which can be deduced from the 1975 inquiry. The percentages of this inquiry are, at best, only indicative, since we are here comparing household wealth rather than the estates left mostly by the elderly. Also — as noted above — very large estates are not fully represented in the 1975 sample, but, certainly, very large inheritances were underrepresented before as well. It seems, however, that we can accept that the concentration of assets remained very high, but that there is a reduction following the First World War and, even more, after 1950. After a quarter of a century of this trend the main beneficiaries have been the owners of middle-sized fortunes, their proportion having increased considerably. But it would be inaccurate to conclude that the position of the poor has deteriorated. For example, 'the equivalent of retirement rights appears to be a powerful factor in the deconcentration of patrimonies: in fact, whereas 10 per cent of the richest households in 1975 held more than 50 per cent of the traditional patrimony [*patrimoine traditionnel*], when we take into account the capital representing retirement rights [*droits à la retraite*] they had only 30 per cent of the patrimony increased in this way'.[28] Considering the importance of social reform and of various mechanisms of social welfare, the 'real poor', so numerous before 1914 especially in the large towns, who had misery as their only prospect, now became an exception. Neither sickness, nor old age, nor even unemployment could make paupers out of people who had only their labour as their means of sustenance.

Taking as their basis the 1975 sample, the Centre of Economic Research for Savings (*CREP*) has made a retrospective study of the evolution of wealth from 1949 to 1975. This analysis looked at 996 patrimonies divided into twelve social groups covering all age classes from 12 to 103 years. The data is not the result of observations. The past was reconstituted by a series of calculations based on the facts collected for 1975; it was attempted to depict the position of the 26 preceding years by correcting this base year using statistical information available concerning different types of income, savings and indebtedness, the structure of inheritance, gains and losses from various types of investment, the role of gifts and, finally, demographic data relating particularly to social groups and the structure of their ages, mortality rates, number of children and matrimonial patterns.[29] The results are difficult to interpret. At first glance it might be concluded that the inequality between rich and poor and between various social groups increased. But if we consider the assets not taken into account in the 1975 inquiry (cash, foreign holdings, gold, jewellery, durable goods, cattle) on the one hand, and pension rights on the other, we can conclude that inequality was greatly reduced.[30] The reality is even more varied. The study carried out by the Research Centre concluded: 'The quarter century from 1949 to 1975 was the scene of a constant "disequilibrium" of fortunes': an increasing gap between the richest and the poorest, a difference between the very richest (one per cent of the total) and those immediately below, but at the same time a particularly strong increase in the intermediary levels. Although a 'relative impoverishment of the most modest classes' can be discerned because the inheritances of the most disadvantaged increased only slowly, on the other hand the households forming the richest one-tenth of the total became wealthier to a lesser degree than the mean increase for the entire sample.[31] A comment by Babeau explains the complex character of the evolution of the inequality of inheritances. He stresses the very large increase in the mean level of patrimonies, much greater than among the highest levels. But he shows that the social composition of the highest level (the highest 10 per cent of all households) and the lowest level (the lowest 10 per cent) has changed with the years. Among the wealthiest in 1949 were found 75 per cent of farmers (*agriculteurs*) but not more than 30 per cent in 1975. On the other hand, the place of artisans, merchants, industrialists, the liberal professions and managers increased greatly. Concerning the poorest levels, they consisted mainly of young people under 30 years of age — but this apparent poverty is without real significance because they used their savings to buy durable goods, motor cars etc. which were not taken into consideration in the inquiry. Let us add that a certain number of young people do not reside with their families and are in a peculiar position because they live on subsidies from their parents or a similar source without having paid jobs. Along with these young people we must place the elderly, who considerably increased between 1949 and 1975. They are the 'real poor' because their accumulated wealth has been annihilated by inflation.[32]

The character of wealth-holding changed considerably during the twentieth century. After the First World War occurred 'the end of rentiers': i.e. the ruin of all those who invested their capital in fixed-income debentures which melted away and disappeared; these were times of great difficulty as well for the many who obtained depreciated returns from fixed-income bonds and from public loans or real estate rents which produced less than their real value. At the beginning of the Depression the value of houses in the total amount of French inheritances decreased considerably compared with its previous total before 1914, whereas the value of private enterprises and, to a lesser degree, the value of stocks and shares increased, the variations being larger in the Seine *département* than in the whole of France. But inflation did not ruin all Frenchmen. The increase in the price of commercial enterprises underlines the gains for small shopkeepers which continued until 1930; their true difficulties appeared only in 1935. During the years of prosperity the quotations of shares, particularly of foreign shares, was subject to fluctuations which gave certain rich capitalists the chance to grow richer still. Although the Depression was deeply resented by some of them, advantageous investments could still be made by those who had the available capital, thanks to the low price of luxury real estate in Paris, for example. The inter-war period brought about a whole series of regroupings, during the 1920s as well as in the 1930s.[33] Inheritance became precarious. Instability threatened all men of property, even the richest and best-informed. With few exceptions, mere possession was insufficient to make the future safe. One such exception might have been the so-called '200 families', but the historian is denied access to any documents which would allow him to address this matter.

After the Second World War, the composition of wealth changes again. Among inheritances, real estate represented 53 per cent of all assets compared with 40 per cent between the world wars. This proportion climbed to 66 per cent in the sample of patrimonies taken in 1975. Simultaneously, the role of stocks and shares sharply declined:

25-26 per cent before 1939 (as before and after the crisis of 1929),
17 per cent in 1949, about 20 per cent in 1959 and 1962 (years for
which only data for estates of 10,000 francs or more are available), and
10 per cent of fortunes analysed in 1975.

As in the nineteenth century, sheer wealth alone does not wholly
define social position today. In all classes there persists the irregular
arrangement of wealth pyramids noted above. At equal social ranks,
patrimonies can be very different, and, conversely, there are
representatives of the more modest social strata whose assets are as
large as those higher up the social scale. Furthermore, influence and
prestige are dependent not only on wealth but upon family origins
and social relationships (which do not always coincide with the size of
one's assets), as well as upon the personalities and characters of
individuals and households. Nevertheless, an evolution occurred.
Previously it was the case with even the most modest of French
fortunes that it had to contain a piece of land, be it a simple field,
family garden or, if possible, a small house to live in. In the towns it
was the possession of a small enterprise, later a little house, not very
valuable, often at least partly sublet, which usually marked the
beginnings of affluence. Today, as in the nineteenth century, the lower
levels of patrimonies correspond to the situation of those people who
own only a modest reserve in the form, for example, of savings deposits.
But the most important part of the patrimony for most Frenchmen,
even now, is their dwelling: 24 per cent of households, including those
citizens with small patrimonies, mostly salaried people (44 per cent of
the total population), are owners of their own dwellings. At the other
extreme, the urban households with the largest fortunes (4 per cent of
the population) participate in the ownership of all forms of private
property, but they are 'distinguished by owning very great parcels of
stocks and shares'. Of these households, 76 per cent own French
industrial shares, 63 per cent own bonds (*obligations*).[34] In smaller
estates utilitarian possessions, such as a dwelling, increasingly replace
productive capital invested in small enterprises or in land. Among larger
fortunes the development of share capital, at the expense of real estate
for renting, direct investment in business or loans to private individuals,
tends to transform into passive capitalists those who had previously
controlled their assets directly. Stock market speculation becomes more
frequent, but this is more a matter of gambling than of rational
enterprise, except among a handful of capitalists who possess
considerable capital and exceptional information. But normally, the
great majority of shareholders have no influence in the direction of

companies of which they are part-owners. Naturally, this does not apply to the very top wealth-holders. According to certain estimates, there are at present in France about 3,000 personal fortunes greater than 10 million francs, comparable in their size to those of multimillionaires during the age of the gold franc. The greater part of this number is in the hands of the great industrialists, along with representatives of the liberal professions and of the diverse activities connected with public entertainment. While certain names of these wealth-holders are frequently cited, a serious study cannot be undertaken.[35] If we mention these exceptional and little-known cases, it is to formulate the hypothesis that perhaps today there is a gap between people wealthy enough to remain the true masters of their fortunes and the mere wealth of others, despite the importance and the form of their investments, which is closer to modest affluence. But this is an extrapolation which would require access to evidence of a type not available to the historian.

Notes

1. See L. Giraud, A. Prost and R. Gossez, *Les Conseillers Généraux en 1870* (Paris, 1967), pp. 22 ff.
2. See A. Daumard *et al.*, *Les Fortunes Françaises au XIXe Siècle* (Paris, 1973), Ch. I.
3. Ibid., pp. 24-7.
4. Until its recent reform, the Civil Code considered as common assets only the real estate owned by each spouse. A special marriage contract before a notary was necessary in order to establish that moveable possessions were not regarded as common assets.
5. F. Divisia, R. Dupin and R. Roy, *A la Recherche du Franc Perdu* (Paris, 1956), vol. 3. In studying the evolution of the franc, this work relies heavily on C. Colson, *Cours d'Economie Politique* (Paris, 1927), vol. 3, pp. 361 ff.
6. Colson, *Cours d'Economie*, vol. 3, p. 374. See also A. de Foville, *La France Economique Statistique Raisonnée et Comparée* (Paris, 1889), p. 516.
7. P. Cornut, *Répartition de la Fortune Privée en France par Département et Nature des Biens au Cours de la Premiere Moitié du XXe Siècle* (Paris, 1963), pp. 21-9, 45-53.
8. For documentation see A. Daumard, 'Les Statistiques Successorales en France aux XIXe et XXe Siècle', *Pour une Histoire de la Statistique* (Paris, 1977), vol. I, pp. 381-9.
9. The first quantitative use of the notarial archives was that of A. Daumard, *La Bourgeoisie Parisienne de 1815 à 1848* (Paris, 1963).
10. Among the works in which wealth was studied on the basis of this evidence, we mention: Daumard, *Les Fortunes Françaises*; P. Léon, *Géographie de la Fortunes et Structures Sociales à Lyon au XIXe Siècle (1815-1914)* (Centre d'histoire économique et sociale de la région lyonnaise, 1974); F.P. Codaccioni, *De l'inégalité sociale dans une Grande Ville Industrielle. Le Drame de Lille de 1850 à 1914* (Lille, 1976); G. Désert, 'Structures Sociales dans

les Villes Bas-normandes au XIXe Siècle' in *Conjoncture Economique, Structures Sociales. Hommage à Ernest Labrousse* (Paris, 1974), pp. 491-513. See also the section concerning assets and wealth in A. Daumard, *Histoire Economique et Sociale de la France* (5 vols., Paris, 1979), vols. 2 and 4.

11. A. Babeau and D. Strauss-Kahn, *La Richesse des Français* (Paris, 1977).

12. Official statistics term a 'household' any group of persons occupying a separate dwelling. A household can be composed of one or more persons and its head can be a man or a woman. The term was used in this sense by Babeau. The researchers on the nineteenth century (through 1914) have studied only the fortunes of individual persons or of married couples – 'households' in the traditional sense.

13. Evidence provided by M. Malinvaud, Director of INSEE, Colloque de Paris, July 1978.

14. Daumard, *La Bourgeoisie Parisienne*, p. 8.

15. See Daumard, *Les Fortunes Françaises*, p. 136.

16. A. Daumard, 'L'évolution des Structures Sociales en France à l'époque de l'industrialisation, 1815-1914', *Colloque International du CNRS, l'industrialisation en Europe au XIXe Siècle* (éditions du CNRS, Paris, 1972), pp. 315-34.

17. A.J. Tudesq, *Les Grands Notables en France, 1840-1849* (Paris, 1964), vol. I, pp. 95-97, 429-32.

18. See Daumard, *Les Fortunes Françaises*, pp. 257-66.

19. Daumard, *Histoire Economique*, vol. 4, p. 99.

20. We used the general wholesale and retail indices (recorded series) published by INSEE.

21. Cornut, *Répartition*, pp. 45-46.

22. Daumard, *Les Fortunes Françaises*, p. 39.

23. A. Sauvy, *La Vie Economique des Français de 1939 à 1945* (Paris, 1978), p. 169.

24. Another estimate based mainly on income tax data using different available statistics put the mean fortune at 197,000 francs. See R. Lattès, *La Fortune des Français* (Paris, 1977).

25. None of the patrimonies analysed in this inquiry exceeds 4 million francs.

26. Cornut, *Répartition*, p. 410.

27. Daumard, *Histoire Economique*, vol. 5 (forthcoming).

28. Babeau and Strauss-Kahn, *La Richesse*, p. 207.

29. A. Masson and D. Strauss-Kahn, 'Une Etude du CREP. Croissance et Inégalité des Fortunes de 1949 à 1975', *Economie et Statistique* (March 1978), pp. 31-49.

30. L'enrichissement des Français', *CNPF, Patronat, la Revue des Entreprises* (March 1978), pp. 8-15.

31. Masson and Strauss-Kahn, *Etude du CREP*, p. 40.

32. A. Babeau, 'La Complexe Inégalité des Patrimoines', *Le Monde*, 9 May 1978.

33. See Daumard, *Histoire Economique*, vol. 5 (forthcoming).

34. Babeau and Strauss-Kahn, *La Richesse*, pp. 153-57.

35. Lattès, *La Fortune*, pp. 169-70; F. Renard, 'Qui sont les Détenteurs de ces Richesses?', *Le Monde*, 3 March 1978.

3 THE RICH IN A LATE INDUSTRIALISER: THE CASE OF ITALY, 1800-1945

Vera Zamagni

Introduction

The aim of this chapter is primarily that of surveying research and material available in Italy on the subject of wealth and the wealthy in modern times. Given that neither the economic nor the sociological literature has shown interest in the last 20-30 years in such a field of research, the only realistic approach to it had to start from a systematic survey of the direct and indirect contributions provided in the more distant past as well as of the relevant material which can be fruitfully employed. An account will also be given in the last section of an initial attempt of devising an original study of prominent businessmen, which will be further developed elsewhere.

The diffusion of the Enlightment and the rise of the bourgeoisie in Europe in the second half of the eighteenth-century saw Italy, as is well known, still divided into many small states which, after being united into a smaller number of states during the Napoleonic era, were reconstituted with few exceptions in the Restoration and lasted beyond the middle of the nineteenth century. The first section of this chapter is devoted specifically to an account of the laborious and unequal emergence of the bourgeoisie in the various Italian states. It will be seen that bourgeois estates widened all through the eighteenth century and the first half of the nineteenth century everywhere in Italy, though following different patterns, but the attitude of such a rising bourgeoisie towards agricultural practices and, above all, towards the industrial novelties which were spreading in the rest of Europe, was profoundly divergent. To the enterprising business milieu existing in Liguria and Piedmont one can only match the solidity of the economy of Lombardy, with its prosperous, well-irrigated countryside and its flourishing silk trade. For the rest, a rather depressing panorama begins from the decline of Venice and ends with Kingdom of Naples, the *Mezzogiorno*, where the bourgeoisie, far from opposing the landed aristocracy in its behavioural patterns and in its way of thinking, worked actively for the maintenance of the status quo.

The second part of this chapter deals with the consequences in terms of wealth of industrialisation efforts which took place in Italy after unification, ending in the successful take-off of a part of the nation, i.e. the 'little country' formed by Piedmont, Liguria and Lombardy known as the industrial triangle. Details will be given about the trend of wealth, the change in its composition, which reveals the growing importance of non-agricultural activities, its regional distribution as well as the problem of concentration of ownership. It will become apparent that only in the period between the two world wars can one identify the transition from wealth mainly composed of real assets to the predominance of personal assets, with all the related consequences in terms of change in political weight of the various groups of wealth-holders.

As far as regional distribution of wealth is concerned, no tendency is revealed to an overcoming of regional imbalances in the period considered; if anything, the tendency is towards a slight improvement of the central regions, accompanied by a worsening of the North-South gap. One can be far less precise on the trend of concentration of ownership, because of the limitations of the data. Some evidence there points to a decrease in concentration until the First World War, followed by a reversal of the trend in the inter-war period. Hypotheses are advanced about the causes of such 'abnormal' behaviour.

No attempt has been made to treat developments after the Second World War, to avoid the risk of becoming unduly superficial, given the size of the present chapter. International comparisons too, if not completely neglected, are only occasional, because the study of wealth has not given rise to the same body of long-run statistical works as the study of income.

The last section illustrates, in a less systematic way, the main features of the Italian business entourage in the first half of the twentieth century. I am of course perfectly aware of the fact that substantial fortunes were (and are) still owned by great landowners, most of whom belonging to the aristocracy, but the names and activities of members of such an 'agrarian' group, as well as the size of their fortunes, remain quite obscure. This is certainly a virgin field of inquiry. A wider research interest and a more widespread publicity have been won by entrepreneurs and businessmen, even though very few Italian works have been specifically devoted to their socio-political features. The most important entrepreneurial dynasties will be reviewed and some coverage will be given to the phenomenon, peculiar to the Italian industrialisation experience, of public and 'subsidised' entrepreneurship.

Participation by the part of the aristocracy in the financing of industrial enterprises and the concentration of share capital will be briefly touched upon at the end.

The Rise of the Bourgeoisie Before Unification

For centuries Italy had been only a geographical expression, being politically divided in several states, most of which were under successive and culturally heterogeneous foreign rules. On the eve of the bourgeois revolution in the second half of the eighteenth century, the only novelty one could notice was a certain tendency on the part of the rulers of the Italian states, most of whom were foreigners, to show a higher degree of autonomy from Spain, Austria and France. This was made possible more by the deep contrasts existing at the time among the great powers than by an increased economic and military strength of the little states themselves. The exception was represented by the direct rule of Austria over Lombardy.

The Napoleonic conquests were, especially in northern Italy, beneficial in terms of new economic and political experiences, but the only result that, for the time being, was sanctioned by the Congress of Vienna was the definitive disappearance of the two ancient and glorious maritime republics; one, Genoa, was absorbed by the Kingdom of Sardinia and the other, Venice, was annexed to the Hapsburg monarchy. In 1815, therefore, Italy was constituted by six 'independent' states, plus Lombardy and Venetia under direct Austrian rule. Two of the states, however, the Duchy of Parma-Piacenza and that of Modena-Reggio, included between them only 800,000 of the 18 million people living in Italy in 1811. They were located in a rich central area of the Po valley and had a quite productive agriculture, but their cramped and unstable political organisation did not allow them to proceed towards an efficient diversification of their economic structure till well after unification.[1] Setting them aside, we are then left with four states, plus Lombardy and Venetia, with political, cultural and natural differences of great importance, to briefly review separately. Unfortunately, no systematic study exists of a comparative nature which could give account of per capita income, industrial activities, agricultural productivity or the accumulation of wealth. We will therefore resort to local studies and qualitative evidence to derive illustration of the causes of the belated and unbalanced development of Italian capitalism.[2]

The Dynamism of the Sardinian States

Under the quite misleading denomination of the Sardinian states (or the

Kingdom of Sardinia), were comprised three regions: Piedmont, Liguria and the island of Sardinia — with three individual histories, of which only two would actually merge before unification. Sardinia, annexed to Piedmont in the second half of the eighteenth century, remained backward and after unification shared the destiny of the rest of the southern part of Italy. In such an island, feudality ruled undisputed till 1824 and feudalism was actually abolished only in 1835-39, a record unbeaten among the Italian regions, but still in 1840 more than half of the island area had not yet been enclosed. Latifundia were predominant and transhumant sheep-rearing was the main economic activity; land yield per hectare was one-tenth of that of Lombardy. Accumulation of wealth was therefore very modest and the degree of mobilisation of that limited wealth almost non-existent. The remarkable mineral deposits of Sardinia (especially zinc and lead ore) were exploited by Genoese businessmen and by foreigners, mainly however after unification.

If there is no doubt that wealth in eighteenth-century Piedmont and Liguria was mainly concentrated in the hands of the nobility, there is also clear evidence that in both regions the rise of the bourgeoisie was well under way, while interest for business was alive in the aristocratic milieu, be it addressed towards agricultural improvements or towards manufacture and trade. In 1738, 13 per cent of the total value of fortunes greater than 6,000 Genoese lire was in Liguria in the hands of non-aristocratic families,[3] while, according to an estimate made by Bulferetti,[4] only half of the agrarian income from property was around 1750 enjoyed by the nobility and the clergy in Piedmont (the two categories constituted about 3 per cent of the population of Piedmont at that date). From a list of Piedmontese taxpayers reported by the same source for the years 1734 and 1795, one can also pinpoint a number of noblemen engaged in non-agricultural economic activities (wool and silk manufacture, wholesale trade), as well as a growing group of wealthy businessmen — bankers, silk traders, wool and cotton manufacturers and merchants.

The distribution of wealth and income, however, was much less unequal in Piedmont[5] than in Liguria, where the gap between the opulence of the patriciate and the misery of the people was so wide at the end of the eighteenth century that it made inevitable the investment of practically all Genoese capital abroad. No domestic market existed to spur the foundation of manufactures. Behind the Dutchmen, the Genoese were considered the next largest creditors of Europe. But the Genoese speculative investments abroad were wiped away by the French Revolution, which caused bewilderment and stagnation in Liguria till the 1830s. Capital was hoarded waiting for better times,[6] which came about with the evolution of Piedmont towards a more dynamic economic performance around 1840, as a result of the moderate but beneficial reforms of Carlo Alberto.

In the two decades from 1840 to 1860, while the economic unification of Piedmont and Liguria was accelerated, all the previous trends were confirmed: a remarkable mobilisation of capital in industry (mainly textiles[7] and metal manufacture[8]), transport (both railways[9] and shipping[10]), trade and banking.[11] Improvement in agricultural practices was not neglected, with the introduction of fertilisers and the diffusion of drainage and irrigation.[12] All this was accompanied, at the macro-economic level, by a modern and aggressive economic policy which made use of deficit spending to finance productive works, especially infrastructures. The participation of the nobility in this structural change was active; the symbol of this, although by no means the only example,[13] is certainly Count Camillo di Cavour, enlightened landowner directly engaged in the managing of his estates, founder of railway companies, partner in innumerable other enterprises, as well as brilliant politician and successful manager of public finances.[14]

It is certainly not a coincidence that the unification of Italy could be accomplished by the most modern of the Italian states, where the town of Genoa was located, which long remained the wealthiest among the Italian towns.

Lombardy and Venetia under Austria

As anticipated above, the two regions, which were joined in the nineteenth century under the common rule of Austria, had a quite independent historical development, not only before, but also after, the Restoration.

The economic history of Venetia before unification is dominated by the irreversible decline of the maritime power of Venice, accompanied by a stubborn and myopic absenteeism of the Venetian patriciate from the management of the real estate acquired in the mainland as an alternative form of investment of its wealth, no longer profitably employable in the trades and manufactures of the capital.[15] In 1740, 32 per cent of the cultivated land of the region was in the hands of such a Venetian aristocracy, which was made up of no more than 5,000 people, i.e. 0.3 per cent of the population.[16] It was true that at the same date 36 per cent of the real estate was owned by non-aristocratic landowners, but there is no evidence that, if Venetian, they behaved in a different way. A more open attitude is recorded on the part of landowners living in the provinces, but their interest in agricultural practices was all too often only theoretical.[17] Mortmain property was not extensive (9 per cent of real estate in 1740) and showed a tendency to contraction. The decline of Venice is witnessed also by the fact that all the artisans in the town lost labour, with the exception of some services like household servants, hairdressers and tailors.

Passing under Austrian rule, Venetia did not register any substantial improvement: Venice continued to remain stagnant and cut off from the rest of the region. The aristocratic and clerical property shrank, while the two categories did not become less absenteeist. On the basis of the land survey carried out in connection with the formation of a new register of landed property around 1839, one can say that noble real estate accounted for no more than 35-40 per cent of the total, and clerical property for perhaps 3-4 per cent,[18] but the rise of bourgeois property was not accompanied by really innovative behaviour. No business entourage emerged capable of breaking the dormant atmosphere of the region. In the 1850s agricultural productivity was estimated at 60 per cent of the Lombard level. The only industrial activity of any importance was textile-manufacturing. At the eve of unification, Venetia accounted for 13 per cent of the Italian raw silk production, had about 30,000 cotton-spindles and two wool manufactures in Schio, the Marzotto and the Rossi firms, which long remained the only two important firms in the region.

Economic development of Lombardy had been much more substantial and had begun before the eighteenth century, if we are to trust what Cattaneo and Iacini wrote about Lombard agriculture, concerning the fact that its high productivity per hectare (the highest in Italy in the nineteenth century) was not due to natural fertility of the soil, but to a continuous and laborious investment in irrigation works dating back to the Middle Ages, which had made of the Lombard plains a quite original case in the European agricultural evolution.[19]

The initial non-agricultural activities of Lombardy were based precisely on that agriculture: silk manufacture in the first place, which can be really considered the main source of the accumulation of capitals in the region and became a vertically integrated industry – from silk worms to silk cloth.[20] Commercial activities too, linked to the trade of specialised agricultural products – silk, cheese, rice – were flourishing. A statistic of 1829 placed on top of a list of Milanese well-to-do people not belonging to the category of real estate owners 14 'bank and silk dealers' and 13 'silk commissioners'. Caizzi draws the conclusion that 'agricultural activities or trade granted at that time in Lombardy the earliest opportunities of enrichment'.[22] Manufacturing in Lombardy cannot be considered very advanced before unification; however, some diffusion existed in cotton-manufacturing[23] and engineering;[24] the Lombard road system was excellent, due to Austrian investments, and some progress was made in railway-building.[25]

Although the agro-mercantile equilibrium had not yet been shaken because it was still yielding sizeable fruits,[26] one could already notice in Lombardy, both reading the progressive economic reviews which were published[27] and the works of well-known agriculturalists,[28] the entrepreneurial talents and the turn for the solution of technical problems which will mark the role of the region in the subsequent Italian economic development. In Lombardy too, as it has been already noticed in the case of Piedmont, although for different reasons,[29] the aristocracy had actively embraced economic activities, especially since the Napoleonic era.[30] One can find counts and marquises engaged in the introduction of gas lighting, steamboats, new textile machinery, improved agricultural practices and the like,[31] as well as in the diffusion of popular culture through schools and magazines.[32] It is not the case that the bourgeoisie, which was at the time mainly composed of rich tenant farmers, silk merchants and private bankers, was united with the progressive part of nobility in the fight against Austrian rule — on which absentee landowners, who were not completely missing, were compliant, because they viewed foreign domination as the main obstacle to the more rapid development of the cultural and economic potentialities of the region.[33]

Moderatism and Mediocrity in the Grand Duchy of Tuscany

The destiny of Tuscany was marked by the reformist approach of the Austrian princes who governed the region from 1765 to 1859, with substantial consensus on the part of nobility and from the intelligentsia of the region. That reformism, making more tolerable the old power structure, prevented in fact the rise of a new bourgeois class of any importance. In Tuscany all the most unprogressive features of feudalism were cancelled during the eighteenth century but one, which was preserved till recent years. This one remaining feature was sharecropping, which proved compatible with agricultural progress only in the very few cases in which landowners were also active managers of their estates.[34] In general, cultivation remained mixed, aimed to the self-sufficiency of each farm holding, which prevented substantial productivity gains. The low capacity of accumulation of the agricultural sector in turn prevented a sizeable increase of non-agricultural activities,[35] which ended up in a preference toward financial investments by existing capital not re-employed within agriculture,[36] an outlet with a long tradition in the region. The commercial harbour of Livorno could have played a role in Tuscany similar to that of Genoa in Liguria, but it did not find any support from its hinterland, mainly because of the free trade policy which prevailed in Tuscany for the whole period up to unification, unfavourable to domestic production and exports.

Yet the region offered good opportunities for profitable enterprises, because of the centrality of its location and of the existence of raw materials (iron ore, copper, lead, marble, mercury and borax). The only important enterprise initiated before unification was the production of boric acid, due to a French refugee, Francis Larderel, who, in the 1860s, was employing around 1,000 workers.[37] The remaining minerals were mined in limited quantities and mostly exported unrefined.[38] A number of textile firms were also present in the region, but they were of very small size; a few blast furnaces existed, the most important of which were owned by the state. The only other two firms worth mentioning were the paper mill of Cini, whose son Giovanni Cosimo became one of the chief Italian financiers, and the china manufacture in Doccia of Marquis Ginori, founded in 1735.[39]

The *medietas* of Tuscany was maintained in subsequent years and became the main cause of the dependence of the region upon the industrial concentrations formed outside it after unification.

The Decadence of the Papal States

The blame accorded to the administration of Papal states in the nineteenth century is unanimously found in contemporary as well as in more recent literature. What is especially denounced is the exclusive centralisation of power in the hands of clergy and the uncertainty of rights, whatever they were, because they were continuously and systematically infringed by privileges granted by prelates to their protégés, often for very trifling reasons.

The economy of the city of Rome, in particular, was very peculiar: half of the population was supported by public charity,[40] and the rest, excluding the aristocracy and clergy who were the owners of all of the real estate of the town, was living off the business of servicing foreign visitors and pilgrims (they were hosts, hotelkeepers or tradesmen). Agriculture was very backward, latifundia owned by an absentee nobility and clergy were extended, mainly in Latium and Umbria. A separate mention should be made of Romagna and its capital Bologna, where the typical features of Papal lands were less apparent. Bourgeois property was more extensive[41] and agricultural practices were more advanced, yielding levels of productivity similar to those of the rest of the non-Lombard Po valley. But even in that better-off area non-agricultural activities languished, especially manufacturing 'reduced to a mere skeleton, remnant of a thousand destroyed fortunes'.[42] Around 1834 income per capita in Bologna was estimated at 100 lire, of which only 14 per cent was produced outside agriculture.[43]

De Marco supports the thesis of an economic decline of the Papal states in the first half of the nineteenth century, which, if so, would be a unique case in Italy. Evidence is provided by the contraction in the number of wool-manufacturers, the most important industrial activity of the state. Maestri deemed the number of cotton-spindles active in the region around 1860 to be negligible (less than 30,000); cotton-looms (around 12,000) were still hand-operated.[44]

In conclusion, the Papal states presented a stagnant scene with a very low level of capital accumulation, excepting only the area around Bologna, where in the decade 1835-45 a new though very limited circle of businessmen emerged, among them Pizzardi, Rizzoli, Minghetti, Marsili, Calzoni and Bolognini.

Oligarchies and Immobility in the Kingdom of Naples

Thus far, I have mentioned the need for an explicit act of repeal of feudality only in the case of Sardinia, because elsewhere feudalism had evolved already in the course of the eighteenth century, in a more-or-less progressive way, towards a more modern social structure. In the Kingdom of Two Sicilies, instead, the watershed dividing the eighteenth from the nineteenth century was provided by the formal repeal of feudalism, which occurred in the Napoleonic era, in 1806 in the continental South and in 1812 in Sicily; in the latter the terms for the ex-feudatories were much better.[45] The strength of the southern baronage at the end of the eighteenth century was still great. Villani estimates that for the continental South, feudal incomes reached 20 per cent of total income from property, to which another 20-30 per cent must be added as ecclesiastical income and 10 per cent more for other types of income accruing to the same individuals. Thus, overall, around 60 per cent of income from property accrued to the families of lay and clerical barons, numbering only about 650 individuals, of whom 90, or 14 per cent, controlled two-thirds of the population of the

kingdom and only 20, or 3 per cent, one-quarter of it.[46] The highly
interesting, but unfortunately unique, sample survey carried out by
De Meo on three southern towns around the middle of the eighteenth
century suggests similar conclusions about the size of income from
property accruing to the nobility and the clergy.[47] After the repeal of
feudality, the acquisition of real estate by non-nobles accelerated, but
a general consensus exists on the fact that there existed a bourgeoisie
living 'in the shadow of feud', completely devoid of entrepreneurial
talents,[48] showing most of the time a behaviour in all ways similar to
that of the noble barons.

All this prolonged the existence of latifundia surrounded by unviable
minifundia, which considerably slowed down any progress in agriculture.
Around 1860 yield per hectare was estimated at one-third of that in
Lombardy, and the conditions of the peasants, most of whom were
daily labourers, was extremely miserable, mainly because of chronic
unemployment due to the predominance of highly seasonal types of
cultivation unaccompanied by further processing of crops in the slack
season.

As far as non-agricultural activities are concerned, a widespread
handicraft and domestic production existed, especially in textiles, but
only in the area around Naples were a number of large textile and
engineering firms established. The features of these firms deserve a
more detailed description, which is given below for the years
immediately before unification. In cotton-spinning, the firms to be
mentioned are those of Vonwiller (620 workers), Escher, Mayer and
Egg. Power-spindles in the whole kingdom did not total 100,000, less
than in Lombardy alone. In cotton-weaving, firms recorded are those
of Wenner, Zublin-Vonmiller (1,500 workers between the two) and
Egg (1,300 workers, spinning included). Overall, no more than 20,000
looms were at work, most of which operated by hand. In wool-
manufacturing, mention must be made of the following firms: Sava
(500 workers, most of whom were prisoners), Polsinelli, Zino and
Jannuzzi (all of them of limited size), producing mainly uniforms for
the Bourbon army.[49] The engineering firms which are known are Zino
and Henry (then Macry and Henry, 550 workers), Guppy and Pattison
(575 workers), the Arsenal (1,600 workers), the Royal Works of
Pietrarsa (800 workers) and the state shipyard at Castellamare (450
workers).[50]

I have taken some pains in enumerating these enterprises to make
two points: the importance of government as a buyer, sometimes
exclusive, if not as a direct manager of some of the large firms, and the

absolute predominance of foreigners among entrepreneurs, both in textiles (Swiss) and in engineering (English and French). In other Italian states, too, the presence of foreign entrepreneurs was substantial, but in the Kingdom of Two Sicilies it was exclusive in many fields, being a clear token of the fact that industry had not found a hold in the local economic structure. When the first Neapolitan railway was built by the Frenchman Bayard de la Vingtrie with French capital and technicians, the *Annali Civili* in 1839 dared to theorise that it was preferable not to 'consume' local capital in such ventures and not to shake existing equilibria.

As a matter of fact 'Neapolitan industry was neither the creature nor the creator of a class of local entrepreneurs';[51] the richest business community was formed by an oligarchy of a few noblemen, several foreigners and some self-made people, who profited from transport and trade of necessities and from public contracts. That oligarchy did not want to disturb the immobility of a society from which they were gaining large profits. I agree with Davis in the conclusion that 'in fact, southern entrepreneurs and capitalists were the first to be interested, from an economic, social, and political point of view, in the existence and maintenance of the state of backwardness'.[52] If one adds to this the extreme shortage of internal transporation facilities – both roads and railways were scarce – and the primitiveness of the banking network, one can thoroughly understand the weak position in which the Kingdom of Two Sicilies found itself after unification compared to much more dynamic and advanced regions such as Piedmont, Liguria and Lombardy.

Industrialisation and Wealth up to 1945

An Outline of the Economic Development of Unified Italy, 1861-1945

At this point, a brief outline of Italian post-unification economic development seems necessary as a prelude to understanding what follows about wealth and wealth-holders.[53]

The political unification of the country in 1861[54] was accompanied by hopes of a quick economic revival, which did not come about. The factors preventing a rapid industrialisation, from a shortage of capital to the very limited size of the internal market (incomes were generally too low to induce industrial mass production),[55] from the technical and cultural backwardness of the population to the narrowmindedness of the political and economic elite at large, from an inefficient banking system to the lack of raw materials, especially fuels, were simply too numerous.

Economic activities dragged along without a decisive spurt till the end of the nineteenth century, in spite of two short-lived booms in 1871-73 and 1881-87, when some of the major Italian firms which flourished later on were founded. In the meantime, however, most of the previous negative constraints were lifted. The agrarian crisis of the 1880s produced the end of the predominant agrarian interests of the northern bourgeoisie, which turned more daringly towards industry, asking for the introduction of protectionism, effectively adopted in 1887. The excessive speculation in urban real estate, to which capital, not finding better opportunities of investment, had turned, caused, between 1889 and 1894, the bankruptcy of all of the most important industrial banks of the country, affecting seriously even the central bank. The necessary reorganisation of the Italian banking system on a more solid basis took place around 1894 with the help of German and French capital, following the pattern of the German mixed banks. This made possible an extensive channelling of national savings in the financing of manufacturing activities and infrastructures.[56]

Only after these laborious vicissitudes could a true take-off of the industrial triangle (whose angles touched Milan, Genoa and Turin) take place in the years 1896-1913.[57]

Sustained rates of growth were experienced by the metal and engineering industries; the textile industry reached its maturity and some branches of the chemical industry were started. The production of vehicles and the establishment of electrical plants were the leading enterprises of the time and attracted considerable capital and the best entrepreneurial talents.

Large-scale production, however, started only during the First World War and in many cases suffered from the consequence of forced and unnatural growth, due to the pressure of war, which was not concurrent with the general economic level of the country.[58]

The post-war crisis, which affected economies much more solid than the Italian one, could not but be serious and was complicated by a crisis of consensus on the political organisation of the country. After the temporary strengthening of the extreme left, with the occupation of factories and farms on the part of workers, the extreme right-wing reaction followed, with the rise of Mussolini to power in 1922. In spite of deep institutional changes, the pre-fascist economic elite was not set aside, at least until the 1929 crisis, which shook to the foundations the network of personal and structural relations resting on the two biggest mixed banks, the Banca Commerciale[59] and the Credito Italiano, and caused a more direct intervention by the fascist government into economic matters. This intervention moved essentially in two directions: the formation of a substantial nucleus of *public* industrial activities through the founding of IRI,[60] and the organisation of protective barriers sheltering existing large enterprises by means of higher tariffs, syndicates and a policy of autarky. All this naturally favoured the increase of industrial concentration and the deterioration of efficiency levels, due also to the decline in foreign trade. The subsequent economic subjugation to Germany and the ill-conceived and inadequately prepared intervention into the Second World War caused the complete collapse of the country, but not of its economic elite, which reappeared after liberation to head reconstruction and the economic 'miracle' in the 1950s.

Wealth and its Composition

Although little has been written in the past on the wealthy, some important contributions have been made on wealth by Italian economists and statisticians of great renown. Such a literature flourished in the period 1900-40, to be later replaced by research on income and fixed reproducible capital.[61]

We have therefore a number of fragmentary estimates of Italian private wealth covering the period 1874-1938, plus a continuous series for the period 1901-38, which have been systematically gathered in Appendix A. For the years preceding the 1908 estimate by Gini, the two prevailing estimating methods were based on the transfer annuity (Pantaleoni, Nitti and Coletti) and on capitalisation of incomes (Bodio, Spectator and Sensini[62]). Both methods, as Gini showed,[63] were highly arbitrary: the former because of the practical impossibility of accurately estimating tax evasion and the transfer interval,[64] the latter because of the apparent difficulty in the choice of capitalisation rates, variable over time. The result produced by the adoption of such highly imperfect methods of evaluation of Italian private wealth in the years 1874-1905 was a remarkable underevaluation of it, of the order of 25 per cent.[65] Gini employed the method of direct inventory of tangible assets, followed by all the best successive scholars, in particular by Retti Marsani, who produced the continuous series covering the years 1901-34. Lack of some relevant data was made up by ingenious *ad hoc* devices.

Accepting the estimate by Retti Marsani, which was completed for the years 1935-38 by De Vita following the same methods, as the most consistent one, and granting that estimates preceding 1901 have to be raised by 25 per cent, one can draw a picture of the trend in private wealth after converting current into constant prices (this has been done in Appendix B). Between the second half of the 1870s and the second half of the 1880s, per capita wealth at constant prices rose 25 per cent, while per capita income stagnated.[66] The successive crisis affected wealth more (−13 per cent) than income, which remained practically stable. The industrial take-off of the Giolittian era is clearly manifested (+32 per cent in per capita wealth; +36 per cent in per capita income in the period 1898-1914), while the war years witnessed a large decumulation of private wealth (−17 per cent in the years 1914-22), unaccompanied by a similar trend in incomes (+4 per cent in the same period). A period of rapid expansion followed (+15 per cent per capita wealth; +17 per cent per capita income in the years 1922-28), then a deep crisis and a slight recovery towards the end of the 1930s (+6 per cent wealth; +9 per cent income in the years 1928-38). Over a span of about 60 years per capita private wealth grew therefore about 43 per cent, while per capita income grew about 82 per cent.

The discrepancy between the growth of private wealth and the growth of income is due in the long run to two main factors: first, productivity gains due to technical progress raised the income produced by one unit of fixed reproducible capital and land; second, public wealth grows in Western capitalist systems more rapidly than private wealth, and therefore national wealth. The strong decumulation of wealth which occurred at the end of the nineteenth century is a token of the severity of that crisis,[67] while the loss of private wealth registered during and after the First World War was certainly due both to the material destruction and to a forced diversion of private resources to the state.

With industrialisation, therefore, private wealth increased, but neither rapidly nor without contrasts; the period of more intense growth occurred during the six years 1922-28 (average yearly rate of growth of private per capita wealth was 2.36 per cent), but certainly the most significant period in terms of continuity of accumulation must be considered the sixteen-year span of time at the beginning of the twentieth century (when the yearly rate of growth was 1.75 per cent). In this latter period, the industrial basis of the country was built, most of the more successful companies were founded and entrepreneurial dynasties started.

From the above-mentioned works on wealth it is possible to draw exhaustive information about its composition, at least for the two main categories of realty and personalty. Again making use of the Retti

Table 3.1: Percentage Composition of Private Wealth, 1901-34

	1901-14	1915-20	1921-29	1930-34
Land	40.8	35.3	34.9	21.1
Cattle	4.4	6.0	4.6	2.7
Mines and quarries	0.7	0.8	1.0	0.8
Buildings	18.9	14.5	15.0	17.2
Total	64.8	56.6	55.5	41.8
Plants and stocks	11.2	10.5	15.7	23.7
Furniture	10.7	16.9	14.1	13.9
Government bonds	7.6	8.4	7.7	9.8
Money and deposits	5.7	7.6	7.0	10.8
Total	35.2	43.4	44.5	58.2
Overall	100.0	100.0	100.0	100.0

Source: see Appendices A and B.

Marsani estimates, the trend appears as summarised in Table 3.1.

The importance of realty began to decline only during the war and underwent a sharp cut in consequence of the drop in agricultural prices during the 1929 crisis. The trend of wealth from industry and commerce is not adequately revealed by Table 3.1. The weight of this dynamic component of private wealth was only 8.5 per cent in 1901, rose to 14 per cent in 1914, fell back to 9.5 per cent in 1920 and then rose again steadily, with a slight drop in 1932-34; between 1901 and 1934, therefore, its percentage almost trebled. 1930 is the watershed; after that date, personal wealth became irreversibly the dominant component in private wealth.[68] Data on wealth, therefore, confirm that the transition from a mainly agricultural society to an industrial one took place in the middle of the fascist period. The power groups with an agrarian basis, who had always strongly conditioned the economic and political choices of the country, not last the rise of Mussolini to power,[69] were definitively granted a secondary role, not, however, without contradictions and hesitations.

The best proof of this is provided by the fact that only after the Second World War was it possible to introduce agrarian reform in Italy, which had been advocated since unification but never put into effect because of the strong opposition by large landowners. If the results of such a reform were not brilliant in terms of the breaking up of the old socio-political power system, especially with regard to the South, nor in terms of substantial increase in agricultural productivity, the reasons must be found in a complete reversal of priorities at the economic policy level, which saw agriculture almost exclusively in the role of manpower reservoir.

Regional Distribution and Concentration of Wealth

An estimate of regional per capita wealth, built with the real inventory method, exists only for the year 1928 and appears in Table 3.2, together with the percentage of personal assets within the total wealth.

For the period 1902-15 it is possible to calculate the transfer annuity by regions,[70] which has been done in a work published by Savorgnan.[71] Unfortunately, the adoption of such data to the purpose of interregional comparisons of private wealth rests on the assumptions that tax evasion and transfer intervals are the same for every region, which is certainly unrealistic, as was exhaustively proved by Contento for the years 1907-9.[72] I have therefore given up using that source extensively. I limit myself to reporting here that the general trend which emerges from it is that of the stability of the industrial triangle in its predominant position, an improvement by Emilia and, to a lesser extent, by the central regions, matched by a deterioration of the South, with the exception of Sardinia. The North-South gap, therefore, would appear to have widened between the beginning of the century and 1929, which agrees with available estimates of regionally disaggregated per capita income.[73]

Table 3.2: Per Capita Private Wealth by Regions, 1928 (Italy = 100)

		Personal assets (percentage)			Personal assets (percentage)
Piedmont	169	48	Abruzzi	75	29
Liguria	142	58	Campania	78	46
Lombardy	129	53	Puglia	70	34
Venetia	84	38	Basilicata	77	34
Friuli	96	39	Calabria	64	33
Emilia	105	40	Sicily	75	36
Tuscany	102	43	Sardinia	61	27
Marche	76	31			
Umbria	80	27	ITALY	100	43
Latium	127	47			

Source: A. De Vita, 'La ricchezza privata dell'Italia al 1928 e la sua ripartizione regionale', *Vita economica italiana* (1933), with slight adjustments in relation to Liguria and Sardinia.

Table 3.3: Real Per Capita Assets by Regions, Various Years (Italy = 100)

	1907-09	1928	1937
Piedmont	135	159	145
Liguria	145	121	141
Lombardy	122	106	102
Venetia	79	94	83
Friuli	–	96	107
Trentino	–	114	101
Emilia	84	110	132
Tuscany	96	94	103
Marche	71	96	94
Umbria	60	106	109
Latium	104	119	133
Abruzzi	93	97	78
Campania	91	74	65
Puglia	108	83	83
Basilicata	81	93	88
Calabria	76	79	77
Sicily	103	83	88
Sardinia	39	68	59
ITALY	100	100	100
North	111	113	113
Centre	89	103	113
South	92	81	77

Sources: De Vita, 'La ricchezza privata'; A. Contento, 'Sulla ripartizione territoriale della ricchezza privata in Italia', *Giornale degli Economista* (1914); P. Thaon di Revel, 'Il valore della proprieta fondiara in Italia', *Rivita del catasto e dei servizi tecnici erariali* (1938).

More accurate interregional comparisons can be attempted with relation to real assets for which, apart from the already quoted works by De Vita for 1928 and Contento for 1907-09, another short, but well based, contribution exists by Thaon di Revel for 1937.[74] The picture which emerges from such works is detailed in Table 3.3.

Northern Italy kept throughout its predominant position, less marked than when total private wealth is considered, given the larger weight of personal assets in this area; Emilia shows a really remarkable improvement and it can certainly be said that it was the region taking

Table 3.4: Concentration of Fortunes Transferred Free of Charge, 1890-1915

| | Gini's concentration coefficient | Percentage of total wealth owned by deceased with property | | | |
| | | Top | | | |
		1%	2%	10%	20%
1890-91	.8555	48	58	78	83
1900-02	.8326	42	53	77	82
1914-15	.8103	41	51	78	87

Sources: R. Benini, 'Distribuzione probabile della ricchezza privata in Italia per classi di popolazione', *Riforma sociale* (1894); E. Porru, 'La concentrazione della ricchezza nelle diverse rigioni d'Italia, *Studi economico-giuridici dell'Universita di Cagliari* (1912); *Bollettino di Statistica e di legislazione comparata*, various years.

most advantage of the agrarian policies of the fascist régime.[75] Central Italy registered a widespread improvement too, especially in Marche and Latium, while the worsening of the relative position of the South took place both in the value of land and in the value of urban real estate, which reveals a generalised deterioration in the area.

Passing now to concentration of wealth-ownership, relevant data concerning total private wealth are only those derived from the transfer annuity for the years before the First World War. A number of works exist based on such data, because the problem had interested many scholars, among whom Benini,[76] Gini, Porru[77] and Cassola.[78] From the indices[79] reported in Table 3.4, it is possible to conclude that concentration of fortunes was decreasing, though slowly, in the period 1890-1915.

As the concentration of fortunes of deceased persons (from which Table 3.4 is derived) is in general greater than that of total private wealth (because size of fortunes increases with age) the picture presented in Table 3.4 overstates the real concentration of wealth-ownership. Keeping this in mind, a comparison with Great Britain suggests that around 1911-13 concentration of wealth was greater there than in Italy.[80] This conclusion is to be expected on the basis of a generalisation made by Porru, who calculated coefficients of concentration of wealth for all the Italian regions in 1900-2 and found that 'in the various regions, concentration of fortunes decreases almost regularly in correspondence with the decrease in their level of economic welfare'.[81] But it may be incorrect to draw any conclusion

Table 3.5: Concentration of Incomes Paying Income Tax

	Gini's concentration coefficients	
1865-66	.5269	total incomes
1881	.5798	"
1894	.4432	cat. B incomes*
1902	.4678	"
1922	.5507	"
1929	.5192	"

*Joint income from capital and labour (i.e. income from industrial and commercial enterprise).

Sources: 1865-66: my elaborations from data given by P. Maestri, *L'Italia economica nel 1868* (Florence, 1868), p. 256. 1881: data from Benini, 'Distribuzione'. 1894, 1902: Porru, 'La concentrazione'. 1922, 1929: S. Orlandi, 'La distribuzione dei redditi mobiliari in Italia nel 1929', *Vita economica italiana* (1934).

from a correlation between average income and degree of concentration in *different* social and economic contexts.[82]

Reconstruction of incomes seems to have started much later. From income tax returns it is possible to calculate Gini's coefficients of concentration of income, which has been attempted and has given the results reported in Table 3.5.

With the caveat that 1865-66 and 1881 data are not comparable in level with successive data, one can observe a progressive concentration of incomes till the 1920s, when a break in the trend took place.

Something more detailed should be said about the trend of concentration of wealth during the inter-war period, but not much can be extracted from available sources. On the basis of data referring to transfers of *real* assets free of charge,[83] it would seem that concentration of real property was increasing: the Gini coefficient of concentration, in fact, increased between 1927/8 and 1935/6 from .7095 to .7945. The top one per cent of deceased people aged 20 years or older owned 48 per cent of real assets at the former date and 52 per cent at the latter; the top 10 per cent owned respectively 81 per cent and 88 per cent at the two dates.

This could be ascribed both to the 1929 crisis and to fascist policies of consolidation of existing large estates. Unfortunately, other documentation of the real property structure of ownership is very fragmentary. A census of landownership by size of holdings was not

Table 3.6: Per Capita Wealth in Various Countries at the Turn of the Nineteenth and Beginning of the Twentieth Century

	Per capita wealth (French francs)		Ratio between transfer annuity and deceased over 40 years
	Mulhall (1895)	Gini (1914)	
UK	7,650	7,850-9,400 (1909)[a]	21,000 (1908-09)
France	6,400	5,750-7,300 (1907)[b]	11,600 (1906)
Germany	3,950	6,400-7,000 (1908)[a]	9,500 (1908)
Austria	(2,650	3,100 (1911)[a]	–
Hungary	(	2,090 (1911)[a]	2,100 (1907-08)
Italy	2,550	2,570 (1908)[b]	4,000 (1902-10)
Sweden	(2,900	2,920[b]; 3,530 (1908)[a]	–
Norway	(	1,900-2,250 (1911)[a]	–
Denmark	5,800	4,160 (1900)[a]	–
Holland	4,650	5,130 (1909)[a]	–
Belgium	3,900	6,350 (1908)[a]	–
Switzerland	4,150	4,000-5,350 (1910)[b]	–
USA	5,900	6,800 (1904)[a]	–
Canada	4,950	6,350 (1903)[a]	–
Argentina	3,900	5,300 (1909)[b]	–
Australia	6,500	7,230 (1909)[b]	21,900 (1908-10)

[a]National wealth. [b]Private wealth.

Sources: M.C. Mulhall, *Industries and Wealth of Nations* (London, 1896); C. Gini, *L'ammontare e la composizione della ricchezza nazioni* (1914, reprinted Turin, 1962).

made till 1946, in connection with the preparation of the post-war agrarian reform, and its results are only partially useful.[84] What one can conclude from it is that, at that date, 28,876 landowners, i.e. 0.3 per cent of the 9.5 million landowners surveyed, owned 39.4 per cent of the cultivated land of Italy; 61,113 landowners, i.e. 0.6 per cent of the total, owned 47.4 per cent.

The highest concentration of landownership was found in Latium, where 50 per cent of land was in holdings of more than 200 hectares, in the hands of 974 big landowners,[85] and in Tuscany, where 46 per cent of the land was in the hands of 1,640 people. In the South, large properties were in 1946 still more extensive than the national average, but they had undergone already a substantial shrinkage since unification.[86]

What conclusion can be offered about concentration of personal assets in the inter-war period will be deferred to the next section.

Finally, although no attempt has been made in this chapter to draw systematic international comparisons, I have considered it of some interest to present in Table 3.6 an estimate of per capita wealth in various countries prepared by Mulhall and Gini, which can give an idea of the relative position of Italy compared with the other industrialised or industralising countries.

It can be seen that around 1910 Italy showed a per capita wealth only 40 per cent of the French[87] and 30 per cent of the English level. The income gap between Italy and these countries later narrowed (Italian per capita income in 1913 was 60 per cent of the French and 45 per cent of the English income[88]), which has probably to be ascribed to the greater importance in those countries of wealth not directly productive of income and to the existence of large amounts of capital invested abroad.

The Protagonists of Structural Change

Entrepreneurial Dynasties, Bankers and 'Public' Entrepreneurs: Whose Economic Power has Mattered More?

In the decade just after unification, Italian businessmen were disunited and did not share a common entrepreneurial strategy or a coherent political position. The first opportunity of organising themselves as a group came in connection with the industrial survey of 1870-74, which witnessed the rallying of textile-manufacturers from Piedmont, Lombardy and Venetia.[89] One of them, the Venetian Alessandro Rossi, is a widely studied figure for his protectionist battles and his proposals of matching modern industry with the old social values.[90]

Notwithstanding the textile-manufacturers, several of the most important entrepreneurial dynasties of the country had already been founded. Beside the Rossis, Marzottos, Gavazzis and Rivettis in the textile industry, several had emerged in the food and drink industry, among whom were the Bozanos, Ravanos, Buitonis, Agnesis, Galbanis, Peronis, Martinis and Camparis, and some could be quoted in other industries, the Pirellis in rubber, the Pesentis in cement, the Falcks, Gregorinis, Lucchinis, Gnuttis, Redaellis, Tassaras and Berettas in the metal industry, the Orlandos, Oderos and Florios in shipbuilding.[91] Other entrepreneurial families, among the richest in Italy, had laid the foundations of powerful family holdings. Among them, the Ligurian

Piaggios,[92] Bombrinis[93] and Raggios,[94] the Lombard Crespis[95] and the Tusco-Venetian Cinis.[96] There were fewer comparable outstanding entrepreneurial dynasties as successful in engineering (Agnelli and Olivetti) or in chemicals (Parodi Delfino), and these started later, between the end of the nineteenth century and the First World War.

It is probably true that only in textiles and food has there been in Italy a strong predominance of enterprises, often not large, managed by the founder and his heirs; in the remaining industrial sectors the same model of entrepreneur capitalist can only be applied to a few successful cases. How then were the other big firms established before the Second World War organised?

A substantial number of engineering, metal, chemical and even some textile and food firms, after a more or less long period under the control of the founder who did not succeed in making them financially viable, came under the control of the banks which had financed them, and often changed direction, when they were not actually merged with other firms to form stronger units.

Other enterprises, like the most important electrical, electro-technical and infrastructural firms (telephone, gas railways and tramways, when they were not foreign), were from the very start dominated by holdings tied to industrial or mixed banks and to the great holding company formed after the nationalisation of the railways in 1905, the Bastogi.[97]

It is among these 'non-autonomous' firms that one finds those which have belonged to IRI from 1933 onwards as well as the firms which had to be nationalised later on (like electricity in 1963) or are still in great financial troubles today. This large area of subsidised or public firms has originated a whole range of very powerful bankers and public or semi-public managers who make up one of the most obvious anomalies of the Italian entrepreneurial class *vis-à-vis* the experience of the other advanced capitalist countries.

Although this picture is quite clear in its general lines, it is not easy to make it more precise, because research on the quality of Italian entrepreneurship has been discontinuous and unsystematic. To move some steps further in the direction of a more systematic kind of analysis, I have started, with the help of a computer,[98] the examination of two of the volumes which, from 1906 onwards, collect data on the joint stock companies existing in Italy. The two years chosen, 1911 and 1927,[99] provide an account of the Italian spurt of the Giolittian era and the results of the industrial boom of the years 1922-26, before the beginning of the 1927 stabilisation crisis. For a future continuation of this work, 1938 recommends itself as another benchmark year, because it allows the identification of the deep changes which took place as a result of the prolonged 1927-34 crisis and of the foundation of IRI.

Among the various pieces of information supplied by the above-mentioned series of volumes on the Italian joint stock companies, beside the productive sector, the regional localisation of head office and the share capital, I have studied the composition of the board of directors of each company. Given that relevant companies are overwhelmingly organised as joint stock companies, one can reach a fairly accurate knowledge of the business community through the analysis of members of the board.

I am well aware that several other steps should be taken before one can conclude from this analysis who were the richest in Italy and how rich they were. The present analysis, while it completely leaves aside fortunes exclusively made up of urban and rural estates,[100] cannot offer more than a starting-point for the identification of the largest financial and industrial fortunes, as it only provides names of the most important firms and of the people most deeply involved in business. The next step, which has regrettably to be left for a future continuation of this research, would be that of studying the people identified as the most important businessmen in their biographical features and in their personal and real property holdings. However, some conclusions about the rich as a class in Italy can be advanced on the basis of our findings, and with the help of a few other related works.

Some remarks, firstly, on the companies included in the 1911 and 1927 samples. The companies encompassed for 1911 are all those with more than one million lire of share capital, numbering 744, with a total share capital of 4,126 million current lire. They constituted 26.4 per cent of the existing companies,[101] but made up 77 per cent of total company share capital. The companies included in the 1927 sample are, instead, all those with more than 10 million lire of share capital, totalling 635, with 28,072 million current lire. They constituted only 4.8 per cent of all the companies, but accounted for 66.4 per cent of capital. Given that in 1927 inflation stood at a level of 4.78 taking 1911 as 1.0,[102] it can be said that the lower limit of companies considered in 1927 is about twice as large as in 1911.[103] From a comparative point of view, it would have been ideal to consider in 1927 all the companies with more than 5 million lire of share capital, but this would have entailed the inclusion in the computer of about 600 extra firms, which proved impracticable in this first phase of research because of the limitation of time. On the other hand, it did not seem wise to limit the 1911 sample to include only companies with more than 2 million lire in share capital, and therefore the 1911 sample remains more comprehensive.[104] 82 per cent of the capital of companies considered for 1911 and 83 per cent of the 1927 companies belonged to those with head offices in the industrial triangle and in the capital.

We can now see, with the help of Table 3.7, some general features of the members of the boards of the above-described companies. Even when due account is taken of the larger average size of the 1927 companies, the average educational level of directors seems to have increased between 1911 and 1927, while the percentage of directors holding public office has shrunk, no doubt also in consequence of the political events which intervened. Comment on the relationship of nobility to the business milieu is deferred until later.

A matter which can be discussed exhaustively is that of the concentration of seats on boards. In Table 3.8 I have gathered all the relevant data for 1911 and 1927, reporting as well the results of a survey carried out for 1922 on the same source as that studied in the present chapter by the well-known statistician Luzzatto Fegis.[105] At the three dates, about one-fourth of the directors held more than one seat and 12-14 per cent more than two seats, while some directors held as many as 20 or 30. Looking more closely at this one-fourth of the directors we find on average more academics (36.9 per cent and 51.7 per cent, respectively, in 1911 and 1927, of all graduands) and more people holding public offices (5.1 per cent, respectively).

In 1911 one-fourth of the directors with two or more seats were

Table 3.7: Some Features of Members of Boards of Directors, 1911 and 1927

	1911	Percentage*	1927	Percentage*
Total number of seats	5,576		6,277	
Total no. of directors**	3,399		3,542	
With academic title	1,141	33.6	1,571	44.4
Holding public office	118	3.5	85	2.4
Belonging to nobility	285	8.4	292	8.2

*Of total number of directors.
**Managing directors included.

Table 3.8: Concentration of Seats on Boards of Directors

No of seats	1911		1922		1927	
	No.	Percentage	No.	Percentage	No.	Percentage
1	2,501	73.6	7,874	74.7	2,599	73.4
2	464	13.6	1,409	13.4	445	12.6
3	187	5.5	524	5.0	185	5.2
4	72	2.1	263	2.5	104	2.8
5	52	1.5	133	1.3	55	1.5
6	37	1.1	92	.9	31	.9
7	29	.9	52	.5	34	1.0
8	13	.4	47	.4	26	.7
9	16	.5	29	.3	13	.4
10	9	.3	21	.2	6	.2
11-15	14	.4	62	.6	27	.7
16-20	4	.1	14	.1	8	.2
21-29	1	–	12	.1	7	.2
30 and over	–	–	3	–	2	–

members of the boards of banks and held one-third of the seats belonging to directors with more than two seats. Companies having on their board at least one member who also sat on the board of a bank were 60 per cent of the total number of companies considered (with a capital certainly exceeding 60 per cent of the total, because the largest companies were included). Looking through the list of the directors sitting on more than two boards,[106] one meets, aside from entrepreneurs of the stature of Agnelli, Falck, Pirelli, Abegg, Odero, Orlando, Pesenti and Parodi Delfino, all the most important financiers and bankers of the time, as well as a handful of noblemen deeply engaged in business. Indeed, in general, bankers and financiers held the highest number of seats per director.

In 1927, 40 per cent were directors with more than two seats on the board of a bank; they held more than half of the seats belonging to directors with two or more seats. Companies having on their board at least one member also sitting on the board of a bank were 80 per cent of the companies considered. Even taking into account the imperfect comparability of the 1911 and 1927 samples, it can be appreciated that the interlocking between financial and industrial capital had increased. All the largest firms had in 1927 manifold and tight links with banks and holding companies. In 1927, too, directors with the highest number of seats were people belonging to the most powerful banks and holding companies.

Concerning the continuity of the economic elite between 1911 and 1927, of the 209 directors who in 1927 held five or more seats each, eleven belonged to the Triestene group, excluded for obvious reasons in the pre-First World War survey, 100 had sat already in 1911 on two or more boards, 11 on one; moreover, 22 were descendants of members of 1911 boards. In total, more than two-thirds of the directors holding one or more seats in 1927 were persons, or the immediate relatives of persons, included in the 1911 sample.

Moreover, among those who did not appear in 1911, many can be traced back to organisations or power groups well established in 1911. For example, Mario Carbagni (26 seats) and Vincenzo Ardissone (9 seats) were men of the Credito Italiano and of the Banca Commerciale; Carlo Orsi (13 seats) was the Managing Director of the Credito Italiano, Mario Rossello (17 seats) had been Managing Director of the Credito Italiano in the years 1921-24, Giacinto Motta (18 seats) had been Managing Director and then President of the Edison (the largest Italian electrical holding company) since 1918. Also, the two men who made a bright career during fascism, Alberto Beneduce (13 seats in 1927; the organiser and General Manager of IRI) and Antonio Stefano Benni (13 seats, Chairman of the Confindustria, the Italian industrialists' confederation, in the years 1926-33) were tied respectively to the Bastogi (as a longtime Chairman) and to the Banco di Roma (another important mixed bank, tied to the Vatican and rescued by Mussolini in 1923; Benni was also Director of Bastogi).

In substance, there were only two businessmen who tried to build new private conglomerates in the 1920s. These were Gian Giacomo Ponti (21 seats in 1927), Chairman of the Societa Elettrica Piemontese (SIP), and Rinaldo Panzarasa (27 seats), Chairman of the Italgas, both of them swept away by the 1929 crisis. With few qualifications, therefore, we can say that the 1927 economic establishment was clearly rooted in the pre-First World War business structure and witnessed an increase in the power of banks and holding companies.

From the documented importance of financial capital in Italy flow two consequences regarding the very wealthy. First, special attention should be paid to the owners of parcels of shares of banks and holdings, because among those capitalists, sometimes not too well known, the richest people can often be found. We know some of the members of this group: the Crespis (Silvio had 11 seats in 1927, plus another 6 held by other members of the family), the Feltrinellis (Carlo had 24 seats, plus another 7 in the family), the Mazzotti Biancinellis (Ludovico had 35 seats), the Volpis (Giuseppe was not included on 1927 boards, because he was Minister at the time), the Gaggias (Achille had 34 seats), the Cinis (Vittorio had 15 seats, plus 2 held by his 87-year-old father, Giovanni Cosimo) and the Marchis (Carlo had, however, only one seat in 1927). But rich families existed who were lending funds without active participation in business, like the Tonollis (from Milan) and some members of the aristocracy. How many they numbered it is difficult to say.

Second, it can certainly be concluded that a remarkable slice of Italian economic power has always been in the hands of people who were managing somebody else's capital. The two Managing Directors of the Banca Commerciale, Otto Joel (8 seats in 1911) and Giuseppe Toeplitz (28 seats in 1927), have been responsible for economic choices more numerous and crucial than those faced by any among the capitalist entrepreneurs, including Agnelli, who was certainly the most successful among them. From estimates reported by Cianci,[107] in 1930 the Banca Commerciale controlled 17.2 per cent of the total share capital, which must be raised to 25.9 per cent if we add allied groups. Similar estimates for other banks are not available; they were certainly more 'mixed' than the Banca Commerciale, which by 1930 had become a truly industrial bank, but the above-quoted data on composition of boards suggest that at least the Managing Directors of the Credito Italiano (Rava Enrico had 11 seats in 1911, Carlo Orsi 13 in 1927), the Banco di Roma and the Bastogi had a significant slice of responsibility and power.

It is now possible to understand how it was that a substantial number of the managers of the largest firms did not hold such a position because of their accumulated wealth. One can quote in this connection the undisputed head for many years of Montecatini, the largest Italian chemical company, Guido Donegani, who, as is notorious, after his death in the late 1940s left only a very modest fortune, or Giuseppe Genzato, head of SME (Societa Meridionale di Elettricita, which passed under IRI). This is true as well of the generation of less-known 'public' entrepreneurs, first subsidised by banks and then by IRI, who had in their hands the destiny of countless large and not-so-large metal, engineering and chemical firms since the 1920s (and sometimes even before), men like Bocciardo and Sinigaglia.

A good account of the relative importance at the end of the Second World War of the above-mentioned economic groups can be derived from a survey carried out in 1946 for the Constituent Assembly on joint stock companies, to which the next section is devoted.

Concentration of Ownership of Company Shares and Economic Power Groups at the End of the Fascist Régime

It is not a surprise to find in a country like Italy, with a narrow domestic market and a limited export capacity, a great concentration of share capital. First of all, it must be noticed that in 1938 the real value of joint stock company capital accounted for no more than 60 per cent of the stock of capital invested in Italy in the industrial and energy sectors, the rest belonging to the still widespread handicraft sector.[108] From a work by Saibante[109] and from another work prepared for the Constituent Assembly,[110] I have been able to calculate Gini's concentration coefficients of share capital for some years between 1916 and 1941. They appear high and increasing, as it can be noticed in Table 3.9.

But for the purpose of evaluating the degree of concentration of personal property, much more relevant are data on the concentration of shareholdings. Such data have been collected for a large number of companies only for 1945 and have been, as far as I know, only partially elaborated. From an article by Zerini, who made use of the above-quoted survey, it is possible to calculate the usual Gini's concentration coefficient.[111] This does not vary substantially if one considers all the shares or only the shares owned by private shareholders. In the former case, the coefficient is .8968, while in the latter it is .8919. Giving some further illustration of this latter case, 0.44 per cent of shareholders were reported to own 29.3 per cent of the share capital in the hands of private shareholders, 3.79 per cent owned 64.2 per cent of that capital, while 7.63 per cent owned 78.8 per cent.

As far as I know, no systematic elaboration has been made of that survey in relation to the people named in the list of shareholders.

Table 3.9: Gini's Concentration Coefficients of Share Capital at Various Dates

1916*	.7537
1932	.8799
1938	.9028
1941	.9164

*At 1932 prices.

Table 3.10: The Most Powerful Economic Groups Existing in Italy, 1945

	Share capital** (milliards)	No. of companies controlled	No. of workers employed
IRI	16.0	216	185,821
Edison*	6.0	98	25,206
Montecatini	5.3	25	41,301
Eridania	3.3	13	14,318
Pirelli	3.2	34	18,000
Sade*	2.6	65	12,009
IFI-Fiat	2.5	153	88,118
SNIA-Viscosa	2.0	43	10,650
Centrale*	2.0	20	11,075
Bastogi	1.6	31	–
Italgas	1.1	13	6,059
Falck	0.6	18	25,108
Piaggio	0.5	16	8,710
Breda-De Angeli Frua	0.4	8	27,124
Caproni	0.4	21	29,723
Italcementi	0.3	14	8,032
GIM	0.2	2	7,651
Total	48.0	790	518,905

*Electrical companies.
**Share capital of the group.

Sources: My elaborations from CGIL, Ufficio Statistica, *Struttura dei monopoli industriali in Italia* (Rome, 1949); RADAR, *Organizzazione del capitale finanziario italiano* (Quaderno di Critica Economica, Rome, 1948).

Attention has been concentrated on the greatest economic groups existing in 1945, about which I can give further details (see Table 3.10).

As in 1945 share capital totalled 72 milliard lire, the 17 companies listed in Table 3.10 which constituted 0.09 per cent of the 19,067 existing companies, controlled two-thirds of the total share capital. Of such companies, 9 were controlled by easily identifiable families.[112] The other companies showed a complex and often interconnected pattern of shareholding, at the centre of which IRI and Bastogi were located. Looking through the names of recurring private shareholders, one finds the same names appearing on the 1911 and 1927 boards. It is impossible to show this in detail here for obvious reasons of space;

Table 3.11: Shareholding Structure of the Bastogi and the Edison, 1947

Bastogi	Shares owned (percentage)	Edison	Shares owned (percentage)
Fiat	4.62	Bastogi	3.60
IRI	4.16	Pirelli (comp.)	1.17
Assicurazioni Gen.	4.05	Fiat	0.49
Edison	3.30	21 other comps.	12.13
Sade	2.54	Crespi	2.88
Centrale	2.45	Feltrinelli	1.63
Pirelli (comp.)	2.18	Abegg	0.54
28 other comps.	22.70	Borletti	0.41
Marchi	2.90	Casati	0.39
Crespi	1.79	Marchi	0.25
Guida	1.10	Tonolli	0.16
Motta	0.50	Volpi	0.07
Parodi Delfino	0.50	Pirelli (fam.)	0.05
Agnelli G.	0.42	Marinotti	0.06
Conti Ettore	0.41		
Pirelli (fam.)	0.41		
Visocchi	0.40		

Source: See Table 3.10.

I will only report, as examples, the shareholding structure of the Bastogi and the Edison (see Table 3.11).

It is therefore possible to conclude, with the help of an article by Chiesi,[113] that a number of entrepreneurs existed in the private area, of various social origins,[114] who had a high family continuity at the head of important and successful firms, where they certainly accumulated substantial family fortunes.

But the large area of enterprises financed by banks or holdings as well as the explicitly public area have given rise to a substantial number of entrepreneurs whose social origin was in general the middle class, showing a high level of education, a high turnover (very seldom were the descendants of these people able to maintain the same top positions), sometimes holding great power while they were in office, but having relatively modest personal fortunes.

Before drawing some implications from this typically Italian experience (in the concluding section), I will make a few final observations on the role of the aristocracy in business.

The Presence of the Aristocracy in the Business Milieu

It can be seen in Table 3.7 that the directors of the joint stock companies under consideration who were noble were 8.4 per cent of the total in 1911 and 8.2 per cent in 1927. However, we must pay attention to the fact that the 1927 companies sampled were only the largest. In any essay published in 1936,[115] the percentage of noblemen on company boards, estimated for a number of years, was shown to be as follows: 9.8 per cent in 1910; 8.45 per cent in 1912 (which agrees perfectly with my 1911 estimate); 7.88 per cent in 1914; 4.52 per cent in 1930; 4.22 per cent in 1932; 4.21 per cent in 1934. In the above-quoted work by Luzzatto Fegiz, the percentage calculated for 1922 was 4.9. It should be concluded that the percentage of noblemen on boards declined during or immediately after the war; most likely this was because noblemen ready to engage in business were almost fixed in number, while companies increased rapidly after the First World War (with the exception of the years 1929-33).

Several sources suggest that the inclusion of noblemen on boards was often only an attempt to secure prestige. This can be confirmed by the fact that among managing directors the percentage of noblemen fluctuated between 1 and 2, without a recognisable trend. My survey has shown a remarkable recurrence of the most well-known aristocratic names on boards of banks and holding companies, which is a clear indicator of the predominance among the aristocrats of finance among all entrepreneurial activities, though cases of true aristocratic entrepreneurs are not entirely unknown. The same surveys largely confirm that noblemen who engaged in business were more common in Piedmont, Liguria and Lombardy; Venetia, Tuscany and Latium nobility had their representative too, while only exceptional cases can be found in the South.

Conclusion

Italy is a country where only relatively few 'super-rich' families can be found. The non-existence of natural resources to be exploited, the age-old military weakness and the unsuccessful colonial policy of the country have prevented any pre-industrial accumulation of wealth outside the traditional agricultural sector and, to some extent, international trade (especially in the case of Genoa and Venice). Italy's artistic and natural beauties, so much praised by poets and travellers of all times, have not been worth much in monetary terms, at least until the era of mass tourism, and the ingenuity of her scientists and inventors has been more often exploited abroad than used domestically to improve technology and create new wealth.

Not even industrialisation has given rise to a substantial number of very rich industrial dynasties.[116] Few are the cases of single families or groups of families who have been able for a long period of time to undertake, with their personal fortunes alone, the risk entailed by major productive activities in a country like Italy, which started industrialisation late, in presence of a narrow domestic and foreign market, and showed a high level of social conflict. With the exception of the Agnellis, Pirellis, Pesentis, Falcks, Olivettis and a few others, the rest of the great Italian industrial concerns have been managed by true 'capital officials', whose income has been relatively high but whose wealth has been modest. The prevailing category of private entrepreneurs in Italy is that of owners of medium and small-sized industrial and commercial enterprises, which still today constitute the core of the productive structure of the country. They cannot be very rich.

Naturally, this does not mean that Italy is a country where social justice reigns. Rather, it means that inequalities are more pronounced in terms of income than in terms of wealth. The capital officials have always been in general more than generously paid,[117] on one hand to guarantee their attachment to work, which they cannot derive, as in the case of the classical entrepreneur capitalist, from the incentive due to risking personal fortunes, and on the other hand to avert the danger, albeit often with a modest success, of embezzlement of some of that capital, which is not and will never become their own property. On the contrary, until recent years, workers have been underpaid in order to re-establish, through wage compression, the conditions of international competitiveness which could not be based either on abundance of raw materials or on advanced technology.

This peculiar feature of Italian economic development has at least three relevant consequences. In the first place, major components of economic power have in many cases been administered by people who were in strategic positions for reasons other than wealth. This is the case with the great bankers and financiers, as well as with the great public entrepreneurs; but it is also the case of less renowned managers and bankers belonging to the public or subsidised area. Has this fact caused a different way of conducting business, different the classical pattern of the entrepreneur capitalist? And how can one compare the Italian experience with so-called managerial capitalism? These are, at the present stage of research, only stimulating questions asking for further analysis.

The other consequences which I want to mention are, on one side, the strategic role of the middle classes in Italian politics and, on the other side, the belated and insufficient modernisation of state bureaucracy.

It is certainly not by chance that Italy never had a great party of the bourgeoisie, as it existed in other countries. Not even fascism was the party of the great capitalists, but it remained in power so long because it succeeded in organising and expressing the claims – not only economic – of the middle classes. Later on, much of the success of Christian Democracy was due to precisely the same cause.[118]

On the other hand, the obstinate persistence of an inefficient state bureaucracy can be certainly explained by cultural and historical reasons, but also by the existence of a too-limited number of powerful private economic concentrations in a position of imposing a radical change in the public sector. If economic activities are predominantly in the hands of small entrepreneurs who cannot realistically aim at interference with the working of the administrative machine, or by public or semi-public enterprises which do not have an organisation too dissimilar from that of the civil service, it is apparent that there is no incentive towards modernisation of the public sector from this side.

What has been said about the features of the wealthy confirms, from a different perspective, the otherwise well-established distinctive character of the Italian way to modernisation.

Notes

1. For an account of economic development in the two duchies in the first half of the nineteenth century, see P.L. Spaggiari, *L'agricoltura negli Stati Parmensi dal 1750 al 1859* (Milan, 1966) and *Aspetti e problemi del Risorgimento a Modena* (Modena, 1963).

2. Two excellent surveys of the literature existing on the period can be found in M. Romani, *Storia economica d'Italia nel secolo XIX, vol. I, 1815-1859* (Milan, 1968), and A. Caracciolo, 'La storia economica' in *Dal primo settecento all'unita*, vol. 3 of the *Storia d'Italia*, published by Einaudi (Turin, 1973).

3. L. Bulferetti and C. Costantini, *Industria e commercio in Liguria nell'età del Risorgimento 1700-1861* (Milan, 1966), p. 20.

4. L. Bulferetti, *Agricoltura, industria e commercio in Piemonte nel secolo XVIII* (Turin, 1963).

5. G. Prato, *La vita economica in Piemonte a mezzo il secolo XVIII* (Turin, 1908) argues that, comparatively, the distribution of wealth was less concentrated in Piedmont than elsewhere, which favoured a larger circulation of consumption goods.

6. See G. Doria, *Investimenti e sviluppo economico a Genova alla vigilia della prima guerra mondiale. Le premesse (1815-1882)* (Milan, 1969).

7. Around 1855, power-spindles at work in Piedmont-Liguria numbered about 200,000 in cotton and 60,000-70,000 in wool, while power-looms were about 5,000 in cotton and less than 1,000 in wool; textile-manufacturers numbered about 200. Production of raw silk covered 25 per cent of Italian output. See P. Maestri, 'Della industria manufatturiera in Italia', *Rivista Contemporanea, 1858-60*; V. Castronovo, *L'industria laniera in Piemonte nel secolo XIX* (Turin, 1964), and his *L'industria cotoniera in Piemonte nel secolo XIX* (Turin, 1965).

8. The engineering industry had a labour force of about 15,000 workers in the 1850s, mainly concentrated in Turin and Genoa; in this latter town there were a few large firms, among which the Ansaldo (founded in 1853) with 1,000 workers, the Foce shipyard with 1,200 workers and the Arsenal with 1,600 workers. They were building ships, engines, arms, wagons and also locomotives with some modern blast furnaces for the smelting of pig iron.

9. In 1859, 25 per cent of the 1800 km of railway working in Italy belonged to Piedmont and Liguria.

10. Around 1855, 25 per cent of the tonnage of the Italian merchant marine belonged to Liguria, which also registered the highest tonnage per ship.

11. Many among the private bankers remained active after unification; among them the Genoese Oneto, Parodi and Croce, and the Turinese Barbaroux, Casana, Ceriana, Defernex, Deslex, Marsaglia and Segre. Moreover, two important banks were founded in the 1840s, the Banca di Genova in 1844 and the Banca di Torino in 1847; they merged in 1849 to form the Banca Nazionale degli Stati Sardi (which will later become the Bank of Italy) under the direction of the Genoese Carlo Bombrini.

12. One of the most important Italian canals, which was later called after Cavour, was started then in Piedmont.

13. See in this connection what is written in M. Einaudi, 'Le prime ferrovie piemontesi e il conte di Cavour', *Rivista di storia economica* (1938); see also P. Guichonnet, *Cavour agronomo e uomo d'affari* (Milan, 1961), and V. Castronovo, 'Formazione e sviluppo del ceto impreditoriale laniero e contoniero piemontese', *Rivista storica italiana* (1966).

14. There are several publications on Cavour, among them R. Romeo, *Cavour e il suo tempo 1810-1854* (Bari, 1969), and R. Luraghi, *Pensiero e azione economica del conte di Cavour* (Turin, 1961).

15. M. Berengo, *La societa veneta alla fine del '700* (Florence, 1956), pp. 88-89.

16. D. Beltrami, *Storia della popolazione di Venezia dalla fine del secolo XVI alla caduta della repubblica* (Padua, 1954), pp. 71-75.

17. M. Mirri, 'Studi recenti di storia del 700 italiano', *Società* (1953).

18. M. Berengo, *L'agricoltura veneta dalla caduta della repubblica all'unità* (Milan, 1963); the concentration of ownership was high: I have estimated on the basis of data reported by Berengo that 8-9 per cent of landowners owned about 80 per cent of Venetian cultivated land.

19. On Lombard agriculture see the writings by M. Romani, especially *L'agricoltura in Lombardia dal periodo delle riforme al 1859* (Milan, 1957). A. Young in his *Travels during Years 1787, 1788 and 1789* (London, 1792), wrote: 'The richest and most flourishing countries in Europe in proportion to their extent are, probably Piedmont, and the Milanese. All the signs of prosperity are there met with; populousness well employed and well supported; a great export without; a thriving consumption within; magnificent roads, numerous and wealthy towns; circulation active; interest of money low; and the price of labour

high. . .The origin and support of all the wealth of these countries are to be found in agriculture, which is carried to. . .perfection' (pp. 509-10).

20. Around 1860, Lombardy produced 40 per cent of cocoons and 33 per cent of Italian raw silk; about 5,500 silk-looms were operated in the region by 8,000 workers gathered in 94 silk manufacturers.

21. Silk constituted 86 per cent of the value of exports from Lombardy in the period 1851-59. See I. Glazier, 'Il commercio estero del regno lombardo-veneto dal 1815 al 1865', *Archivio economico dell'unificazione italiana*, series I, v, XV (Turin, 1966).

22. B. Caizzi, *L'economia lombarda durante la Restaurazione 1814-1859* (Milan, 1972), p. 102.

23. In 1857 there existed in Lombardy 121,000 power-spindles and 17,000 looms, many of which were hand-operated.

24. Lombard firms were small or medium in size; the most important were Elvetica of Milan, which in 1855 had 350-400 workers; Grondona with 200 workers and Regazzoni of Como with 100-120 workers. Arms-manufacturers existed in the area around Brescia; metal had been long manufactured in Dongo, where in 1840 there arrived from Alsace Giorgio Enrico Falck, whose son was later to found near Milan the Acciaierie e ferriere lombarde, the largest metal firm in Lombardy. Other metal-manufacturers existed in Lecco, Bellano and other places. It is, however, difficult to estimate the overall labour force employed in the sector. For other details, see B. Caizzi, *Storia dell'industria italiana* (Turin, 1965), pp. 247-54.

25. 29 per cent of the existing railway network belonged to Lombardy.

26. S. Jacini, *La proprietà fondiaria e le popolazioni argicole in Lombardia* (Milan, 1857), estimated the value of real property to be 2,424 million lire around 1851-52, distributed among 350,000 owners (making about 6,900 lire per real assets owner).

27. Among the most important magazines, I mention *Annali universali di statistica, Annali di commercio, Ape delle cognizioni utili, Bollettino di notizie statistiche ed economiche, Politecnico* and *Rivista Europea.*

28. For example Cattaneo, Jacini, Dandolo and Gioia.

29. N. Quilici, *Origine, sviluppo e insufficienza della borghesia italiana* (Ferrara, 1932), argues that Lombard aristocracy turned to business for lack of diplomatic and military opportunities (p. 46).

30. A good work on nobility and property in the Napoleonic era is G. Zaghi, 'Proprieta e classe dirigente nell'Italia giacobina e napoleonica', *Annuario dell'Istituto storico italiano per l'età moderna e contemporanea, 1971-72* (Rome, 1975), where one can find, among other things, a list of the 300 wealthiest landowners in the Cisalpine Republic (then Kingdom of Italy), with their respective rent income.

31. See the numerous references made by K.R. Greenfield, *Economics and Liberalism in the Risorgiment. A Study of Nationalism in Lombardy 1815-1848* (Baltimore, 1934).

32. See R. Ciasca, 'L'evoluzione economica della Lombardia dagli inizi del secolo XIX al 1860' in *La Cassa di risparmiio delle province lombarde nella evoluzione economica della regione* (Milan, 1923), pp. 386-87.

33. It is worthwhile mentioning that in 1861 the percentage of illiterates in Lombardy was the lowest among the Italian regions (53.7 per cent), followed closely by that in Piedmont-Liguria (54.2 per cent). All the other Italian regions had much higher percentages, ranging from 75 per cent to 90 per cent. Lombardy, moreover, was the only Italian region where popular participation in the Risorgiment was substantial.

34. I am referring to Baron Bettino Ricasoli, Marquis Cosimo Ridolfi and

Ferdinando Bartolommei.

35. C. Pazzagli, *L'agricoltura toscana nella prima metà dell'800* (Florence, 1973), underlines the lack of expansion of the internal market due to the sharecropping system which was impoverishing, relatively, landowners too, who were deriving from their estates, often very large, inadequate incomes.

36. See G. Giorgetti, *Capitalismo e agricoltura in Italia* (Rome, 1977), p. 417.

37. It is interesting to note that, to make acceptable such an industrial enterprise to the local paternalistic views, Larderel had to build near borax fields a new village, Larderello, where he provided a house, an orchard and other services to his workers. See I. Imberciadori, *Economia toscana nel primo '800. Dalla Restaurazione al regno, 1815-1861* (Florence, 1961).

38. See data on the foreign trade of Tuscany in G. Parenti, 'Il commercio estero del Granducato di Toscana dal 1851 al 1859', *Archivio economico dell'unificazione italiana*, series I, v, VIII (Turin, 1959).

39. Details on these and other minor industrial enterprises can be found in L. Dal Pane, *Industria e commercio nel granducato di Toscana nell'età del Risorgimento* (Bologna, 1973).

40. D. De Marco, *Il tramonto dello Stato pontificio. Il papato di Gregorio XVI* (Turin, 1949), writes 'When charity was not at work, the government tried to mitigate unemployment using the unemployed for useless public works' (pp. 97-98).

41. In 1802, 32 per cent of the Bolognese plain was in the hands of the bourgeoisie and only 2 per cent was owned by the clergy. See R. Zangheri, *La proprietà terriera e le origini del Risorgimento nel bolognese* (Bologna, 1961). The very large landowners were, however, all noble (Hercolani, Segni, Tanari, Malvezzi, Aldrovandi, Spada, Isolani, Ranuzzi, Pepoli, Marsigli, Bentivogli and Marescotti).

42. L. Dal Pane, *Economia e società a Bologna nell'età del Risorgimento* (Bologna, 1969), p. 398.

43. Ibid.

44. Maestri, *Industria manufatturiera*.

45. R. Ciasca, 'Borghesia e classi rurali del Mezzogiorno nell'età del Risorgimento' in *Il movimento unitario nelle regioni d'Italia* (Bari, 1963), speaks of an 'excellent bargain' for Sicilian barons.

46. P. Villani, *Mezzogiorno tra riforme e rivoluzione* (Bari, 1973), pp. 195-97. The richest families were those of Pignatelli dukes of Monteleone, Caracciolo, Doria, Acquaviva, Carafa, Tocco, Ruffo, Monastero and Sangro.

47. G. De Meo, 'Distribuzione della ricchezza e composizione demografica in alcune citta dell'Italia meridionale alla metà del secolo XVIII', *Annali di Statistica*, series VI (1931). He analyses the towns of Castellamare di Stabia, Foggia and Barletta, and finds that nobility and clergy absorbed 64 per cent of incomes from property.

48. Take for instance the case of the Sicilian *gabellotto*, who were a greedy intermediary strata between peasants and the absentee landlord rather than an entrepreneurially minded tenant farmer. See, in this connection, E. Sereni, *Il capitalismo nell campagne* (Turin, 1948), pp. 184-86.

49. F. Milone, 'Le industrie del Mezzogiorno all'unificazione dell'Italia' in *Studi in onore di G. Luzzatto* (Milan, 1950), v. III.

50. L. De Rosa, *Iniziativa e capitale straniero nell'industria metalmeccanica del Mezzogiorno 1840-1904* (Naples, 1968).

51. J. Davis, 'Oligarchia capitalistica e immobilismo economico a Napoli (1815-1860)', *Studi Storici* (1975), n. 2, p. 379. See also by the same author, *Società e impreditori nel regno barbonico, 1815-1860* (Bari, 1978).

52. Ibid., p. 426. He estimates at no more than 20-30 the main families

belonging to that oligarchy, whose 'power derived from the fact of owning capital in a place where it was scarce'.

53. For a detailed and well-informed survey of the economic history of post-unification Italy, see V. Castronovo, *La storia economica* in *Storia d'Italia*, v. 4 (Turin, 1975).

54. Note that Venetia was annexed in 1866, Latium in 1870, Trieste and Trentino after the First World War.

55. Income per head was in 1861 around 315 current lire. See P. Ercolani, 'Documentazione statistica di base' in G. Fuà (ed.), *Lo sviluppo economico in Italia* (3 vols., Milan, 1969), vol. 3.

56. On the developments of the Italian banking system from 1861 to 1906 three well-documented volumes exist today written by A. Confalonieri, *Banca e industria in Italia 1894-1906* (Milan, 1974-76).

57. Various indicators confirm that it is not possible to speak of an *Italian* industrial take-off: all the most advanced lines of production were concentrated in the Piedmont-Liguria-Lombardy area which, having 27 per cent of the entire population of Italy, produced at the eve of the First World War 57 per cent of electricity and consumed 69 per cent of it. For further details, see V. Zamagni, *Industrializzazione e squilibri regionali in Italia. Bilancio dell'età giolittiana* (Bologna, 1978).

58. See a good account of such a transition in the essay by A. Caracciolo, 'La crescita e la trasformazione della grande industria durante la prima guerra mondiale' in Fuà, vol. 3.

59. E. Cianci, *Nascita dello stato imprenditore in Italia* (Milan, 1977), estimates that share capital controlled by the Banca Commerciale and its allies was, around 1930, 25 per cent of all the share capital of Italian joint stock companies.

60. On the origin and development of IRI, beside the already quoted Cianci, see M.V. Posner and S.J. Woolf, *Italian Public Enterprise* (Harvard University Press, 1967).

61. The only article I have been able to find on wealth written in the post-Second World War period is the one by A. Giannone, 'Evaluations of Italian National Wealth in the last 50 Years', *Banca Nazionale del Lavoro Quarterly Review* (December 1963), where the author briefly reviews the most important works written on the topic and offers an estimate of Italian *national* wealth for 1938 and 1961. The 1938 estimate is compatible with the estimate of *private* wealth that will be adopted in what follows.

62. For a systematic survey of these and other works on wealth till 1917, see L. Maroi, 'Come si calcola e a quanto ammonta la ricchezza d'Italia e delle altre principali nazioni', *Rivista delle società commerciali* (1919).

63. C. Gini, *L'ammontare e la composizione della ricchezza delle nazioni* (Turin, 1962; originally 1914), Chs. 2-4.

64. Gini estimated that around 1908 tax evasion was at least 50 per cent of the true value of real and personal assets transferred and that the transfer interval was 31 years. With such parameters, his evaluation of private wealth based on the transfer annuity was not far from the estimate obtained through the real inventory method.

65. Evaluation based on the comparison between the Retti Marsani series and the Tivaroni-Nitti estimates for the years 1900-3.

66. Income data are taken from Ercolani, 'Documentazione statistica' in Fuà, vol. 3.

67. It can be hypothesised that wealth not directly productive of income was mainly destroyed during the crisis.

68. Between 1929 and 1930, value added in manufacturing, building and

electricity equalled value added in agriculture. Naturally, the large productivity gap between the two sectors is responsible for the fact that employment was larger in agriculture.

69. The rise of Mussolini to power is a complex phenomenon, as it is accurately explained by A. Lyttelton, *The Seizure of Power, Fascism in Italy 1919-1929* (London, 1973). But, if one could weigh the influence of the agrarian elite *vis-à-vis* the industrial elite, certainly the former would reveal a larger importance than the latter. In 1922 the industrial crisis had already been overcome, while the agrarian problems had not shown any substantial improvements. When Mussolini was in power, the agrarian elite supported him without any reservation, while the industrial elite was more independently minded, as it is well documented in R. Sarti, *Fascism and the Industrial Leadership in Italy 1919-1940*(Berkeley, 1971).

70. See data published in *Bollettino di statistica e di legislazione comparata,* 1901/2-1914/15.

71. F. Savorgnan, 'La ripartizione regionale della ricchezza privata italiana', *Metron* (1920-21).

72. A. Contento, 'Sulla ripartizione territoriale della ricchezza privata in Italia', *Giornale degli economisti* (1914). The author supports with his findings the conclusions reached by Gini, *L'ammontare*, Ch. 5, with relation to the North-South gap, which disagreed with the more pessimistic conclusions given by F.S. Nitti in *La ricchezza d'Italia* (Naples, 1905). The pioneering work by M. Pantaleoni, 'Delle regioni d'Italia in ordine alla loro ricchezza ed al loro carico tributario', *Giornale degli economisti* (1891) was also disproved. Both Gini and Contento were excluding, on the basis of their estimates of regional wealth, the existence of a fiscal discrimination against the South, which constituted one of the more polemical arguments of the meridionalistic battle made by Nitti.

73. See Zamagni, *Industrializzazione*, Ch. 4. A few estimates of regional wealth exist; see references in De Vita, 'La ricchezza privata'.

74. P. Thaon di Revel, 'Il valore della proprietà fondiaria in Italia', *Rivista del catasto e dei servizi tecnici erariali* (1938). The author was at the time Minister of Finance and had to survey anew the value of real estate to estimate revenue from an extraordinary tax on real property which the fascist government wanted to (and in fact did) levy.

75. According to the data reported in the works by De Vita and Thaon di Revel, one hectare of cultivated land had seen its value increased in Emilia between 1928 and 1937 by more than 40 per cent (at constant prices).

76. R. Benini, 'Distribuzione probabile della ricchezza privata in Italia per classi di popolazione', *Riforma sociale* (1894).

77. E. Porru, 'La concentrazione della ricchezza nelle diverse regioni d'Italia', *Studi economico-giuridici dell'Universita di Cagliari* (1912).

78. C. Cassola, *La proprietà e la distribuzione della ricchezza* (Milan, 1914).

79. The formula adopted to calculate the Gini's coefficient of concentration is the following:

$$R = \frac{\overset{r}{\Sigma}(i_k + i_{k-1} - 1)S_k}{(n-1)A_n} - 1 \quad \text{where}$$

R = number of classes
i_k = number of people with income (or wealth) < than the upper limit of class
i_{k-1} = number of people with income (or wealth) < than the lower limit of class
S_k = total income (or wealth) in class k
A_n = total income in all classes   n = total number of people considered.

The coefficient varies from 0 (when income or wealth, is equally distributed) to 1 (when total income, or wealth, is owned by one person only).

80. See H.F. Lydall and D.G. Tipping, 'The Distribution of Personal Wealth in Britain', *Bulletin of the Oxford Institute of Economics and Statistics* (1961), republished in A.B. Atkinson (ed.), *Wealth, Income and Inequality* (London, 1973).

81. Porru, 'La concentrazione', p. 115.

82. For instance, from data reported by R. Lampman, 'Changes in the Share of Wealth held by Top Wealth Holders 1922-56', *Review of Economics and Statistics* (1959), one can see that the US, having a higher per capita income than Britain in the inter-war period, had a lower degree of concentration.

83. See *Bollettino di statistica e di legislazione comparata*, 1928-37.

84. As it is well known, cadastral data are of limited use in connection with the problem of concentration of landownership, because one owner can own properties which are not contiguous (and are therefore separately recorded). The 1946 'census' took this into account aggregating all the estates owned by one landowner within the boundaries of each commune, without attempting an aggregation between communes too. See *Annuario statistico dell'agricoltura italiana*, 1947-50, and G. Medici, *La distribuzione della proprietà fondiaria in Italia* (2 vols., Rome, 1956). Interesting observations can be found also in *Rapporto della Commissione economica presentato all'Assemblea Costituente, I. Agricoltura. Relazione* (Rome, 1947).

85. The estates of the old Roman nobility, such as those belonging to Princes Corsini and Torlonia (amounting to tens of thousands hectares each) were still very extensive.

86. Take the case of Sicily. Around 1906, G. Bruccoleri, 'Un po' di luce sulla distribuzione della proprietà in Sicilia', *Giornale degli economisti* (1910), estimated that about 1,000 landowners owned 50 per cent of the island. To reach more or less the same extension of land, in 1946 one had to group at least 6,000 landowners.

87. The distance between Italian and French average per capita wealth can also be appreciated comparing data on the transfer annuity per deceased (or per inhabitant). Taking data for France 1826-1913 from A. Daumard, *Les Fortunes Françaises au XIXe Siècle* (Paris, 1973), p. 44, and those for Italy from the above-quoted works, one can see that Italy appears 'retarded' by about 70 years with respect to France.

88. Income data are taken from P. Bairoch, 'Europe's Gross National Product 1800-1975', *Journal of European Economic History* (1976).

89. See the recent book by R. Romano, *Borghesia industriale in ascesa, Gli imprenditor tessili nella inchiesta industriale 1870-74* (Milan, 1977). On the rise of industrialists organisations, the only book full of names and factual references still existing concerns Lombard entrepreneurs: L. Vidotto, *L'organizzazione industriale lombarda nell'ultimo conquantennio* (Milan, 1959).

90. Among the several works on A. Rossi, see what is said in G. Baglioni, *L'ideologia della borghesia industriale nell'Italia liberale* (PBE, 1974), Ch. 4.

91. The only recent and extended biography of an entrepreneur written by an academician is that of *Giovanni Agnelli*, written by V. Castronovo (Turin, 1971), where there is however no attempt of estimation of the fortunes of the family. A few entries exist in the *Dizionario biografico degli italiani*, published only till the letter C, plus some old laudatory volumes. Of some interest is the book by V. Poggiali, *I conquistatori di miliardi* (Milan, 1967), which includes only fifteen Italian names, arranged in rapid sketches. Some basic information on the economic milieu in the period 1914-31 can also be derived from the book by G. Mori, *Il capitalismo industriale in Italia* (Rome, 1977).

92. In Doria,˙*Investmenti a Genova*, an appendix is devoted to the reconstruction of shareholdings of the most important Genoese entrepreneurs. The Piaggios are among the richest families, with an average shareholdings of 10-14 million lire in the years 1906-14, plus substantial real properties.

93. From the same source, we know that the Bombrinis·had been the only owners of Ansaldo (one of the greatest Italian metal and engineering firms) till 1903; then they formed a joint stock company and diversified their shareholdings, keeping an average of 10-16 million lire of shares in the pre-war years.

94. The Raggios, shipowners and ironworks owners, beside large landowners, were probably the richest family in Genoa before the First World War. They are reported in Doria, *Investmenti a Genova*, to own castles and palaces in Genoa and shares worth an average of 15-20 million lire in pre-First World War years.

95. Unfortunately I do not have for the Crespis even the slim quantitative estimates available for the Genoese families. Their fortune included, anyway, textile firms as well as electrical companies, plus the most important national newspaper, the *Corriere della Sera*.

96. The Cinis started their fortunes in Tuscany with a paper mill already in the eighteenth century, but they expanded it mainly with Vittorio in the fascist period in connection with the development of the industrial port of Venice at Porto Marghera.

97. The proper name of the company was Societa per le strade ferrate Meridionali, but it used to be called Bastogi from the name of the Tuscan financier who had founded it as a railway company in 1861.

98. I wish here to warmly thank my friend Professor Giorgio Gozzi, of the University of Parma, who built and operated for me a very complex and unusual programme. Without his help I would never have been able to proceed in the laborious elaboration of the data used in the present section.

99. The publications used are Credito Italiano, *Notizie statistiche sulle principali società per azioni* (Milan, 1912), and Società Italiane per Azioni, *Notizie statistiche* (Milan, 1928).

100. Some hints concerning the links between agrarian wealth and industrial development will be found below.

101. See G.M. Sfligiotti, 'Un tentativo di valutazione statistica dello sviluppo e del risparmio delle società italiane per azioni' in Fuà, vol. 3.

102. Derived from ISTAT, *Il valore della lira dal 1861 al 1965* (Rome, 1966).

103. The average size of companies in 1927, however, given inflation, is only 60 per cent higher than in 1911.

104. The 1911 publication on joint stock companies included a total of 793 companies, few of which have therefore been excluded.

105. P. Luzatto Fegiz, 'Il consiglio di amministrazione e l'interdipendenza della imprese', *Giornale degli economisti* (1928). His sample included all the companies with more than one million lire of share capital, which numbered 2,829, totalling 20,317 million lire of capital, equal to 94 per cent of all the 1922 share capital.

106. Such list cannot be published here for reasons of space, but it will certainly be given more adequate space elsewhere.

107. Cianci, *Nascita dello stato imprenditore in Italia*.

108. Output produced by joint stock companies was, however, reaching 70-75 per cent of the total, because of higher productivity.

109. M. Saibante, 'Nuovi dati statistici sulle Società italiane per azioni', *Vita economica italiana* (1934).

110. 'Le società per azioni' in Ministero per la Costituente, *Rapporto della Commissione economica. II. Industria, I. Relazione* (Rome, 1947), vol. 2.

111. E. Zerini, 'L'economia capitalistica ed i vari aspetti delle egemonie

economiche in Italia', *Critica economica* (1947). The author derives this data from the extraordinary survey on companies carried out in 1946, which I have not seen.

112. The IFI, holding company of the FIAT group, was 100 per cent controlled by the Agnelli family; Pirelli had 39 per cent of its shares in the hands of the Pirelli family; Falck was 73 per cent owned by the Falck family; the GIM was owned by the families Orlando and Bruno; the Eridania by the families Cevasco, Oberti, Stoppani, Parodi and Acquarone; the Caproni was 75 per cent owned by Gianni Caproni. The Breda and the Italcementi had a lower percentage of their shares in the hands of the families who were controlling them, respectively the De Angeli Frua with 18.9 per cent of the shares, and the Pesenti with 10 per cent.

113. A.M. Chiesi, 'Una ricerca sulle biografie imprenditoriali nell'Italia liberale e fascista', *Quaderni di sociologia* (1977).

114. Some of them, especially in the textile and engineering sectors, came from the working class.

115. M. Boldrini and A. Alberti, 'Il patriziato italiano nelle categorie dirigenti' in *Contributi del laboratorio di statistica dell'Universita Cattolica del Sacro Cuore di Milano* (1936).

116. The existence of a large 'petty industrial bourgeoisie' as a 'specific feature of the Italian situation, which cannot be found, with the same relevance, in any other capitalistic advanced country (with the exception, perhaps, of Japan)' is quite apparent to M. Paci in his essay 'La struttura di classe della società italiana', published in the *Capitalismo e classi sociali*, edited by M. Paci (Bologna, 1978), p. 367. The lack of formulation of an industrial strategy by entrepreneurs, due among other things to the limited number of people belonging to that class, is the main theme of Ch. 2 of Baglioni, *L'ideologia della borghesia*.

117. In a quite peculiar article published in 1932 in the *Riforma sociale* (R. Levis, 'Sulle rimunerazioni percepite dagli amministratori di società anonime'), one can read data on the average yearly compensation of a director of 40 joint stock companies (chosen among the largest and medium-sized ones) in 1930. That average was 57,630 lire, but in some cases compensation reached as much as 160,000 lire. One can compare this with the average yearly wage for a worker employed in an advanced industry which totalled only 3,200 lire. It must also be recalled that the office of director was quite generally cumulated with other offices of the same type or other activities. Moreover, the director was usually given extra money, in one way or another, under various titles.

118. The importance of the middle classes in Italy has been quite clearly underlined in a booklet by a renowned Italian economist, which has raised much debate: P. Sylos Labini, *Saggio dulle classi sociali* (Bari, 1974).

Appendix A: Estimates of Private Wealth in Italy, 1874-1938 (milliards of current lire)

Years	Pantaleoni (1)	Bodio (2)	Sensini (3)	Spectator (4)	Coletti (5)
1874					
1875					
1876	44.7				
1877		45.5	45.4	46.2	
1878					
1879					
1880					
1881	49.0				
1882		51.1		51.5	
1883			51.1		
1884					
1885					
1886	54.7				45.7
1887		54.4	54.6		
1888				54.7	
1889					
1890					
1891					
1892			55.0		
1893				50.1	47.2
1894					
1895					
1896					
1897			50.9	54.4	45.7
1898					
1899					
1900					

Appendix A *(contd.)*

Years	Tivaroni	Gini	Degli Espinosa	Retti Marsani	De Vita
	(6)	(7)	(8)	(9)	(10)
1901[a]	60.0			73.6	
1902				74.3	
1903				74.8	
1904				73.7	
1905				78.1	
1906				82.2	
1907				86.8	
1908[b]		80-5		87.4	
1909				89.8	
1910[c]				93.4	
1911				98.8	
1912[d]	74.1			104.0	
1913	74.9			102.9	
1914[e]	100.0	111		107.4	
1915				115.6	
1916				129.5	
1917				154.3	
1918				201.4	
1919				248.1	
1920				333.8	
1921[f]				365.1	
1922				387.9	
1923				406.5	
1924	500.0			458.7	
1925		550		526.2	
1926[g]				544.0	
1927				521.4	
1928[h]	470.0		475	498.5	510
1929				479.5	
1930				460.8	
1931	400.0			433.3	
1932				408.8	
1933				401.5	
1934				407.1	
1935					426.3
1936			539		430.7
1937			621		546.4
1938					566.7

Appendix A *(contd.)*

Notes:

a. For 1901-3 another estimate exists (65 milliards) by F.S. Nitti, *La ricchezza d'Italia* (Naples, 1905).
b. The estimate by L. Princivalle is 61-65 milliards, see *La ricchezza privata in Italia* (Naples, 1909).
c. Estimate by M. Santoro (74.5 milliards) in *L'Italia nei suoi progressi economici dal 1860 al 1910* (Rome, 1911); for 1910-11 and 1913-14 estimates exist by N. Colajanni (80 and 100 milliards, respectively) in 'L'aumento della ricchezza italiana', *Nuova Antologia* (1915).
d. Estimate by C. Gabriel-Wiseman (93.2 milliards) in 'L'agricoltura nell' economia nazionale e sociala dell'Italia', *Nuova Antologia* (1915).
e. Estimate by G. Dettori (95 milliards) in *Lezioni di statistica economica per l'anno 1917/18* (Genoa, 1918).
f. Estimate by U. Pellegrini (353 milliards) in *Il risorgimento economico dell'Italia della constituzione del Regno al 1921* (Milan, 1922).
g. Estimate for 1925-26 by A. Sacerdote (547 milliards) in *Ricchezza e reddito privati in Italia* (Pinerolo, 1928).
h. Estimate by G. Lasorsa (455 milliards) in 'La ricchezza e il reddito privato dell'Italia e delle sue ripartizioni', *L'economia italiana* (1937).

Sources:

1. Pantaleoni, 'Della ricchezza privata in Italia dal 1872 al 1889', *Giornale degli economisti* (August 1890).
2. D. Bodio, *Di alouni indici misuratori del moviemento economico in Italia* (Rome, 1891).
3. G. Sensini, *Le variazioni dello stato economico d'Italia nell'ultimo trentennio del secolo XIX* (Rome, 1904).
4. Spectator, 'Rivista economico finanziaria dell'Italia nel periodo 1885-1901', *Riforma sociale* (1902).
5. F. Coletti, 'La determinazione della durata della generazione ed il calcolo della ricchezza privata in un paese', *Riforma sociale* (1907).
6. J. Tivaroni, 'Contribuzione e reddito dei privati in Italia dalla proclamazione del Regno ai nostri giorni', *Metron* (1926) and 'La pressione tributaria in Italia attraverso il tempo' in *Trattato elementare di statistica* (Milan, 1933), vol. 4.
7. C. Gini, *L'ammontare e la composizione della ricchezza delle nazioni* (Turin, 1914) and *Ricchezza e reddito* (Turin, 1959).
8. A. Degli Espinosa, 'La ricchezza privata degli italiani nel 1928', *Metron* (1929) and 'Il reddito e la ricchezza degli italiani nel 1936-37', *Economia* (1939).
9. S. Retti Marsani, 'Variazioni annuali della ricchezza italiana dal 1901 ai giorni nostri', *La vita economica italiana* (1936 and 1937).
10. A. De Vita, 'La ricchezza privata dell'Italia al 1928 e la sua ripartizione regionale', *La vita economica italiana*, 1933 and 'Nota sulle relazioni nel tempo tra ricchezza privata e delitti contro il patrimonio', *Atti della III riunione della Societa Italiana di Statistica* (Rome, 1941).

Appendix B: Retti Marsani-De Vita Series of Italian Private Wealth, 1901-38, at Constant Prices (1938 prices)

Years	Private wealth		Years	Private wealth	
	Total (milliards)	Per capita (lire)		Total (milliards)	Per capita (lire)
1901	362.5	11,100	1920	411.7	11,400
1902	371.2	11,300	1921	380.8	10,100
1903	357.3	10,900	1922	407.9	10,700
1904	350.4	10,600	1923	429.0	11,100
1905	371.2	11,200	1924	467.7	12,000
1906	383.4	11,500	1925	477.7	12,100
1907	386.4	11,500	1926	457.7	11,500
1908	393.4	11,600	1927	479.9	12,000
1909	415.6	12,200	1928	495.1	12,300
1910	420.8	12,200	1929	468.6	11,500
1911	434.3	12,500	1930	465.1	11,300
1912	453.0	12,900	1931	484.3	11,700
1913	447.3	12,700	1932	469.0	11,300
1914	466.9	12,900	1933	489.5	11,700
1915	469.5	12,800	1934	523.4	12,400
1916	420.4	11,500	1935	540.3	12,700
1917	354.3	9,700	1936	507.7	11,800
1918	331.3	9,300	1937	588.1	13,600
1919	402.1	11,200	1938	566.7	13,000

Sources: See Appendix A; the deflator used has been the cost of living index published by ISTAT, *Il valore della lire dal 1861 al 1965* (Rome, 1966).

4 WEALTH IN AMERICA BEFORE 1865

Edward Pessen

Great wealth has been a significant feature of American life since
before the American Revolution. Nor were American fortunes
minuscule or paltry in comparison to European. Such American
accumulators as John Jacob Astor, Stephen Girard and Peter Chardon
Brooks in the North-east, and the great slave-owning planters in the
South, possessed real and personal property of a magnitude and value
comparable to the estates amassed by the Rothschilds in England and
Gabriel Julien Ouvrard in France before the middle of the nineteenth
century.[1]

Almost all societies produce wealth and wealthy men of sorts. It
is a statistical inevitability that some will have more than others and
come to possess that relative abundance of material things that passes
for wealth in its most marginal sense. In North America, almost from
the time of its colonial beginnings, small but significant numbers of
men and families carved out material fortunes that would have been
appraised anywhere as true riches, affording those who enjoyed them
material comfort and luxury, sumptuous possessions, a corps of
servants and retainers, much leisure time and attractive and expensive
ways of spending or using it.

If the fact comes as somewhat of a surprise if not a shock to
European readers, it is because of the prevalence of persistent myths
attesting to American exceptionalism, in wealth-holding as in other
respects. Alexis de Tocqueville's *Democracy in America*, based on his
brief visit to the country in 1831-32, was the most influential source
in perpetuating the legend that great wealth was non-existent in the
early history of the United States.

Tocqueville's thesis was a marvel of logic and internal consistency.
But, as Sainte-Beave, John Stuart Mill and even his colleague and
collaborator Gustave Beaumont observed, Tocqueville was indifferent
if not oblivious to mere mundane facts about the actual United States
of the antebellum era. Given the equality of material condition that
ostensibly prevailed almost everywhere in the America of his
imaginative devising, it followed that no true fortunes could emerge:
American riches were thus riches only in a manner of speaking. Since
Tocqueville's *démocratie* was a kaleidoscopic society ruled by flux,

those who did manage to come into inordinate wealth did not long enjoy the possession of it. Riches in the United States were supposedly limited in extent and ephemeral in duration. The American 'rich' had only yesterday been poor and were likely to return to that dismal state in the near future. And in view of the insecurity attendant on the possession of wealth in America, Tocqueville found it altogether unsurprising that wealth there commanded what he said was slight prestige and influence. In the land where Tocqueville's 'tyranny of the masses' purportedly obtained, men of wealth were reduced to political impotence.[2] Scholars over the past decade have adduced substantial evidence that undermines, if it does not demolish entirely, every part of Tocqueville's fragile and empirically anaemic intellectual structure.[3]

Advised by several of his American informants that the law of entail and primogeniture no longer operated in the United States, Tocqueville leaped to the erroneous conclusion that a great equalisation of estates and possessions had therefore ensued. As a matter of fact, entail and primogeniture had lost what little force they ever had in this society a century prior to Tocqueville's arrival. Their demise owed far less to a spirit of confiscation or social democracy than it did to the lack of necessity for traditional signeurial encumbrances in a nation blessed with treasures of untapped land resources and at first cursed with insufficient labour to exploit this vast acreage.[4]

Outmoded feudal institutions were not needed by the great landowners of the Chesapeake Bay colonies, South Carolina and the Hudson River valley in order to carve out and maintain within their families huge estates of baronial dimension. The laws of private property and inheritance, combined with the predominant influence of socially and economically elite families over early American politics, sufficed to ensure that wealth earlier amassed by family founders would not easily be dissipated by their heirs in later generations. This is not to say that all of the fiefdoms pressed on early grantees remained intact within their own families over the course of the next two centuries. It is only to say that the Tocquevillean notions of a nineteenth-century America marked by a rough equality of condition and therefore by the absence of true wealth are not borne out by the historical evidence.

A dramatic inequality of condition long antedated Tocqueville's visit to America. If the overwhelming preponderance of the colonial population were small farmers, who eked out a living in the subsistence agricultural regions of the back country and who experienced, at best, a modest prosperity, in the commercial coastal areas, indentured

servants, itinerant labourers, town mechanics and black slaves, men of
families the value of whose possessions ranged from nothing at all to
most modest sums, a small number of men and families, in contrast,
commanded wealth of an altogether different sort. In the century
prior to the American Revolution, colonies in every geographical
section of British North America witnessed the emergence of families
possessed of substantial real and personal property.

No one in America possessed larger estates than those that the
Crown granted the Hudson River valley manor lords in New York
province at the end of the seventeenth century and the beginning of
the eighteenth. Accompanied by signeurial lordship privileges, the
patents of Rensselaerswyck, Livingston and Cortlandt manors and
Philipsburgh covered approximately 1.5 million acres. The non-
manorial estates of the Bayard, DeLancey, DePeyster, Heathcote,
Johnson, Morris, Nicoll, Pell, Rapelye, Remsen, Schuyler, Smith,
Stuyvesant and Beekman families, each of them embracing 50,000
acres or more, provided their owners with wealth and a style of living
that differed hardly at all from the lifestyle of the manorial grantees.[5]
North Carolina was neither a very wealthy colony nor one known for
the kind of wealthy class that played so important a part in Virginia
to its north and South Carolina to the south. Yet in the early decades
of the eighteenth century men like the Earl Granville and other
proprietors and merchants each controlled several hundred thousand
acres in the province. As for the Virginia patriciate, it has been
estimated that by the time of the Revolution the wealthiest 100 were
each worth at least £10,000 and owned about 100 slaves. While heroic
land accumulators like Robert Beverly, William Byrd and King Carter
each controlled hundreds of thousands of acres, most of the 'first
families' of Virginia owned more modest estates of about 10,000 acres
in the Tidewater counties in the Potomac and James River valleys.[6]

Colonial wealth was based on diverse sources, by no means confined
to land alone. True, land, as Leonard Labaree has observed, 'was the
fundamental source of wealth in provincial America and the produce
of the land the principal origin of income'.[7] Yet great landowners in
all geographical sections of the North American colonies were by the
mid-eighteenth century typically involved in additional economic
affairs. For that matter landed wealth was exploited in a variety of
ways. New York's land magnates, as Sung Bok Kim has pointed out,
were not a homogeneous group, since some were interested in land for
speculative purposes, others would combine promotion with
speculation, while a third group 'regarded the land primarily as a source

for commercial development'.[8] Aubrey Land has drawn attention to
great planters in the Chesapeake region who were involved in 'industrial
enterprises that ranged from relatively simple products such as
coperage to complex and costly establishments like ironworks'. Nor
was commercial wealth lacking in interest to them. For, as Jackson
Turner Main has shown, 'many Charlestonians were merchant-planters
and the combination was common throughout the South'.[9] The
'combination' was by no means confined to the South. Large northern
landowners were 'basically commercial in orientation', their land
operations 'more or less subsidiary to their mercantile activities'. Great
New England merchants, on the other hand, who accumulated
fortunes in domestic and overseas trading and shipbuilding,
characteristically put much of their capital into land, whether for
speculation or other purposes.[10]

    Modern quantitative studies have gone beyond impressionism to
reveal the inordinate proportion of their communities' wealth that was
owned by the wealthy class in British North America before the
Revolution. Relying on such sources as wills, probate inventories, and
above all on tax assessment data, scholars have disclosed not only the
dimensions of early American fortunes and the numbers of persons
commanding true wealth, but the comparative portions of wealth
controlled by the rich and other elements in society. The wealth
distributions were not all of a piece, their patterns shaped largely by
the community's level of economic advance and sophistication.
Backwater subsistence areas divided what little wealth they had fairly
equally. Commercial farming areas and cities and towns from early in
the seventeenth century onwards produced more skewed distributions.
Whatever their precise nature, however, American communities without
exception witnessed increasing concentration or maldistribution of
wealth with the passage of time.

    In Boston, for example, at the time of the Glorious Revolution in
England the richest one per cent of the community held 10 per cent
and the richest 10 per cent owned about 40 per cent of the wealth,
while the poorest 50 per cent of the population controlled slightly
more than 10 per cent of the property. Almost a century later, just
before the American Revolution, the upper one per cent had doubled
their portion, while the wealthiest 10 per cent now controlled almost
60 per cent of the wealth. Similar trends have been revealed for Chester
County, Pennsylvania, Philadelphia, rural and tidewater Maryland and
other communities in colonial America, with an increase both in the
share of wealth owned by top wealth-holders and in the proportion of

the population without property.[11]

At a time, the 1770s, when a fortune of no more than £5,000 and an income one-tenth as great enabled one, in Jackson Main's phrase, to buy what he chose, to furnish lavishly an elegant home maintained by a corps of servants, several thousand Americans had no difficulty in living in such style. Those baronial estates ranging from many tens of thousands to hundreds of thousands of acres, included land the value of which was more than £6 per acre. Great merchants, such as William Bingham and Thomas Willing in Philadelphia and others like them in the other commercial centres of the North-east, matched the grandees of Maryland, Virginia and South Carolina in the opulence of their lifestyles.

One explanation of the size of the greatest American fortunes by the late eighteenth century is that they were accumulated over the course of generations. Only a handful of the 100 wealthiest Virginians, for example, were the 'self-made men' of American legend, with more than 90 per cent of them having inherited the bulk of their large estates from parents and grandparents before them.[12] The absence of primogeniture and entail by no means deflected the course of increasing wealth concentration. More modest holdings, on the other hand, were amassed by 'new men' in impressive numbers during the era. That perhaps one-third of small merchants in some cities had been born to modest agricultural and artisan families testified to a high rate of upward economic mobility in late-eighteenth-century America. It did not mean that great wealth or true riches were easily attained by those not born to it.

Wealth in colonial America conferred great influence and political power as well as lofty social status on those who possessed it. At a time when almost all means of obtaining riches, including smuggling and land speculation, were equally honorific, the hierarchy of social prestige was almost identical with the hierarchy of property-holding. The great landowners and merchants and the professionals who served them were precisely the 'better sort' who alone composed the society's upper crust and by their endogamous marriages confined it to their own families. These were the men who in the South sat as vestrymen, controlling their Anglican parishes, in New England engrossed influence in their Congregationalist churches, and everywhere were alone designated 'gentleman' or 'esquire'. As for the political influence and power of the rich during the era, at no time since has it been so complete or so direct.

From the beginnings of formal government in British North America, offices at whatever level were almost invariably occupied by men of property and standing. As a modern historian has observed, there was an expectation in seventeenth-century New England that the very rich would be very active in government.[13] The expectation was largely realised, as was its corollary, that political offices would be controlled by the affluent. This is not to say that such modest posts as town selectmen were filled by truly rich men. It is rather to say that even the most insignificant positions were held, as in seventeenth-century Connecticut, by men from 'old families notable for piety, public service, wealth, and familiarity with power'. In an era when power, wealth and social status were closely linked, 'lesser men were expected to stay out of government', with men of small means and insignificant background not expected to become even selectmen.[14] Early New England fulfilled the intention that John Winthrop had imputed to God, that 'in all times some must be rich, some poor', with the former 'highe and eminent in power and dignitie', the latter 'meane and in subjection'. As Bernard Bailyn concludes, 'riches, dignity, and power were properly placed in apposition, they pertained to the same individual', in New England life as in Winthrop's thought. And the same patterns prevailed in the middle and southern as in the New England colonies. Political office in early Pennsylvania was occupied by the social and economic elite or by those 'the leading men saw fit to propose'. In early Virginia, too, low office, like high, was the preserve of the 'leading men of the country', as was true as well in Maryland and the Carolinas.[15]

What John R. Pole has called the oligarchic nature of colonial politics in the seventeenth century was not diminished during the eighteenth. In Labaree's pithy summary, in almost every colony a small, wealthy ruling class 'dominated the local political machinery [and] filled all or nearly all the important local offices'. Some scholars have recently discovered that the colonial suffrage was far more widespread than had earlier been believed. Smallholdings were sufficiently pervasive to permit something close to one-half of the white male adults to meet the era's property requirements for voting. As Jack P. Greene has wryly observed, that the colonial 'franchise was considerably wider than had previously been supposed [only] demonstrated that the predominance of the upper classes in politics did not depend upon a restricted franchise'. For all their right to vote, men of modest property were in effect priced out of active participation in politics by the high costs of such involvement. Then, as later, political campaigning was expensive, particularly in an era

which expected competitors for office to reach into their own and
their backers' pockets and spend lavishly on liquid refreshments and
other treats for their constituencies.[16] In eighteenth-century New
York, Henry Beekman began to ply his tenant voters with great
quantities of food and drink two days before the polls opened, while
in Albany as much as £40 was sometimes required to buy the support
of a voter. In the presence of such practices it is not surprising that
rich men monopolised political office. Ingrained habits of deference
also explain the acceptance by the 'common sort' of rule by their social
and economic superiors. For whatever the reasons, provincial or
colonywide as well as local, political offices, elective and appointive,
were the private preserve of large property-owners.

Before the American Revolution most of the colonies were under
the direct control of the Crown, with the others controlled either by
corporations, as was Rhode Island, or great proprietors, as were
Pennsylvania and Maryland. Whether royal, corporate or proprietary,
all had essentially the same form of government: a governor assisted
by a council combining the executive and judicial powers and an
assembly controlling most legislative authority, subject to the veto
power wielded both by the provincial governor and the Crown.
Governors may in some instances have been of families whose stars
were fading in England, but without exception they had lustre enough
to shine at least as brightly as did any others in the colonial social
firmament. As for the councils, 'a list of all the men who served on the
various colonial councils for the one hundred years before the
Revolution would certainly include ninety per cent of the names of
the great "first families" of colonial America'.[17] Nor were the
assemblies markedly less elitist in their make-up, for all their character
as the sole provincial body in any sense representative of local as
against British interests. Jackson Main estimates that in the mid-
eighteenth century less than one-fifth of the membership of the six
colonial assemblies he examined were the farmers and artisans who
constituted the bulk of their populations, with the others prestigious
merchants, lawyers and large landowners. The latter 'economic elite'
furnished at least 85 per cent of the assemblies.[18]

Not only were the rich and prestigious numerically predominant in
colonial legislatures. As Michael Zuckerman, Robert Zemsky,
J.R. Daniell and others have shown, small groups, in some cases single
individuals, were by their exalted prestige able to command an
influence that equalled if it did not surpass the influence of dozens of
other members, themselves of the upper crust.[19] These inordinately

influential men were invariably of families whose social prestige was matched by their great wealth.

Since, in Jack Greene's phrase, colonial politics everywhere were 'primarily elitist in nature', conflicts when they did arise in the assemblies, represented something other than discontent among the lower classes. Instead of following class lines, political divisions revolved around the ambitions of rival upper-class factions, with the popular interest drawn in only to support one or the other elite clique.[20]

Conservative and pluralist political scientists quite rightly point out that the social and economic characteristics of office-holders do not necessarily establish either their political ideologies or their pattern of public behaviour. It is conceivable that officials and legislators of a particular social background would not necessarily legislate in the interests of their class. The evidence for colonial America offers slight comfort to this theory. If the men who controlled all important offices were almost without exception of a single social and economic grouping, their public performance betrayed slight concern for the needs and interest of other groupings. In numerous instances, as most notably perhaps in New Hampshire, New York and Virginia, prominent men 'used their political power to get lucrative public offices and extensive amounts of land'. In Labaree's phrase, political activity 'was a very profitable occupation' to those on the 'inside'. The political pre-eminence of the great families enabled them to 'exploit their position for the benefit of their own class'. Even in North Carolina, regarded by many as the most socially democratic of the colonies, when during the 1760s the insurgent Regulator movement protested against the 'high and inequitable tax burden', the 'large landed and mercantile elements' in control of the colony succeeded in having the assembly deflect any movement for 'real reform of the tax structure'.[21]

As was true too of the Parliament of the mother country, perhaps more significant than the practice of some individuals to use office in their own narrow, private and family interest was the prevalent pattern by which the uncommonly wealthy and prestigious men who controlled colonial politics clearly took it as axiomatic that the primary purpose of political power was to maintain and enhance the position in society of those who best thrived within it.

It is a fair summary that over the course of the colonial era several thousand families, constituting less than one per cent of the American population, had amassed great riches based on diverse sources, lofty social prestige and a near monopoly of influence and power which they appear to have regarded both as a fitting recognition of their possessions and eminence and as a means of promoting their own personal interests and those of their class.

The last quarter of the eighteenth century witnessed cataclysmic political changes as first the colonies established their independence as a new nation and then, in 1787-88, after several years of subordinating national power to the power of the states, created a brilliant and flexible new federal system that significantly shifted the balance.

For a long time the American Revolution was evaluated by American historians as purely and simply a war for independence, lacking in the class conflicts that characterised revolutions elsewhere. True, the Americans were divided, with 'patriots' taking drastic measures against the persons and property of loyalists. But if estates were confiscated, it was not because they were the property of the rich but because they were the property of Tories or loyalists. Then, slightly more than a half century ago, such 'progressive' historians as Carl L. Becker, J. Franklin Jameson and Arthur M. Schlesinger offered a new and increasingly influential interpretation, highlighting the importance of social tensions and discords, a jockeying for political control between divergent classes, and sweeping social and humanitarian reforms that ostensibly reflected the growing influence of the lower orders and the have-nots in revolutionary America.[22] If modern historians have been retreating from the progressive version of revolutionary America, it is because the evidence sustaining it remains fragmentary and unimpressive.

The point is not that late-colonial American society was lacking in internal strains. It is rather that the removal of British rule over the colonies not only did not topple the colonial ruling classes from their former position of wealth and eminence, but that the struggle was largely led by members of those classes. George Washington, Thomas Jefferson, James Madison, Alexander Hamilton, John Adams and John Hancock were men of the upper crust, if not by birth then by marriage and by their own achievement. Adams's father may have been a resident of the small community of Braintree, Massachusetts, but he was universally regarded as its second leading citizen, in part no doubt because of his marriage into the wealthy and prestigious Boylston family.

Inevitably the Revolution did create rich economic openings for new men. Robert Morris, the near financial dictator of America during the late years of the war, was one of many who amassed fortunes out privateering and the other opportunities times of crisis open up to the bold and the able. But, as Robert East pointed out a generation ago, Tory losses apart, old fortunes for the most part remained intact and swelled, supplemented by a sprinkling of new fortunes. Former Tory lands accumulated not so much in the hands of small purchasers as in the hands of wealthy speculators. For that matter, the great leaders of the revolutionary cause — the Founding Fathers — were themselves not above engaging in what the historian Thomas P. Abernethy called 'rapacious speculation'.[23]

Discarding their status as colonial provinces under a foreign monarchy, the newly independent states wrote indubitably liberal state constitutions and formed a republican system under the first national charter, the Articles of Confederation. But, liberating as all this no doubt was, it did not deflect the trend toward increasing concentration of wealth that continued to operate, impervious to the great international strains that shook the Empire. Interestingly, at the very moment that the Continental Congress proclaimed its egalitarian ideals out of a 'decent respect to the opinions of mankind', it struck down an attack on slavery and slave property in the original draft of the Declaration of Independence out of what Jefferson later described as its unwillingness to offend slave-owners in the South and slave-traders elsewhere. One state alone, Pennsylvania, for a while toyed with the idea of criticising large accumulations of property for their pernicious political effects, in the preamble to its state constitution, but ultimately it thought better of the idea.

In writing about the 'critical period' that followed the end of the fighting, Merrill Jensen has depicted an America in which democratic friends of debtors and small property-owners were temporarily ascendant.[24] Fear of their increasing domination ostensibly led the friends of private property and social order to champion a political change that would remove power from state governments too sympathetic to the interests of have-nots and place it instead in the hands of a central government more attuned to the interests of the haves. The suggestion in Jensen's thesis that riches or private property were in jeopardy in post-war America is misleading. Laws congenial to debtors were passed in Rhode Island, while for a moment in Massachusetts Daniel Shays and his 'embattled farmers' threatened to take over the state capital. But debtors, as Joseph Dorfman has shown, were by no means confined to society's have-nots. As for the small band of Shaysites, they were easily suppressed, their chief historical significance turning out to be not the serious challenge they posed to

the powers that were, for they posed no such challenge, but the
pretext their pathetic movement provided the friends of a more
powerful central government everywhere for ditching the Articles of
Confederation.

The new federal constitution that was framed in 1787 and took
effect the following year was described by Charles A. Beard two
generations ago as a superb economic document created above all
by the great personalty and slave-owning interests of the nation in
order to secure their immediate and long-range economic interests.[25]
Beard's many detractors have effectively demolished the notion that
the new charter of government was the product of simple economic
determinism. The fact remains that private wealth was now placed on
a surer foundation than ever before in the youthful nation's history.
And the men who at first controlled political power under the new
charter, above all Alexander Hamilton, the Secretary of the Treasury
in Washington's administrations, took pains to cement a close alliance
between national government and the great propertied classes through
fiscal, banking and tariff policies that even Hamilton's critics
subsequently found very difficult to dismantle. The new federal
judiciary, and for that matter most state judiciaries, proved sympathetic
to the interests of private property and hostile to attempts by
government to impair property rights.

At the turn of the century the Jeffersonian party that took
command of the state, like the Jacksonians who followed them a
generation later, had a reputation for radicalism that derived largely
from their adoption of a style of public rhetoric that seemed to be
faintly hostile to aggregates of great wealth. Appearances were
deceiving. The men who led the major parties that monopolised
politics and office in the years before the Civil War were cut of the
same inordinately prestigious and economically privileged cloth and
they did nothing likely to jeopardise great wealth-holdings.

Manuscript census and tax assessment data, wills and probated
inventories of estates reveal that the dimensions of American private
fortunes expanded drastically during the first half of the nineteenth
century. The upsurge resulted from a series of economic and
technological changes that created opportunities above all for the men
and families who alone had sufficient capital to take advantage of these
opportunities. What George R. Taylor has called a 'transportation
revolution' opened new markets at home and abroad for the producers
and the merchants who shipped American agricultural and industrial
products. The characteristic pattern was one in which men who had

inherited substantial property enlarged their holdings through diverse investments. Transportation projects, public and private banking, marine and general insurance, importing and exporting, purchase or speculation in western lands and urban lots, the new factories springing up at first primarily in New England and the North-east, were among the economic activities that attracted the investment dollars of American — and European — investors. The local directories that are so useful to antebellum historians, for listing the male heads of families in pre-Civil War communities and alongside their names their 'occupations', are seriously misleading in suggesting that the era's capitalists made their wealth primarily through one or another kind of economic activity. The private papers of many hundreds of the greatest accumulators reveal that typically each of them engaged in various forms of investment simultaneously.[26]

The fabled John Jacob Astor, known for his great western fur empire as for the shipping fleet he controlled, in fact made greater profits out of his investments in New York City lots than from any other source.[27] The retired merchant Philip Hone's private diary, two dozen folio volumes filled with invaluable detailed information on the personal and social life as well as the myriad economic pursuits of Hone himself and the hundreds of great merchants and wealth-holders who constituted his circle, reveals the great variety of economic involvements that took up the time and money of Hone and his friends.[28]

Historians, the present author included, had earlier alluded to the alleged conflict of interests between different types of wealth, particularly commercial and industrial. In view of the actual versatility of antebellum capitalists, with factory investment in the era heavily dependent on money made in trade and finance, it now appears that these divergences have been overdrawn. While such Massachusetts families as the Appletons and Lawrences came to be increasingly sensitive to their manufacturing involvements, becoming for example ever more sympathetic to a protective tariff, they remained close, economically as well as socially, with their fellows among the New England merchant class who, unlike them, did little more than dabble in factory investment. For that matter, the ties between these 'lords of the loom' and their fellow merchants in the North extended to the great cotton-planters of the South. Fissures in the national political realm caused above all by the issue of slavery and its extension to the territories conquered in the Mexican War, were not paralleled by like splits among the wealth-holding classes in the sections. The southern

elite consorted socially and intermarried with the great families
of the North, precisely as in affairs of the market their mutual
interdependence appears if anything to have grown greater.

The fortunes of antebellum America's greatest wealth-holders were
ample by any standard. In the North-east the scope of the greatest
holdings is only hinted at by the tax assessment data that provide the
best evidence on the wealth owned by individuals. The assessments
have a number of weaknesses, the chief one being their undervaluation
of the estates, particularly the personal estates, of wealthy men.[29] Tax
officials bemoaned the practice of great merchants, men known to be
owners of vast real estate holdings and substantial shareholders in banks
and insurance companies, coolly to swear that they possessed no
personal wealth whatever. Who could gainsay them in view of the
incorporeality, and the impossibility of tracking down, this form of
wealth? Boston's property-owners may have been unusual in disclosing
to assessors much personal wealth, yet officials even in that highly
moral city were rightly convinced that property there was assessed
substantially below its market value. The consoling feature of the sums
disclosed by the tax records is that they are solid bedrock. Charles
Hoyt in 1841 was worth at least the $242,226 Brooklyn's assessors
of his real property said he was; Hezekiah B. Pierrepont was worth at
least the $629,000 that his many lots were assessed for – although, if
the poor chap could be believed, he had not a penny in liquid assets.

Even when the assessed valuations are taken at face value, New
York City at the time of Tocqueville's visit had about 100 persons
each worth $100,000 or more, while Boston had 75 worth at least that
sum. A decade later New York City's tax data disclosed that John
Jacob Astor and Peter G. Stuyvesant were millionaires, while 300 other
persons were each $100,000 or more. Boston by then had 150
individuals worth the latter sum, in addition to Peter Chardon Brooks,
the millionaire. While Philadelphia's assessments, in not distinguishing
between owners and users of real property, do not indicate the total
assessed wealth owned by citizens within the city, reliable if indirect
evidence suggests that the proportion of wealthy men in the city was
comparable to the proportions in New York and Boston.

The $100,000 figure that many hundreds of North-easterners were
assessed at may not appear to be an impressive sum. Yet even if one
makes the unrealistic assumption that the assessment figures accurately
recorded the extent of an individual's wealth, the sums in question
were hardly paltry. According to John Jacob Astor's grandson – and he
was in a good position to know – a member of the 'exclusives' in 1850

could have devoted himself entirely to the good life, including leisurely
travel in Europe, on ten thousand a year — in 'dollars not pounds', as
he hastened to add.[30]

The dollar of the 1830s was capable of wondrous things. William E.
Dodge was able to rent a two-storey house on Bleecker Street in New
York City for an annual rental of $300, while one or two hundred
dollars more could pay for an elegant place on 'aristocratic Park Place
among the Motts, Hones, Costers, Haggertys, Austins, Beekmans, and
Hosacks', the *crème de la crème* of New York society. Room and board
at the new Astor House cost $1.50 in 1836, that sum paying for four
meals consisting of 'all the delicacies of the season. . .served in a most
ample manner'. Philip Hone, who was sufficiently demanding a gourmet
to have found the famed Delmonico's Restaurant wanting, thought
the fare at the Astor House capital; he had never seen 'a table better
set out, better provided, or a dinner better cooked'. A wealthy
Philadelphian of mid-century held that $50 'constituted the
millionairism of money aristocracy of those days', since this sum
enabled a man to keep a carriage. According to the socialite Sidney
George Fisher of Philadelphia, his annual income of less than $3,000
gave him 'a comfortable house — servants, a good table — wine — a
horse — books — 'country quarters' — a plentiful wardrobe — the ability
to exercise hospitality', while an additional one thousand would have
enabled him to live like a truly rich man. Since, in the rule of thumb
relied on by modern specialists, a man's income ranges from between
one-fifth to one-third of his wealth, one can understand better why
contemporaries regarded wealth assessed at $100,000 as a great fortune.
And there is good reason to think that men assessed at that figure were
typically worth many times $100,000.

In the absence of income taxes, as well as the presence of a local tax
that characteristically took less than one per cent of what a man
claimed to be worth, assessed wealth of $100,000 made him a
functional millionaire several times over, in terms of modern costs and
prices. His real estate in the local community was undervalued
conservatively by half. Personal estate, regarded by tax authorities and
insiders as equal in value to real, was almost totally masked. Possessions
and investments outside the city were treated by assessors as non-
existent. Not one penny was yielded up to a federal tax bureau that in
modern times appropriates a substantial portion of a rich man's wealth.
In view of the fact, finally, that the dollar of 1840 appeared to be
worth something between a half-dozen and several dozen times as much
as the dollar of the 1970s — depending on the times compared — wealth

that 130 years ago was assessed at $100,000 is the equivalent of a gross
amount between fifty and several hundred times that figure in our own
day.

Even before the end of the eighteenth century Thomas Willing, the
Philadelphia financier, and William Bingham had each accumulated
millions. By a half-century later, hundreds of families in the nation's
north-eastern cities had amassed fortunes of similar magnitude based
on commerce, insurance, finance, shipbuilding, manufactures, land-
holding, real estate speculation and the professions. The resources and
the style of living enjoyed by the Astors, Stuyvesants, Lenoxes and
Whitneys in New York City, the Brookses, Appletons, Greenes, Otises,
Searses and Shaws in Boston, the Girards, Ridgways, Biddles, Shippens
and Whartons in Philadelphia, and the great landed families of the
antebellum South, were very far from scanty and would have been
regarded as substantial wealth anywhere in the world. By almost any
criterion opulent Americans lived lives comparable to those enjoyed
by their English and Continental counterparts and were evidently able
to do so with significantly smaller expenditures of money. (The
$10,000 per annum said by Charles Astor Bristed to be required for
lavish living was evidently from one-third to one-quarter the amount
needed to achieve a similar standard abroad.)

The town houses of David Sears, Nathaniel Prime, William B. Astor,
William Bedlow Crosby, Peter Schermerhorn, Samuel Ward, Harrison
Gray Otis or Henry Brevoort would have been judged as magnificent
anywhere. Squadrons of servants, impressive libraries, elaborate
furniture, sumptuous furnishings, stores of the finest wines and
expensive works of art filled the interiors of the homes of the American
economic elite. In the warm weather months the rich retreated to the
delights of the Rockaways and other ocean resorts, or to the waters of
Saratoga, and they regularly travelled to Havre in ships filled with their
own kind, blessed with lavish accommodations and, in Hone's words,
with 'every day as good a table as the most fastidious gastronome
could desire'. Their lives at home during the workaday year were
enlivened by a constant round of expensive parties, dazzling balls,
extravagant fêtes and excursions, binding more closely together the
leading families both within and between the great cities.

A fashionable marriage, such as the one uniting Charles A. Heckscher
and the daughter of John G. Coster in late 1834, triggered off a round
of balls and parties that left even inveterate pleasure-seekers somewhat
exhausted and a trifle dismayed at their extravagance. The great ball
given by Henry Brevoort on 28 February 1840 excited widespread

attention for its opulence, but much space in Hone's more than
10,000 pages is given over to descriptions of many dozens of smaller-
scale but equally exclusive and splendid affairs. A *fête champêtre* of
unusual elegance, such as that held at Thomas W. Ludlow's villa on the
Hudson, in Phillipsburgh on 26 June 1845, could attract several
hundred of the leading 'judges, lawyers, merchants, men of leisure and
millionaires' of New York City to a 'picnic' adorned with 'every
delicacy', fine band music for outdoors, waltzes, polkas and cotillions
inside the house, the entire scene enlivened by the presence of several
private yachts that circled the private steamer hired for the occasion
by Ludlow to carry his guests to and from the festivities. Theatre,
Italian opera, soirées and musical evenings also occupied the elite.
Fastidious foreign visitors mocked the pretentiousness of the American
elite's highlife, but there could be no denying its expensiveness.

Those who referred to the paltriness of American fortunes doubtless
had European wealth in mind. I have elsewhere argued that vast though
the estates of such great accumulators as Nathan Meyer Rothschild,
Gabriel Julien Ouvrard, the Duke of Bedford, Sir Robert Peel and Lord
Overstone may have been, they appear to have been approximated by
those of the wealthiest Americans. John Jacob Astor's wealth was close
to Rothschild's. Dozens of Americans commanded riches similar to
what has been attributed to Ouvrard and the Barings. For that matter,
Alexander Baring's fortune had been substantially abetted both by his
marriage to William Bingham's eldest daughter and by his purchase of
Bingham's vast Maine properties.

European landed wealth was of course much older than American,
a fact that possibly led contemporaries to question the extent as well
as the vulgarity of the Yankee *nouveaux riches.* Herman Thorn, a
fashionable New Yorker, who, in marrying the niece of William Jauncey,
had also come into much of the latter's fortune, stayed in Paris during
the 1830s. Thorn was said to have 'lived in a style of princely splendor
that eclipsed all rivalry, to the great astonishment of the French, who
failed to comprehend where in America he had acquired such funds'.
In 1836 he was reported 'to have spent $8,000 on a single fancy dress
ball in his Paris home' (actually a splendid palace). According to Philip
Hone, his friend Thorn talked 'about hundreds of thousands with the
air of a man who has been brought up in the midst of gold, silver and
precious stones'. Yet although Thorn was a rich man, there were almost
100 families in New York City alone whose wealth surpassed his. The
notion that antebellum America lacked substantial fortunes is not
borne out by the evidence, primarily because of its faulty assumption

concerning the alleged distribution of 'resources to all the members of the community',[31]

In contrast to Tocqueville, who claimed that what rich Americans there were typically had been born poor, the English visitor J.S. Buckingham believed that 'the greater number' of wealthy Americans had inherited much of their wealth. Detailed evidence on the backgrounds of the rich in the great cities of the North-east and such smaller North-western towns as Detroit and Chicago confirms the accuracy of Buckingham's observation. As was the case with the wealthiest Virginians of two generations earlier, fewer than 10 per cent of the antebellum rich could in any sense have been described as the 'self-made men' Americans liked to think they were.

Nor does the Tocquevillean notion that fortunes in America were insecure, circulating with 'inconceivable rapidity', as they ostensibly passed through the hands of many individuals during their adult careers, fare any better than do his companion ideas that American fortunes were 'scanty' and that those who possessed them had been born poor. A friend of the famous statesman Henry Clay observed that in America, 'money and property among us are constantly changing hands'. Evidence on the alleged rise and fall of fortunes during the lifetimes of the antebellum rich does not substantiate this notion of intragenerational flux. In the short run, as in the long, those who controlled large properties managed to hold on to their wealth. Since the mid-nineteenth-century population had increased substantially, the enlarged ranks of the later rich necessarily had to be filled by many individuals who earlier had not been among the wealthiest one per cent of their communities. Yet these 'newcomers' were almost invariably younger members of rich and prestigious families. The pursuit of wealth during the era was marked not by fluidity but by stability, if not rigidity. Great fortunes earlier accumulated held their own through all manner of vicissitudes, not excluding the financial panics and depressions of the late 1830s and 1840s.[32]

Tocqueville opened his *Democracy in America* with the observation that nothing struck him more forcibly there than the general inequality of condition that he said prevailed. Alas, yet again the facts refute the brilliant visitor. Wealth was more unequally distributed by the mid-nineteenth century than it had been at any earlier period in American history. Census data for the nation as a whole reveal that the wealthiest one per cent of property-owners owned almost one-third, the richest 10 per cent held almost three-quarters, while the poorest 60 per cent were worth only one per cent of the nation's real wealth.[33]

The decades before the Civil War were once widely known as the 'era of the common man' or the 'age of egalitarianism'. For, in addition to the equality of opportunity and condition that were long thought to have prevailed during the period, a 'tyranny of the masses', in Tocqueville's famous phrase, also was thought to obtain. The rich supposedly suffered a vast loss of influence in an increasingly democratic milieu, whose commoners were said to possess a power compared by Tocqueville to that of the Deity over the universe. There can be no question but that the suffrage and opportunities for office-holding were significantly democratised, as religious and property requirements were brushed aside, at least for white males, at all levels of government. Then, no more than now, however, did the democratisation of paper constitutions ensure that the newly enfranchised voters would in fact achieve political power.

It is true that with the passage of time truly wealthy men had retreated from the kind of direct participation in government that had earlier been a feature of American politics. But this change betokened not so much their loss of power as their growing assurance that American politics, whether on the local, state or national level, posed no threat to, and was unlikely to jeopardise, their most vital interests. For all the era's reputation as a time of turbulence and class war, the demagogic rhetoric indulged in by Andrew Jackson and other master politicos was not matched by deeds commensurate with their overheated language. In vetoing the bill calling for the recharter of the Second Bank of the United States, for example, Jackson gave the impression that he was hostile to 'bloated accumulations of wealth'. As a matter of fact, when examined closely, his words promised nothing more than governmental neutrality toward rich and poor alike. His policy was supported by numerous wealthy men for the good reason that it was not uncongenial to their interests. Similarly, the famous Supreme Court decision in the Charles River Bridge case of 1837 gave the unwary the impression that it was an attack on capital, when in fact it urged the casting aside of state-imposed obstacles to the expansion of opportunity for businessmen and investors.

None of this should be occasion for surprise, since the major parties that controlled American politics were led by uncommonly wealthy men sympathetic to the inequitable social arrangements that prevailed in the nation. If they were for the most part themselves not among the nation's rich or super-rich, dozens of detailed studies of their measurable social and economic characteristics disclose that candidates and party managers were inordinately wealthy and of the most prestigious occupations. More importantly, they subscribed to an ideology that differed hardly at all from the social beliefs held by the great wealth-holders themselves.[34]

In antebellum America, as elsewhere, the rich did not constitute a monolithic class of single mind or interest. Their divergent preferences with regard to the innumerable issues that arise in life were paralleled by the lively arguments dividing the major parties in the political arena. Behind the inevitable controversy over the day-to-day issues of politics lay a consensus with regard to the society's fundamental arrangements. The era's mock-political battles, as one modern historian has observed, 'never threatened the distribution in society of property or power'.[35]

Influence and power are of course not manifested in politics alone. This was particularly true for an age in which *laissez faire* came close to being an article of faith. 'All communities are apt to look to government for far too much,' President Martin Van Buren told the nation, at a time when it was reeling from the effects of the worst financial panic and depression it had yet experienced. In local communities, where a host of problems pressed in on governments that were neither willing nor financially capable of dealing with the overcrowding, ethnic tensions, poverty and threats to order that now beset them, private or 'voluntary' associations stepped into the breach to supplement the actions of mayors, councils and aldermen.

Dozens of studies reveal that in all sections of the country government was run 'by the propertied for the propertied'. As for the voluntary associations, they were led invariably by the wealthiest members of their communities and they acted accordingly. I have elsewhere noted that the motives of wealthy altruists were as varied and complex as those of other men. Yet the policies and actions undertaken by the era's diverse benevolent organisations make clear that they took for granted Malthusian and other theorems upholding inequality and holding the poor responsible for their own misery: the causes of social distress, they insisted, lay in the flaws of human character, not in the flaws of capitalistic society. That they sincerely held to such beliefs did not make these ideas any the less comforting to the nation's wealthiest classes. And recent examinations of power in its varied manifestations, economic, social, intellectual and even religious, suggest that the power of the rich in America was not confined to politics.[36]

The outbreak of the great fratricidal war in 1861, a war sought by rich men neither in the North nor the South, indicated clearly that for all the extent and depth of their power in antebellum America their control was a good deal less than complete. Historians long ago shook off Charles Beard's inspired but slightly documented contention that the Civil War was engineered by the political spokesmen of the industrial capitalists in order to subdue the great rival interest ostensibly thwarting their dreams of national hegemony. The state, whatever it may have been in the United States on the eve of the Civil War, was not quite the executive committee of the ruling class. In any case, neither the distribution of wealth nor the allocation of influence among the social orders within American society appears to have shifted significantly during the years of the fighting. Indubitably, the wealth of the South plummeted sharply; this represented not the destruction of great estates but the stark statistical fact that slave wealth simply disappeared from existence. The national expansion of machine industry and the factory system, the near completion of the nation's railway network and the emergence of fortunes of unprecedented dimension, followed the end of the war, but modern historians have discounted earlier suggestions that these vital developments were due primarily to the war's liberating influence.

The way was paved for the great industrialised society of the late nineteenth century primarily by steady technological, financial and commercial developments occurring earlier in American history, rather than by the dramatic war that ended black slavery.

Notes

1. For a discussion of the sources underlying these generalisations, see Edward Pessen, 'The Egalitarian Myth and the American Social Reality: Wealth, Mobility, and Equality in the "Era of the Common Man"', *American Historical Review*, 76 (October 1971), pp.999-1004.

2. Alexis de Tocqueville, *Democracy in America* (2 vols., New York edition, 1954), vol. 1, pp. 53-54; vol. 2, pp. 105, 138, 164, 199, 234, 237, 239, 250, 251, 258 and 263.

3. For a critical discussion of the recently disclosed evidence and the literature in which it appears, see Edward Pessen, *Riches, Class, and Power Before the Civil War* (Lexington, Mass., 1973), and *Jacksonian America: Society, Personality, and Politics* (revised edition, Homewood, 1978), Ch. 5 and the Bibliographical Essay, particularly pp. 399-41.

4. C. Ray Keim, 'Primogeniture and Entail in Colonial Virginia', *William and Mary Quarterly*, 25 (October 1968), pp. 585-86.

5. Sung Bok Kim, *Landlord and Tenant in Colonial New York: Manorial Society, 1664-1775* (Chapel Hill, 1978); Leonard Woods Labaree, *Conservatism in Early American History* (Ithaca, 1972), pp. 16-17.

6. Jackson Turner Main, 'The One Hundred', *William and Mary Quarterly*, 11 (July 1954), pp. 354-84.

7. Labaree, *Conservatism in Early American History*, p. 40.

8. Sung Bok Kim, 'A New Look at the Great Landlords of Eighteenth-century New York', *William and Mary Quarterly*, 27 (October 1970), p. 595.

9. Aubrey C. Land (ed.), *Bases of the Plantation Society* (New York, 1969), p.125; Jackson Turner Main, *The Social Structure of Revolutionary America* (Princeton, 1965), p. 139.

10. Kim, *Landlord and Tenant in Colonial New York*, p. 161.

11. James Henretta, 'Economic Development and Social Structure in Colonial Boston', *William and Mary Quarterly*, 22 (January 1965), pp. 79-92; James T. Lemon and Gary B. Nash, 'The Distribution of Wealth in Eighteenth-century America: A Century of Changes in Chester County, Pennsylvania, 1693-1802', *Journal of Social History*, 2 (Fall 1968), p. 13; Main, *The Social Structure of Revolutionary America*, p. 42; Alice Hanson Jones, 'Wealth Distribution in the American Middle Colonies in the Third Quarter of the Eighteenth Century', paper presented at the annual meeting of the Organization of American Historians, in New Orleans, 17 April 1971.

12. Main, 'The One Hundred'.

13. Sumner Chilton Powell, *'Puritan Village: The Formation of a New England Town* (Middletown, 1963), p. 100.

14. Richard L. Bushman, *From Puritan to Yankee: Character and the Social Order in Connecticut, 1690-1765* (Cambridge, 1967).

15. Gary B. Nash, 'The Framing of Government in Pennsylvania: Ideas in Contact with Reality', *William and Mary Quarterly*, 23 (April 1966), pp. 183-209; and *Quakers and Politics: Pennsylvania, 1681-1726* (Princeton, 1968); Land, *Bases of Plantation Society*.

16. See Charles E. Sydnor, *American Revolutionaries in the Making: Political Practices in Washington's Virginia* (New York, 1965), p. 102.

17. Labaree, *Conservatism in Early American History*, p. 4.

18. Jackson Turner Main, 'Government by the People: The American Revolution and the Democratization of the Legislatures', *William and Mary Quarterly*, 23 (July 1966), pp. 396-97.

19. Robert Zemsky, *Merchants, Farmers, and River Gods: An Essay on Eighteenth-Century American Politics* (Boston, 1971); Michael Zuckerman, *Peaceable Kingdoms: New England Towns in the Eighteenth Century* (New York, 1970); Jere R. Daniell, 'Politics in New Hampshire under Governor Benning Wentworth, 1741-1767', *William and Mary Quarterly*, 23 (January 1966), pp. 76-77.

20. Jack P. Greene, 'Foundations of Political Power in the Virginia House of Burgesses, 1720-1776', *William and Mary Quarterly*, 16 (October 1959), pp. 485-506. See also M. Eugene Sirmans, 'The South Carolina Royal Council, 1720-1763', *William and Mary Quarterly*, 18 (July 1961), pp. 373-92.

21. Daniell, 'Politics in New Hampshire', pp. 85-86; Sydnor, *American Revolutionaries in the Making*, p. 14; Labaree, *Conservatism in Early American History*, pp. 24, 33-34; M.L.M. Kay, 'The Payment of Provincial and Local Taxes in North Carolina, 1748-1771', *William and Mary Quarterly*, 26 (April 1969), p. 240.

22. Carl L. Becker, *The History of Political Parties in the Province of New York, 1760-1776* (Madison, 1909); J. Franklin Jameson, *The American Revolution Considered As a Social Movement* (Princeton, 1926); Arthur M. Schlesinger, *The Colonial Merchants and the American Revolution, 1763-1776* (New York, 1918).

23. Robert A. East, *Business Enterprise in the American Revolutionary Era* (New York, 1938); Harry B. Yoshpe, *The Disposition of Loyalist Estates in the Southern District of the State of New York* (New York, 1939); Thomas Perkins

Abernethy, *Western Lands and the American Revolution* (New York, 1937).

24. Merrill Jensen, *The Articles of Confederation: An Interpretation of the Social-constitutional History of the American Revolution, 1774-1781* (Madison, 1940); Jensen, *The New Nation: A History of the United States During the Confederation, 1781-1789* (New York, 1967).

25. Charles A. Beard, *An Economic Interpretation of the Constitution of the United States* (New York, 1913).

26. See, for example, Pessen, *Riches, Class, and Power Before the Civil War*, Ch. 4, and 'The Egalitarian Myth and the American Social Reality', Appendix, pp. 1031-34.

27. Kenneth W. Porter, *John Jacob Astor, Business Man* (2 vols., New York, 1931).

28. Edward Pessen, 'Philip Hone's Set: The Social World of the New York City Elite in the "Age of Egalitarianism"', *New York Historical Society Quarterly*, 56 (October 1972), pp. 285-308, discusses the reliability and the usefulness of Hone's evidence.

29. For a discussion of the strengths and weaknesses of tax data as a clue to the wealth of individuals, see Edward Pessen, 'The Wealthiest New Yorkers of the Jacksonian Era: A New List', *New York Historical Society Quarterly*, 56 (October 1972), pp. 148-52.

30. Charles Astor Bristed, *The Upper Ten Thousand: Sketches of American Society* (New York, 1852), p. 18. According to Bristed, an upper ten thousand was a great exaggeration, 'for the people so designated are hardly as many hundreds' (p. 271).

31. For detailed documentation of all the assertions bearing on the lifestyle of the rich see Pessen, 'The Egalitarian Myth and the American Social Reality', pp. 995-1004.

32. Pessen, *Riches, Class, and Power Before the Civil War*, pp. 130-50.

33. Lee Soltow, *Men and Wealth in the United States, 1850-1870* (New Haven, 1975). For additional evidence on the maldistribution of wealth in different areas, see Pessen, *Riches, Class, and Power Before the Civil War*; Gavin Wright, *The Political Economy of the Cotton South: Households, Markets, and Wealth in the Nineteenth Century* (New York, 1978); Randolph B. Campbell and Richard G. Lowe, *Wealth and Power in Antebellum Texas* (College Station, 1977).

34. See Pessen, *Jacksonian America: Society, Personality, and Politics*, pp. 171-96.

35. Ronald P. Formisano, *The Birth of Mass Political Parties: Michigan, 1827-1861* (Princeton, 1971), pp. 42-43, 55.

36. Edward Pessen, 'Who Rules America? Power and Politics in the Democratic Era, 1825-1975', *Prologue: Journal of the National Archives*, 9 (Spring 1977), pp. 5-26; and 'Who Has Power in the Democratic Capitalistic Community? Reflections on Antebellum New York City', *New York History*, 58 (April 1977), pp. 129-55.

5 THE GILDED ELITE: AMERICAN MULTIMILLIONAIRES, 1865 TO THE PRESENT

Frederic Cople Jaher

The Greek historian Herodotus and the *New Yorker* cartoonist Peter
Arno had a common interest. The chronicler of Midas and Croesus and
the satirist of Park Avenue millionaires bear witness to Western
society's protracted fascination with the very rich. This chapter deals
with the wealthiest Americans during the period when the United
States moved from youthful to mature capitalism and then into the
so-called post-industrial age where leisure and consumption bid to
replace work and production as reigning social values. The investigation
of the great fortunes and their creators and inheritors focuses on the
individual, the family, the different enclaves within the highest strata
of affluence, and the super-rich as an entity and a subgroup of society.
The development of characteristic multimillionaire types and their
illustration through representational and suggestive evidence convey
the varieties in lifestyle, outlook and personality that are the subjects
of the first and last parts of this study. The middle sections, dealing
with the sources and forms of wealth and presenting a collective trait
profile of the rich, required a more systematic analysis through
statistical tables. Underlying the impressionistic and systematic
approaches is the essential element of historical studies, the impact of
changes over time on the behaviour of the multimillionaires.

Psychological Typology

Psychologists trace the compulsive quest for money, symbol of and
means to the ownership and control of esteemed and scarce resources,
to interrelated desires for self-regard and nurturance. If these needs are
not fulfilled by love and affection or if cultural conditioning identifies
self-worth with successful contention for goods, services, prestige and
dominance, then defences may emerge that preclude self-affirmation
through healthier channels. Failure to achieve personal acceptance may
thus lead to the pursuit of external goals, often in competition with
and at the expense of others. Possessions and acquisitions, fame,
fortune and influence, then, become the essence of the self and a
substitute for interpersonal commitments. Those who take this route
embark on a journey without rest or end, on a mission in which their

189

sense of worth depends on their latest triumph and may be forfeited by their last defeat.

Single-minded pursuit of money, or the things it buys, stems from attempts to overcome feelings of loss and weakness that arise from withheld or conditional parental love. Freudians even claim that compulsive money-makers are 'anal types' whose stunted emotional growth drives them to hoard cash, profits or goods. Greedy, frugal, introverted, repressed, and distrustful of themselves and others, they become calculating and controlling in their relationships. Affluence makes acquisitive types independent from other human beings at the cost of overdependence upon material things; consequently they never attain autonomy. Wealth-gathering permits no rest because its ceiling is limitless, and poor judgements, high living, and bad luck or other uncontrollable forces may destroy a fortune.

The dehumanisation involved in gaining entry into the economic elite results from the necessity to exploit others as well as to deny and manipulate the self. Great wealth is not spontaneously generated – when Jay Gould, J.P. Morgan, Andrew Carnegie and John D. Rockefeller called the tune, someone else paid the piper. Depriving competitors, employees, investors and the public did not necessarily evoke guilt in the tycoons. What they did unto others, however, made them worry what others, if they had the chance, might do unto them. This saturnine expectation reflected a realistic assessment of the prevalent savagery in business conduct and reinforced the combative cynicism that brought them pre-eminence in that Hobbesian world. Sound judgement dictated that the tactics and qualities vital to commercial success were equally necessary to stay on top. Conquests and riches, therefore, did not generally relax their vigilance, curtail their efforts or warm their hearts. Indeed, they raised yet another barrier to human contact, and intensified self-alienation. Having won their fortunes, the accumulators could now brood over whether they were valued for themselves or their gains. This anxiety doubtless encouraged the monied elite to seek companionship (and frequently to find spouses for their children) among their peers, who presumably would not be drawn to them solely to share their possessions. Until they acquired affluence, self-made multimillionaires were spared the awareness that the hounds might become the hares. Their heirs, however, from childhood lived with the possibility that people sought them not for what they were but for what they had.[1]

It may be objected that this psychological model of the multimillionaire magnate focuses too narrowly upon money-making, thus excluding from consideration other important incentives and aims. The urge for power and status, for example, rivalled pecuniary ambition in motivating the builders of America's largest fortunes. In the modern capitalist culture, however, the acquisitive personality embraces these aspirations. An impoverished emotional life induces compulsive desires for authority and celebrity as well as money. Recognition, wealth and dominance are simply overlapping, reinforcing and mutually facilitating objectives for acquisitive types.

The founders of gigantic fortunes were burdened with another anxiety when they contemplated what might happen to their accomplishments after they left the scene. Death represents the ultimate challenge to self-identity, and many try to avoid this confrontation by seeking immortality through their offspring. The accumulators worried that gains made and traits honed in contests for possessions, place and power could not be perpetuated in an atmosphere of unearned opulence.

If the accumulation of wealth generates emotional strains, its inheritance does not create carefree individuals. The progeny of the rich laboured under a parentally imposed obligation to adopt the attributes and continue the accomplishments of the previous generation. As models, the fortune-hunters created staggering problems for their children. Could they live up to the expectations and match the attainments of such predominant figures? Coming to maturity at a time when the deeds of their fathers fell into disfavour should they even aspire to emulate the idols of the acquisitive society? If they continued the paternal pattern were they betraying themselves and exploiting the public? If they lived differently were they betraying their fathers or fleeing family and social responsibility because they were pale replicas of titanic progenitors?

The frustrations involved in living up to the standards set by the great American capitalists were compounded by the drawbacks of the acquisitive personality and Victorian patriarchy. Fathers dedicated to wordly success and money-making were often too busy or incapable of nurturance and intimacy. Deprived of warmth and affection in their own childhoods, they had difficulty in giving love and support to their sons and daughters. Marital friction and the preoccupation of many rich wives with society matters intensified parental remoteness and neglect. The authoritarian urge and aloof stance legitimised in the Victorian patriarch role, and the interposition in upper-class households of servants and governesses, widened the distance between the nursery and the den or drawing-room. The custom of sending youths to elite boarding-schools raised yet another barrier to intimacy. Tensions in the family generated guilt and conflicts on all sides and often led to a repressive discipline that might stifle the traits which fathers tried to encourage, or to an equally abortive indulgence of the younger generation in idleness and luxury which proved self-defeating to the elders and self-destructive to their children.

Public resentment toward inherited wealth increased the agony of self-doubt and intergenerational friction. Bequeathed fortunes attracted more widespread and uncompromising opposition than did the spoils of the robber barons. The tainted treasures of the tycoons had at least been amassed through their own efforts. Hostile critics sometimes conceded that the multimillionaire moguls enhanced the economy and affirmed the American Dream of 'making it'. These redeeming features could not be discovered in the richly born. Indeed, the emergence of coupon-clippers and rentiers contradicted capitalist norms and republican ideals.

Market-place realities, capitalist canons and social sanctions imposed a relatively uniform behaviour pattern upon the entrepreneurial originators of the gigantic American fortunes. Their legatees, subject to the conflicting impulses of imitation and independence, the fluctuating reputations of their forebears, and the disapprobation of derived affluence, displayed no such cohesion. Some followed ancestral lifestyles and careers. Others retained the values of the older generation but chose other spheres of action. A large number, however, fled individual achievement or responsibility and damaged themselves and their fortunes through extravagance, drinking, drug addiction, promiscuity and disastrous marriage. Many, in fact, travelled productive and destructive routes, assuming different roles or going through various stages, in a lifelong search for inner peace or basic survival.[2]

The acquisitive personality is not a recent phenomenon. Down through the ages traders, conquerors, courtiers, priests, pirates, bandits, nobles and soldiers schemed, fought and flattered for money, goods, place and power. Modern capitalism did not invent the psychological sources of its triumphs, but it rationalised these impulses and focused them more exclusively upon monetary and business achievement. Lacking feudal traditions and an established church, and without a peasantry, aristocracy or radical group with a pre- or anti-entrepreneurial vision, the United States achieved the purest type of acquisitive society. The quintessence of capitalism, by 1900 America had the highest per capita standard of living, the most advanced and powerful national economy, and the largest number of multimillionaires.

Capitalism is the macrocosmic equivalent of the acquisitive individual. It transposes into public virtues the inner drives of this personality type: Thrift and self-denial become the basis for capital formation, diligence leads to productivity, interpersonal calculation is rational behaviour, compulsive pecuniary ambition is transformed into the profit motive, possessiveness is determination and aggression is leadership. The profit margin is the 'bottom line' in the ledger and wealth the ultimate standard of personal excellence.

Even in the United States, however, the terrain of the psyche extends far beyond the boundaries of the market place. Consequently, affluence and its associated satisfactions do not dispel the storms and shadows in the interior landscape. In fact, capitalism rationalises the pursuit of wealth in ways that heighten ego anxiety. Accumulation is linked with spiritual righteousness and expenditure with social responsibility. Money-making signifies obedience to the grim deities of duty, service, striving, self-improvement, thrift and hard work. Incessant labour in a chosen commercial calling, and self-denial in order to devote energy and pecuniary surplus to commercial expansion or philanthropic endeavour, were the rigorous conditions, joyless compulsions and uncompromising ideals imposed upon, if not wholly accepted by, multimillionaire magnates.[3]

The virtues of wealth never received greater acclaim than in the heroic age of American capitalism. Between the Civil and First World Wars the captains of industry and finance seemed to confirm the capitalist creed. With rare exceptions they were prudent, competitive and industrious men who demonstrated supreme skill and dedication in the entrepreneurial calling. Most of the leviathan fortunes belonged to these business chieftains, a testament to the alleged equity of free enterprise. Monumental wealth was widely considered a just reward for those presumed responsible for the United States becoming the richest and mightiest nation. Many tycoons rose from humble beginnings and a few became celebrated as generous philanthropists. These circumstances offered further evidence for the identification of massive personal wealth with national power and prosperity, public service and individual achievement. Immense fortunes, especially when self-made seemed to validate the political as well as the economic system. A democratic society ensured equality of opportunity, thus enabling virtuous, talented and useful citizens to assume leadership, assure the public good and receive merited rewards.

Individual commercial triumphs, monetary accumulations and publicity mark the heroic stage of capitalism. The robber barons achieved commercial pre-eminence and accumulated enormous fortunes by prudently husbanding their resources and frugally reinvesting their surpluses. Conspicuous consumption, despite the anxieties of the acquisitive personality and the sanctions of the capitalist ethic, also reached elephantine proportions. Now the rich magnates, sometimes of their own volition, but more frequently prompted by their wives and children, engaged in extravagant expenditure. Luxurious living was even more extensive in heirs several generations removed from the progenitors of their seemingly inexhaustible resources. If the emperors of free enterprise were entitled to their gains because of exemplary character and services why should not they, or their spouses and descendants, spend millions on mansions, yachts, liveried servants, furnishings, art, mistresses, marriages and divorces?

Neither industry nor indulgence ultimately gratified the founders or inheritors of the colossal fortunes. During the decades when accumulation, largesse or display attracted unprecedented praise and defence, most multimillionaires endured damaged egos. Nervous breakdowns, family conflicts, alcoholism and suicide intruded the renaissance palaces along New York's Upper Fifth Avenue or Chicago's Near North Side.

Inner wounds were exacerbated by public ambivalence. Accolades and respect mingled with doubt and hostility.[4] For many Americans the very rich embodied the aspirations and validated the virtues of democratic capitalism. Others thought that ruthless tycoons, wanton playboys, pompous dowagers, frivolous heiresses and affluent skinflints had crossed the thin line between thrift and miserliness, pride and arrogance, remuneration and greed, leadership and repression, shrewdness and deceit. Some even argued that the very existence of huge fortunes precluded widespread prosperity, equal opportunity and genuine democracy. For this minority the pursuit of material gain and the free enterprise system impoverished the soul and endangered the republic.[5]

Emotional strains bred by the quest for wealth and public ambivalence about its fulfilment, made multimillionaires feel disquieted and even beleaguered. Progressive reformers, and an even stronger outcry in the Depression and in the 1960s radical upsurge, discredited the pursuit and exhibition of great affluence as socially regressive and personally degrading. The emphasis on family life in the 1950s and early 1960s and the current hedonistic self-preoccupation has further tainted the acquisitive spirit. Crusaders for contradictory goals of domesticity and self-realisation look upon this impulse as a neurotic surrender to joylessness, compulsiveness, rigidity and other dehumanising traits. Finally, the partial displacement of the multimillionaire proprietor by the corporate manager in the realm of business leadership reduced the influence and repute of mammoth fortunes.

Did these developments blunt the acquisitive drive and constrict the accumulation of immense fortunes? The resolution of this issue requires an assessment of the number of rich Americans from 1865 to the present and of the possible changes in the size of the group over this time period.

Determining the number of affluent Americans and the size of their fortunes is a complicated task involving judgements of how to translate ownership of goods into dollars and of how many dollars constitute great wealth. How accurate is the measurement of these assets? How long must they be held? A net worth of one million dollars is the colloquial base-point distinguishing opulence from prosperity. To the multimillionaire this level of wealth barely secures the necessities of life; to nearly everyone else it represents unattainable and virtually unimaginable abundance.

Body counts of the fabulously rich first appeared in the late 1880s when society queens and robber barons reached the summit of their prominence. *Forum* magazine in 1889, the *New York Tribune* in 1892, and ten years later the *New York World* compiled lists of American millionaires.[6] Based on hearsay evidence and with considerably different conclusions, these compilations have dubious value. The 1892 list of 4,047, derived from information provided by corporate lawyers and others with knowledge about American fortunes, was the most credible assessment.

Better studies resulted from improved research methods and more detailed record-keeping due to the advent in 1913 of federal income and estate taxes. Ferdinand Lundberg, then the outstanding scholar of great wealth, estimated that 7,500 American millionaires existed in 1914 and that huge war profits and the feverish prosperity of the 1920s enlarged the total to 38,889 in 1929. This spectacular advance was reversed in the Depression – by 1936 the monied elite numbered no more than the 11,800 of 1917.[7] Despite Lundberg's pioneering and monumental *America's Sixty Families* (1937), a reliable historical accounting of affluent Americans appeared only within the last decade. Lundberg, for example, accepted the *Tribune* speculation and made no independent measurements of late-nineteenth-century millionaires. Economist Robert E. Gallman, adding data from census samples to impressionistic information from contemporary lists of rich people, estimated that in 1890 there were 2,000-4,000 millionaire families in the United States.[8]

Lee Soltow has recently published the most comprehensive and rigorous history of affluent Americans. He used 1866 federal income tax returns, probate and manuscript census records and Internal Revenue Service tax reports, and controlled for changes in consumer prices and population growth. Soltow concluded that the ratio of millionaires to the entire population was almost as high in 1866 (possibly higher if underestimated income was taken into account) as in 1914 and larger in these years than in 1965. The proportion of millionaires in the national populace, considering demographic and price index changes, remained constant between 1870 and 1962, although fluctuations occurred in the size of the group within shorter timespans during this period. Soltow estimates, using manuscript census samples, that in contemporary dollar value of property 40 millionaires existed in 1860, 545 in 1870, 5,904 in 1922, and 60,000-67,000 in 1962. The Board of Governors of the Federal Reserve System agreed with the upper range of Soltow's 1962 ascertainment; the Internal Revenue Service, on the basis of a sophisticated statistical formula, projected a 1962 figure of 59,662 for that stratum.[9]

Soltow's investigation omitted the years between 1922 and 1962 and thereafter, but experts ventured estimates for various times in this period. The National Bureau of Economic Research calculated the number of millionaires at 13,000 in 1948 and 27,000 in 1953. James D. Smith and Staunton K. Calvert, employing the estate multiplier technique[10] (the same method used in the IRS 1962 finding), declared that in 1958 over 40,000 Americans had a net worth of at least one million dollars. This finding received support in the IRS estate multiplier projection of 47,827 gross estates of that amount for the same year.[11] Recent estimates based upon estate sampling were 102,700 millionaires in 1969, according to Smith and two other colleagues, and 120,652 in an IRS projection for that year. The latest IRS calculation (1972) is 180,000.[12]

The assessments of 1969 and 1972 indicate a far greater increase in the number of millionaires than could be expected from the concurrent rise in the national population or the inflated dollar. This recent and short-term growth of the very rich, however, does not necessarily disprove Soltow's conclusion that the millionaire segment in the general population remained constant over a long period. Between 1962 and 1972 the nation enjoyed economic prosperity, but the subsequent

sharp recession, especially the steep decline in the stock market, has
undoubtedly reversed the expansionary trend in the millionaire group.
In any case, millionaires have always constituted an infinitesimal share
of the population. Gallman claimed that in 1890 they made up 0.016
to 0.031 per cent of American families. During the prosperous decade
of 1962-72 their share of the total population, as derived from
calculations based on estate sampling, amounted to 0.1 per cent.[13]

Lifestyle

A million dollars is an unscalable peak for almost all who make the
difficult climb toward material success. Even Ward McAllister,
majordomo of the New York Four Hundred, a late-nineteenth-century
ensemble of multimillionaire swells and *grandes dames* that included
the Astors, the Vanderbilts and others among America's monied elite,
recognised that 'to be worth a million of dollars [in the 1870s] was to
be rated as a man of fortune'. In that decade 'there were not more
than one or two men in New York who spent, in living and entertaining,
over 60,000 dollars a year'. This outlay did not greatly exceed the
antebellum '50,000 a year' that Mrs John King Van Rennselaer, by
birth and marriage a member of New York's aristocracy of old Dutch
and English families, claimed 'not more than a couple of families' spent
'on their living expenses'.[14]

By the 1890s the pinnacle of one million dollars was a mere foothill
when overlooked from the summit of vast wealth. 'New York's ideas
as to values leaped boldly up ten millions, 50 millions, 100 millions,'
pontificated McAllister. Due 'to the rapid growth of riches' in the last
20 years 'millionaires are too common to receive much deference; a
fortune of a million is only respectable poverty'.[15] His pompous but
truthful pronouncement reflected the emergence and multiplication of
phenomenal fortunes and proclaimed the reality that a mere million no
longer fulfilled the primary functions of immense personal wealth.
Even $ 10 million was inadequate to support the resplendence, supply
the largesse and consolidate the economic dominance that constituted
the distinguishing features and self-definition of the super-rich.

The extravagance of the wealthiest people titillated and horrified
contemporary commentators and subsequent historians. While the
repeatedly recorded catalogue of stupendous expenditure need not
here be extensively recounted, some examples of lavishness indicate
the extraordinary resources necessary to belong to the highest circle of
affluence.

An age of baroque luxury supplanted the modest brownstones and subdued dinner-parties of earlier decades. Private homes, usually copies of renaissance châteaux and palazzos and stocked with priceless European antiques and paintings, were the costliest items in the world of unlimited purses. Kinship rivalries and contention for social prominence took the form of outbuilding, outentertaining and outmarrying competitors. Among the Vanderbilt mansions were a New York townhouse costing $2 million to construct and $9 million to decorate, and a Newport domicile and a North Carolina plantation each involving an outlay of $7 million. Henry Clay Frick lived near several Vanderbilts in a $5 million establishment on Fifth Avenue. These expensive monuments were not restricted to the 1890s or to New York. In 1916 Henry Ford was housed for $2 million in a Detroit suburb. The residences of Philip D. Armour and Samuel Insull, located near Chicago, cost respectively $5 million and $7 million. William Randolph Hearst's California barony, San Simeon, with its zoo, furnishings, gardens and grounds one-third the size of Rhode Island, was the most ostentatious of these temples to Mammon. Those at the topmost rung of the monied elite did not stop with one dwelling. They typically had a townhouse, a home at one of the fashionable resorts like Newport or Palm Beach, and a country estate or European manor. Here, too, Hearst led the field with seven homes at a total investment of over $40 million. The collective expenditure of the wealthiest families is even more incredible than these individual outlays. Lundberg estimates that the Vanderbilt mansions were worth $120 million, the duPont homes $150 million, the Rockefeller residences $50-75 million, and the Morgan estates at least $30 million.[16] Apart from construction and furnishing, the upkeep alone was more than a millionaire could afford. The great New York townhouses cost $200,000-300,000 yearly to run and an additional $100,000 was necessary to maintain a Newport mansion. Much of this expense went to pay a staff that averaged 24 servants. Country homes could involve considerably higher expenses. John D. Rockefeller's Pocantico estate in Tarrytown, New York, had 350 employees and cost $400,000 per annum during the 1930s.[17]

These mansions were social fortresses whose costly splendour and antique ornaments gave their owners social credentials that compensated for an *arriviste* status. They were the armouries in the contests for pre-eminence waged in the opulent enclaves of New York, Detroit, San Francisco and elsewhere. The citadels of society queens, with scores of rooms and liveried servants, did not house an intimate family life; they were designed for the *beau monde* of formal dinners and dances. The most expensive events were costume balls. Alva

Vanderbilt in 1883 elevated the family into the Four Hundred by giving a $200,000 fancy-dress ball in her $3 million New York mansion and fortified this triumph by setting aside $300,000 for entertainment during the Newport season. She initiated new heights of expenditure. Turn-of-the-century costume balls occasionally exceeded $200,000 (the costliest of these events was the $370,000 Bradley Martin affair in 1897), and Newport hostesses now regularly allotted several hundred thousands of dollars for the summer social swirl.[18]

Expenditures on private art and artefact collections sometimes surpassed residential disbursements. Andrew Mellon, the richest American in the 1920s, spent $31 million on paintings and Hearst over $50 million on art and antiques. Mellon's and J.P. Morgan's acquisitions were each worth over $50 million when they died. Throughout history expensive art assemblages have been a favourite hobby of the affluent, and wealthy capitalists have collected pictures and sculpture with the same avidity that they gathered money or corporations. A recent survey of Americans worth at least $100 million claimed that art collecting was the costliest item of conspicuous consumption in this enclave. At least ten owned collections valued at a minimum of $20 million. Centimillionaires like Los Angeles banker Howard F. Ahmanson, conglomerate czar Norton Simon of the same city, uranium magnate Joseph H. Hirshorn and billionaire oilman J. Paul Getty have collections that cost $50 million.[19]

Yachts, jewellery, racing stables, prestigious marriages and expensive divorces accounted for other huge monetary outlays in the in the flamboyant lifestyle. *Corsair*, J.P. Morgan's ship, cost $2 million, and the vessels of banker George F. Baker, William K. Vanderbilt, Vincent Astor and A.P. Sloan Jr of General Motors, were priced between one and two million dollars. Annual operating costs for these ocean-going steamships amounted to $50,000. Yachts were a rich man's hobby, an instrument of social status in their own right and for entry into the elite urban yacht clubs. For several wealthy and unhappy husbands they also became a refuge from (and in some cases a *demi-monde* alternative to) the fashionable set dominated by their wives. Women with the resources and wishes to become idols of conspicuous consumption spent as much on jewellery as did their husbands or brothers on yachts. In the early 1900s three Vanderbilt wives had collections of jewels worth over a million dollars. The daughter-in-law of Wall Street speculator Jay Gould possessed gems that approached this level of value, and Mrs Collis P. Huntington, wife of the railway tycoon, owned eleven necklaces aggregately appraised at $3.5 million. Wealthy devotees of the 'sport of kings' pursued their passion with the same magnificence as multimillionaires dedicated to rule the quarterdeck or sparkle in society. Belmonts, Whitneys, Phippses, Millses, Vanderbilts and Hartfords had stables involving investments of $1-5 million. Their racing silks appeared at the English and Kentucky Derbies, the Grand Prix and other renowned contests, and they got further recognition from belonging to exclusive jockey clubs. The paraphernalia of conspicuous display in the 1890s also included private railway carriages priced at $85,000-125,000 and boxes in the Diamond Horseshoe of New York's Metropolitan Opera House purchased for $60,000.[20]

The struggle for status brought the super-rich into contact with people who neither feared nor worshipped them. Titled Europeans who embellished the parties in Fifth Avenue mansions and at fashionable spas regarded multimillionaire heiresses as quarries in a quest for cash to refurbish tarnished crests. Fortune-hunters viewed daughters and granddaughters of robber barons, not unlike the way great capitalists looked upon their own enterprises, as investments of time, energy and skill that would, if properly handled, yield maximum profits. The newly risen, searching for unassailable credentials to expunge *arriviste* origins, made alliances that exchanged capital assets for genteel attachments. The linking of the daughter of a rail magnate or a meat-packer with a duke or a count guaranteed family respectability and social acceptance. Such mergers were the social equivalent of corporate mergers. Between 1874 and 1909 approximately 500 American girls wedded titled Europeans, and $220 million changed hands as a result of these vows. Whitneys, Vanderbilts and Goulds from New York, Leiters from Chicago and Washington, DC, Thaws from Pittsburgh, Wards from Detroit and Longworths from Cincinnati were among the prize catches in the transatlantic matrimonial market. Many of these matches, like their analogues in the business world, were disreputable, unhappy, impermanent and costly: Gladys Vanderbilt's marriage to a Hungarian count and her cousin Consuelo's connection with the Duke of Marlborough set back the family respectively $12 million and $10 million, and Jay Gould's daughter Anna conferred $5.5 million upon an Italian count before that union dissolved.[21]

Nearly half the women who married European aristocrats came from New York, a little more than 10 per cent were Philadelphians, under 9 per cent were Bostonians and none of the brides came from Charleston.[22] Herein lies a tale of different cities. Patricians in Philadelphia, Charleston and Boston were more secure in their inherited ascendancy than the newly risen rich. Their modest fortunes prohibited the luxurious indulgence exhibited in New York, Chicago or modern-day Los Angeles, Dallas and Houston. Godfrey Lowell Cabot, a Boston blueblood, was the only figure from that city to make the 1957 *Fortune* list of Americans worth at least $75 million.[23] None the less, Cabot adhered to the abstemious lifestyle associated since the early national period with the upper class in that city. As a child he never had toys, luxuries or money other than a 50¢ weekly allowance. The wealthy manufacturer imposed ancestral and group values of thrift and self-denial upon his own offspring. Like many other Boston brahmins he detested the showy self-glorification of the Four Hundred and was content with a house that he built for $18,000.[24] Parvenu elites, however, depended upon publicity and costly display to elevate themselves and upon imported or imitated European titles, artefacts and styles to substitute for their own lack of rooted credentials and conventions.[25]

The urban gentry congregated in the old cities along the Atlantic seaboard here deserve mention only to note that not all metropolitan elites were fabulously or wantonly wealthy. After the First World War, however, social commentators perceived a slackening of profligacy even among the most flagrant spenders. The premiums on luxury increased due to mounting wages paid to servants, inflated costs of upkeep on yachts and mansions and soaring prices for artistic objects. These debits rose at the same time that dissipation and a natural multiplication of heirs diminished many great fortunes. Economic collapse and the dramatic ascension of income and inheritance taxes during the 1930s threatened other mammoth accumulations. The Depression, accompanied by a rise in social consciousness during the New Deal and the Second World War, made indulgence appear more unseemly than in previous decades. The family 'togetherness' crusade of the 1950s and early 1960s, and the political and social reform movements of the late 1960s and early 1970s, further inhibited extravagance. The café society that flourished between the wars and the 'beautiful people', 'jet setters' and 'radical chic' enclaves of the post-war and contemporary eras brought the very rich into contact with intellectuals, writers, actors, actresses and political activists whose achievements did not necessarily involve entrepreneurial triumphs, gigantic fortunes or lavish expenditures. Many of the celebrities in these groups showed little desire to emulate or admire pecuniary aggrandisement and display. Their fame and charisma offered models of aspiration and behaviour that muted gaudy impulses in the multimillionaires who mingled with them. A similar effect resulted from the withdrawal from money-making or wanton leisure of a number of great capitalists and their children or grandchildren in favour of social welfare or public service activities. During the 1890s John D. Rockefeller retired from Standard Oil and began to devote much of his energy and money to benevolence. His only son and oldest grandson made a career of administering the Rockefeller charities. In 1900 Andrew Carnegie left the steel business to concentrate exclusively upon the benefactions flowing from his immense fortune. Wall Street speculator Bernard Baruch in the First World War, financier Herbert H. Lehman in the late 1920s, fledgling capitalist Nelson Rockefeller and banker W.A. Harriman, son of E.H. Harriman, in the 1930s, gave up business activity for lifelong government service. After the Second World War, several Rockefellers and the sons of multimillionaire capitalist Joseph Kennedy became prominent political figures.[26]

These developments moderated sumptuous living. Beginning in the 1920s, famous American châteaux were closed down, sold off, turned into museums or donated to public and private institutions. Whitneys, Fords, Clarks and Mellons, who could afford to maintain their estates, and some of the Vanderbilts, who could not, vacated these mansions because of taxes, upkeep costs and preference for smaller homes.[27] The Depression curtailed expenditure in the fashionable sets in New York and Chicago, then the capitals of conspicuous consumption. Arthur Meeker, Chicago socialite and son of a millionaire bankrupted in the stock market crash, reported that the economic crisis had ended the posh Assembly and Twelfth Night Balls, that cocktail-parties had replaced formal dinners, and that debutante affairs were simpler and cheaper. *Fortune* noted that New York debuts in the 1930s, the most expensive of the cities, averaged $9,500. Although the very rich spent up to $60,000, the norm was substantially below the $11,500 mean of pre-Depression years.[28] When prosperity returned luxurious expenditure did not regain its old heights. Responses to a 1957 *Fortune* survey of men with $50 million and above, revealed that half of the respondents owned only one house or apartment, that only one-quarter had three or more residences, that they averaged only three domestic servants and none had more than 15, that the cost of running their largest abode varied between $6,000-75,000 yearly, and that most of those queried disliked ornate living. Eleven years later *Fortune* studied America's centimillionaires and concluded that most of them did not conform to the stereotypes of McAllister's Gilded Age of F. Scott Fitzgerald's Jazz Age multimillionaires.[29] Another example of the relative modesty of the modern multimillionaires was the notoriety in

1959 regarding Henry Ford's $100,000 coming-out party for his daughter. George J. Gould spent $200,000 on his daughter's 1912 debut, when the dollar had considerably more buying power, without attracting nearly as much attention.[30] The group to watch for a possible reappearance of extravagance on the Gilded Age scale was the Texas oil magnates, who amassed the largest fortunes in recent times. Despite their reputed expansiveness, they spent less magnificently than did their eastern predecessors. H.L. Hunt and John W. Mecom, in 1957 allegedly worth respectively $400-700 million and $100-200 million, had residences that cost less than $100,000. In the 1950s a Texas home costing a million dollars was a rare sight. During that decade the most expensive party given in this enclave cost $120,000, and debuts averaged between $10,000 and $25,000.[31]

The lowered level of expenditure and the rising social awareness among the super-rich led social critic David Riesman, society novelist Louis Auchincloss, the *New York Times*, *Fortune*, *Time*, the editors of the *Wall Street Journal* and several multimillionaires to claim that flamboyance and excess no longer stigmatised the monied elite. According to these commentators the affluent were now drawn to family life, worked hard at the office or on the boards of cultural and benevolent organisations, or aspired to political careers. Many preferred cosy houses or apartments to rambling estates, small suppers with family or friends to formal dinners, discotheques to ballrooms, square dances to costume dances, jeans to tuxedos, casual parties to stilted society affairs, backpacking to Palm Beach or the Riviera, and anonymity to notoriety. Multimillionaires decorated their own homes, cooked their own meals and dressed modestly.[32]

Many of the wealthiest Americans did indeed forsake extravagance; others continued to squander their resources. High living, in fact, actually contributed to the humbler image of the post-1918 multimillionaire. Profligacy curtailed or disposed of several big spenders and made many fortunes vulnerable to the stock market crash which dimmed the splendour of Fifth and Park Avenues in New York, the Near North Side of Chicago, and Newport and Palm Beach. Financial reverses, compounded by a mania to revel in luxuries and precious objects, forced Hearst, America's champion consumer, in the 1930s to cut back his $15 million annual personal outlay. Unwise investments, poor corporate strategy, a stable of chorus girls and other diversions caused George Gould to lose his father's rail empire. In 1933 his estate amounted to only $324,630. Mrs Edward T. Stotesbury of Palm Beach, a luminary of conspicuous display, had a million-dollar collection of

emeralds and spent $50,000 a month on entertainment. By 1938 her
husband had lost almost nine-tenths of his $100 million fortune of
1929. In the 1950s his granddaughter ran an inn and his great-grandson
pumped gas in the vicinity of his magnificent former estate. Multiple
divorces, alimony, precious gift giving, law suits, riotous parties,
resplendent mansions and parasitic entourages eroded the patrimonies
of Horace Dodge Jr, Evelyn Walsh McLean, Atwater Kent and John
Jacob Astor VI. These individual cases of pecuniary self-destruction
are overshadowed by the Vanderbilt record. Family founder Cornelius
Vanderbilt in 1877 and his son in 1885 left what were then the largest
legacies in American history. Although the aggregate family assets
remained huge, dissipation, divorces and a natural multiplication of
heirs drastically shrunk individual inheritances. In the fourth and fifth
generation (in the 1920s) no Vanderbilt appeared among the ten
wealthiest Americans and only three made the list of 274 United
States taxpayers with incomes of one million dollars or above in
1923.[33] The wreckage of the Vanderbilt fortunes doubtlessly prompted
fifth-generation Cornelius Vanderbilt Jr to remark in the 1930s: 'In
another ten years there won't be a single great fortune left in
America.'[34]

Vanderbilt was wrong. Taxes did not redistribute wealth, most of
the colossal fortunes escaped ruin by wanton expenditure, and
prosperity returned to revivify old accumulations and generate new
ones. The modern monied elite may not have made as grotesque or
magnificent a show as did the Four Hundred, but their living standard
was still far beyond the capacity of the mere millionaire. The gaudy
recklessness of glamorous ex-debs Doris Duke and Barbara Hutton, the
$250,000-300,000 annual entertainment budget of Grace Wilson
Vanderbilt (successor to her mother-in-law as queen of high society)
and the racing stables of the Whitneys, Vanderbilts, Wideners and
Phippses, survived the world wars and the Depression. In 1938,
according to one estimate, 36 American women had jewellery worth
at least a million dollars, by 1965 over 50 had gems of this value.
Nieman-Marcus, the Dallas department store that caters to the Texas
millionaires, listed in its 1950s Christmas catalogues 'his and her' planes
priced respectively at $149,000 and $27,000. During that decade
Mecom bought a jet for $1.3 million which became the flagship of his
ten-plane squadron. Marjorie Merriweather Post, daughter of the
breakfast-food tycoon and perhaps the biggest of the recent big
spenders, in the 1960s budgeted $2 million a year, of a $200-300
million fortune, on three houses, numerous cars and boats, a four-

engine plane and other living expenses.[35]

The departure of the titanic entrepreneurs coincided with the decline of the gargantuan consumers. But the heroic age of luxury lasted longer and did not end as abruptly as the heroic age of capitalism.

Social Responsibility

Spectacular expenditures were not restricted to vulgar or lordly opulence nor motivated solely by profligacy, gluttony or the glitter of high society. Indeed, the trophies of conspicuous consumption, magnificent estates, libraries and art collections, ultimately served socially redeemable ends when donated to altruistic organisations. While many affluent Americans devoted themselves mainly to sensual pleasures and comforts, others enlisted their resources and efforts in what they deemed humanitarian service.

Glandiose acts of charity, like grandiose manifestations of luxury, proclaimed pecuniary pre-eminence. The pillars of philanthropy, however, rarely overlapped with celebrities of conspicuous display. A generation ago Texas multimillionaire and renowned benefactor Hugh Roy Cullen bluntly stated the disharmony of these priorities: 'I have taught my children that if they feel like buying some jewelry, they should find out how much it costs and then go out and give that amount to a school or a hospital.'[36] Education and medical care did not preoccupy the minds and purses of the Four Hundred. In 1882-83, perhaps its most brilliant social season, about 4 per cent of the *beau-monde* affairs (30 out of 849 events, exclusive of weddings) appearing in the society pages of the *New York Tribune* were organised for charitable purposes. The 1900 social season followed by only a few years a severe depression, yet the fashionable set only doubled its percentage of benevolent activities.[37] Members of the Astor crowd evinced no greater sense of public responsibility individually than as a unit. A tradition of niggardliness passed intact from family founder John Jacob to his grandsons. Three consecutive generations of heads of that family left not more than 2.5 per cent of their estates to philanthropic causes.[38] The Vanderbilts, rivals of the Astors in self-indulgence and social prominence, equalled them in beneficence. Here, too, the originator of the family fortune set the tone. Cornelius Vanderbilt feared that 'if I was to begin that business' (alms-giving) a deluge of supplicants would engulf him. Believing that 'if you give away the surplus [money], you give away the control', the crusty 'commodore' kept all but about a million dollars in lifetime earnings for himself and his heirs. This ancestral example was faithfully followed by his son and grandson, the chief inheritors of the family fortune, who willed less than 2 per cent of their legacies to the public welfare.[39] The Astors and the Vanderbilts were not the only stars in the *fin-de-siècle* extravaganza to discover that frugality, when applied to other people's needs, was not a vice. 'I'll never be remembered for the money I've given away,' remarked Collis P. Huntington. Huntington, together with barbed-wire monopolist and stock speculator John W. ('Bet A Million') Gates, a famed sport of his Gilded Age, William C. Whitney and J.P. Morgan, acquired fortunes in the range of $21-78 million. They spent lavishly on townhouses and country estates, yachts, the turf and collections of old masters and other *objets d'art*, but left little or nothing to charity. Morgan alone of this group made sizeable donations while still alive.[40]

Multimillionaires who begrudged the needy were also found among those who lived relatively modestly or denied themselves the pleasures of vast wealth. Moses Taylor, the last of the notable general entrepreneurs, Jay Gould and his friend and associate Russell Sage, Hetty Green, 'the witch of Wall Street', and several Texas oil tycoons, had fortunes above $50 million, yet they contributed sparingly while alive and little or nothing posthumously to altruistic endeavours. Gould and Taylor lived comfortably but moderately for men of their wealth, Sage reluctantly spent money, even on himself, and Green was a downright miser. The latter became the richest American woman of her time, but a self-consuming pursuit of money made her a veritable caricature of the acquisitive type. Born into a rich but frugal household, she wore old clothes, lived in cheap hotels, and refused to pay for medical assistance when her son contracted an infection, an economy which cost him a leg. This stringent budget, based on $67-100 million worth of railway and real estate investments, allowed not a penny for organised charity.[41]

Gould, Sage and Green were money-making machines, supremely specialised predators in the market place, with the instincts of sharks in the sea. On the other hand, Andrew Carnegie and John D. Rockefeller, the foremost industrialists of their era, pioneered modern upper-class philanthropy. The magnitude of their donations was unprecedented, and they initiated the technique of grants through specialised or multipurpose charity bureaucracies. Rockefeller believed in 'the necessity to organize and plan this department [philanthropy] of our daily tasks on as distinct lines of progress as we did our business affairs'. He proposed to 'erect a foundation, a Trust, and engage directors who will make it a life work to manage, with our personal

cooperation, this business of benevolence properly and effectively'.[42]
These charity trusts, called institutes, foundations or, occasionally,
corporations, resembled the steel and oil trusts and coincided with the
modern trends of making social work a profession and modelling
welfare agencies on business bureaucracies.

Carnegie, a typical example of the self-made tycoon, began his
mammoth campaign of benevolence in the 1890s, after his fortune and
industrial primacy were invulnerable. 'I resolved to stop accumulating,'
the steel-manufacturer said, justifying his retirement in 1901, 'and
begin the infinitely more serious and difficult task of wise distribution.'
He gave away $350 million (90 per cent of his fortune) before death
and left two-thirds of the remainder chiefly to universities, libraries and
institutions for scientific research, acting mostly through foundations
rather than personally as had been the tradition of wealthy benefactors.
The Carnegie Corporation of New York (1911), until it was surpassed
in 1947 by the Ford Foundation, had more capital than any other
philanthropic organisation.[43]

Rockefeller, like Carnegie, detested the sensational extravagance of
high society, believed in the stewardship of wealth and became a great
humanitarian in the 1890s after gaining a gigantic fortune, unassailable
leadership and a reputation as a ruthless industrial capitalist. Both men
had familial models of social consciousness: Carnegie's father and
grandfather were Scottish artisans who supported democracy and
labour reform, and the steel magnate was once a youthful abolitionist
and free-soiler. Rockefeller's maternal grandparents were abolitionists
and they and his mother systematically contributed part of their
modest incomes to charity. But Rockefeller, unlike Carnegie, began
giving in the 1850s when he became a wage-earner. Before death the
oil tycoon's largesse amounted to more than half his fortune, which
peaked at one billion dollars in 1913. He also set up foundations and
institutes to channel most of his funds; as in the case of the Carnegie
organisations, these were formed between 1900 and 1914. The
Rockefeller Foundation (1913), like the Carnegie Corporation, a
multipurpose contributing agency, was the centre of the Rockefeller
charity empire. Carnegie left only one daughter, but Rockefeller's
benevolence became dynastic. 'I have been brought up to believe,' said
John D. Rockefeller Jr, 'that giving ought to be entered into in just the
same careful way as investing – that giving is investing, and that it
should be tested by the same intelligent standard.' Dedicated to the
principles of his father, the younger Rockefeller made a vocation of
administering the family foundations, and between 1917 and 1958

gave away $450,901,000, approximately $100 million less than the
founder. John D. Rockefeller III, his eldest son, undertook the
management of the clan's good samaritanism.[44]

Similarities between Carnegie and Rockefeller were numerous and
important, but one significant difference deserves mention. Carnegie
liquidated his business interests in order to undertake benevolence on
a full-time basis, and then committed his capital to altruism. The
Rockefellers, despite their greater dispensations, retained their
industrial and financial enterprises, and their fortune continued to
grow.[45]

The Carnegie-Rockefeller example was imitated by many titanic
accumulators imbued with the social obligations of great wealth.
Hearst, Alfred I. duPont, Charles Hayden, Marshall Field III, James B.
Duke, Payne Whitney and Julius Rosenwald gave between $50 million
and $100 million, personally or through foundations, in their lifetime
and in bequests. Alfred P. Sloan, Cullen, George Eastman, James A.
Chapman, Clint Murchison and Edward S. Harkness contributed more
than $100 million. Andrew Mellon and Henry Ford donated over
$200 million, and William P. Moody created a foundation funded in
excess of $400 million.[46]

These philanthropists emulated the method as well as the magnitude
of alms-giving associated with Carnegie and Rockefeller. Only 36
foundations with a minimum of $100,000 in assets appeared before
1910. Between 1910 and 1929, when estate and income taxes began,
another 163 were founded. During the 1930s, when benevolent
institutions were used more extensively as tax shelters and to retain
control of corporate stock against steepening death and income
imposts, 288 were formed. Well over half of the American foundations
were organised after 1952. By 1962 there existed 14,685 foundations,
fourteen years later there were 26,000. In 1976 the 2,818 foundations
with assets of at least one million dollars or grant dispensations of
$100,000 or more had total assets exceeding $28.6 billion. The top
ten, with aggregate assets of $8.2 billion, included those founded by
the richest Americans. The Ford Foundation (1936), with resources
of $2,354 million was the largest in this group; the smallest was the
Carnegie Corporation with assets of $240,196,000.[47]

The divergence between the socially responsible and the skinflints
or wastrels indicates the extreme difficulty of generalising about the
generosity of the very rich. A study of the proportion of large estates
reserved for public or charitable purposes discloses variations over time
as great as the differences in motives for, and magnitude of,

beneficence. Between 1922 and 1933 gross estates of $10 million and above averaged $27,480,000 per estate tax return. Deductions for charity averaged $1,398,000 per return for net estates worth $10 million or more.[48] Allowing for the disparity between gross and net estates, during these years 5-10 per cent of the wealth in this class was willed to philanthropy. Table 5.1 shows the extraordinary subsequent fluctuations in the public welfare bequests of the wealthy. These disparate figures do not seem to result from changes in the tax structure or the economic situation. If anything, they reflect a distribution of selfishness and community spirit among the affluent determined by individual tastes, familial dictates and subgroup identifications that resist any overall trends.

Lifetime giving, as might be expected, involved proportionately smaller outlays. Of 52 Americans with gross estates, according to tax returns in 1957 and 1959, of $10 million or more, 50 made philanthropic contributions before death. The total value of the gross estates in these two years amounted to $1,112 million; $78 million (7 per cent) was donated for lifetime benevolence. But charitable bequests totalled over 30 per cent of the probated estates at this level of wealth in these years.[49]

Those moved by the social responsibilities of vast wealth did not act from purely humanitarian principles. The relationship between commercial and charitable trusts was closer than a merging of methods. The US Treasury Department reported in 1962 that many donors rented property to and from their foundations, sold and bought assets from them, borrowed or lent money to and from them, retained income from their foundations and delayed or gave small grants to divert allegedly philanthropic resources to business capital or private income. Benefactors manipulated their foundations to amass other assets, for investment purposes, tax shelters, and to keep or gain control of business corporations through foundations acquiring stock in companies created by the founders or in which the donors sought to expand their interests. Through extensive ownership of stock and heavy concentration of capital the foundations became a strong force in the economy. In the 1950s, for example, the 534 largest (by assets) foundations had a greater after-tax income and net worth than the 50 top (by assets) American banks.[50]

A more enlightened version of self-interest led philanthropists to improve the local environment and support other projects that enhanced their business interests. Inventor and manufacturer George Eastman, the Mellons and the DuPonts funded schools, hospitals, parks,

Table 5.1: Philanthropic Bequests of Gross Estates of $10 Million or More Filed in 1940, 1950, 1963 and 1972-73

Year	Total number	Number with charitable bequests	Total value of estates (thousands of dollars)	Total given to philanthropy (thousands of dollars)	Percentage of estate left to philanthropy
1940	8	–	126,099	30,979	24.6
1950	4	–	56,264	1,785	3.2
1963	32	23	576,485	25,085	4.4
1972-3	89	67	1,899,638	592,317	31.2

Sources: Internal Revenue Service, *Statistics of Income for 1939*, pp. 264-65; *1949*, Part 1, pp. 364-65; *Fidicuary, Gift and Estate Tax Returns, 1962*, p. 60; *Estate Tax Returns, 1972*, pp. 14-15 (Department of the Treasury, US Government Printing Office, Washington, DC, 1942, 1954, 1965, 1975).

symphonies and social welfare agencies in Rochester, Pittsburgh and Delaware respectively. Eastman and the duPonts contributed generously to the Massachusetts Institute of Technology, a university attended by several duPonts and many Kodak and E.I. duPont de Nemours employees. Another case of self-serving beneficence was the Mellon Institute, an industrial research centre whose patents and discoveries swelled profits in the family enterprises. Eastman candidly explained the motives behind these donations in expressing his reasons for contributing to the University of Rochester Medical School and Hospital: from 'the standpoint of making Kodak Company an enduring institution, safe against the assaults of competition for expert services and labor, I have felt that the best thing that could be done was to help make Rochester the best place in the country to live in. This has been one of the controlling ideas in my gifts to Rochester'.[51]

If benefactors were seldom motivated by unadulterated altruism, material self-interest provided a limited, though powerful, explanation for philanthropy. Civic pride and community obligation, as well as the desire to advance business interests, prompted the Eastman, duPont and Mellon disbursements. Before the advent of income and inheritance taxes in 1913 Carnegie and Rockefeller gave away several hundred millions, and California rail magnate Leland Stanford donated $30 million, the bulk of his fortune, to found Stanford University. In an era when many foundations were devices of commercial and pecuniary aggrandisement, the creator of the Julius Rosenwald Fund (1923) mandated its liquidation in 25 years through grants to public causes.[52]

Preservation of property constituted an incentive for philanthropy even when not directly connected with corporate involvements or tax strategies. Public endowments attested to the merit of the multimillionaire and to the benefits that immense personal wealth conferred upon the relatively deprived, often indigent and sometimes angry masses. Carnegie, the most articulate of the heroic philanthropists, felt that personal assets should be given away while their possessors still lived in order to prevent mammoth accumulations from corrupting inheritors and to demonstrate the public spirit of rich donors. Largesse was the 'antidote for the temporary unequal distribution of wealth'. *Noblesse oblige* reconciled the rich and the poor under 'a reign of harmony in which the surplus wealth of the few will become, in the best sense, the property of the many, because administered for the common good'.[53] Carnegie's assertion that rich benefactors could reduce economic inequality, further the common good and create harmony among the haves and the have-nots disclosed an historical anxiety harboured by the affluent — the ever present possibility that the poorer majority would dispossess the favoured few. Such defensiveness made benevolence, as in the case of the well-publicised Rockefeller dispensations, a design to launder a public image stained by the ignoble acts necessary to acquire money and power.[54] Automobile-manufacturer Henry Ford, who succeeded Carnegie and Rockefeller as the nation's premier industrialist and by the 1930s compiled a fortune of between $500 million and $700 million, assured the public that men of his rank were 'servants of the people', whose 'tenure' would be 'very short' unless they fulfilled their 'responsibility' to make 'their activities beneficial to the people as a whole'.[55] Marshall Field III, grandson of the richest and most powerful nineteenth-century Chicagoan, had in 1930 an estimated $300 million. A rare multimillionaire with liberal views, he looked upon wealth as 'a privilege Western society has traditionally granted to its stronger or more fortunate members, and, like every privilege, it carries with it certain obligations as a kind of payment for the privilege. Those who neglect the obligations, I am convinced, speed the day when this privilege will be curtailed or perhaps denied.'[56]

Resisting criticism or even more dangerous attacks, the affluent used charity as a means of social control. Funds flowed into educational and religious institutions and welfare agencies that disseminated values justifying the existence of the monied elite and that superficially relieved the deprivations of the many while defending the system which showered rewards upon the few. Ford, Rockefeller and Carnegie argued that their kind of beneficence reinforced the social system and enabled many to emulate successful capitalists.[57] Philanthropy as an instrument of social control was far more than a means of buying protection for great fortunes. Benevolence was an exercise in community leadership by those accustomed to commercial mastery and social dominance. Success in America has primarily been associated with business achievement and measured by money, and those who piled up the most assets were considered the best experts in distributing them to advance the public welfare. Carnegie claimed that 'the millionaire' could administer wealth 'for the community far better than it could or would have done for itself', Rockefeller agreed that the rich should choose how to employ their money for the public good. Ford felt that 'the leaders of business are as responsible for the welfare of the people as the generals of any army are responsible for the welfare of the soldiers'.[58]

Pride as well as power stimulated egocentric philanthropy. James B. Duke gave over $20 million to Trinity College in Durham, North Carolina, on condition that it become Duke University. Henry Huntington in 1924 bequeathed his library and art gallery, a $13 million gift, to the state of California because ' It represents the reward of all the work I have ever done and the realization of much happiness.' Frick posthumously donated his home, art collection and a trust fund, a contribution worth between $50 million and $60 million, to establish a public museum 'to be my monument'.[59]

Philanthropy proceeds from honourable and self-serving impulses that are inseparable in the soul of the benefactor. Carnegie, Rockefeller, Ford and Field repeatedly described their property in terms of 'trust', 'tenure', 'privilege', 'duty' and 'responsibility'. These words express the stewardship of wealth; a belief that vast fortunes are given to individuals by God or by the community, and are acquired by superior character to serve divine or public purposes. Carnegie, in a characteristic formulation of this creed, deemed wealth 'a sacred trust, to be administered by its possessor, into whose hands it flows, for the highest good of the people'. Although an agnostic, his best-known essay was entitled 'The Gospel of Wealth', Rockefeller 'believe[d] the power to make money is a gift from God. . .to be developed and used to the best of our ability for the good of mankind'. Gratitude for boons from the Almighty, in addition to obligations to the Ultimate Benefactor, inspired rich donors. 'God has blessed me so lavishly,' declared banker and philanthropist Jacob Schiff, 'that had I done less. . .I should feel no respect for myself.'[60] These feelings derived from the Judaeo-Christian ethic of labouring for the Lord, a conviction that made charity a religious and public duty and a private responsibility. A faith that decreed that money spent in enjoyment or consumption was at best a stigma of human frailty, sanctified, by making charity a sign of salvation, the self-denying urges of the acquisitive personality. This moral imperative impelled Godfrey Lowell Cabot to subscribe over one-quarter of his company's stock to benevolent endeavour. Imbued with ancestral puritanism and a brahmin tradition of public service, he felt that 'You ought to give money away when you're alive, when it costs you something.'[61]

Charity was not always invoked by the awesome burdens of divine judgement or the stewardship of wealth. Many premier benefactors retired from the battlefields of the market place to discover in philanthropy a less taxing source of gratification in their later years. They may, as Erik Erikson suggests, have reached full maturity in attaining the age of nurturance. Philadelphia publisher Edward Bok, who shared an estimated $180 million with his associate and father-in-law Cyrus H.K. Curtiss, obviously reached this stage. 'Too many men make the mistake, when they reach the point of enough,' Bok observed in explaining his retirement at 56 years of age, of 'accumulating more money, grasping for more power until either a nervous [or physical] breakdown', or an 'early grave' stops them. 'They cannot seem to get the truth into their heads that as they have been helped by others so should they now help others: as their means have come from the public, so now they owe something in turn to that public.'[62] Their quest for power, success and wealth satisfied beyond their wildest dreams, several multimillionaires now found joy in helping others. 'It is more fun to give money than to will it,' said Eastman. Cullen, who before death parted with 90 per cent of a fortune, estimated at over $200 million, 'desire[d] to spend [for benevolence] all the money I possibly can during my life, so that I may get a selfish pleasure out of spending it'.[63]

Ethnic and religious identity provided another humanitarian motive. Schiff liberally endowed Jewish organisations and causes, and Wall Street broker Thomas Fortune Ryan bestowed a tenth of his $200 million fortune upon the Catholic Church. An even more touching sentiment spurred the mother of deceased alumnus Harry Widener to give Harvard a library and Leland Stanford to create Stanford University in memory of his son.[64]

A final incentive, never publicly articulated but undoubtedly significant, was a lack of heirs, particularly male offspring, to divert resources from benevolence. Eastman never married, Carnegie and Duke each had one daughter and Stanford's only child did not survive him.

This survey discloses several trends in beneficence among the affluent. A major transformation occurred after 1900 from individualistic contributions to support for organised efforts on behalf of public welfare. The foundations, the vehicles of this innovation, over time changed the distribution of their assets. Between 1921 and 1930 aggregate allocation of foundation funds for education increased from over two-fifths to more than one-half of total disbursements. Sums devoted to health and welfare correspondingly diminished. In 1962, as compared to 1930, education still received the highest outlay but its share shrunk to 46 per cent of total grants, health dispensations decreased by one-half, religious gifts multiplied fivefold and welfare contributions fell slightly.[65] Recent domestic turmoil generated an expansion of support for civil rights and anti-poverty groups at the cost of more traditional disbursements, but in the last few years these priorities have shifted.

More subtle revelations await further investigation of a subject badly in need of illumination. Guideposts for exploration involve the following unsolved (and even unraised) problems. Little is known, for example, beyond the truism that like frequently gives to like, of how ethnicity and residential location influence the type and magnitude of upper-class philanthropy. Were Jewish multimillionaires, who belonged to a faith notable for its charity, more likely to be generous donors than rich members of other religions? Were immigrants or children of newcomers more benevolent than affluent Americans whose remote ancestors had settled in this country? Were the monied enclaves in newer or older cities, in the North or the South, in towns where the elite had or lacked a tradition of social service more or less apt to devote a larger share of their assets to public causes? The impact of vintage of wealth, personality traits, family outlook and other factors upon wealthy givers also deserves attention. Does the putative *noblesse-oblige* attitude of inherited riches and status encourage a more open purse than a fortune presumably less secure in tenure because of its recent formation? Conversely, are the self-made more generous because of their less-established claims to acceptance and deference? Or does the accumulation of more numerous heirs and higher fixed costs, and the possibly slower growth that often erodes older fortunes, make the *nouveaux riches* more generous donors? The complex elements that shape benevolence are illustrated by the dissimilar philanthropic performances in rich families. Duke, once poor, allocated over half his fortune to altruism; his daughter Doris chooses to spend her money in other ways. William C. Whitney preferred self-indulgence to alms-giving, but his son Payne left more than a quarter of his fortune to charity. A similar situation occurred in the Gould family. Jay Gould's eldest son emulated the public parsimony of his father; another son, after a lifetime of handsomly supporting benevolent causes, left half his fortune to community welfare efforts.[66] The Rockefellers, unlike these other clans, demonstrated intergenerational cohesion in philanthropy.

Property and Power

Great fortunes brought their owners public prominence, gross and refined pleasures, and even the chance to do good. But the ultimate gift of colossal wealth, at least for the founders of the richest families, was power. Money begat authority — and authority, money. Accumulation and domination are interlocking drives in the acquisitive personality, and individuals captivated by such compulsions cannot separate these quests. Vanderbilt's identification of his desire for money with his need for power has already been noted. A century later Howard Hughes, whose fortune fluctuated from $100 million to over one billion in the course of a labyrinthine business career, voiced the same sentiment. Liberally endowed with both resources, Hughes declared that 'Money is the measuring rod of power. . .The effective use of money can bring power. The effective use of power can bring money.' James Stillman amassed some $200 million and with George F. Baker and J.P. Morgan composed the holy trinity of Gilded Age high finance. In a last reflection upon the leading bankers and entrepreneurs of his era, Stillman said: ''Twasn't the money we were after, 'twas the power. We were all playing for power. It was a great game.'[67]

The lions in the jungle of American capitalism fulfilled their search for money and power by owning and operating the nation's major railways, mines and steel mills, oil fields and pipe lines, car factories, newspaper chains, insurance firms and department stores. A widespread assumption exists that the largest American business organisations have for the last two generations been managed by corporate bureaucrats who do not own the companies they direct. In fact, many of the titanic enterprises founded in the heroic age of capitalism are still headed and owned by descendants of the original proprietors: a Rockefeller grandson chairs the board of Chase Manhattan, the nation's third-largest

bank and a longtime family-controlled institution; a Ford grandson
rules the Ford Motor Company; Hearst's children run his publishing
empire; Andrew Mellon's son-in-law and nephew administer that clan's
industrial and financial interests. More systematic studies confirm these
examples of rich-family commercial dominance. One such study was an
examination of 1959 stock-ownership in the 250 biggest industrial, the
18 largest investment, and the top 18 insurance companies (ranked by
total assets in 1960). The 99 directors, who each had over $10 million
in shareholdings in the firms on whose boards they sat, possessed nearly
12 per cent of the aggregate market value of the stock of the 286
corporations.[68]

Three publications contain significant information on the vast power
and wealth of some American families. The Temporary National
Economic Committee survey, *The Distribution of Ownership in the
Largest 200 Nonfinancial Corporations*, was based on 1937 data from
the 200 greatest (by assets) American firms, exclusive of banks. In that
year this group collectively had 45 per cent of the total assets of US
non-financials and 25 per cent of the total assets of all US corporations.
'Stock Ownership and the Control of Corporations', a report in *New
University Thought*, dealt with 1959 shareholding in the 286 biggest
business establishments of 1960. *Interlocks in Corporate Management*,
an Anti-Trust Subcommittee Staff Report of the Committee on the
Judiciary of the US House of Representatives, explored the overlapping
board memberships of the 20 foremost (by 1962 sales) industrial
corporations and ten other industrial leviathans, including the American
Telephone and Telegraph Company, the 15 most prominent commercial
and the ten largest savings banks (by 1962 deposits), and the top ten
fire and casualty insurance conpanies (by 1962 assets).[69]

The TNEC survey found that the duPont, Mellon and Rockefeller
1937 shareholdings comprised nearly $1.4 billion, which directly or
indirectly (i.e. the corporations that they dominated in turn controlled
other companies) gave the three clans control of more than $8 billion
in assets, 11 per cent of the total assets of the top 200 non-financial
concerns. Thirteen families (including the above three) owned $2.7
billion worth of stock, over 8 per cent of the total stock issued by the
200. Except for the Mellons, who diversified their proprietorship, the
family holdings concentrated in the enterprises where the family
fortunes were made. The majority or substantial minority (more than
10 per cent) shareholdings of the duPonts gave the family control of
E.I. duPont de Nemours (8th largest), General Motors (25th) and US
Rubber (105th). By the same means the Mellons dominated Gulf Oil

(36th), Koppers United (60th), Pullman Inc. (74th) and the Aluminum Company of America (79th), as well as three other concerns in the second 100. Rockefeller stock-ownership preponderated in oil firms ranked second, 14th, 21st and 32nd in the top 100 companies, and one establishment in the second 100. In approximately 40 per cent of the top 200 corporations, one family or a small number of families owned a majority or a controlling minority share of the stock.[70]

The investigation of stock distribution in the gargantuan corporations of 1960 reveals little change in wealthy family proprietorship from the earlier period. Table 5.2 compares the holdings of the Mellons, duPonts and Rockefellers, individually or by family trusts, holding companies and foundations, in some of the leading corporations in 1937 and the 1950s.

An even more extensive interrelationship between the richest families and the largest stockholders in the top companies is shown by the fact that ten of the thirteen family groups in 1937 with stock valued in excess of $50 million in the 200 greatest non-financial corporations belonged to Ferdinand Lundberg's group of the 60 American families or individuals with a minimum wealth of $30 million in 1937. The persisting wealth of the thirteen family groups is manifested by their representation on the *Fortune* lists of the 76 Americans in 1957 with $75 million or more in assets and the 66 in 1968 with a minimum of $150 million. Of the richest individuals, 23 (30.2 per cent) in 1957 and 18 (27.3 per cent) in 1968 came from the top shareholding clans of 1937.[71]

Ownership confers potential influence, but actual control depends upon management of property. The proportion of wealthy family members represented in the administration of the large corporations in which they were extensive stockholders indicates whether power accompanied proprietorship. The TNEC study disclosed that 13 (21.6 per cent) of Lundberg's rich enclave were directors or officers in 1939 in the top 200 non-financial firms of 1937. The Anti-Trust Subcommittee report on directorships of the foremost US business establishments supports a contention that the rich families continued to exert influence in the companies where they were large stockholders: 15 of Lundberg's group had at least one family member on the 1962 boards of the largest American companies and 5 of Lundberg's enclave or their direct descendants, served in two or more directorships. Of the 76 richest Americans in 1957, 37 (48.7 per cent) were directors or similarly related to directors of the 1962 companies and 8 (10.8 per cent) held at least two directorships; 25 of the 66 wealthiest Americans

Table 5.2: Mellon, duPont and Rockefeller Stock-ownership in Large American Corporations

Family	Company	Percentage of common stock owned	
		1937	1950s
Mellon	Aluminum Co. of America	29.7	27.6
Mellon	Gulf Oil	70.2	30.9
duPont	E.I. duPont de Nemours	38.5	33.3+
duPont	General Motors	20.3	22.8
Rockefeller	Standard Oil of California	12.3	8.3
Rockefeller	Secony Mobil Oil	16.3	13.2
Rockefeller	Standard Oil of Indiana	11.4	6.8
Rockefeller	Standard Oil of New Jersey	13.5	60.8

Sources: Raymond W. Goldsmith and Rexford C. Parmelee, *The Distribution of Ownership in the Largest 200 Nonfinancial Corporations*, monograph no. 29 (Temporary National Economic Committee, US Government Printing Office, Washington, DC, 1940); Donald Villarejo, 'Stock Ownership and the Control of Corporations', *New University Thought*, 2 (Fall 1961).

of 1968 (37.8 per cent) were or were related to board members in these corporations and 6 (9.1 per cent) held at least two directorships.[72]

Final evidence of the merger of money and management is revealed by the portion of shareholder directors who owned more than $50 million worth of stock in 1959 in the largest American companies of 1960. Fifteen of these 28 directors (53.6 per cent) appeared on the *Fortune* list of 1957 and another had a father on this compilation. Eight of the directors (28.6 per cent) made the *Fortune* roster of 1968 and four other board members had immediate relatives on this list. Conversely, 22 of the 76 richest Americans of 1957 (28.9 per cent) and 17 of the 66 wealthiest of 1968 (25.8 per cent) were or were related to the directors of 1959.[73]

Office-holding, a stronger indication of power than is extensive stock-ownership, does not offer conclusive evidence of control. Executives and directors can participate in varying degrees in decision-making. A multitude of case studies is necessary to supply accurate information on the real influence of affluent officers and shareholders. This account of the distribution of ownership and directorships reveals that a major part of the property of the very rich involved extensive proprietorship in the leading US corporations and that members of these wealthy stockholding families frequently assumed supervisory posts in the largest American corporations. In these ways the monied elite acquired a potential to shape policy in key business establishments and to determine the course of the national economy.

The uppermost rank of wealth established its economic base, procured influence and elevated its prestige, primarily through entrepreneurship and secondarily through philanthropy and politics. The power urges, commercial interests and status yearnings of this enclave led it into political activity. This well-known aspect of the behaviour of the richest Americans needs only brief summary here. Affluent capitalists and their clans secured advantageous tariffs, land and mineral grants, protection of interests in foreign countries, turned government force against labour unions, avoided anti-trust, mining and railway regulations, obtained relief from taxation and got many other important favours by occupying public posts, putting their representatives in office and financing political parties and campaigns.

Mentioned below are prominent capitalists who held high office and had pre-1914 fortunes that exceeded $25 million, or who appeared on the Lundberg and *Fortune* lists. Wall Street investor Bernard Baruch supervised the mobilisation effort during the First World War as Chairman of the War Industries Board. During the New Deal Joseph Kennedy, another Wall Street wizard, chaired the Securities and Exchange Commission, and Texas banker and realtor Jesse H. Jones headed the Reconstruction Finance Corporation. William C. Whitney served as President Grover Cleveland's Secretary of the Navy, Andrew Mellon was Secretary of the Treasury from 1921 to 1930, Ogden Mills succeeded him, while C. Douglas Dillon held that office under President John F. Kennedy and Jones and W. Averell Harriman became Secretaries of Commerce. Sage and Hearst were elected to the US House of Representatives. Stanford, copper magnates Simon Guggenheim and William A. Clark, silver-mining tycoon James G. Fair, land baron Stephen B. Elkins and Henry A. and T. Coleman duPont sat in the US Senate. In 1907, 18 millionaires were in that chamber.[74]

Many of these 'statesmen' unabashedly used political office to advance their business interests. Mellon, in a notorious example of self and class service, reduced excess profits, income and estate taxes, thereby saving millions for himself and his companies, and hundreds of millions for his peers in the highest circles of wealth and commerce.[75] Office-holding, however, constituted a supplementary role for great entrepreneurs. Most of the premier capitalists after the 1860s, unlike those of earlier eras, did not assume government positions. Nearly all who did served for a few years and then returned to their primary vocations. Multimillionaires undertaking full-time political

careers – the Kennedys, Averell Harriman who was New York
Governor, US Senator, Ambassador to Russia and Secretary of
Commerce, Herbert Lehman, another New York Governor and US
Senator, and Nelson Rockefeller, a third New York Governor and
Vice-President of the United States – were almost invariably men of
inherited wealth. Family-founding entrepreneurs preferred bribery or
hired aides to advance their interests in the state capitals and
Washington. Elihu Root, Secretary of War in President William
McKinley's Cabinet, was an attorney for Thomas Fortune Ryan,
J.P. Morgan, and E.H. Harriman. Philander C. Knox, a US Senator
from Ohio and McKinley's Attorney General, was Frick's political and
legal handyman and conducted a crucial reorganisation of the Carnegie
Steel Company. Henry B. Payne, another US Senator from Ohio, was
a partner in the Standard Oil trust.

The government influence and political positions of the rich largely
derived from their contributions to political organisations. The
Lehmans, Fricks, Ryans, Rockefellers, Mellons and Whitneys
perennially were the chief donors to candidates and organisations
especially, but by no means exclusively, on the Republican side.

Through office-holding, employing specialists in politics in the same
manner as they did lawyers, accountants or engineers, and particularly
through funding candidates and parties, the super-rich influenced the
federal government and treated as fiefs the towns and states where
their enterprises were located. The reigns of the Guggenheims in
Colorado, the Elkins in West Virginia, the duPonts in Delaware, the
Fricks and Mellons in Pennsylvania and the Rockefellers in Ohio,
exemplify the considerable sovereignty acquired by wealthy
capitalists.[76]

Enumeration

This discussion of multimillionaires has concentrated thus far upon
types and individuals, but a more precise and comprehensive depiction
requires aggregate analysis. Early attempts to enumerate Americans
with upwards of $10 million, such as the series of articles in the 1889
issues of *Forum* or the 1913 list in the *New York World*, contained no
evidential references or explanations of methodology.[77] They omitted
individuals as wealthy as those included and sometimes underestimated
the resources of those listed. Conversely, they inflated the property-
holdings of several figures included in these compilations. Until more
accurate assessments appeared in the 1930s, the yearly Internal
Revenue Service's *Statistics of Income* provided the most accessible

and reliable information on the number of multimillionaires. Federal
tax returns, however, constitute an imperfect index of wealth. Assets
may be hidden to avoid imposts and some sources of income can
legally remain fully or partially undeclared. High income, particularly
declared earnings, also tends to greater fluctuation than does vast
wealth. The former is highly sensitive to changes in the law, interest
rates and capital gains and losses. The latter is composed of more
constant property values in the form of stock-ownership, government
bonds, real estate, *objets d'art* and fixed capital investments. Earnings
in the higher tax brackets represent only a segment of the property
which generates the income. Thus stock dividends and capital gains
provided over two-fifths and sometimes over 90 per cent of the annual
tax reported income in the range of one million dollars or above in
every year since the IRS began keeping these records. Since these
sources of income were notoriously undertaxed, those reporting a
minimum income of one million dollars generally possessed
considerably more than $10 million in wealth.[78] The number of
Americans in the one million dollars and above gross-income bracket
(a more reliable measure than net earnings, which are easier to
underdeclare for purposes of tax evasion), therefore, approximates the
uppermost rank of wealth. In 1914, 60 gross incomes of at least one
million dollars were reported to the IRS, 65 were reported in 1919,
207 in 1925, 513 in 1929, 93 in 1934, 45 in 1939, 71 in 1945, 120
in 1949 and 291 in 1954.[79]

Scholarly studies of great wealth and the estate multiplier technique
provided more reliable appraisals of the ionosphere of wealth.
Supplementing IRS data with information on corporate profits and
ownership of stock and other assets, Lundberg claimed that 60
American families or individuals had reached or surpassed the $30
million mark. In 1957 a treasury official said that between 150 and
500 Americans possessed assets of at least $50 million; the editors of
Fortune were reasonably certain that 155 of their countrymen had
achieved that distinction. Eleven years later *Fortune* asserted, on the
basis of public records and interviews, that 153 Americans were worth
a minimum of $100 million.

A more accurate measure of great wealth, the estate multiplier
technique, was first employed in 1958 when a study using this method
concluded that 2,000 residents of the United States had fortunes of
between $10 million and $20 million, and that an additional number
ambiguously stated at less than 1,000 had a net worth of or above $20
million. The IRS, through the same analysis, estimated that 1,784

people in 1962 and 3,413 in 1969 had $10 million or more, and that 11,300 in 1972 were worth at least $5 million (the highest category mentioned in the latest IRS report).[80]

These various sources show that, as in the case of millionaires, the number of richest Americans rose in prosperous years and fell when the national economy lagged. But the multimillionaire group has never surpassed its 1914-21 growth rate.

Immense accumulations have historically multiplied in size as well as in number. John Jacob Astor in the 1840s and Cornelius Vanderbilt a decade later amassed $20 million, the largest American antebellum fortunes. William B. Astor and dygoods retailer Alexander T. Stewart in the 1870s had double that amount, and Cornelius Vanderbilt attained the unprecedented height of $100 million. In the next decade William H. Vanderbilt achieved another level of pre-eminence by acquiring riches of $200 million. John D. Rockefeller in 1913 became the first billionaire, an accomplishment unequalled for another 40 years and exceeding the combined family fortunes of the Astors, Vanderbilts, Carnegies, Harrimans and Morgans.[81]

The IRS reports do not distinguish these levels of wealth and the Lundberg and *Fortune* rolls do not cover the entire period under study. Hence it is necessary to compile, from biographical and historical accounts and published tax records and wills, a catalogue of Americans who, between 1865 and the present, arrived at these ranks of affluence. Evaluating titanic accumulations presents problems. 'I cannot even judge the extent of my own fortune with any degree of accuracy,' observed J. Paul Getty in commenting upon *Fortune* designating him the first American billionaire since Rockefeller, 'the values of a businessman's holdings fluctuate greatly.'[82] Public and private gifts, to meet social or familial obligations or to avoid inheritance and income taxes, self-indulgence and fluctuating economic conditions, especially variations in corporate stock values, significantly modified the holdings of the super-rich. Enormous changes have also occurred in constant dollar values over time in the national price and corporate stock indexes. A fortune of $20 million in current dollars obviously does not have the prominence, power or infrequency that this sum had in the 1890s.[83]

Taking account of these changes and, even more important, of the personal resources commanded by the leading entrepreneurs, philanthropists, society figures and conspicuous consumers at different times since the Civil War, necessitates an enumeration of those worth at least $20 million between 1865 and 1919, those with assets of $30 million or more between 1920 and 1945, and those with a minimum of

$75 million after the Second World War. Longevity of fortune is another criterion for inclusion. Those who made a fortune and quickly lost it usually did not keep their gains long enough to qualify as luminaries of capitalism, charity or the world of society and celebrity. Continuity, however, does not present a major difficulty; the holdings of the fabulously endowed rarely evaporated in rapid fashion. Finally, to unify standards and allow for shrinkages that resulted from transfers of assets to public, institutional or private recipients, this inventory of pre-eminent wealth is based upon maximum lifetime property concentration.

From 1865 to the present day, 310 Americans have been found to meet these criteria. Of the 300 with ascertained dates of birth, 27 (9.0 per cent) were born before 1830, 105 (35.0 per cent) between 1830 and 1864, 113 (37.7 per cent) between 1865 and 1899, and 55 (18.3 per cent) in the twentieth century (only one after 1930).[84]

Collective Biography

Enumeration precedes the important task of systematic evaluation. But this sequential strategy rarely guides historical interpretations of American multimillionaires. Generalisations about the monied elite usually proceed from impressionistic reasoning and incomplete evidence. While intuition sometimes yields striking insights, it frequently substitutes for rigorous research. Several collective trait analyses, however, based on careful assessments of massive accumulations of data, provide useful comparisons to the monied elite here examined. Pitirim Sorokin's 'American Millionaires and Multi-Millionaires' (1925) was the first statistically sophisticated group profile of the very rich. Chester M. Destler's 'Entrepreneurial Leadership Among the "Robber Barons"' (1946), the next cumulative biography, dealt with a smaller, but in the present context, a highly relevant assemblage of multimillionaires. The most valuable of these aggregate portraits appeared in *The Power Elite* by C. Wright Mills (1956). Mills defined the degree of wealth with greater precision than did Sorokin, and explored more variables and covered a longer timespan than did the other scholars.[85]

Sorokin selected a sample of 668 living and dead millionaires and multimillionaires, mostly well-known businessmen whose careers peaked after the Civil War. Destler focused on the social background of 43 leading Gilded Age capitalists; the overwhelming majority of these tycoons are also included in this analysis of affluent Americans. Mills surveyed biographical data on 90 Americans worth at least $30 million

in 1900 and 95 and 90 individuals at that wealth level in 1925 and
1950 respectively.

Similar findings appeared for the analytic categories common to
the three studies. Nearly 90 per cent of Sorokin's, Detler's and
Mills's 1900 cohorts were native born; 98 per cent of Mills's 1950
group also originated in the United States. The proportions of native
Americans in the ranks of the affluent were significantly higher than
in the national population at these times. The fathers of these privileged
groups were more likely to follow callings associated with greater
wealth and higher status than the contemporary vocational-frequency
distribution in the United States. Over three-fifths of the fathers of
Sorokin's sample were businessmen and another one-seventh were
professionals; less than 5 per cent were artisans and 13 per cent were
farmers. Destler found that one-third of the magnates were at least
second-generation entrepreneurs and that an additional one-sixth were
sons of professionals; 35 per cent were children of farmers and 5 per
cent came from working-class families. Some 70 per cent of the male
parents of Mills's cohorts were urban entrepreneurs, 10 per cent were
professionals and another 10 per cent were wage-earners, either white
or blue collar.

Sorokin and Mills probed more extensively into the social
background of their subjects than did Destler. Variables investigated
by both authors showed substantial agreement. The high frequency of
remunerative and prestigious paternal vocations reflected the
comparatively (to the general population of their time) privileged
origins of the rich. Of Sorokin's millionaires, 28 per cent were born
poor while 42 per cent came from wealthy families and the remainder
from moderate circumstances. The living and generally younger group
showed a markedly greater trend toward inherited wealth and away
from humble beginnings. Mills had similar findings. The upper-class
(nine-tenths of whom inherited fortunes with a minimum value of
$500,000) and lower-class parentage of the 1900 enclave were evenly
balanced, each representing 39 per cent of the total. The well-born
rose to 68 per cent and the Horatio Alger types fell to 9 per cent of
the 1950 echelon.

These two studies also agreed upon the domestic geographical
distribution of the monied elite. Seven-eights of Sorokin's deceased
millionaires and four-fifths of Mills's 1900 group, came from the
eastern seaboard states. Slightly over two-thirds of Sorokin's living
millionaires and a similar share of Mills's 1950 monied elite were born
in that region. The Atlantic coast representation among the affluent far

exceeded its share of the national population. The second-largest source of rich Americans, the Chicago-Cleveland-Detroit industrial area, produced 9 per cent of Sorokin's dead and 21 per cent of his living millionaires. The same region provided the birthplaces of 16 per cent of Mills's 1900 group and 19 per cent of the 1950 class. This geographical distribution reflects the primacy of the North-east, particularly New York and Pennsylvania, in American capitalism. In more recent decades the North-east retained dominance but its lead over other sections gradually diminished. As revealed by Mills's figures, the Midwest increase did not account for this drop-off. Most of the shift in birthplace frequency was due to the upsurge of the South-west, especially the emergence of cattle and oil tycoons in Texas. This region contributed one per cent of Mills's 1900 enclave and 10 per cent of his 1950 group.

In another concordant finding, Sorokin and Mills showed that the percentages of the very rich who attended institutions of higher learning far exceeded the national averages for the relevant time periods. In Sorokin's sample 54 per cent attained that level of education; 31 per cent of Mills's 1900 enclave and 68 per cent of his 1950 group graduated from college.[86]

Other traits were not examined by both authors; therefore, the aggregate analyses of these attributes did not receive independent confirmation. Sorokin provided evidence that, relative to national frequencies between 1890 and 1920, the pre-eminently wealthy wedded later and had considerably higher rates of marriage and divorce. He showed that the monied elite also had more children and lived much longer than the contemporary national averages. Compared to their percentages in the general population, Jews were heavily overrepresented and Catholics significantly underrepresented among the millionaires. Sorokin's sample achieved success at an early age: over half of those from poor or moderately propertied families made at least $300,000 by the time they reached their forties and almost five-sixths of those with inherited wealth became presidents or vice-presidents of major corporations before the age of forty. Finally, manufacturing was the largest single vocation of the millionaires and half of the total group were industrialists or bankers and brokers.[87]

Sorokin and Mills sought to depict the social characteristics of the super-rich. Mills, however, also emphasised their elite status and aristocratic orientation. While Sorokin discussed family size, marital status and longevity, Mills stressed prestigious institutional affiliations. One-third of the college graduates in Mills's study went to Harvard or

Yale. The uppermost rank of wealth also belonged to the most
fashionable religions: half worshipped in the Episcopalian faith and
one-quarter were Presbyterians. Economic and social elites considerably
overlapped. Half the descendants of the richest people of 1900
appeared in the social registers of Boston, New York, Philadelphia and
Chicago in the 1950s. The super-rich were unified by shared
experiences of great wealth, social prominence and membership in
high-status institutions. Group cohesion was more intimately fortified,
as in the case of other upper classes, by extensive kinship networks and
intermarriage: one-third of the 1925 enclave was related to the 1900
group and over three-fifths of the premier wealth-holders of 1950 were
similarly connected to those in the two earlier intervals. Family ties
influenced business activity, a development that further integrated the
highest rank of affluence. Nearly two-fifths of the 1950 group held
high positions in ancestrally founded firms. These patrician elements
in the monied elite did not, however, create a leisured upper class.
Although the proportion of rentiers increased from 14 per cent in 1900
to 26 per cent in 1950, the vast majority, even at the later date, were
engaged in gainful employment.[88]

Unlike Sorokin, Destler and Mills, Frederick Lewis Allen's profile
of leading turn-of-the-century multimillionaire capitalists is based on
too small a sample to validly represent the super-rich. But nine of the
ten individuals he studied are included in the data base for the collective
biography presented in this chapter. More important, Allen highlights
some significant trends not covered by the other scholars. Although
only one of the magnates went to college, their 15 sons who lived to
an eligible age attended institutions of higher learning and 12 went to
Harvard or Yale. Jacob Schiff alone, the sole Jew, was not listed in the
social register. The other nine averaged 9.4 club memberships; only
four, however, belonged to the most prestigious associations. As in
education, their sons acquired more extensive patrician credentials:
two of the fathers and six of the sons belonged to the Knickerbocker,
New York's top-ranked social club.[89] Larger groups of equal affluence
exhibited the same tendencies, but their aristocratic aspirations were
not always fully realised. Inheritors were more likely than accumulators
to enter elite social and academic institutions. Indeed, money, especially
when properly aged, facilitated admission into the upper class, and the
desire for high status often intensified the drive for pecuniary
aggrandisement.

These surveys contain useful information and insights, but different
concerns and limitations of scope and method necessitate yet another

endeavour in collective trait analysis. Sorokin's investigation ends in
1920 and insufficiently distinguishes birth cohorts and levels of wealth.
Destler deals with too small a sample, too narrow a timespan, too few
biographical variables, and selects for entrepreneurial performance
rather than size of fortune. Mills's time intervals omit the first and last
generation of great wealth since 1865. His study does not allow for
substantial fluctuations in money values and numbers of great
accumulators over a 50-year period. The same number of dollars define
titanic fortunes for a half-century and the three groups of
multimillionaires are kept approximately uniform in size. Fortunately,
the IRS annual *Statistics of Incomes, Estates,* and *Personal Wealth*
contain aggregate data on asset distribution, gender, marital status, age
and residence for larger numbers of the rich in more recent years and
at more specifically and objectively determined wealth levels. Tables
5.3 to 5.8 construct, through IRS statistics on these variables, a
collective profile of the wealth elite.

Table 5.3 dramatically reveals a crucial difference in property
holding between the affluent and the lesser endowed. Pre-Civil War

**Table 5.3: The Percentage of Stock-ownership as a Source of Income
for Those with Minimum Net Earnings of $1 Million in 1914, 1919 and
1929, and as a Source of Wealth for Those with a Minimum Net Worth
of $10 Million in 1958, 1962 and 1969, and $5 Million* in 1972**

Year	Percentage of net income or wealth
1914	73.8
1919	97.8
1929**	78.7
1939	70.3
1949	76.7
1958	91.7
1962	86.0
1969	52.9
1972	48.9

*The highest rank of wealth measured in that year.
**Stock-ownership was underrepresented because dividends from foreign stock
  and from sale of stock and capital gains from stocks held less than two years
  were not included in the income statistics.
Sources: IRS: *Statistics of Income for 1919*, p. 33; *1929*, p. 5; *1939*, pp. 26-28;
  1949, pp. 23-24; *Supplemental 1962*, pp. 59, 190; *Supplemental 1969*, p. 19;
  Supplemental 1972, p. 12.

228   *The Gilded Elite*

fortunes came largely from such tangible assets as land, building, ships, inventories and firms. Since the late nineteenth century, stock-ownership accounts for the major share of great personal wealth. Recently, this form of wealth has somewhat diminished because modification in tax laws makes other types of investment, for example municipal bonds, more attractive. Wages and salaries, on the other hand, compose the bulk of the sparse resources of the masses.

Males preponderated in the highest class and had an edge in the top net worth rank. This dominance is underscored by the obvious fact that males have composed about half of the national population. Females did better in the net worth than in the income brackets because they lived longer, thus more often inheriting money upon the deaths of spouses than did males. The smaller feminine representation in the high-earning group is also due to the fact that incomes peak at a lower age than does net worth, therefore favouring men over women, and to social conventions that inhibit female earning power.

Single individuals were rarer among the very rich than in the total population. In 1920, 58.2 per cent, in 1940, 58.9 per cent, in 1960, 67.3 per cent and in 1970, 62.7 per cent of Americans fourteen years and older had spouses.[90] The comparison between the national and

Table 5.4: Gender of Those with Minimum Gross Incomes of $1 Million in 1919, 1929, 1939 and 1949, and of Those with a Minimum Net Worth of $10 Million in 1962 and 1969, and $5 Million in 1972

Year	Total number	Males		Females	
		No.	%	No.	%
1919	65	57	87.7	8	12.3
1929*	513	365	71.7	148	28.9
1939	44	32	72.7	12	27.3
1949*	120	90	75.0	30	25.0
1962	1,784	1,173	65.8	611	34.2
1969	3,412	1,635	47.9	1,777	52.1
1972	11,300	6,700	59.3	4,600	40.7

*Eighty-five per cent of joint and community property returns in 1929 and 1949 were assigned to males because they accounted for 86.8 per cent and 82.9 per cent respectively of separate returns for spouses in 1945 and 1949.

Sources: IRS: *Statistics of Income for 1919*, pp. 48-49; *1929*, pp. 70-71; *1939*, pp. 110-13; *1949*, p. 141; *Supplemental 1972*, p. 15.

Table 5.5: Marital Status of Those with a Minimum Gross Income of $1 Million in 1919, 1929, 1939, 1949 and 1954, and Those with a Minimum Net Worth of $5 Million* in 1962, 1969 and 1972

Year	Total number	Married No.	%	Single** No.	%
1919	65	47	72.3	18	27.7
1929	501***	357	71.2	144	28.8
1939	44	33	75.0	11	25.0
1949	120	89	74.1	31	25.9
1954	201	146	72.6	55	27.4
1962	4,457	3,281	73.6	1,176	26.4
1969	9,239	6,125	66.3	3,197	33.7
1972	11,300	7,200	63.7	4,100	36.3

*Highest designated bracket.
**Widowed, divorced or never married. In 1939 this category included separated spouses.
***Twelve community property returns did not specify marital status.
Sources: IRS: *Statistics of Income for 1919*, pp. 48-49; *1929*, pp. 70-71; *1939*, pp. 110-113; *1949*, pp. 141-45; *1954*, pp. 59-60; *Supplemental 1962*, p. 22; *1969*, pp. 22-23; *1972*, pp. 15-17.

multimillionaire proportions of married people favours the latter because of the inclusion of teenagers in the former group. But this distortion is balanced by the concentration of the rich in old-age levels where spousal deaths are more frequent. The divergence in marital status between the wealthy and the general average resulted from better physical and emotional health, greater vocational opportunities and other advantages that accompany money. At the very least the problem of making ends meet would not cause divorces or prevent marriages among the affluent.

Table 5.6 reflects the fact that longevity is associated with great fortunes and marriage. The vastly higher proportions of rich Americans, compared to the national frequencies in the old-age bracket (8.1 per cent of the population was 65 years and older in 1950, 9.1 per cent in 1960 and 9.9 per cent in 1970) was due to better living conditions and medical care in the affluent enclave.[91] Despite the strains involved in accumulating or inheriting a fortune, comparative longevity also stems from a healthier emotional disposition in the rich. Wealth aids the psyche by facilitating vocational choice, leisure, enjoyment and personal esteem, and by reducing the likelihood of self-isolation.

Table 5.6: Number and Percentage of Decedents Seventy Years and
Older with Minimum Net Estates of $5 Million Filed in 1950 and
$10 Million Filed in 1954. Number and Percentage of Americans
Sixty-five Years and Older with a Minimum Net Worth of $5 Million
in 1962 and 1972, and $10 Million in 1969

Year	Minimum net worth* ($ million)	Total number	Oldest age bracket	No. in oldest age bracket	Percentage in oldest age bracket
1950	5	12	70	9	75.0
1954	10	17	70	15	88.2
1962	5	4,457	65	1,364	30.6
1969	10	3,414	65	854	25.0
1972	5	11,300	65	4,400	38.9

*Highest designated bracket.

Sources: IRS: *Statistics of Income for 1949*, p. 379; *1953*, p. 82; *Supplemental 1962*, p. 19; *1969*, pp. 31-32; *1972*, pp. 24-25.

Physical and emotional fitness, in turn, enhance the acquisition of wealth. Hence, the self-made contingent of the multimillionaires constitutes a pre-selected substratum that expands the aggregate lifespan of the group.

Tables 5.7 and 5.8 relate the geographical distribution of one million dollars minimum incomes to regional shares of the national population. A shift of high incomes from the North-east, the historical centre of personal wealth, is disclosed in the post-Second World War upsurge in the West South Central and Pacific coast states and the corresponding decrease in the New England and Middle Atlantic areas. Although New York remains the leading home of one million dollars minimum income-earners, its national salience has declined and Pennsylvania no longer ranks second in this category. Since the early 1940s the great incomes have increasingly clustered in Texas in the West South Central division and California on the Pacific coast. Eastern affluence derived chiefly from older mercantile and industrial enterprises; lately the most lucrative pursuits tend to be independent oil operations, recreational and aerospace activities, and other facets of economic growth in the Sunbelt.

Annual IRS accounts give a reasonably precise depiction of the collective social dimensions of great personal wealth. The accuracy of these data, however, is marred by undeclared or devalued assets in

Table 5.7: Regional Location of $1 Million Minimum Gross Income Earners, Selected Years

Region	1919		1929		1939		1949	
	No.	%	No.	%	No.	%	No.	%
New England	5	7.7	31	6.0	–	–	3	2.5
Middle Atlantic	36	55.4	337	65.7	27	61.4	57	47.5
East North Central	14	21.5	90	17.5	6	13.6	13	10.8
West North Central	1	1.5	8	1.6	–	–	3	2.5
South Atlantic	5	7.7	23	4.5	11	25.0	17	14.2
East South Central	–	–	4	0.8	–	–	3	2.5
West South Central	2	3.1	7	1.4	–	–	13	10.8
Mountain	–	–	1	0.2	–	–	1	0.8
Pacific	2	3.1	12	2.3	–	–	10	8.3
Total	65	100	513	100	44	100	120	100
New York State	25	38.5	276	53.8	16	31.6	45	37.5

Region	1954		1963		1972*	
	No.	%	No.	%	No.	%
New England	9	4.5	16	4.3	60	5.9
Middle Atlantic	83	41.3	120	32.4	289	28.4
East North Central	20	10.0	50	13.5	184	18.0
West North Central	5	2.5	20	5.4	48	4.7
South Atlantic	31	15.4	69	18.6	124	12.2
East South Central	1	0.5	5	1.3	23	2.2
West South Central	25	12.4	33	8.9	105	10.3
Mountain	5	2.5	14	3.8	17	1.7
Pacific	22	10.9	42	11.3	166	16.3
Other Areas	–	–	2	0.5	3	0.3
Total	201	100	371	100	1,019*	100
New York	56	27.9	85	22.9	181	18.7

*Arkansas, Idaho, Mississippi, New Hampshire, North Carolina, South Carolina and Vermont did not segregate incomes above $500,000. West Virginia and Montana did not segregate incomes above $200,000. Since 28 per cent of the former bracket and 4.5 per cent of the latter bracket earned at least $1 million, the total number of $1 million minimum incomes from each of these states was estimated according to the national percentages of the uppermost rank in the $500,000 minimum class and the $200,000 minimum class. In any case these were relatively small and poor states and do not significantly affect the national geographic distribution of $1 million minimum income-earners.

Sources: IRS: *Statistics of Income for 1919*, pp. 64-97; *1929*, pp. 80-151; *1939*, pp. 176-201; *149*, pp. 162-74; *1963*, pp. 100-17; *1972*, pp. 240-66.

Table 5.8: Regional Percentage Distribution in the National Population, Selected Years

Region	Year					
	1920	1930	1940	1950	1960	1970
New England	7.0	6.7	6.4	6.2	5.9	5.8
Middle Atlantic	21.1	21.4	20.9	20.0	19.1	18.3
East North Central	20.3	20.6	20.2	20.2	20.2	19.8
West North Central	11.9	10.8	10.3	9.3	8.6	8.0
South Atlantic	13.2	12.8	13.5	14.1	14.5	15.1
East South Central	8.4	8.1	8.2	7.6	6.7	6.3
West South Central	9.7	9.9	9.9	9.6	9.5	9.5
Mountain	3.1	3.0	3.2	3.4	3.8	4.1
Pacific	5.3	6.7	7.4	9.6	11.8	13.1
Total	100.0	100.0	100.0	100.0	100.0	100.0
New York State	9.9	10.2	10.2	9.8	9.4	9.0

Sources: *Statistical History*, p. 21; *US Census of Population 1960*, p. 19;
    1970, p. 51.

earnings and estates returns in order to escape taxes. The reports do not record the vital factor of continuity in great fortunes because they do not identify, and seldom trace from year to year, large income-earners, estate-leavers or individuals of huge net worth. Moreover, the IRS statistics on income were not issued before 1914 and on net worth before 1962. Correcting for these distortions and omissions necessitates an aggregate trait analysis of the list of American multimillionaires compiled in this chapter. Tables 5.9 to 5.26 present data for the 310 richest Americans on source of fortune, birthplace, paternal occupation, vintage of wealth, kinship, educational level, religious affiliation, gender, age, marital status, number of children, political party membership and government office-holding. These findings are organised by birth cohort to disclose changes over time, and related to national frequencies to compare the group with the entire population.[92]

Table 5.9 confirms Sorokin's evidence regarding the importance of industrial enterprise in the acquisition of mammoth fortunes. Before the Civil War, land, trade and banking accounted for most vast accumulations of wealth. Beginning in the 1820s, manufacturing, especially textiles, and rail became a major source of great fortune. During the generation after the Civil War America became the leading

Table 5.9: Primary Source of Wealth and Birth Cohort of the Richest Americans

Birth cohort	Primary source of wealth						
	Finance capitalism	Steel	Oil	Mining	Rail	Automobiles	Other manufacturing
Pre-1830							
Number	5	—	1	2	8	—	5
Percentage*	(18.5)	—	(3.7)	(7.4)	(29.6)	—	(18.5)
Percentage**	[12.5]	—	[2.1]	[10.5]	[32.0]	—	[5.7]
1830-65							
Number	15	4	12	11	11	3	22
Percentage	(14.3)	(3.8)	(11.4)	(10.5)	(10.5)	(2.9)	(21.9)
Percentage	[37.5]	[66.7]	[25.0]	[57.9]	[44.0]	[18.8]	[25.0]
1866-99							
Number	11	1	23	4	6	9	37
Percentage	(9.7)	(0.9)	(20.4)	(3.5)	(5.3)	(8.0)	(32.7)
Percentage	[27.5]	[16.7]	[47.9]	[21.1]	[24.0]	[56.3]	[42.0]
1900-							
Number	9	—	10	2	—	4	18
Percentage	(16.4)	—	(18.2)	(3.6)	—	(7.3)	(32.7)
Percentage	[22.5]	—	[20.8]	[10.5]	—	[25.0]	[20.5]
Unknown							
Number	—	1	2	—	—	—	6
Percentage	—	(10.0)	(20.0)	—	—	—	(60.0)
Percentage	—	[16.7]	[4.2]	—	—	—	[6.8]
Total							
Number	40	6	48	19	25	16	88
Percentage	(12.9)	(1.9)	(15.5)	(6.1)	(8.1)	(5.2)	(28.4)
Percentage	[100.0]	[100.1]	[100.0]	[100.0]	[100.0]	[100.1]	[100.0]

Table 5.9 *(contd.)*

	Utilities	Other transportation	Real estate	Trade	Publishing	General capitalism***	Other****	Total
Pre-1830								
Number	—	—	4	1	—	1	—	27
Percentage	—	—	(14.8)	(3.7)	—	(3.7)	—	(99.9)
Percentage	—	—	[23.5]	[7.1]	—	[11.1]	—	[8.7]
1830-65								
Number	5	—	7	8	4	2	1	105
Percentage	(4.8)	—	(6.7)	(7.6)	(3.8)	(1.9)	(1.0)	(100.2)
Percentage	[62.5]	—	[41.2]	[57.1]	[36.4]	[22.2]	[20.0]	[33.9]
1866-99								
Number	3	3	2	5	5	2	2	113
Percentage	(2.7)	(2.7)	(1.8)	(4.4)	(4.4)	(1.8)	(1.8)	(100.2)
Percentage	[37.5]	[75.0]	[11.8]	[35.7]	[45.5]	[22.2]	[40.0]	[36.5]
1900-								
Number	—	1	3	—	2	4	2	55
Percentage	—	(1.8)	(5.5)	—	(3.6)	(7.3)	(3.6)	(100.1)
Percentage	—	[25.0]	[17.6]	—	[18.2]	[44.4]	[40.0]	[17.7]
Unknown								
Number	—	—	1	—	—	—	—	10
Percentage	—	—	(10.0)	—	—	—	—	(100.0)
Percentage	—	—	[5.9]	—	—	—	—	[3.2]
Total								
Number	8	4	17	14	11	9	5	310
Percentage	(2.6)	(1.3)	(5.5)	(4.5)	3.5	(2.9)	(1.6)	(100.0)
Percentage	[100.0]	[100.0]	[100.0]	[99.9]	[100.0]	[99.9]	[100.0]	[100.0]

*Percentages in parentheses indicate the contribution of each source to the total in that birth cohort.

**Percentages in square brackets indicate the contribution of each cohort to the total source.

***General capitalism indicates more than one source of wealth.

****Includes 1 rancher, 2 insurance underwriters, 1 lawyer, 1 film, TV and radio figure.

Table 5.10: Birthplace and Birth Cohorts of the Richest Americans

Birth cohort	New England	Middle Atlantic	East North Central	Birthplace West North Central	South Atlantic	East South Central	West South Central
Pre-1830							
Number	1	19	1	—	1	—	—
Percentage*	(3.7)	(70.4)	(3.7)	—	(3.7)	—	—
Percentage**	[4.0]	[16.0]	[2.1]	—	[3.6]	—	—
1830-65							
Number	15	43	19	—	8	1	2
Percentage	(14.4)	(41.3)	(18.3)	—	(7.7)	(1.0)	(2.0)
Percentage	[60.0]	[36.1]	[39.6]	—	[28.6]	[33.3]	[13.3]
1866-99							
Number	6	39	18	11	16	2	9
Percentage	(5.6)	(36.1)	(16.7)	(10.2)	(14.8)	(1.9)	(8.3)
Percentage	[24.0]	[32.8]	[37.5]	[78.6]	[57.1]	[66.7]	[60.0]
1900-							
Number	3	16	10	3	3	—	3
Percentage	(6.7)	(35.5)	(22.2)	(6.7)	(6.7)	—	(6.7)
Percentage	[12.0]	[13.4]	[20.8]	[21.4]	[10.7]	—	[20.0]
Unknown							
Number	—	2	—	—	—	—	1
Percentage	—	(66.7)	—	—	—	—	(33.3)
Percentage	—	[1.7]	—	—	—	—	[6.7]
Total							
Number	25	119	48	14	28	3	15
Percentage	(8.7)	(41.5)	(16.7)	(4.9)	(9.8)	(1.0)	(5.2)
Percentage	[100.0]	[100.0]	[100.0]	[100.0]	[100.0]	[100.0]	[100.0]

Table 5.10 (contd.)

Pre-1830	Mountain	Pacific Coast	Canada	Foreign	Known total	Group total***	New York
Number	—	—	1	4	27	27	14
Percentage	—	—	(3.7)	(14.8)	(100.0)	(100.0)	(51.9)
Percentage	—	—	[33.3]	[16.7]	[9.4]	[8.7]	[18.9]
1830-65							
Number	—	1	1	14	104	105	28
Percentage	—	(1.0)	(1.0)	(13.5)	(100.2)	(99.0)	(26.9)
Percentage	—	[20.0]	[33.3]	[58.3]	[36.2]	[33.9]	[37.8]
1866-99							
Number	2	1	1	3	108	113	21
Percentage	(1.9)	(0.9)	(0.9)	(2.8)	(100.1)	(95.6)	(19.4)
Percentage	[66.7]	[20.0]	[33.3]	[12.5]	[37.6]	[36.5]	[28.4]
1900-							
Number	1	3	—	3	45	55	11
Percentage	(2.2)	(6.7)	—	(6.7)	(100.1)	(81.9)	(24.4)
Percentage	[33.3]	[60.0]	—	[12.5]	[15.7]	[17.7]	[14.9]
Unknown							
Number	—	—	—	—	3	10	—
Percentage	—	—	—	—	(100.0)	(30.0)	—
Percentage	—	—	—	—	[1.0]	[3.2]	—
Total							
Number	3	5	3	24****	287	310	74
Percentage	(1.0)	(1.7)	(1.0)	(8.4)	(99.9)	(92.6)	(25.8)
Percentage	[100.0]	[100.0]	[100.0]	[100.0]	[99.9]	[100.0]	[100.0]

*Percentages in parentheses indicate the contribution from each birthplace to the total birth cohort.
**Percentages in square brackets indicate the contribution of each birth cohort to the total of birthplaces.
***Percentages in group total indicate the proportion of the known total of the entire group.
****One born in China and the rest in Europe.

Table 5.11: Regional and New York Residential Percentages and Foreign-born Percentage of the US Population, 1800, 1830, 1860, 1890 and 1910

Region	Year				
	1800	1830	1860	1890	1910
New England	23.2	15.2	10.0	7.5	7.1
Middle Atlantic	26.4	27.9	23.7	20.2	21.0
East North Central	1.0	11.4	22.0	21.4	19.8
West North Central	–	1.1	6.9	14.2	12.7
South Atlantic	43.1	28.3	17.1	14.1	13.3
East South Central	6.3	14.1	12.8	10.2	9.1
West South Central	–	1.9	5.6	7.5	9.6
Mountain	–	–	0.6	1.9	2.9
Pacific	–	–	1.4	3.0	4.5
Total	100.0	99.9	100.1	100.0	100.0
New York	11.1	14.9	12.3	9.5	9.9
Foreign-born	–	–	13.2	14.7	14.7

Source: *Statistical History*, p. 66.

industrial power, a development reflected in the primacy of manufacturing as a source of colossal personal affluence.

The birthplace distribution of the richest Americans confirms the Sorokin and Mills findings, although the proportion of the monied elite originating along the Atlantic seaboard was not as high as in their studies. Another finding of these earlier investigations verified by Table 5.10 is the decline of these sections (New England, Middle and South Atlantic) as a source for multimillionaires in the post-1830 birth cohorts. The North-east (New England and the Middle Atlantic states) ceased to contribute a majority of the super-rich after the 1830-65 birth cohort; in the twentieth-century birth cohort the Atlantic coast no longer furnished a majority of the birthplaces. In every birth cohort, however, the Middle Atlantic section by far had the largest single contingent of birthplaces. Its predominance was largely due to the primacy of New York State. The last column in Table 5.10 shows that this state, despite a steep fall off after the pre-1830 cohort, retained its pre-eminence among the states as a birthplace for multimillionaires.

A comparison between Tables 5.10 and 5.11 shows which sections of the country at which times, by dint of their share of the national population, are overrepresented or underrepresented as birthplaces for the richest Americans. The same procedure relates the percentages of foreign-born in the entire population and among the multimillionaires.

The birthplace frequencies in the monied elite were determined by the flow of national settlement and the geographical concentration of great industrial and financial enterprises. Throughout the first three birth cohorts the nation's populace, factories, banks and railways were primarily located in the North-east. When the Midwest (East North Central states) emerged as a population, industrial, transportation and banking centre it assumed greater prominence as a progenitor of the fabulously wealthy. In the last two birth cohorts this section ranked second to the North-east in business and population, a development reflected in the fact that in the post-1830 birth cohorts the East North Central stood next to the Middle Atlantic area as a birthplace for the richest Americans.

A comparison of Tables 5.10 and 5.7 indicates that the Middle Atlantic and East North Central regions will further decline as progenitors of the affluent. Table 5.7 shows the representation of the former section steadily dwindling as a residential locus for the monied elite and the displacement since 1929 of the East North Central states as the second-ranked location for multimillionaires. The South and Far West have correspondingly gained in importance as havens for the opulent. If the population (as shown in Table 5.8 and 5.11) and economic growth of the United States continue to drift southward and westward, current and future birth cohorts of rich Americans will increasingly originate as well as locate in these areas.

Table 5.12 explores the family background of the wealthiest Americans. The survey of paternal vocations, in substantial agreement with Sorokin and Mills, shows that over three-fifths of the multimillionaires' fathers pursued business careers and that three-quarters were either professionals or businessmen. In this, as in other respects, the monied elite's origins were considerably more privileged than the generality of Americans. In 1870, 2.4 per cent of the gainfully employed males in the United States were professionals and 12 per cent (including the professionals) worked in white-collar occupations, 53.3 per cent were manual labourers and the rest were farmers. Thirty years later 3.3 per cent were professionals, 17 per cent (including the professionals) had white-collar occupations, the proportion of blue-collar workers remained unchanged and the remainder were farmers.[93] Moreover, the proportion of the monied elite with fathers in high status and income callings increased with each subsequent birth cohort.

Table 5.12: Father's Occupation and Birth Cohorts of the Richest Americans

Birth cohort	Father's occupation				
Pre-1830	Business	Professions	Farmer	Skilled labourer	Unskilled labourer
Number	13	2	8	–	1
Percentage*	(54.2)	(8.3)	(33.3)	–	(4.2)
Percentage**	[8.0]	[5.9]	[20.0]	–	[50.0]
1830-65					
Number	50	17	18	6	–
Percentage	(52.6)	(17.9)	(18.9)	(6.3)	–
Percentage	[30.9]	[50.0]	[45.0]	[37.5]	–
1866-99					
Number	62	10	14	8	–
Percentage	(63.9)	(10.3)	(14.4)	(8.2)	–
Percentage	[38.3]	[29.4]	[35.0]	[50.0]	–
1900-					
Number	34	4	–	2	1
Percentage	(82.9)	(9.8)	–	(4.9)	(2.4)
Percentage	[21.1]	[11.8]	–	[12.5]	[50.0]
Unknown					
Number	3	1	–	–	–
Percentage	(75.0)	(25.0)	–	–	–
Percentage	[1.8]	[2.9]	–	–	–
Total					
Number	162	34	40	16	2
Percentage	(62.1)	(13.0)	(15.3)	(6.1)	(0.8)
Percentage	[100.1]	[100.0]	[100.0]	[100.0]	[50.0]

Pre-1830	Government official	Farmer and business	Known total	Group total
Number	–	–	24	27
Percentage	–	–	(100.0)	(88.9)
Percentage	–	–	[9.2]	[8.7]
1830-65				
Number	2	2	95	108
Percentage	(2.1)	(2.1)	(99.9)	(88.0)
Percentage	[50.0]	[50.0]	[36.4]	[33.9]
1866-99				
Number	1	2	97	113
Percentage	(1.0)	(2.1)	(99.9)	(85.8)
Percentage	[50.0]	[50.0]	[37.2]	[36.5]
1900-				
Number	–	–	41	55
Percentage	–	–	(100.0)	(74.5)
Percentage	–	–	[15.7]	[17.7]

240   *The Gilded Elite*

Table 5.12 *(contd.)*

Pre-1830	Government official	Farmer and business	Known total	Group total
Unknown				
Number	–	–	4	10
Percentage	–	–	(100.0)	(40.0)
Percentage	–	–	[1.5]	[3.2]
Total				
Number	3	4	261	310
Percentage	(1.1)	(1.5)	(99.9)	(84.2)
Percentage	[100.0]	[100.0]	[100.0]	[100.0]

*Percentages in parentheses indicate the contribution from each occupational category to each cohort.
**Percentages in square brackets indicate the contribution of each birth cohort to the total in each occupational category.

Business and the professions (columns 1 and 2) contributed one-third of the fathers of the pre-1830 enclave and steadily climbed to more than nine-tenths of the male parents of the twentieth-century birth enclave.

Table 5.13 accords with the findings of Sorokin and Mills on the vintage of wealth. The monied elite came from considerably more affluent backgrounds in the aggregate than did the less fortunate mass of the population, a phenomenon closely related to the relatively high income and status occupations of their fathers. The strong representation of self-made figures (the first-generation column), however, indicates that a large proportion of the multimillionaires derived from families of moderate and a few from families of humble circumstances. This group, however, came from sources significantly more advantaged than did the general population: two-thirds of the first generation of great wealth had fathers in business, 20 per cent of the male parents were professionals and only 16 per cent were blue-collar workers. The trend, as disclosed in each successive birth cohort, was in the direction of inherited wealth, a development also revealed by the data of Sorokin and Mills. Related to this shift was the progressively larger proportion of comparatively old wealth (the second, third and fourth columns) in the vintage distribution. America's gigantic fortunes were, in the main, perpetuated through several generations of descendants.

Tables 5.14 and 5.15 measure kinship cohesion among the wealthiest Americans by determining the percentages of those interrelated by

Table 5.13: Vintage of Wealth and Birth Cohort of the Richest Americans

Birth cohort			Generation of wealth			
Pre-1830	First	Second	At least second	Three or more	Known total	Group total
Number	15	6	2	3	26	27
Percentage*	(57.7)	(23.1)	(7.7)	(11.5)	(100.0)	(96.3)
Percentage**	[11.4]	[10.5]	[10.0]	[4.1]	[9.2]	[8.7]
1830-65						
Number	56	19	9	21	105	105
Percentage	(53.3)	(18.1)	(8.6)	(20.0)	(100.0)	(100.0)
Percentage	[42.4]	[33.3]	[45.0]	[28.8]	[37.2]	[33.9]
1866-99						
Number	43	24	6	27	100	113
Percentage	(43.0)	(24.0)	(6.0)	(27.0)	(100.0)	(88.5)
Percentage	[32.6]	[42.1]	[30.0]	[37.0]	[35.5]	[36.5]
1900-						
Number	15	6	3	20	44	55
Percentage	(34.1)	(13.6)	(6.8)	(45.5)	(100.0)	(80.0)
Percentage	[11.4]	[10.5]	[15.0]	[27.4]	[15.6]	[17.7]
Unknown						
Number	3	2	–	2	7	10
Percentage	(42.8)	(28.6)	–	(28.6)	(100.0)	(70.0)
Percentage	[2.3]	[3.5]	–	[2.7]	[2.5]	[3.2]
Total						
Number	132	57	20	73	282	310
Percentage	(46.8)	(20.2)	(7.1)	(25.9)	(100.0)	(90.1)
Percentage	[100.1]	[99.9]	[100.0]	[100.0]	[100.0]	[100.0]

*Percentages in parentheses represent the contribution of each generational vintage to the total vintage distribution of wealth for that birth cohort.
**Percentages in square brackets represent the contribution of each birth cohort to the total of each generation of wealth.

blood or marriage within each birth cohort and those in one birth cohort who had ancestors in earlier cohorts or descendants in later cohorts. Table 5.14 reveals a considerable degree of familial connections within the cohorts and for the entire group. These ties account for most of the large segment of inherited wealth in the monied elite as shown in Table 5.13.

The measures of horizontal (Table 5.14) and vertical (Table 5.15) kinship integration in the wealth elite, respectively one-third and two-fifths of the whole group, indicate that analysis of the rich must encompass families as well as individuals. The highest rates of both

Table 5.14: Relatives and Birth Cohorts among the Richest Americans

Birth cohort	Interrelated by birth or marriage	Group total
Pre-1830		
Number	8	27
Percentage*	–	(29.6)
Percentage**	[7.5]	[8.7]
1830-65		
Number	51	105
Percentage	–	(48.6)
Percentage	[48.1]	[33.9]
1866-99		
Number	30	113
Percentage	–	(26.5)
Percentage	[28.3]	[36.5]
1900-		
Number	17	55
Percentage	–	(30.9)
Percentage	[16.0]	[17.7]
Total		
Number	106	310***
Percentage	–	(34.2)
Percentage	[99.9]	[100.0]***

*Percentages in parentheses represent the share of relatives in each birth cohort.
**Percentages in square brackets represent the contribution of each birth cohort
   to the total of relatives.
***Includes the 10 in the unknown birth cohort, none of whom were related.

types of cohesion occurred in the 1830-65 birth cohort, a sign of the
mutually reinforcing relationship between these facets of integration:
a multiplicity of rich relatives within one generation increases the
chances of perpetuating the family fortune. The founders of many
great family fortunes, the Mellon, Harriman, Rockefeller and Whitney
dynasties, were born during this period. This birth cohort may have
been better able than the subsequent cohort to perpetuate its gains.
The 1830-65 enclave placed more descendants in the post-1900 echelon
than did the 1866-99 class, despite the more immediate time link
between the latter two birth cohorts. This conclusion, however, must
remain tentative because of the longevity of the rich. Many
multimillionaires born at the end of the 1866-99 cohort still live and
may not yet have bequeathed enough of their assets to permit their
descendants to enter the stratospheric wealth bracket of the twentieth-

Table 5.15: Members of One Birth Cohort with Relatives in Other Cohorts

Birth cohort	Known total	Group total
Pre-1830		
Number	11	27
Percentage*	–	(40.7)
Percentage**	[8.6]	[8.7]
1830-65		
Number	54	105
Percentage	–	(51.4)
Percentage	[42.2]	[33.9]
1866-99		
Number	44	113
Percentage	–	(38.9)
Percentage	[34.4]	[36.5]
1900-		
Number	16	55
Percentage	–	(29.1)
Percentage	[12.5]	[17.7]
Unknown		
Number	3	10
Percentage	–	(30.0)
Percentage	[2.3]	[3.2]
Total		
Number	128	310
Percentage	–	(41.3)
Percentage	[100.0]	[100.0]

*Percentages in parentheses represent the contribution of those in one birth cohort with relatives in other birth cohorts.

**Percentages in square brackets represent the contribution of each birth cohort to the total of those with relatives in other birth cohorts.

century birth cohort. This possibility, of course, may also influence the frequency of those in the latest birth group with relatives in the previous cohorts.

Table 5.16 provides further evidence for the privileged aggregate background of the wealthiest Americans. In 1870, 1.7 per cent of the national population between 18 and 21 years old was enrolled in institutions of higher learning, and 2 per cent of the Americans aged 17 had graduated from high school. In 1900 the percentages attaining these levels of education in these age groups were respectively 4 and 6.4; 30 years later they were 12.4 and 29.0.[94] The educational advantages possessed by the monied elite relative to the entire

Table 5.16: Educational Level and Birth Cohort of the Richest Americans

Birth cohort	Educational level			
	College, seminary, business school, professional training and other post-secondary school education	Secondary school and below	Known total	Group total
Pre-1830				
Number	10	17	27	27
Percentage*	(37.0)	(63.0)	(100.0)	(100.0)
Percentage**	[5.9]	[14.8]	[9.5]	[8.7]
1830-65				
Number	46	59	105	105
Percentage	(43.8)	(56.2)	(100.0)	(100.0)
Percentage	[27.2]	[51.3]	[37.0]	[33.9]
1866-99				
Number	76	31	107	113
Percentage	(71.0)	(29.0)	(100.0)	(94.7)
Percentage	[45.0]	[27.0]	[37.7]	[36.5]
1900-				
Number	37	7	44	55
Percentage	(84.1)	(15.9)	(100.0)	(80.0)
Percentage	[21.9]	[6.1]	[15.5]	[17.7]
Unknown				
Number	–	1	1	10
Percentage	–	(100.0)	(100.0)	(10.0)
Percentage	–	[0.9]	[0.4]	[3.2]
Total				
Number	169	115	284	310
Percentage	(59.5)	(40.5)	(100.0)	(91.6)
Percentage	[100.0]	[100.1]	[100.0]	[100.0]

*Percentages in parentheses indicate the contribution of each educational level to each cohort.
**Percentages in square brackets indicate the contribution of each birth cohort to the total in each educational level.

population, a phenomenon noted by Sorokin and Mills and characteristic of the affluent groups, were obviously associated with collectively superior status and income occupations of their fathers and the large segment of inherited affluence compared to the whole population.

Religious affiliation constitutes another variable that distinguishes the multimillionaire group from the rest of the population. Tables 5.17

Table 5.17: Religious Affiliations and Birth Cohort of the Richest Americans

Birth cohort	Religious affiliation					
	Episcopalian	Presbyterian	Methodist	Baptist	Quaker	Congregationalist
Pre-1830						
Number	6	3	—	—	1	—
Percentage*	(35.3)	(17.6)	—	—	(5.9)	—
Percentage**	[8.7]	[8.8]	—	—	[33.3]	—
1830-65						
Number	25	13	3	2	2	2
Percentage	(32.9)	(17.1)	(3.9)	(2.6)	(2.6)	(2.6)
Percentage	[36.2]	[38.2]	[30.0]	[18.2]	[66.7]	[66.7]
1866-99						
Number	30	15	3	3	—	1
Percentage	(41.1)	(20.5)	(8.2)	(4.1)	—	(1.4)
Percentage	[43.5]	[44.1]	[60.0]	[27.3]	—	[33.3]
1900-						
Number	8	3	1	6	—	—
Percentage	(33.3)	(12.5)	(4.2)	(25.0)	—	—
Percentage	[11.6]	[8.8]	[10.0]	[54.5]	—	—
Unknown						
Number	—	—	—	—	—	—
Percentage	—	—	—	—	—	—
Percentage	—	—	—	—	—	—
Total						
Number	69	34	10	11	3	3
Percentage	(36.1)	(17.8)	(5.2)	(5.8)	(1.6)	(1.6)
Percentage	[100.0]	[99.9]	[100.0]	[100.0]	[100.0]	[100.0]

Table 5.17 *(contd.)*

	Unitarian	Other Protestant	Non-sectarian (attending several Protestant Churches)	Catholic	Jewish	None	Known total	Group total
Pre-1830								
Number	—	2	—	3	1	1	17	27
Percentage	—	(11.8)	—	(17.6)	(5.9)	(5.9)	(100.0)	(63.0)
Percentage	—	[25.0]	—	[16.7]	[5.0]	[20.6]	[8.9]	[8.7]
1830-65								
Number	5	3	2	10	6	3	76	105
Percentage	(6.6)	(3.9)	(2.6)	(13.2)	(7.9)	(3.9)	(99.8)	(72.4)
Percentage	[83.3]	[37.5]	[50.0]	[55.6]	[30.0]	[60.0]	[39.8]	[33.9]
1866-99								
Number	1	2	2	4	8	1	73	113
Percentage	(1.4)	(2.7)	(2.7)	(5.5)	(11.0)	(1.4)	(100.0)	(64.6)
Percentage	[16.7]	[25.0]	[50.0]	[22.2]	[40.0]	[20.0]	[38.2]	[36.5]
1900-								
Number	—	—	—	1	5	—	24	55
Percentage	—	—	—	(4.2)	(20.8)	—	(100.0)	(43.6)
Percentage	—	—	—	[5.6]	[25.0]	—	[12.6]	[17.7]
Unknown								
Number	—	1	—	—	—	—	1	10
Percentage	—	(100.0)	—	—	—	—	(100.0)	(10.0)
Percentage	—	[12.5]	—	—	—	—	[0.5]	[3.2]
Total								
Number	6	8	4	18	20	5	191	310
Percentage	(3.1)	(4.2)	(2.1)	(9.4)	(10.5)	(2.6)	(100.0)	(61.6)
Percentage	[100.0]	[100.0]	[100.0]	[100.1]	[100.0]	[100.0]	[100.0]	[100.0]

*Percentages in parentheses indicate the contribution of each religious affiliate to each birth cohort.
**Percentages in square brackets indicate the contribution of each birth cohort to the total in each religious affiliation.

Table 5.18: Percentage Distribution of Selected Religious Affiliations of the US Population, 1826, 1860, 1891, 1927 and 1951

Year	Religious affiliation				
	Episcopalian	Presbyterian	Methodist	Catholic	Jewish
1826	–	1.1	3.1	–	–
1860	–	0.9	5.3	–	–
1891	–	1.2	5.5	12.9	–
1927	1.5	1.6	6.1	16.4	–
1951	1.7	1.6	5.9	18.6	3.2

Source: *Statistical History*, pp. 228-29.

and 5.18 show that the representation of wealthy Americans in sects associated with high social and/or economic and occupational status (Episcopalian, Presbyterian and Jewish) was much larger than the percentage of these enclaves in the national population. Conversely, multimillionaire adherents of sects associated with low status and low wealth (Methodist and Catholic) were at or below the shares of these religious bodies in the total population.

Tables 5.19 to 5.23 present the vital statistics, gender, age, marital status and number of children of the richest Americans. The first of these statistical surveys discloses the overwhelming majority of males in the group. The founders of the nation's great fortunes, except for Hetty Green, were men. Many families followed the custom of bequeathing most of their property to male heirs in order to keep the money within the clan, a device sanctioned by custom and made necessary by laws, which until relatively recently gave husbands substantial control over the assets of their wives. The slight but steady trend of women to increase their representation in each birth cohort is due to legislation which enabled females to control their property, to the growth, over time, of smaller shares of wealth into substantial holdings, and to the longer lifespan of women. Table 5.19 is occasionally at variance with Table 5.4, this difference partially lies in the fact that at any given time female heirs, especially wives, will have a greater representation among the wealth elite than they will over the major timespan of the fortune. The reason for this disparity is that wives, usually outliving their husbands, will inherit the bulk of the estate. Upon their death, however, most of the property will then revert to male heirs. Another and perhaps more permanent and important explanation is that Table 5.4 concentrates exclusively upon a more

Table 5.19: Gender and Birth Cohort of the Richest Americans

Birth cohort	Gender		
	Male	Female	Group total
Pre-1830			
Number	27	0	27
Percentage*	(100.0)	(0.0)	(100.0)
Percentage**	[9.3]	[0.0]	[8.7]
1830-65			
Number	103	2	105
Percentage	(98.1)	(1.9)	(100.0)
Percentage	[35.4]	[10.5]	[33.9]
1866-99			
Number	107	6	113
Percentage	(94.7)	(5.3)	(100.0)
Percentage	[36.8]	[31.6]	[36.5]
1900-			
Number	47	8	55
Percentage	(85.5)	(14.5)	(100.0)
Percentage	[16.2]	[42.1]	[17.7]
Unknown			
Number	7	3	10
Percentage	(70.0)	(30.0)	(100.0)
Percentage	[2.4]	[15.8]	[3.2]
Total			
Number	291	19	310
Percentage	(93.9)	(6.1)	(100.0)
Percentage	[100.1]	[100.0]	[100.0]

*Percentages in parentheses indicate the contribution of each gender to each
  birth cohort.
**Percentages in square brackets indicate the contribution of each birth cohort
  to the total in each gender.

recent era in the history of the very rich.

Table 5.20 affirms Table 5.6 in showing the longevity of the very
rich relative to the national population. Over three-fifths of the monied
elite attained 70 or more years of life. In addition to the reasons
previously given, early deaths did not comport with massive fortunes
because the acquisition of vast assets almost invariably took several
decades and potential heirs had to await the death or old age of long-
lived accumulators.

Tables 5.5 and 5.22 indicate, for reasons already discussed, that the
monied elite was far less likely to remain single than was the total
population. A comparison of Tables 5.21 and 5.22 shows that the

Table 5.20: Age and Birth Cohort of the Richest Americans

Birth cohort	Age***							Known total	Group total
	30-39	40-49	50-59	60-69	70-79	80-89	Over 90		
Pre-1830									
Number	—	—	1	9	9	6	2	27	27
Percentage*	—	—	(3.7)	(33.3)	(33.3)	(22.2)	(7.4)	(99.9)	(100.0)
Percentage**	—	—	[3.3]	[13.6]	[10.6]	[8.6]	[10.5]	[9.7]	[8.7]
1830-65									
Number	—	3	13	23	29	30	7	105	105
Percentage	—	(2.9)	(12.4)	(21.9)	(27.6)	(28.6)	(6.7)	(100.1)	(100.0)
Percentage	—	[50.0]	[43.3]	[34.8]	[34.1]	[42.9]	[36.8]	[37.9]	[33.9]
1866-99									
Number	1	2	12	16	28	34	10	103	113
Percentage	(1.0)	(2.0)	(11.7)	(15.5)	(27.2)	(33.0)	(9.7)	(100.1)	(91.2)
Percentage	[100.0]	[33.3]	[40.0]	[24.2]	[32.9]	[48.6]	[52.6]	[37.2]	[36.5]
1900-									
Number	—	1	4	18	19	—	—	42	55
Percentage	—	(2.4)	(9.5)	(42.9)	(45.2)	—	—	(100.0)	(76.4)
Percentage	—	[16.7]	[13.3]	[27.3]	[22.4]	—	—	[15.2]	[17.7]
Total									
Number	1	6	30	66	85	70	19	277	310****
Percentage	(0.4)	(2.2)	(10.8)	(23.8)	(30.7)	(25.3)	(6.9)	(100.1)	(89.4)
Percentage	[100.0]	[100.0]	[99.9]	[99.9]	[100.0]	[100.0]	[99.9]	[100.0]	[100.0]

*Percentages in parentheses indicate the contribution of each age group to each birth cohort.
**Percentages in square brackets indicate the contribution of each birth cohort to the total in each age group.
***Age at death or, if still living, as of 1978.
****Includes 10 with unknown dates of birth.

Table 5.21: Marital Status and Birth Cohort of the Richest Americans

Birth cohort			Marital status			
	Married	Single	Divorced	Separated	Known total***	Group total
Pre-1830						
Number	27	–	–	–	27	27
Percentage*	(100.0)	–	–	–	(100.0)	(100.0)
Percentage**	[9.4]	–	–	–	[9.1]	[8.7]
1830-65						
Number	100	5	11	3	105	105
Percentage	(95.2)	(4.8)	(10.5)	(2.9)	(100.0)	(100.0)
Percentage	[35.0]	[41.7]	[22.9]	[75.0]	[35.2]	[33.9]
1866-99						
Number	106	5	22	1	111	113
Percentage	(95.5)	(4.5)	(19.8)	(0.9)	(100.0)	(98.2)
Percentage	[37.1]	[41.7]	[45.8]	[25.0]	[37.2]	[36.5]
1900-						
Number	48	1	15	–	49	55
Percentage	(98.0)	(2.0)	(31.3)	–	(100.0)	(89.1)
Percentage	[16.8]	[8.3]	[30.6]	–	[16.4]	[17.7]
Unknown						
Number	5	1	–	–	6	10
Percentage	(83.3)	(16.7)	–	–	(100.0)	(60.0)
Percentage	[1.7]	[8.3]	–	–	[2.0]	[3.2]
Total						
Number	286	12	48	4	298	310
Percentage	(96.0)	(4.0)	(16.1)	(1.3)	(100.0)	(96.1)
Percentage	[100.0]	[100.0]	[100.0]	[100.0]	[99.9]	[100.0]

*Percentages in parentheses indicate the contribution of each marital status to
  each birth cohort.
**Percentages in square brackets indicate the contribution of each birth cohort
  to the total in each marital status.
***Columns 1 and 2.

privileged group also had astronomically higher divorce rates than did
the national population. Sorokin noted both of these differences in his
study of the very rich. Emotional problems associated with the
acquisition and inheritance of phenomenal wealth, concentration in the
cities, and, even more significantly, the absence of economic need,
accounts for the relative frequency of dissolved marriages among the
affluent. Table 5.22 underrepresents the percentage of failed unions in
the country because it excludes couples, usually in the poorer classes,
who did not marry and later parted and those who left spouses without
legal ratification of terminated relationships. But divorce rates and

Table 5.22: Percentage of Marital Status of US Population, 1890, 1920 and 1957

Year	Marital status			
	Single	Married*	Divorced	Total
1890	39.1	60.6	0.3	100.0
1920	33.3	65.9	0.7	99.9
1957	21.1	76.8	2.0	99.9

*Includes widowed.

Source: *Statistical History*, p. 15.

Table 5.23: Number of Children per Richest Americans and Birth Cohort

Birth cohort		Number of children	
	Total number of children	Known total of richest Americans	Number of children per richest American
Pre 1830	106	25	4.24
1830-65	307	98	3.13
1866-99	250	94	2.66
1900-	124	40	3.10
Unknown	8	1	8.00
Total	789	258	3.06

Table 5.24: Number of Children Born per Ever-married US Women (Survivors of Birth Cohorts of 1835-39, 1855-59, 1875-79, 1895-99 and 1900-04): 1910, 1940 and 1950

Birth year of women	Census year	Age of women	Number of children per women
1835-39	1910	70-74	5.39
1855-59	1910	50-54	4.97
1875-79	1940	60-64	3.46
1895-99	1940	50-54	2.70
1900-04	1950	45-49	2.49

Source: *Statistical History*, p. 24.

similar *ad hoc* arrangements are also underrepresented in Table 5.21. Public biographical data, especially when furnished by the subjects, were less likely to include notification of divorce than of marriage. Moreover, separate living conditions without divorce or legal separation frequently occurred because vast wealth permitted the mismatched to maintain individual living quarters.

Tables 5.23 and 5.24 provide the data for a comparison between the number of children born to the super-rich and the population as a whole. Only one of the monied elite was born after 1930, therefore future reproduction among the multimillionaires is unlikely to affect the statistics presented even in the latest birth cohort. Moreover, the divorce rate was low enough among the affluent and their spouses to permit a valid comparison between them and the ever-marrieds in the lower economic strata. Table 5.24 does not contain enough information for twentieth-century conclusions, but the evidence clearly shows that throughout most of the nineteenth century the birth rate of the wealthiest echelon was appreciably smaller than for lesser-endowed contemporaries. This disparity may be explained by the same factors that created differences in the divorce rate between the wealthiest stratum and the less-endowed Americans. Lower birth rates, as with higher divorce rates, are commonly associated with urban life and higher levels of education. The multimillionaires were primarily city-dwellers who had considerably more schooling than the national average. Until the First World War more than half the population lived in rural areas and up to the 1870s the majority of gainfully employed Americans engaged in farming, an occupation in which children are an economic advantage. The self-made component of the multimillionaire enclave may also have depressed the fertility rate in the group by adopting the typical bourgeois strategy of limiting family size in order to promote upward mobility. The birth-rate differential between the super-rich and the rest of society undoubtedly created room at the top for the newly risen.

Tables 5.25 and 5.26 explore another, but not unrelated, aspect of the behaviour of multimillionaires. The overwhelming Republican affiliation of the group is unsurprising in view of the historically Democratic tendencies of Southerners, Catholics and most lower wealth levels and national minorities, all underrepresented or unrepresented among the monied elite. With the advent of the New Deal, when the Democrats were poorer classes, the proportion of Republicans among the very rich became nearly universal. Although the Republicans were the majority party throughout much of the post-Civil War period

Table 5.25: Political Party Affiliation and Birth Cohort of the Richest Americans

Birth cohort	Party affiliation				
	Republican	Democrat	Independent	Known total	Group total
Pre-1830					
Number	14	4	1	19	27
Percentage*	(73.7)	(21.1)	(5.3)	(100.1)	(70.3)
Percentage**	[11.4]	[9.8]	[20.0]	[11.2]	[8.7]
1830-65					
Number	41	15	4	58	105
Percentage	(70.7)	(25.9)	(3.4)	(100.0)	(55.2)
Percentage	[33.3]	[36.6]	[40.0]	[34.3]	[33.9]
1866-99					
Number	47	20	2	69	113
Percentage	(68.1)	(29.0)	(2.9)	(100.0)	(61.1)
Percentage	[38.2]	[48.8]	[40.0]	[40.8]	[36.5]
1900-					
Number	20	2	–	22	55
Percentage	(90.1)	(9.1)	–	(100.0)	(40.0)
Percentage	[16.3]	[4.9]	–	[13.0]	[17.7]
Unknown					
Number	1	–	–	1	10
Percentage	(100.0)	–	–	(100.0)	(10.0)
Percentage	[0.8]	–	–	[0.6]	[3.2]
Total					
Number	123	41	5	169	310
Percentage	(72.8)	(24.3)	(3.0)	(100.1)	(54.5)
Percentage	[100.0]	[100.1]	[100.0]	[99.9]	[100.0]

*Percentages in parentheses indicate the contribution of each political party affiliation to each birth cohort.
**Percentages in square brackets indicate the contribution of each birth cohort to the total in each political party affiliation.

(1896-1932), the party's greatest triumph, when it outpolled the Democrats by 54.0 to 28.8 per cent in the 1924 presidential election, fell far short of its share of the multimillionaires.[95]

The wealthiest Americans shared with other economic elites a decline in office-holding during the nineteenth century, especially in state and local government and in elective posts. Their displacement, reflected in Table 5.26, was mostly due to the emergence of ethnic minority candidates, voters and party machines in the north-eastern states. Nevertheless, one-fifth of the entire group, and no less than one-sixth in the lowest birth cohort, held public office: substantial

Table 5.26: Government Office-holding and Birth Cohort of the Richest Americans

Birth cohort	US Cabinet	US Sub-Cabinet	High federal official	Offices Ambassador	US Senate	US House	Governor
Pre-1830							
Number	—	—	—	1	4	3	1
Percentage*	—	—	—	(6.7)	(26.7)	(20.0)	(6.7)
Percentage**	—	—	—	[11.1]	[30.8]	[42.9]	[20.0]
1830-65							
Number	3	1	1	3	5	3	—
Percentage	(8.8)	(2.9)	(2.9)	(8.8)	(14.7)	(8.8)	—
Percentage	[42.9]	[25.0]	[7.1]	[33.3]	[38.5]	[42.9]	—
1866-99							
Number	3	1	10	3	3	1	2
Percentage	(9.4)	(3.1)	(31.3)	(9.4)	(9.4)	(3.1)	(6.3)
Percentage	[42.9]	[25.0]	[71.4]	[33.3]	[23.1]	[14.3]	[40.0]
1900-							
Number	1***	2	3	2	1	—	2
Percentage	(7.1)	(14.3)	(21.4)	(14.3)	(7.1)	—	(14.3)
Percentage	[14.3]	[50.0]	[21.4]	[22.2]	[7.7]	—	[40.0]
Total							
Number	7	4	14	9	13	7	5
Percentage	(7.4)	(4.2)	(14.7)	(9.5)	(13.7)	(7.4)	(5.3)
Percentage	[100.1]	[100.0]	[99.9]	[99.9]	[100.1]	[100.1]	[100.0]

Table 5.26 (contd.)

Pre-1830	State Legislature	High state official	Mayor	Local Council	High local official	Total offices	Total rich holding office****
Number	3	—	—	3	—	15	8
Percentage	(20.0)	—	—	(20.0)	—	(100.1)	(29.6)
Percentage	[37.5]	—	—	[33.3]	—	[15.8]	[13.3]
1830-65							
Number	5	1	2	4	6	34	24
Percentage	(14.7)	(2.9)	(5.9)	(11.8)	(17.6)	(99.8)	(22.8)
Percentage	[62.5]	[20.0]	[50.0]	[44.4]	[60.0]	[35.8]	[40.0]
1866-99							
Number	—	3	1	2	3	32	18
Percentage	—	(9.4)	(3.1)	(6.3)	(9.4)	(100.2)	(16.8)
Percentage	—	[60.0]	[25.0]	[22.2]	[30.0]	[33.7]	[31.7]
1900-							
Number	—	1	1	—	1	14	9
Percentage	—	(7.1)	(7.1)	—	(7.1)	(99.8)	(16.4)
Percentage	—	[20.0]	[25.0]	—	[10.0]	[14.7]	[15.0]
Total							
Number	8	5	4	9	10	95	60
Percentage	(8.4)	(5.3)	(4.2)	(9.5)	(10.5)	(100.1)	(19.4)*****
Percentage	[100.0]	[100.0]	[100.0]	[99.9]	[100.0]	[100.0]	[100.0]

*Percentages in parentheses indicate the contribution of each office to each birth cohort

**Percentages in square brackets indicate the contribution of each birth cohort to the total in each office.

****Includes Vice-President Nelson Rockefeller.

****Percentages in parentheses indicate the percentage of each birth cohort holding office. Percentages in square brackets indicate the contribution of each birth cohort to the total holding office.

*****Includes the 10 unknown dates of birth for a group total of 310.

evidence of considerable overlap between economic and political elites. A more extensive interlock would emerge if multimillionaires of lesser magnitude who were related to the mammoth fortune-holders, a Vanderbilt governor, a Guggenheim senator and a host of duPonts in Congress and high state offices, and if the political bosses and party officials among the richest Americans had been included.

Personality Analysis

Collective trait analysis identifies aggregate attributes by statistical investigation of 'what' and 'where' questions. 'Why' problems, however, do not yield as easily to numerical evaluation. Tabulations of tangible variables vaguely indicate the emotional drives and human relations that determine the actions and personalities of the very rich. The murky realm of mood and motive, the subjective source of objective data, is best explored through a sensibility attuned to temperamental nuances and contradictions.

A group defined solely by magnitude of personal fortune creates hazards in the search for encompassing psychological interpretation. 'In my opinion,' said Andrew Mellon, 'you will find no typical case' of the extremely affluent.[96] Certain claims, emotional experiences and character traits recur often enough in this enclave to suggest a degree of convergence that contravenes Mellon's contention. Great fortune-holders assured others and perhaps themselves that they possessed conventional virtues of optimism, determination, self-confidence, efficiency, industry, thrift, altruism, leadership and love of family.[97]

Self-praise, however, frequently hid a grim reality. Harriman 'never stayed awake a night in my life about business', yet suffered from overwork, nervous strain and a gastric ulcer. 'There is nothing [that] really bothers me much,' asserted Philip D. Armour, 'I am that sort of make-up, that I throw off cares easily.' The serene Chicago meat-packer claimed to be most contented at home. His family doctor, however, never remembered seeing a happy rich man, and Arthur Meeker, son of a multimillionaire business and social associate of the Chicago tycoon, reported that Armour was unhappily married. James J. Hill professed a devotion to his wife and children, but his son-in-law announced that the multimillionaire Minnesota rail magnate sometimes would not speak to his spouse for a whole week. An ageing and retired Rockefeller publicly confessed to having been a 'slacker' who 'never. . .let business engross all my time and attention'. He admitted to his wife, however, that 'all the fortune I have made has not served to compensate me for the anxiety of' the 1870s. 'Work by day and worry by night. . .If I had foreseen the future I doubt whether I would have had the courage to go on.' By 1890 'I worked myself almost to a nervous breakdown.' In fact he endured recurrent digestive disorder and an emotional and physical collapse that, a few years later, made him leave Standard Oil. 'I am. . .one of the happiest of men,' John D. Rockefeller Jr told an interviewer. In the same interview he noted that 'I had no opportunity to shape my life', and even his hagiographer stated that he was uneasy with people and unsure of himself.[98]

Customary testaments to a healthy outlook and a happy life sometimes expressed cultural norms rather than true circumstances. Good form dictated public reticence about personal and family matters, and admission of emotional distress might entail disrespect and commercial disadvantage. Few wish to risk being labelled a 'loser' or a 'whiner' as a result of violating the American canon of cheerfulness. Nor were many, in an activist and pragmatic society, inclined to the self-contemplation necessary to confront or even recognise inner conflicts. But the biographical data reveal that the virtually obligatory 'upbeat' portrayals concealed extensive agitation based upon a similitude of negative ways in which the wealthy experienced themselves, their relations and their money.

Personality analysis appropriately begins with an inquiry into parent-child interaction. A considerable number of accumulators and inheritors of vast fortunes had unhappy relationships with their elders. Self-made multimillionaires were often closer to their mothers and regarded their fathers as aloof and harsh. Those with a birthright of affluence were frequently alienated from both parents. Vanderbilt, Stillman, Rockefeller, Cullen, Armour and mining magnate William Boyce Thompson were favoured by their mothers and found their fathers fearsome, distant, stern, critical and unreliable. Their fathers dead or deserters, W. Clement Stone, who amassed over $150 million as an insurance underwriter, Charles B. Thornton, head of Litton Industries and possessor of $100 million, and Joseph Hirshorn, another self-made centimillionaire, were raised solely by their mothers. Frick, Gates, Harriman and Gould had similarly troubled relations with their male parents without any apparent maternal support. Rockefeller's bigamous father, an extreme case, deserted the family and lent his son money at exorbitant interest.[99]

Children of rich parents, like Hearst, Schiff and Hughes, were also alienated from their fathers while being affirmed by their mothers. But a larger number did not get on either with their mothers or with both parents. Barbara Hutton hated her father and Mellon endured patriarchal coldness apparently without countervailing maternal affection. Both parents of Green and Cabot were parsimonious. Peggy Guggenheim, neglected by a mismatched father and mother, was brought up by governesses and terrorised by nurses. Eleanor Medill (Cissy) Patterson, a member of the Medill-McCormick-Paterson publishing dynasty, went through life scarred by bitterness toward her mother, the spectacle of an alcoholic father and the effects of a disastrous parental marriage. Mrs Harold F. McCormick, the unhappily wedded daughter of Rockefeller, saw her children only by appointment. The offspring of the Rockefeller grandchildren frequently rebelled against their fathers and the tradition and money of the clan. They found their parents rigid, formal, cold and judgemental, and their own identity was stifled at home. Successive generations of Vanderbilts were plagued with miserable childhoods that resulted from a long sequence of matrimonial catastrophies and the stunted emotional growth of their elders. The old Commodore emulated his father in being distant and brutal toward his own offspring. He tried to best one son in a business deal and disinherited another. Friction continued in the male line. 'Every Vanderbilt son has fought with his father,' declared third-generation Cornelius Vanderbilt II after a long conflict that resulted in a small paternal bequest. The maternal side afforded little relief. 'I forced her to marry the Duke,' explained social climber Alva after her daughter's divorce and their reconciliation. 'I have always had absolute power over my children. . .When I issued an order, nobody discussed it,' Society queen Grace similarly dominated her children while seeing them only on the rare moments between social engagements. Vanderbilts were not the only sires who resorted to disinheritance to vent displeasure with their offspring. The son and daughter who snubbed William C. Whitney after his second marriage were left little money, Thomas F. Ryan cut his son out of his will, and Astors who wedded against the wishes of their elders received small legacies.[100]

Material and emotional indigence created unhappy childhoods. Sage, Bok, California rail magnate George Crocker and Standard Oil partner and Florida resort-developer Henry M. Flager claimed that poverty and toil robbed them of boyhoods.[101] John D. Rockefeller Jr, Barbara Hutton, Hughes, several Vanderbilts and Peggy Guggenheim recalled early years of intense loneliness. 'Every time I was hurt or lonely as a child, I wished I had a father living, and a mother who loved me and loved him,' remembered Gloria Vanderbilt, pawn in a sensational custody fight in the 1930s between her mother and aunt. 'Rich children can be lonely, very lonely.'[102]

Talent, luck and character compensated the accumulators. They claimed that youthful ambition, diligence, prudence, frugality and self-confidence enabled them to avoid difficulties, surmount obstacles and seize opportunities.[103] An early aptitude for arithmetic contrasted sharply with the indifferent scholarship of most great capitalists and signified an acute intelligence easily adapted to the market place. Morgan, Stillman, Benton, Carnegie, Rockefeller, Gould, Gates, Joseph P. Kennedy, Jones, Cabot and General Motors executives Charles F. Kettering and Alfred P. Sloan excelled in mathematics. Interested in business and adept at figures, Carnegie and his partner Frick, Gould, William and John D. Rockefeller, Baruch, steel tycoon Henry Phipps, Minnesota Mining and Manufacturing executives Archibald G. Bush and William L. McKnight, retail chain-store merchandiser S.S. Kresge and West Coast rail pioneer Mark Hopkins were book-keepers in the beginning of their careers. Keeping accounts, as J.D. Rockefeller pointed out, prepared the apprentice entrepreneur for commercial success by inculcating the habit of systematic attention to detail and by providing comprehensive knowledge of a firm's operations.[104]

If self-made multimillionaires owed their success to exceptional talent and an acquisitive drive stimulated by familial conflict and emotional and material deprivation, the richly born were burdened with psychological problems less likely to foster worldly gain. Renowned accumulators, as in the cases of Commodore Vanderbilt, Stillman, Cabot, Mellon, Green and Alfred I. duPont, often had emotional deficiencies which condemned them to inflict upon their spouses and children the remote and reproachful attitudes of their own fathers. A number of parents, Gould, Gates and several Astors and Vanderbilts, indulged their offspring in luxuries instead of giving them time and attention, thereby ill-fitting them for the responsibilities of wealth or the demands of the market place. Descendants of rich, powerful and famous figures, like William K. Vanderbilt and John D. Rockefeller Jr, were further plagued with the agony of being overshadowed by their formidable forebears and the feeling that inherited wealth and status robbed them of an independent identity. 'My life was never destined to be happy,' said the Commodore's disgruntled grandson. 'It was laid out along lines which I could foresee almost from earliest childhood. It has left me with nothing to hope for, with nothing definite to see or strive for. Inherited wealth is a real handicap to happiness. . .certain death to ambition.' He could not even enjoy his money because 'the first satisfaction, and the greatest, that of building the foundation of a fortune, is denied'.

John D. Rockefeller Jr also regretted that he 'never had the
satisfaction of earning my own way. . .I envy anybody who can do that.
I never had that kind of reassuring experience.'[105]

The inheritors' feelings of inferiority were not ill-founded. The
remarkable mental and emotional qualities that made for brilliant
entrepreneurship did not regularly recur in the next generation. Indeed,
many sons shared the problems of J. Ogden Armour, who was
compelled by his father to undertake a business career for which he
lacked skill or temperament. Frazier Jelke, heir of a Chicago
oleomargarine fortune, undoubtedly had these circumstances in mind
when he reported that 'the Chicago tradition' of rugged entrepreneurship
'was hard on the second generation. . .It is a matter of record that few
sons of outstanding success made names for themselves or kept pace
with their fathers'. The sons were pale replicas of their fathers because
'they had inherited their. . .fortunes, ready made — there was little
more to struggle for'. Several of the fabulously successful Texas oilmen
expressed similar sentiments in noting that the offspring of self-made
tycoons conducted the family business without the nerve or drive of
the originators.[106] For every Morgan, duPont, Ford or Watson who
expanded, or at least did not destroy, a family empire, there were
Gould, Green, Gates and Armour scions who lost the businesses and
depleted the legacies of their sires.[107]

The relationship of John D. Rockefeller Sr and Jr is sometimes cited
as an exemplary interaction between creator and inheritor. A seemingly
affectionate and harmonious bond united father and son. The latter
patterned himself after the former and lived up to the obligations of
wealth instilled in him by the founder. The younger Rockefeller, in
turn, transmitted to his children, not without some success, the values
of their grandfather. Below the surface, however, throbbed wounds
that desolated many rich men's children. An overriding sense of
worthlessness impelled the son to seek paternal approval through an
exaggerated form of father worship that amounted to virtual self-
abasement. 'Of my ability I have always had a very poor opinion,'
wrote junior to senior, but 'it is wholly and absolutely devoted to your
interests.' The most pathetic of many declarations of effacement
through filial servility begins with the assertion: 'From my earliest
years I have had but one thought and desire, namely to be helpful to
Father in every way in my power'; Rockefeller Jr had 'ever been proud
to lay the credit for things accomplished at his feet, where alone it
belonged'. The son 'glorified in the greatness of his [father's]
unparalleled achievements in industry and his world-wide service to

humanity', but 'never sought anything for myself'.[108] Abject devotion, however, could not reassure Rockefeller. At sixteen he suffered a nervous breakdown. After graduating from Brown University he entered The Standard Oil Company feeling 'my own sense of unfitness. I didn't have any confidence in my own ability'. Unfortunately this foreboding materialised and his father had to rescue him from unwise speculations. After his failure, which undoubtedly sharpened his dissatisfaction at not achieving financial independence, he left the firm and tended the family philanthropies. Throughout life he was uncomfortable with people and driven by a compulsive sense of duty regarding the affluence passed on to him. Although pangs of conscience made him a relatively model multimillionaire, little joy warmed his life. A great benefactor, and son of an even greater benefactor, he raised his children in the manner he had been brought up — to be ever watchful of the moral obligations of money and to guard against using the family fortune for mere personal pleasure.[109]

Riches, power and prominence may have reinforced the egos of the monied elite but did not eliminate the self-destructive tendencies prefigured in their tormented childhoods. Connubial friction, not rare among the creators and their spouses, became legion in subsequent generations. 'More marriages were failures than were not,' observed Meeker of his father's crowd, the self-made Chicago tycoons.[110] Sibling rivalry and other kinship clashes over the distribution and administration of estates and control of family firms fragmented the Vanderbilt, Gould, Hill, duPont, Green, Hughes and Guggenheim clans. 'The deplorable family quarrels which so often afflict the rich,' commented Carnegie, 'generally have their rise in sordid differences about money.' Astors and Vanderbilts also waged internecine wars for social precedence as bitter as their interfamilial struggles for the same purpose.[111]

Family feuds were not the only nor the severest signs of inner turmoil. Mental instability, digestive disorders, alcoholism and suicide appeared among the possessors of gigantic fortunes. Creators of great wealth generally had stronger egos and more affirmative experiences of life than did the inheritors, consequently they were less susceptible to the breakdowns that harassed their heirs. Nevertheless, the strains of competitive entrepreneurship and unresolved early conflicts wrought havoc among the self-made multimillionaires. Gould, Harriman, Rockefeller Sr and Kennedy suffered from dyspepsia or ulcers, Green, Morgan and Stillman from chronic headaches, Harriman and Stillman from nervous tension, Gould from neuralgia and insomnia and Morgan from fainting spells, skin eruptions and exhaustion. More acutely afflicted were Fair, who became a drunkard, and Rockefeller Sr, Stanford and breakfast cereal king Charles William Post, who underwent nervous breakdowns. The irrational behaviour of Green and Hughes, going far beyond neurosis, suggested psychotic compulsions. The former lived like a beggar while acquiring a vast fortune, imagined that her father, husband and aunt had been murdered, and carried a pistol in the delusive expectation of imminent kidnapping or assassination. The latter also had paranoid fixations: he was morbidly secretive, suspicious, reclusive and fearful of germ-induced diseases. Suicide, the ultimate act of self-destruction, ended the emotionally blighted existences of Eastman and Post.[112]

The very rich and their intimates were aware of the considerable incidence of malaise in the affluent enclave. Meeker observed that 'several' Chicago magnates 'went quietly insane. . .and took their lives for business or personal reasons'. Dr Frank Billings, a distinguished Chicago and Palm Beach physician to the wealthy, asserted that he never saw a happy multimillionaire because family, woman or other kinds of troubles disturbed their lives. Direct testimony of widespread misery amidst opulence came from several fortune-founders. 'Millionaires who laugh are rare,' wrote Carnegie. 'We are all slaves,' said Gould of himself and the other robber barons, 'and the man who has one million dollars is the greatest slave of all, except it be he who has two million.' A middle-aged Stillman grieved that 'I have never in all my life done anything I wanted and cannot now.' Divorced and alienated from his sons, upon his deathbed the banker lamented that 'I ought to have been praised more. I ought to have been kinder.' H.H. Rogers did not 'know of anyone who has been successful, but that he has been compelled to pay some price for success. Some get it at the loss of their health; others forego the pleasure of home and spend their years in the forests or mines; some acquire success at the loss of their reputation; others at loss of character.' The 'price that I have never known any successful man to escape. . .is the jealousy of many of the community in which he moves'. Similar agonies tormented morose mining magnates Thompson and Fair, recluse Howard Hughes and Norton Simon.[113]

The conflicts, failures and ailments of the founders, though extensive, paled in contrast to the anguish of their heirs. Unsustained by a sense of achievement and lacking the toughness of their elders, the inheritors show even more widespread instability. Drunkenness, divorce and neurosis reached epidemic proportions among the

Vanderbilts, Astors, Goulds, McCormicks, Pattersons, Guggenheims, Dukes, Fairs, Stillmans, Rockefellers, Woolworths and other fabulously wealthy American families. Numerous suicides, compared to the family founders, indicated the widespread existence of disrupted personalities among the inheritors. Sons of Commodore Vanderbilt, Marshall Field, Fair, car-maker, Horace Dodge, Thomas Fortune Ryan and publisher Walter Annenberg killed themselves. Guggenheim, Gould, duPont and Ryan grandsons and several Guggenheim grandchildren also committed suicide.[114]

This solemn account of the emotional impact of great wealth documents the discussion which opened the chapter. The circle closes with an inquiry into a specific aspect of the outlook of the multimillionaires. Their attitude toward money highlights the psychological ramifications of making or inheriting monumental fortunes. Creators, like Carnegie, Rockefeller, Ford and Philip Armour, and inheritors, like Rockefeller Jr, Vincent Astor, Alfred I. duPont and J. Ogden Armour, asserted that vast accumulations usually rewarded character, productivity and leadership, and that extensive property-ownership led to economic growth, national power, mass prosperity and social well-being. Many multimillionaires argued that money-making was a by-product of creative and useful work, of striving to succeed and of altruistic aspiration. Large concentrations of personal assets were rendered harmless by self-regulating defences indigenous to their formation and dispersion: inherited wealth destroyed itself by promoting indolence and waste; poverty encouraged prosperity by promoting diligence and thrift. Thus did the rich assure themselves and the people that an economic hierarchy did not threaten equal opportunity and republican government, that immense personal profits did not undermine entrepreneurship, innovation or other shibboleths of capitalism, and that material gain did not corrupt the sacred virtues of self-discipline and individual achievement.[115]

In public statements about money, as in other proclamations, multimillionaires frequently expressed views at variance with their essential (and sometimes unconscious) convictions. Money-making and keeping, not adorned or rationalised by nobler explanations, actually constituted a powerful force in the lives of the very rich. As boys Thompson and Rockefeller vowed to accumulate a fortune. Thompson, Carnegie and Gates promised themselves to retire after reaching a certain level of wealth, but kept pushing onward. Rogers, a Rockefeller disciple and associate, said that the Standard Oil partners made the profit motive a 'religion', a faith 'taught' them by 'Mr Rockefeller'.

Billionaire Texas oil operator H.L. Hunt worshipped at the same shrine, and taciturn banker George F. Baker found true happiness in his estimated net worth of $200 million.[116]

The obvious importance of money to the rich, as manifested by their resistance to taxes, avidity for profits, costly lifestyle and pride in ownership of precious objects, made many assume that disavowals of materialistic incentives were hypocritical devices. These allegedly self-serving denials were designed to assuage mass envy, prevent attacks upon wealth, relieve guilty consciences and hide the lust for lucre in order to facilitate its gratification. The well-endowed were undoubtedly attached to their assets (the gains of the fortune-founders symbolised their manhood and were deemed by themselves and others the rewards of courage, aggressiveness and indomitable will), but their relationships to things were no less ambivalent than their human interactions. They treated their property as extensions of themselves, and thus their attitude towards money became, in those subject to inner conflict, another facet of a fragmented personality.

Disclaimers about the pecuniary incentive disclosed a defensiveness partly grounded in the awareness that great wealth was distrusted, feared and envied, a realisation that discomfited J. Ogden Armour, Otto H. Kahn, Vincent Astor and several Rockefeller great-grandchildren when they contemplated their own resources or the holdings of their peers.[117] A variety of more personal disappointments left other multimillionaires dissatisfied with their wealth. Baruch grew 'restless and discontented' with Wall Street and turned to public service because his father, a public health physician whom he admired, 'held ethical values and usefulness to the community in higher esteem' than 'money-making'. Gould, Thompson and Nevada Comstock Lode proprietor John W. MacKay complained that their money had brought them misery. Flagler worried that 'ninety-five percent' of those who sought him out 'love my money, not me'. Hetty Green's son, Thompson, Getty and Stanford felt 'besieged', 'tormented' and 'cheated' by multitudinous pleas for contributions or other schemes to separate them from their fortunes. Getty found money 'often a bar' to love, family life and 'personal happiness'.[118]

The inheritors exhibited similar dismay. W.K. Vanderbilt and J.O. Armour regarded their heritages as blights on their lives. Steven, son of Nelson Rockefeller, shared Flager's suspicion that people responded to him and his cousins for their money instead of their selves. Several of his cousins also expressed frustrations with their privileged birthrights. Abby, daughter of David Rockefeller, who attempted to renounce her patrimony, eloquently stated the difficulties that alienated her generation from the family fame and fortune:[119]

> Early on I picked up the idea that I shouldn't be proud of the money. Should I be grateful? No, that was wrong too. So was pride and contentment. There was no attitude in our childhood that we were allowed to have with respect to that money that was appropriate. We weren't allowed to discuss it; we weren't allowed to gloat; we couldn't do anything. And so it was like a festering sore. Like a thing that was going to pop later on.

Disquieted by the acquisitive spirit that pushed them to the pinnacle of opulence, alarmed over attacks made on the corruption and irresponsibility of the great fortune-holders, and aware of the emotional problems rooted in affluence, a few multimillionaires took steps to prevent the evils of wealth from infecting their children. Cabot, three generations of Rockefellers and John Jacob Astor IV imposed a regimen of sparse allowances, strict accounting and, given the family resources, a spartan lifestyle, on their youngsters. In this way the parents hoped to instil the self-control and sense of responsibility that would protect their offspring from the temptations of wealth. 'I know that you and Abby will be careful to educate the children in financial matters as we sought to educate you,' wrote Rockefeller Sr to Rockefeller Jr, 'that they may understand the value of money and make the very best use of it.' Paternal example and advice was always faithfully followed. The son shielded his family from publicity, made the children earn money, gave them small stipends and required that they keep a ledger of their expenditures and give regularly to charity. 'I was always so afraid that money would spoil my children,' remarked the younger Rockefeller, 'and I wanted them to know its values and not waste it or throw it away on things that weren't worthwhile.' William Benton, when listed in *Fortune* as having $150-200 million, warned his children that 'you're not rich by the standards of the rich. Please don't change your attitude because of this unfortunate and unhappy and unwarranted and illegitimate publicity.'[120]

Ruminations on the discontent induced by great wealth, anxieties regarding public disapproval of huge fortunes and efforts to shield children from the undesirable consequences of immense inheritances laid bare the tribulations of the super-rich. The compulsions that obsessed self-made multimillionaires with pecuniary aggrandisement were intensified by the fulfilment of that ambition. Affluence, once achieved or inherited, encouraged attitudes that conflicted with accumulative traits. Instead of diminishing the insecurities embedded in the acquisitive personality, these attitudes compounded ego damage. This paradox suggests an answer to the question that lurks behind all investigations of monied elites: how do they differ from the rest of us? While most aspects of the human condition are shared by people in various walks of life, only the supremely wealthy experience the gratifications, frustrations and contradictions involved in the attainment or heritage of vast fortunes.

Notes

I would like to thank Charles F. Moss and Michael Goldschmidt for their efficient and tireless assistance in gathering data for this essay. I would also like to thank Professors Carol S. Dweck and Blair B. Kling for reading the manuscript and making many invaluable suggestions for its improvement.

1. Psychologists and psychiatrists have rarely investigated the personality traits involved in wealth-gathering. The best study, 'The Drive to Amass Wealth' by renowned psychoanalyst Otto Fenichel, appeared in *The Psychoanalytic Quarterly*, 7 (1938), pp. 69-95.

2. For investigations by professionals into the lives of rich children, including case studies, see Charles McArthur, 'Personality Differences Between Middle and Upper Classes', *The Journal of Abnormal and Social Psychology*, 50 (March 1955), pp. 247-54; Roy R. Grinker Jr, 'The Poor Rich', *Psychology Today*, 11 (October 1977), pp. 74-76, 81; Burton W. Wixen, *Children of the Rich* (New York 1973); Robert Coles, *Privileged Ones. The Well-off and the Rich in America* (Boston, 1978). Historical studies of this subject include John Tebbel, *The Inheritors. A Study of America's Great Fortunes and What Happened to Them* (New York, 1962); Michael H. Stone and Clarice J. Kestenbaum, 'Maternal Deprivation in Children of the Wealthy: A Paradox of Socio-economic vs. Psychological Class', *History of Childhood Quarterly*, II (Summer 1974), pp. 79-106.

3. Robert L. Heilbroner, *The Quest for Wealth* (New York, 1956), is an excellent discussion of money-making in the context of modern capitalism.

4. For the mixed public reception see Sigmund Diamond, *The Reputation of the American Businessman* (New York, 1966); Albert W. Atwood, *The Mind of the Millionaire* (New York, 1926), pp. 1-14, 45-50.

5. For an illuminating examination of the animus toward the very rich see Heilbroner, *Quest*, pp. 168-70, 202-03, 213-15, 238-42; 'Trying to Make Sense of It', *New York Times*, 10 October 1977.

6. Thomas G. Shearman, 'Henry George's Mistakes', *Forum*, 8 (September 1889), pp. 40-52. For further elaboration of these findings see Shearman's articles in *Forum*: 'The Owners of the United States', (November 1889), pp. 262-73; 'The Coming Billionaire', 10 (January 1891), pp. 546-57. The *New York Daily Tribune* and *New York World* studies are reprinted in Sidney Ratner (ed.), *New Light on the History of Great American Fortunes* (New York, 1953), pp. 85-91, 141-43.

7. Ferdinand Lundberg, *America's Sixty Families* (New York), 1937), p. 44.

8. Robert E. Gallman, 'Trends in the Size Distribution of Wealth in the 19th

Century' in Lee Soltow (ed.), *Six Papers on the Size Distribution of Wealth and Income* (Studies in Income and Wealth, National Bureau of Economic Research, 33, New York, 1969), pp. 12-15.

9. Lee Soltow, 'Evidence of Income Inequality in the United States, 1866-1965', *The Journal of Economic History*, 29 (June 1969), pp. 281-85; *Men and Wealth in the United States. 1850-70* (New Haven, 1975), p. 112. The United States Internal Revenue Service (hereafter cited as IRS) found that between 1953-62 those with a net worth of at least one million dollars composed a constant share of those worth at least $60,000; see *Supplemental Statistics of Income, Personal Wealth Estimated from Estate Tax Returns 1962* (US Government Printing Office, Washington, DC, 1967), p. 57. For the Board of Governors finding see Herman P. Miller, 'Millionaires are a Dime a Dozen', *New York Times Sunday Magazine*, 28 November 1964. For the IRS assessment see IRS, *Supplemental Statistics 1962*, p. 12.

10. The estate multiplier technique ascertains the number of living Americans at a given level of wealth at a given time by extrapolating from the proportion of deaths at that wealth level among a sample of probated estates at all wealth levels in that year.

11. The National Bureau of Economic Research estimation was reported in Miller, 'Millionaires', p. 41 and in 'Now There are 90,000 Millionaires in the United States', *U.S. News & World Report*, 59 (October 1965), p. 119; James D. Smith and Staunton E. Calvert, 'Estimating the Wealth of Top Wealth-Holders from Estate Tax Returns', *Proceedings of the Business and Statistical Section of the American Statistical Association* (1965), p. 251. IRS, *Supplemental Statistics 1962*, p. 59.

12. James D. Smith, Stephen D. Franklin and Douglas A. Wion, *Financial Concentration in the United States* (The Urban Institute, Washington, DC, 1975), p. 8. IRS, *Supplemental Statistics 1969*, p. 19; *1972*, p. 12.

13. Gallman, 'Trends', pp. 12-15; Smith *et al.*, *Financial*, p. 8. Estate multiplier findings underestimate the actual number of millionaires because estates are undervalued to avoid inheritance and estate taxes, but an accurate account of such property would still leave the very rich a tiny segment of the national population.

14. Ward McAllister, *Society As I Have Found It* (New York, 1890), pp. 157, 349. For similar views by another member of the fashionable set see Frederick Townsend Martin, *The Passing of the Idle Rich* (Garden City, 1911), pp. 5-58, 71-72; and *Things I Remember* (New York, 1913), pp. 77-80, 90, 289-92; Mrs John King Van Rensselaer, *Newport Our Social Capital* (Philadelphia, 1905), pp. 29-36.

15. McAllister, *Society*, p. 349; Interview in the *New York Daily Tribune*, 25 March 1888.

16. Merrill Folsom, *Great American Mansions and Their Stories* (New York, 1963); W.A. Swanberg, *Citizen Hearst. A Biography of William Randolph Hearst* (New York, 1961), p. 489; Conrelius Vanderbilt Jr, *Queen of the Golden Age. The Fabulous Story of Grace Wilson Vanderbilt* (New York, 1956), pp. 162, 540-44.

17. Gustavus Myers, *The Ending of Hereditary American Fortunes* (New York, 1939), p. 151; Atwood, *Mind*, p. 161; Folsom, *Great*, p. 110; Vanderbilt, *Queen*, pp. 287-90.

18. Myers, *Ending*, p. 151; Cleveland Amory, *The Last Resorts* (New York, 1952), p. 209; Elizabeth Drexel Lehr, *King Lehr and the Gilded Age* (Philadelphia, 1935), pp. 70-71, 138; Dixon Wecter, *The Saga of American Society. A Record of Social Aspiration. 1607-1937* (New York, 1970), pp. 227, 368-71; Vanderbilt, *Queen*, pp. 146, 156, 277; Folsom, *Great*, pp. 260-62. For

an analysis of the values of the super-rich of this era see Frederic Cople Jaher (ed.), *The Rich, The Well Born and the Powerful* (Urbana, 1973), pp. 258-84.

19. Lundberg, *America's*, pp. 364-69; E. Digby Baltzell, *Philadelphia Gentlemen: The Making of a National Upper Class* (Glencoe, 1958), p. 212; George Harvey, *Henry Clay Frick. The Man* (New York, 1928), pp. 333-34; Lewis Corey, *The House of Morgan. A Social Biography of the Master of Money* (New York, 1930), pp. 412-13; Lucius Beebe, *The Big Spenders* (Garden City, 1966), p. 292; John Tebbel, *The Life and Good Times of William Randolph Hearst* (New York, 1952), pp. 267-68; Arthur M. Louis, 'America's Centimillionaires', *Fortune*, 77 (May 1968), p. 196; Kenneth Lamott, *The Moneymakers* (Boston, 1969), pp. 249-51, 264.

20. For these varied items of expenditure see Lundberg, *America's*, pp. 349-50, 429, 438; Myers, *Ending*, p. 151; Wecter, *Saga*, pp. 451-55, 464; Vanderbilt, *Queen*, pp. 1, 44; Edwin P. Hoyt, *The Goulds. A Social History* (New York, 1969), pp. 290-91; Beebe, *Big*, p. 263; Harvey O'Connor, *The Astors* (New York, 1941), p. 178.

21. Arthur E. Hartzell, *Titled Americans* (New York, 1915); Elizabeth Eliot, *Heiresses and Coronets* (New York, 1959); Wector, *Saga*, pp. 407-15.

22. Hartzell, *Titled*.

23. Richard Austin Smith, 'The Fifty Million Dollar Man', *Fortune*, 56 (November 1957), p. 177.

24. Leon Harris, *Only to God. The Extraordinary Life of Godfrey Lowell Cabot* (New York, 1967), pp. 51, 56, 159-60, 179-80.

25. For a fuller discussion of the differences among wealth elites in various cities and references from which these generalisations are drawn see Jaher, *The Rich*, pp. 258-60, 280-81, 283-84; 'Nineteenth Century Elites in Boston and New York', *Journal of Social History*, 6 (Fall 1972), pp. 32-77; and my forthcoming study on the upper classes of Boston, New York, Charleston, Chicago and Los Angeles.

26. For discussions and reports of the more modest lifestyle of the very rich see *Fortune*, 16 (December 1937), pp. 123-29, 180, 183-84, 186; *Fortune*, 18 (December 1938), p.126; Smith, 'Fifty Million', pp. 226-28, 230, 233-36; David Riesman (ed.), *Abundance For What & Other Essays* (Garden City, 1964), p. 126; *Time*, 84 (December 1964), pp. 54-67; *Time*, 88 (December 1965), pp. 88-92; Michael Demarest, 'The Hot New Rich', *Time*, 109 (June 1977), pp. 72-83; *New York Times*, 17 December 1967; Arthur Meeker, *Chicago With Love* (New York, 1955), pp. 273, 277; Atwood, *Mind*, pp. 166-68; Cleveland Amory, *Who Killed Society?* (New York, 1960), pp. 132-35, 140-43, 186-88, 207-10; the Editors of the *Wall Street Journal*, *The New Millionaires and How They Made Their Fortunes* (New York, 1961), pp. 15-16, 185; Louis Auchincloss, Introduction to the 1970 edition of Wecter, *Saga*, xvi, xviii.

27. Atwood, *Mind*, pp. 166-68. Folsom, *Great*; Amory, *Last*, p. 174.

28. Meeker, *Chicago*, p. 273; *Fortune*, 18 (December 1938), pp. 48, 125-26.

29. Smith, 'Fifty Million', pp. 228, 230; Louis, 'America's Centimillionaires', p. 196.

30. Beebe, *Big*, p. 120.

31. Smith, 'Fifty Million', p. 177; John Bainbridge, *The Super-Americans* (Garden City, 1961), pp. 158-60, 178, 180, 203-04, 208.

32. See references in note 26.

33. Swanberg, *Citizen*, pp. 390-91, 484-87; Gustavus Myers, *The History of the Great American Fortunes* (New York, 1936), pp. 466-503; Hoyt, *Goulds*, pp. 95-96, 121-32, 141, 194-95, 213-21, 231-34; Tebbel, *Inheritors*, pp. 72-73, 86, 121-25, 129-33, 146; Amory, *Last*, pp. 300-02, 305, 380, 396; Lundberg, *America's*, pp. 412, 416; Stewart H. Hobrook, *The Age of the Moguls. The Story*

of the Robber Barons and the Great Tycoons (Garden City, 1954), p. 356; Wayne Andrews, *The Vanderbilt Legend* (New York, 1941), pp. 277 ff; Edwin P. Hoyt, *The Vanderbilts and Their Fortunes* (Garden City, 1962), pp. 362-63, 370-72, 377-79, 396-97; Gloria Vanderbilt and Thelma Lady Furness, *Double Exposure. A Twin Autobiography* (New York, 1958), pp. 90, 118-19, 137, 150, 164-65.

34. Cornelius Vanderbilt Jr, *Farewell to Fifth Avenue* (New York, 1935), p. 376.

35. Beebe, *Big*, pp. 174-82, 260-70; Lundberg, *America's*, pp. 412, 430-31; Amory, *Who*, pp. 169-77; Tebbel, *Inheritors*, pp. 93-104; Vanderbilt, *Queen*, pp. 2, 277; Bainbridge, *Super-Americans*, p. 36; Louis, 'America's Centimillionaires', pp. 156, 196.

36. Hugh Roy Cullen quoted in Bainbridge, *Super-Americans*, p. 121.

37. Gabriel Almond, 'Plutocracy and Politics in New York City', unpublished doctoral dissertation, University of Chicago, 1938, pp. 156, 158, 272.

38. O'Connor, *Astors*, pp. 83-85, 125, 191, 231-32.

39. Cornelius Vanderbilt quoted in Walter J. Lane, *Commodore Vanderbilt. An Epic of the Steam Age* (New York, 1942), p. 313. For the Vanderbilt charity dispensations see ibid., pp. 184, 314, 316-17; Andrews, *Vanderbilt Legend*, pp. 85, 169-71, 173, 230-31, 236, 354.

40. Lloyd Wendt and Herman Kogan, *'Bet-A-Million!' The Story of John W. Gates* (Indianapolis, 1948), pp. 328-29. For Collis P. Huntington's giving see Oscar Lewis, *The Big Four* (New York, 1951), pp. 212-13, 236-39, 261-65, 276; Mark D. Hirsch, *William C. Whitney, Modern Warwick* (New York, 1948), p. 599. For Morgan see Myers, *History* (1936 edition), p. 636.

41. Daniel Hodas, *The Business Career of Moses Taylor. Merchant, Financial Capitalist and Industrialist* (New York, 1976), pp. 197-98, 279-80; Richard O'Connor, *Gould's Millions* (Garden City, 1962), pp. 12, 290-91; Paul Sarnoff, *Russell Sage: The Money King* (New York, 1965), pp. 310-11, 327-28; Boyden Sparks and Samuel T. Moore, *Hetty Green. A Woman Who Loved Money* (Garden City, 1930), pp. 147-53, 160, 182, 189, 211, 214-16, 218, 258, 330-31, 336-37; Bainbridge, *Super-Americans*, p. 350.

42. John D. Rockefeller, *Random Reminiscences of Men and Events* (Garden City, 1933), pp. 156, 188.

43. Andrew Carnegie, *Autobiography of Andrew Carnegie* (Boston, 1924), p. 255. For the Carnegie charity see ibid., pp. 259-86; Joseph Frazier Wall, *Andrew Carnegie* (New York, 1970), pp. 805, 815-16, 827-40, 882-84, 960-65, 1,042-43.

44. John D. Rockefeller Jr quoted in Tebbel, *Inheritors*, p. 298. For the Rockefeller charities see Alan Nevins, *John D. Rockefeller, The Heroic Age of American Enterprise* (2 vols., New York, 1940), vol. I, p. 106; vol. II, pp. 474-85, 615, 648, 665, 720; Peter Collier and David Horowitz, *The Rockefellers. An American Dynasty* (New York, 1976), pp. 48-49, 52, 61-67, 140-48, 276-90, 649; Raymond B. Fosdick, *John D. Rockefeller, Jr.: A Portrait* (New York, 1956), pp. 122, 433.

45. Ferdinand Lundberg, *The Rich and the Super Rich. A Study in the Power of Money Today* (New York, 1968), pp. 187, 190-91, 739.

46. Myers, *History* (1936 edition), pp. 503, 693, 704; Myers, *Ending*, pp. 279, 285, 327; Lundberg, *America's*, pp. 356-58, 363-64, 399-400; Lundberg, *Rich*, pp. 46, 59-60, 62, 74-77; Bainbridge, *Super-Americans*, pp. 351, 356; Tebbel, *Inheritors*, pp. 256, 301; M.R. Werner, *Julius Rosenwald, The Life of a Practical Humanitarian* (New York, 1939), p. 366; Marquis James, *Alfred I. DuPont, The Family Rebel* (Indianapolis, 1941), pp. 532-36; Edward Kilman and Theon Wright, *Hugh Roy Cullen. A Story of American Opportunity* (New York, 1954),

pp. 199, 231, 249-50; Tebbel, *The Marshall Field* (New York, 1947), pp. 262, 271; Robert F. Durden, *The Dukes of Durham, 1865-1929* (Durham, 1975), pp. 244-50; Carl W. Ackerman, *George Eastman* (Boston, 1930), pp. 315, 324, 348, 453-54, 466-67, 482.

47. Lundberg, *Rich*, pp. 46, 59-60, 74-75, 199-200, 470-81; Lundberg, *America's*, pp. 363-64; Bainbridge, *Super-Americans*, pp. 351-52, 356; *New York Times*, 4 April 1976, 6 November 1977; F. Emerson Andrews, *Philanthropic Giving* (New York, 1950), pp. 92-93; F. Emerson Andrews, *Philanthropic Foundations* (New York, 1950); *US Treasury Department Report on Private Foundations*, Committee on Ways and Means, US House of Representatives, 89th Congress, 1st Session US Government Printing Office, Washington, DC, 1965), pp. 1,107, 1,109, 1,112, 1,130-32; Edward C. Lindeman, *Wealth and Culture* (New York, 1936), pp. 10, 14, 16-17, 20, 24, 29, 31.

48. William L. Crum, *The Distribution of Wealth. A Factual Survey Based Upon Federal Estate Tax Returns* (Boston, 1935), pp. 20, 23; Ackerman, *George Eastman*, pp. 315, 324, 348, 453-54, 466-67, 482.

49. Carl S. Shoup, *Federal Estate and Gift Taxes* (Washington, DC, 1966), pp. 20-21, 180, 220-27. For another examination of charity among the wealthy see William S. Vickery, 'One Economist's View of Philanthropy' in Frank G. Dickinson (ed.), *Philanthropy and Public Policy* (New York, 1962), pp. 52-53.

50. *US Treasury Report*, pp. 1,039-43, 1,048-97; Lundberg, *Rich*, pp. 472-76, 479.

51. Lundberg, *America's*, pp. 357-58, 364, 400-01; Ackerman, *George Eastman*, pp. 324-26, 353, 384, 439, 453-54; William H.A. Carr, *The duPonts of Delaware* (New York, 1964), pp. 199, 295-97, 346-48; George Eastman quoted in Ackerman, *George Eastman*, pp. 443-44.

52. George T. Clark, *Leland Stanford* (Palo Alto, 1931), pp. 392-93; Lewis, *Big Four*, p. 186; Julius Rosenwald, 'The Burden of Wealth', *Saturday Evening Post*, 5 January 1929.

53. Andrew Carnegie, *The Gospel of Wealth and Other Timely Essays* (New York, 1901), p. 12.

54. Collier and Horowitz, *Rockefellers*, pp. 65-66.

55. Henry Ford and Samuel Crowther, *Moving Upward* (Garden City, 1930), pp. 6-7, 107-08. For his fortune see Keith Sward, *The Legend of Henry Ford* (New York, 1968), p. 479.

56. Marshall Field, *Freedom is More than a Word* (Chicago, 1945), p. ix. For his fortune see Myers, *History* (1936 edition), p. 210.

57. Carnegie, *Gospel*, pp. 16-18, 22-40; Rockefeller, *Random*, pp. 142, 150-53; Henry Ford and Samuel Crowther, *Today and Tomorrow* (Garden City, 1926), pp. 179-85; *My Life and Work* (Garden City, 1932), pp. 209-21; *Moving*, pp. 118-119.

58. Carnegie, *Gospel*, pp. 18, 42; Rockefeller quoted in Collier and Horowitz, *Rockefellers*, p. 47; Ford and Crowther, *Moving*, p. 64.

59. Durden, *Dukes*, pp. 244-46; John E. Pomfret, *The Henry E. Huntington Library and Art Gallery from its Beginning to 1929* (San Marino, 1969), pp. 51-52, 59; Huntington quoted in Robert C. Schad, *Henry Edwards Huntington. The Founder and the Library* (San Marino, 1948), p. 32; Harvey, *Henry Clay Frick*, pp. 333-34, Frick quoted on 336.

60. Andrew Carnegie, *The Empire of Business* (Garden City, 1902), p. 143; John D. Rockefeller quoted in Collier and Horowitz, *Rockefellers*, p. 47; Schiff quoted in Cyrus Adler, *Jacob Henry Schiff. A Biographical Sketch* (New York, 1921), p. 65.

61. Cabot quoted in Harris, *Only*, pp. 292-93.

62. Edward Bok, *The Americanization of Edward Bok* (New York, 1930),

p420. For the Bok fortune see Lundberg, *America's*, p. 26.

63. Eastman quoted in Ackerman, *George Eastman*, p. 382; Cullen quoted in Kilman and Wright, *Hugh Roy Cullen*, p. 227. For Cullen's fortune and charities see Kilman and Wright, *Hugh Roy Cullen*, pp. 226, 239; Lundberg, *Rich*, pp. 75-77.

64. Adler, *Jacob Henry Schiff*, pp. 21-22, 30, 32, 35-43, 59; Clark, *Leland Stanford*, pp. 392-93; Tebbel, *Inheritors*, p. 136.

65. Lindeman, *Wealth*, p. 24; Andrews, *Philanthropic Foundations*, p. 278; *US Treasury Report*, p. 1,133.

66. Hoyt, *Goulds*, p. 300.

67. Howard Hughes, *My Life and Opinions* (Best Books Press, 1972), p. 202. For his fortune see *New York Times*, 20 June 1977; James Stillman quoted in Anna Robeson Burr, *The Portrait of a Banker: James Stillman, 1850-1918* (New York, 1927), pp. 278-79. For his fortune see John Winkler, *The First Billion. The Stillmans and the National City Bank* (New York, 1934), p. 256. For the views of other super-rich magnates on money, commercial success and power see James Duke quoted in Atwood, *Mind*, pp. 28-29; Edward H. Harriman quoted in George Kennan, *E.H. Harriman. A Biography* (2 vols., Boston, 1922), vol. I, p. 195; Otto Kahn, *Edward Henry Harriman* (New York, n.d.); *Reflections of a Financier* (London, 1921), pp. 399-424; W. Clement Stone quoted in Lamott, *Moneymakers*, p. 91.

68. Donald Villarejo, 'Stock Ownership and the Control of Corporations', *New University Thought*, 2 (Fall 1961), p. 53.

69. Raymond W. Goldsmith and Rexford C. Parmelee, *The Distribution of Ownership in the Largest 200 Nonfinancial Corporations, Temporary National Economic Committee*, monograph no. 29 (US Government Printing Office, Washington, DC, 1940), pp. 3-4; Villarejo, 'Stock Ownership', *Interlocks in Corporate Management*, Staff Report to the Anti-Trust Subcommittee of the Committee on the Judiciary, US House of Representatives, 89th Congress, 1st Session (US Government Printing Office, Washington, DC, 1965), pp. 111, 116, 178, 191. Other studies of the concentration of power and wealth in the big corporations are Anna Rochester, *Rulers of America. A Study of Finance Capital* (New York, 1936); Victor Perlo, *The Empire of High Finance* (New York, 1951). More information on this issue may be found in Lundberg, *Rich*; Myers, *History of the Great American Fortunes* (3 vols., Chicago, 1911-17), vols. II and III and in the 1936 edition; Lundberg, *America's*, pp. 34-37, 60-80.

70. Goldsmith and Parmelee, *Distribution*, pp. 105-06, 116-30, 1,488-89, 1,508-28.

71. Ibid., p. 116; Lundberg, *America's*, pp. 26-27; Smith, 'Fifty Million', p. 177; Louis, 'America's Centimillionaires', p. 156.

72. Goldsmith and Parmelee, *Distribution*, pp. 533-38; Lundberg, *America's*, p. 27; Staff Report, *Interlocks*, pp. 254-70; Smith, 'Fifty Million', p. 177; Louis, 'America's Centimillionaires', p. 156.

73. Villarejo, 'Stock Ownership' (Winter 1962), p. 63; Smith, 'Fifty Million', p. 177; Louis, 'America's Centimillionaires', p. 156.

74. Harvey O'Connor, *The Guggenheims. The Makers of an American Dynasty* (New York, 1937), pp. 346-47.

75. O'Connor, *Mellon's Millions. The Biography of a Fortune* (New York, 1933), pp. 124-33; Louis Eisenstein, *The Ideologies of Taxation* (New York, 1961), pp. 65, 94-95, 104.

76. Standard accounts of the political power of the rich entrepreneurs and their families are Lundberg, *America's*, pp. 51-203, 236-37, 419, 455, 480, 484; Lundberg, *Rich*, pp. 81, 202-03, 416-49, 508-09; Myers, *History*, vols. II and III and 1936 edition; Mathew Josephson, *The Robber Barons. The Great American*

Capitalists, 1861-1901 (New York, 1934); Holbrook, *Age*; Frederick Lewis Allen, *The Lords of Creation* (Chicago, 1966); William Damhoff, *The Higher Circles. The Governing Class in America* (New York, 1971); Carl Solberg, *Oil Power. The Rise and Fall of an American Empire* (New York, 1976), pp. 8-9, 45-50, 166-72, 217; Louis Overacker, *Money in Elections* (New York, 1932); *Presidential Campaign Funds* (Boston, 1946); Jasper B. Shannon, *Money and Politics* (New York, 1959); Herbert E. Alexander, *Financing the 1960 Election* (Princeton, 1962); *Financing the 1964 Election* (Princeton, 1966). For specific accounts of political activity in this group see more specialised studies and biographies in the notes.

77. Shearman, 'Owners', pp. 265-66; 'Henry George', pp. 41-42; 'Coming', pp. 546-47; *New York World* list reprinted in Appendix to the *Congressional Record*, 63rd Congress, 1st Session (US Government Printing Office, Washington, DC, 1913), p. 124.

78. IRS, *Statistics of Income 1915-72*. For the sources of wealth for large estates see George E. Lent, *The Ownership of Tax-Exempt Securities, 1913-1953* (New York, 1955), p. 114; IRS, *Supplemental Statistics 1962*, p. 19; *1969*, p. 19; *1972*, pp. 13-14; Robert J. Lampman, *The Share of the Top Wealth-Holders in National Wealth, 1922-1956* (Princeton, 1962), p. 170.

79. *Statistics of Income 1916*, p. 14; *1919*, pp. 4, 21; *1929*, p. 32; *1939*, pp. 14, 59-60; *1945*, pp. 13, 69, 230-32; *1949*, Part 1, pp. 13, 300; *1954*, p. 33.

80. Lundberg, *America's*, pp. 26-27, 44-45; Smith, 'Fifty Million', pp. 176-77; Louis, 'America's Centimillionaires', pp. 152, 156; Smith and Calvert, 'Estimating', p. 251; IRS, *Supplemental Statistics 1962*, p.19; *1969*, p. 19; *1972*, p. 12. An estate multiplier finding of 2,500 Americans in 1969 at the level of $10 million or more appeared in Smith, Franklin and Wion, *Financial Concentration*, p. 8.

81. Lane, *Commodore*, pp. 184, 318; Collier and Horowitz, *Rockefellers*, p. 649.

82. J. Paul Getty, *My Life and Fortunes* (New York, 1963), pp. 259-60, 263. For a similar statement by William Benton, whose net worth was possibly as high as $400-500 million, see Sidney Hyman, *The Lives of William Benton* (Chicago, 1969), p. 508.

83. For changes in the money value of the top one per cent of estates and in the corporate stock index see Lampman, *Shares*, pp. 217, 221-27; Lawrence H. Seltzer, *The Nature and Tax Treatment of Capital Gains and Losses* (New York, 1951), pp. 159-63. Alan A. Tart, *The Taxation of Personal Wealth* (Urbana, 1967), p. 49. For changes in the consumer price index from 1865 to 1965 see Tart, *Taxation*, p. 49; William Isbell King, *The National Income and Its Purchasing Power* (New York, 1930), p. 170; *The Statistical History of the United States* (Stanford, n.d.), pp. 126-27; Soltow, *Men*, pp. 112-13; 'Evidence', p. 283.

84. The data from which this enumeration derives can be found in obituaries, wills, and estates reported in the *New York Times* and the *Chicago Tribune*. Compilations and evaluations of the wealthy in Smith, 'Fifty Million', pp. 176-78, 226, 228, 230, 233-34, 236, 238; Louis, 'America's Centimillionaires', pp. 152-57, 192, 195-96; 'Richest US Women', *Fortune*, 14 (November 1936), pp. 115-20, 192, 194-96, 198, 200, 202; 'Land of the Big Rich', *Fortune*, 37 (April 1948), pp. 98-103, 182-88; Lewis Beman, 'The Last Billionaires', *Fortune*, 94 (November 1976), pp. 132-37; Myers, *History*, vols. II and III and 1936 edition; *Ending*; Lundberg, *America's*; *Rich*. National, regional, and ethnic accounts of the rich in Amory *Who*; *Last*; Tebbel, *Inheritors*; Beebe, *Big*; Bainbridge, *Super-Americans*; Stephen Birmingham, *'Our Crowd' The Great Jewish Families of New York* (New York, 1967); Atwood, *Mind*; Folsom, *Great*; Wecter, *Saga*; Ruth Knowles, *The*

Greatest Gamblers. The Epic of American Oil Exploration (New York, 1959); 'They Gamble at 9 to 1 Odds', *Business Week* (24 March 1956), pp. 141-48; Richard O'Connor, *The Oil Barons. Men of Greed and Grandeur* (Boston, 1971); Amory, 'The Oil Folks at Home', *Holiday*, 21 (February 1957), pp. 52-56, 133-34, 136, 138, 141-42. Collections of biographies of the rich in Laura E. Holloway, *Famous American Fortunes* (New York, 1889); William O. Stoddard, *Men of Achievement. Men of Business* (New York, 1894); James Burnley, *Millionaires and Kings of Enterprise* (London, 1901); B.C. Forbes (ed.), *Men Who are Making America* (New York, 1926); *America's Fifty Foremost Business Leaders* (New York, 1948); George F. Redmond, *Financial Giants of America* (2 vols., Boston, 1922); n.a., *Famous Fortunes* (Springfield, Mass, 1931); Theodore J. Grayson, *Leaders and Periods of American Finance* (New York, 1932); n.a., *The Mirrors of Wall Street* (New York, 1933); Josephson, *Robber Barons; The Money Lords. The Great Finance Capitalists. 1925-1950* (New York, 1972); Arthur D. Howden Smith, *Men Who Run America* (Indianapolis, 1935); Holbrook, *Age*; the Editors of *Fortune, The Art of Success* (Philadelphia, 1956); Goronwy Rees, *The Multimillionaires. Six Studies in Wealth* (New York, 1961); Lamott, *Moneymakers*; Allen, *Lords*. The most important sources were biographies, autobiographies and memoirs cited throughout the notes: *The National Cyclopedia of American Biography* (70 vols., New York, 1898-1972); *Dictionary of American Biography* (26 vols., New York, 1928-74); *Who's Who in America* (Chicago, 1899-1977); *Who Was Who in America* (7 vols., Chicago, 1967-76). Unfortunately, publishing costs have made the inclusion of the appendix impossible.

85. Pitirim Sorokin, 'American Millionaires and Multi-Millionaires', *The Journal of Social Forces*, 3 (May 1925), pp. 628-39; Chester M. Destler, 'Entrepreneurial Leadership Among the "Robber Barons": A Trial Balance', *The Journal of Economic History*, supplement IV (1946), pp. 28-49; C. Wright Mills, *The Power Elite* (New York, 1956), pp. 102-17, 375-80.

86. The findings here discussed are in Sorokin, 'American', pp. 633-37; Destler, 'Entrepreneurial', p. 36; Mills, *Power*, pp. 104-07.

87. Sorokin, 'American', pp. 628-34, 638-39.

88. Mills, *Power*, pp. 106-10.

89. Allen, *Lords*, pp. 83, 85, 98-99.

90. *Statistical History*, p. 14; US Bureau of the Census, *US Census of Population 1860* (US Government Printing Office, Washington, DC, 1961), I, Part A, p. 155; *1970*, I, Part 1, Section 1, p. 311.

91. *Statistical History*, p. 8; *US Census 1960*, p. 146; *1970*, p. 263.

92. The references for Tables 9-26 are in note 84.

93. Jocelyn Ghent and Frederic Cople Jaher, 'The Chicago Business Elite: 1830-1930. A Collective Biography', *The Business History Review*, 50 (Fall 1976), p. 305. For comparable analysis in the study of other economic elites, of the variables investigated in Tables 9-26 see ibid., pp. 288-328 and Jaher, 'Nineteenth Century Elites', pp. 32-77.

94. *Statistical History*, pp. 207, 210-11.

95. Ibid., pp. 686-88, 692.

96. Mellon quoted in Atwood, *Mind*, p. 10.

97. These themes were commonplace assertions in the writings of Carnegie and Rockefeller and in quotations reproduced in interviews with, and biographies, articles and books about, the super-rich previously cited in the notes. For additional examples of these sentiments see Philip D. Armour quoted in Harper Leech and John C. Carroll, *Armour and His Times* (New York, 1938), pp. 23-24, 88, 281; Clint Murchison quoted in Freeman Lincoln, 'Big Wheeler-Dealer from Dallas', *Fortune*, 47 (January 1953), p. 120; George Curtis quoted in Edward W. Bek, *A Man From Maine* (New York, 1923), pp. 223-24. Several multimillionaires,

274   *The Gilded Elite*

in addition to those already cited, expressed these attitudes in their own books:
Edward Bok, *Twice Thirty* (New York, 1927); Bernard Baruch, *The Public Years*
(New York, 1960), p. 416; Napoleon Hill and W. Clement Stone, *Success
Through a Positive Mental Attitude* (Englewood Cliffs, 1962); Stone, *The Success
System That Never Fails* (Englewood Cliffs, 1962); William H. Danforth, *I Dare
You* (privately printed, 1969).

98. Harriman quoted in Kennan, *E.H. Harriman*, vol. II, p. 394; for his
medical symptoms see vol. II, p. 346; Armour quoted in Leech and Carroll,
Armour, pp. 88, 101. For contradictory evidence see Meeker, *Chicago*, p. 97;
Clarence W. Barron, *They Told Barron* (New York, 1930), p. 272. For Hill's
alleged devotion see Pyle, *James J. Hill*, vol. II, pp. 393-94. For his son-in-law's
comment see Barron, *They Told*, p. 61; Rockefeller quoted in Forbes, *Men*,
p. 299; Nevins, *John D. Rockefeller*, vol. I, p. 627; Rockefeller, *Random*, p. 156.
For Rockefeller's symptoms see Nevins, *John D. Rockefeller*, vol. II, pp. 266,
287, 427-28; Collier and Horowitz, *Rockefellers*, pp. 44-46; J.D. Rockefeller Jr
interview with Atwood in Atwood, *Mind*, pp. 240-41. For Rockefeller Jr's
insecurity see Fosdick, *John D. Rockefeller, Jr.*, pp. 418-27.

99. Smith, *Commodore Vanderbilt*, pp. 21-26; Andrews, *Vanderbilt Legend*,
pp. 5-7; Rockefeller, *Random*, pp. 41, 46-48; Collier and Horowitz, *Rockefellers*,
pp. 8-11; Herman Hagedorn, *The Magnate. William Boyce Thompson and His
Time* (New York, 1935), pp. 21-22, 67; Leech and Carroll, *Armour*, p. 41;
Kennan, *E.H. Harriman*, vol. I, pp. 3-9; Winkler, *First Billion*, pp. 24-29; Burr,
Portrait, p. 51; Harvey, *Henry Clay Frick*, pp. 24, 32; O'Connor, *Gould's
Millions*, p. 23; Wendt and Kogan, *'Bet-A-Million'*, pp. 24-25; Stone, *Success
System*; Lamott, *Moneymakers*, pp. 56, 165, 169.

100. Cornelius Vanderbilt II and Alva Vanderbilt quoted in Vanderbilt Jr,
Queen, pp. 301, 45; for further evidence of parent-child difficulties see pp. 162,
165, 204, 219, 225, 227, 230, 263-64, 277, 298, 301, 306, 310; Hoyt,
Vanderbilts, pp. 79, 101-03, 109-10, 139-40, 142-44, 169, 190, 244, 289-91,
305-08, 350; Lane, *Commodore*, pp. 80-81, 201. For similar friction in rich
families see Birmingham, *'Our Crowd'*, pp. 155-57; Sparks and Moore, *Hetty
Green*, pp. 3-50; Swanberg, *Citizen*, p. 3; Hughes, *My Life*, p. 46; O'Connor,
Mellon's Millions, pp. 11-17; O'Connor, *Astors*, pp. 87-120; Harris, *Only*,
pp. 36-54; Alibe Albright Hoge, *Cissy Patterson* (New York, 1966), pp. 3-27;
Amory, *Who Killed*, pp. 172-73; Tebbel, *Inheritors*, pp. 121-25, 131, 136;
Emmet Dedmon, *Fabulous Chicago* (New York, 1953), pp. 302-04; Peggy
Guggenheim, *Out of This Century* (New York, 1946), pp. 7-21; Collier and
Horowitz, *Rockefellers*, pp. 503-619; Hirsch, *William C. Whitney*, pp. 570-71.

101. Bok, *Americanization*, pp. 120-21, 124, 270; Sage quoted in Sarnoff,
Russell Sage, p. 8; Charles Crocker quoted in Lewis, *Big Four*, p. 53; n.a., *In
Memoriam. Henry Morison Flagler* (New York, n.d.), p. 8.

102. Gloria Vanderbilt quoted in Tebbel, *Inheritors*, p. 131. For the other
examples of unhappiness see Fosdick, *John D. Rockefeller, Jr.*, pp. 34-35;
Guggenheim, *Out*, pp. 7-21; Amory, *Who Killed*, p. 173; John Keats, *Howard
Hughes* (New York, 1972), p. 13. Vanderbilt Jr, *Queen*, pp. 204, 219, 225, 227,
230.

103. For representative statements of this theme see Bok, *Twice Thirty*,
pp. 42-62, 142-43, 167-70; Bok, *Americanization*, pp. 120-21, 124, 270;
Standard Oil partner Archbold, J.B. Duke and Frick quoted in Forbes, *Men*,
pp. 68-69, 133, 436, 441; Frick quoted in Jennings, *Dozen*, p. 113; Carnegie,
Autobiography, pp. 3, 14, 42-43, 54, 91, 97-98; Rockefeller quoted in Burnley,
Millionaires, p. 20; Armour quoted in Leech and Carroll, *Armour*, pp. 18, 23-24.

104. Rockefeller, *Random*, pp. 21, 36-37; Rockefeller quoted in Forbes,
Men, pp. 304-05.

105. W.K. Vanderbilt quoted in Tebbel, *Inheritors*, p. 133; J.D. Rockefeller Jr quoted in Fosdick, *John D. Rockefeller, Jr.*, p. 87.

106. Frazier Jelke quoted in Dedmon, *Fabulous*, p. 194; Meeker, *Chicago*, p. 98. For the similar sentiments of the Texans see Bainbridge, *Super-Americans*, p. 364.

107. For the problems of some inheritors see O'Connor, *Gould's Millions*, pp. 46-47, 258-60; Collier and Horowitz, *Rockefellers*, pp. 80, 84, 97, 136; Meeker, *Chicago*, p. 98; Leech and Carroll, *Armour*, pp. 81-82; 'Armour Fortune', *Fortune*, 3 (April 1931), pp. 49-57, 158; Hoyt, *Vanderbilts*, p. 336; Fosdick, *John D. Rockefeller, Jr.*, pp. 190-201; Winkler, *First Billion*, pp. 8-9; Burr, *Portrait*, pp. 273-74; Wendt and Kogan, *'Bet-A-Million'*, pp. 139-40, 266-67, 310, 319-20; Harris, *Only*, pp. 172, 178-87, 190, 253-54, 283-84, 299, 321-23, 329-31; Sparks and Moore, *Hetty Green*, pp. 120, 166; James, *Alfred I. DuPont*, pp. 112-13, 194-95, 199, 202-19, 370, 374-77; Amory, *Who Killed*, pp. 361-62; Bainbridge, *Super-Americans*, pp. 360-64.

108. J.D. Rockefeller Jr quoted in Fosdick, *John D. Rockefeller, Jr.*, pp. 191-92; Collier and Horowitz, *Rockefellers*, p. 136.

109. Collier and Horowitz, *Rockefellers*, pp. 84, 87, 116, 181-86; Fosdick, *John D. Rockefeller, Jr.*, pp. 418-27.

110. Meeker, *Chicago*, p. 60.

111. Andrew Carnegie, *Problems of Today* (New York, 1908), p. 35. For family conflicts among the rich see Hoyt, *Vanderbilts*, pp. 208-09, 218-24, 249-50, 252, 286-96, 339, 352-53; Vanderbilt Jr, *Queen*, pp. 135, 141, 144-45, 246; Hoyt, *Goulds*, pp. 283-84; O'Connor, *Gould's Millions*, pp. 311-12, 317; O'Connor, *Astors*, pp. 106-07, 145, 177-78; O'Connor, *Guggenheims*, pp. 356, 358; Carr, *duPonts*, pp. 247-76; Winkler, *The DuPont Dynasty* (New York, 1935), pp. 177-228; Tebbel, *Inheritors*, pp. 139-41; Barron, *They Told*, pp. 248-49; Hughes, *My Life*, pp. 52-54; Sparks and Moore, *Hetty Green*, p. 103.

112. O'Connor, *Gould's Millions*, p. 262; Kennan, *E.H. Harriman*, vol. II, p. 346; David E. Koskoff, *Joseph P. Kennedy, A Life and Times* (Englewood Cliffs, 1974), p. 233; Burr, *Portrait*, p. 40; Herbert L. Satterlee, *J. Pierpont Morgan. An Intimate Portrait* (New York, 1939), pp. 158, 172; Lewis, *Silver Kings. The Lives and Times of MacKay, Fair, Flood and O'Brien. Lords of the Nevada Comstock Lode* (New York, 1946), p. 177; Rockefeller, *Random*, p. 156; Collier and Horowitz, *Rockefellers*, pp. 44-46; Clark, *Leland Stanford*, p. 342; Sparks and Moore, *Hetty Green*, pp. 76, 165, 214-15, 235, 265-66, 268; Hettie Leitch Major, *C.W. Post. The Hour and the Man* (Washington, DC, 1963), pp. 15, 27-29, 144-45; Barron, *More They Told Barron* (New York, 1931), pp. 281, 305. Keats, *Howard Hughes*, pp. 175, 245, 292, 334-36; Jennings, *Dozen*, pp. 181-82.

113. Meeker, *Chicago*, p. 60; Frank Billings quoted in Barron, *They Told*, p. 272; Carnegie, *Problems*, p. 35; Gould quoted in Robert I. Warshaw, *Jay Gould. The Story of a Fortune* (New York, 1928), p. 180; Stillman quoted in Burr, *Portrait*, p. 40; Winkler, *First Billion*, p. 254; Fair quoted in Lewis, *Silver Kings*, p. 178; Thompson quoted in Hagedorn, *Magnate*, pp. 174, 320; Hughes quoted in Keats, *Howard Hughes*, pp. 198, 335; Rogers quoted in Amory, *Last*, p. 345; Simon quoted in Lammot, *Moneymakers*, p. 251.

114. Hoyt, *Vanderbilts*, pp. 318, 341, 343-47, 352-53, 358, 362, 270-71, 377-82, 385, 388-91, 393-94; Vanderbilt Jr, *Queen*, pp. 44-45, 131, 218; Tebbel, *Inheritors*, pp. 70-80, 93, 98-104, 121-24, 137-41, 234-35, 248-49, 268-69; Hoyt, *Goulds*, pp. 256, 279, 281, 293, 305, 318-19, 325-26; O'Connor, *Gould's Millions*, pp. 312-13; Lewis, *Silver Kings*, pp. 179-80, 206-08; Winkler, *First Billion*, pp. 10, 65; Amory, *Who Killed*, pp. 169-72, 354-56, 361, 378, 380-86, 437; Collier and Horowitz, *Rockefellers*, pp. 72, 220, 254-57, 317-18, 503-619; Guggenheim, *Out*, pp. 29 ff; O'Connor, *Guggenheims*, pp. 466-67, 472, 480; Frederick Morton, 'The Guggenheims', *New York Times Book Review*,

26 February 1978; Hoge, *Cissy Patterson*, pp. 3-43, 83, 214. Duke, *DuPonts*, pp. 209-10; Birmingham, *'Our Crowd'*, p. 275.

115. For statements of these sentiments see the previously cited writings of Ford, Carnegie, Rockefeller, Kahn, Bok, Getty, Rosenwald and Stone. See also remarks of the super-rich in Forbes, *Men*; Atwood, *Mind*; Louis, 'America's Centimillionaires', pp. 195-96. For additional examples in books written by multimillionaires and in interviews with them see Kahn, *High Finance* (New York, 1916), p. 331; Andrew W. Mellon, *Taxation: The Peoples' Business* (New York, 1924); Alfred P. Sloan, *Adventures of a White Collar Man* (New York, 1949), p. 170; Vincent Astor interview with John B. Kennedy in Kennedy, 'His Money Makes Him Work', *Collier's*, 76 (19 December 1925), p. 26; Marshall Field III, 'Field on Work' *New York Times*, 31 December 1920.

116. Rockefeller quoted in Collier and Horowitz, *Rockefellers*, vol. II; Rogers quoted in C.B. Glasscock, *The War of the Copper Kings* (Indianapolis, 1935), p. 304; Gates quoted in Wendt and Kogan, *'Bet-A-Million'*, p. 90; Carnegie, *Autobiography*, pp. 157n-58n; Hagedorn, *Magnate*, pp. 68-69, 113; Hunt quoted in Bainbridge, *Super-Americans*, p. 303; Baker quoted in Amory, *Last*, p. 119. For another multimillionaire's unabashed pursuit of money see Stone and Hill, *Success*; Stone, *Success System*, pp. 12-13, 39, 51.

117. J.O. Armour quoted in Forbes, *Men*, p. 5; Armour to Atwood, Summer 1920, Atwood, *Mind*, p. 252; Astor interview with Kennedy in Kennedy, 'His Money', p. 26; Kahn, *High Finance*, pp. 23-24, 33; *Edward Henry Harriman*, pp. 22-24; Collier, *Rockefellers*, pp. 526, 580, 604-05, 619.

118. Baruch, *Public*, p. 2; *My Own Story* (New York, 1957), p. 178; Stanford quoted in Lewis, *Big Four*, p. 173; Edward Green quoted in Sparks and Moore, *Hetty Green*, p. 193; John W. MacKay quoted in Lewis, *Silver Kings*, pp. 55-56; Gould quoted in Warshaw, *Jay Gould*, p. 180; Thompson quoted in Hagedorn, *Magnate*, pp. 154, 174; Flagler quoted in n.a., *In Memoriam*, p. 18; Getty, *My Life*, pp. 110, 260-63.

119. Vanderbilt quoted in Tebbel, *Inheritors*, p. 133; Armour quoted in Forbes, *Men*, p. 5. For the disenchantment of Steven Rockefeller and his cousins see Collier and Horowitz, *Rockefellers*, pp. 526, 580, 605, 613, 617, 619; Abby Rockefeller quoted on p, 523.

120. Rockefeller quoted in Nevins, *John D. Rockefeller*, vol. II, p. 685; Rockefeller Jr and Abby and Steven Rockefeller quoted in Collins and Horowitz, *Rockefellers*, pp. 180-81, 523, 613; William Benton quoted in Hyman, *Lives*, p. 571; Astor interview with Kennedy in Kennedy, 'His Money', p. 26; Harris, *Only*, pp. 172, 178-200, 253-54, 283-84, 299, 321-23, 329-31.

NOTES ON CONTRIBUTORS

Adeline Daumard is Professor of Contemporary History at the University of Amiens, France, and also teaches at the Ecole de Hautes Etudes en Sciences Sociale in Paris. She is the author of *La Bourgeoisie Parisienne de 1815 à 1848* (1963), recognised as one of the greatest works of modern French history, and of *Les Fortunes Françaises au XIXᵉ Siècle* (1973), a momumental study of nineteenth-century French wealth-holding, and has written or contributed to five other books as well. Previously she taught at the University of Brest and currently she has close ties with several Brazilian universities.

Frederic Cople Jaher is Professor of History at the University of Illinois in Champaigne-Urban, Illinois. He received his BA from CCNY in 1955 and his PhD from Harvard University in 1961; he has taught at Long Island University and the University of Chicago prior to coming to the University of Illinois. He is the author or editor of four books, including (with Leonard Dinnerstein) *Aliens; A History of Ethnic Minorities in America* and *The Rich, the Well-born, and the Powerful*, as well as more than a dozen articles, and received the 1976 Newcomen Award in business history.

Edward Pessen is Distinguished Professor of History at Bauch College and the Graduate Center, City University of New York. He is the author of *Riches, Class, and Power Before the Civil War* (1973), *Most Uncommon Jacksonians: The Radical Leaders of the Early Labour Movement* (1967), *Jacksonian America: Society, Personality, and Politics* 1969), and is the editor of *New Perspectives on Jacksonian Parties and Politics* (1969) and *Three Centuries of Social Mobility in America* (1974), as well as numerous articles.

William D. Rubinstein is lecturer in the School of Social Sciences at Deakin University, Geelong, Victoria, Australia. He received his BA from Swarthmore College in 1968 and his PhD from Johns Hopkins University in 1975. He has worked as Research Associate to Professor Harold Perkin of the University of Lancaster, England, and was Research Fellow in Sociology at the Australian National University in Canberra, Australia, before taking up his present position in 1978. He

277

is the author of numerous articles which have appeared in such journals as *Past and Present*, *The Journal of Contemporary History*, *Australian Economic History Review* and *Economic History Review*, the last of which jointly won the T.S. Ashton Prize of the Economic History Society in 1977.

Vera Zamagni is presently Professor of Economic History at the University of Florence, Italy, and Visiting Professor of Economics at the Bologna Centre of the Johns Hopkins University. She graduated from the Catholic University of Milan, and received a DPhil from Oxford University, working under Professor R.M. Hartwell. She is the author of *Industrialyzazione e squilibri regionali in Italia, Bilancio dell'età giolittiana* (1978), and other articles on Italian economic history.

INDEX

279